INQUISITION

Toby Green is the author of three previous books, *Saddled with Darwin*, *Meeting the Invisible Man* and *Thomas More's Magician*, and his work has been translated into six languages. He has travelled widely in Africa and Latin America, and now lives with his family in the west of England.

'Toby Green is a sensitive and disciplined historian, who eloquently recovers lost stories, experiences and emotions'
Sunday Telegraph

'An exceptional study of the original terror states'
Scotsman

'A powerful study of intolerance . . . Just as Arthur Miller used the Salem witchcraft trials of 1692 to comment on McCarthyite America, so in this book Green appears to be using the Inquisition to comment obliquely on the "war on terror"'
Guardian

'A cracking read'
Sunday Herald

'Toby Green's book is a tour de force which shows that when fear takes a grip it does not easily let go and that many suffer until it does. It is a real lesson for us from history'
Tribune

Also by Toby Green

SADDLED WITH DARWIN

MEETING THE INVISIBLE MAN

THOMAS MORE'S MAGICIAN

TOBY GREEN

INQUISITION

THE REIGN OF FEAR

PAN BOOKS

First published 2007 by Macmillan

First published in paperback 2008 by Pan Books
an imprint of Pan Macmillan Ltd
Pan Macmillan, 20 New Wharf Road, London N1 9RR
Basingstoke and Oxford
Associated companies throughout the world
www.panmacmillan.com

ISBN 978-0-330-44335-7

1 3 5 7 9 8 6 4 2

A CIP catalogue record for this book is available from the British Library.

Typeset by SetSystems Ltd, Saffron Walden, Essex
Printed and bound in Great Britain by
Mackays of Chatham plc, Chatham, Kent

For Ian,
always an inspiration

For all those who suffered
at the hands of the Inquisitions
of Portugal and Spain

First they came for the Jews
and I did not speak out because I was not a Jew.
Then they came for the Communists
and I did not speak out because I was not a Communist.
Then they came for the trade unionists
and I did not speak out because I was not a trade unionist.
Then they came for me
and there was no one left to speak out for me.

Pastor Martin Niemöller

Picture Acknowledgements

Credits are by page number in order from left to right and top to bottom.

1 – Biblioteca Nacional, Madrid / The Bridgeman Art Library; British Library. 2 – Mary Evans Picture Library. 3 – Libro Rojo, Archivo General de la Nación (Mexico) / Cambridge University Library; Mary Evans Picture Library. 4/5 – Real Academia de Bellas Artes de San Fernando, Madrid / The Bridgeman Art Library. 6/7 – Mary Evans Picture Library (all). 8 – Mary Evans Picture Library (both). 9 – British Library; Mary Evans Picture Library. 10 – Brown University Library, Providence, Rhode Island / The Bridgeman Art Library. 11 – Mary Evans Picture Library; British Library. 12 – British Library. 13 – Libro Rojo, Archivo General de la Nación (Mexico) / Cambridge University Library (all). 14 – Bonhams, London / The Bridgeman Art Library. 15 – Prado, Madrid / The Bridgeman Art Library (both). 16 – Bibliothèque des Arts Décoratifs, Paris / The Bridgeman Art Library; Bibliothèque Nationale, Paris / The Bridgeman Art Library.

Contents

Acknowledgements

This book is the fruit of over four years' research, and almost fifteen years of living, travelling in and thinking about the Iberian worlds in Africa, America and Europe. Countless people have contributed directly and indirectly to it, and to my sadness I can only give thanks to a few of them here.

This book would never have been written without the consistent support of my wonderful agents Jamie Crawford and Maggie Pearlstine. They believed that I could write it before I did, and spent many hours working with me to make sure that it became a reality. This was crucial input at a stage where I still struggled with the idea.

At Macmillan, Richard Milner has proved again what a wonderful editor and friend he is. Not everyone would have dragged themselves through a bout of tonsillitis to make sure we could work together on this idea. In the editorial process he has contributed key suggestions which have fundamentally improved the book. I know how lucky I am to have had him steering this difficult ship. I would also like to thank Lorraine Baxter, Georgina Difford and Bruno Vincent for helping to move the book towards publication, and Hugh Davis for a very helpful copy-edit.

Two of my biggest debts are to my teachers and friends Paulo Farias and Tom McCaskie. Their comradeship, wit and generosity guided me through difficult patches. They have always succeeded in imparting their intellectual honesty and showing me in countless ways how to become a historian.

For a variety of reasons, the writing of this book occurred at a difficult moment in my life. I would like to thank Bob Fowke, Fuschia Fowke and Caroline Glanville for giving up some of their time so that I could get it done. The Arts and Humanities Research Board provided funding during which some of the relevant research was undertaken; Rahul Jacob commissioned my articles on southern Europe and so helped me to fund some more of it; Mark Epton came up with a great idea at an important moment.

My work has benefited greatly from discussion of ideas with the historians Michael Alpert, Francisco Bethencourt and Philip Havik, among others. A big thank you too to the many librarians and archivists who have helped me locate the relevant information: to the staff of the British Library and the Main Library of Birmingham University; and at the archives of the Archivo Histórico Nacional in Madrid, the Archivo Generalde las Indias in Seville, the Instituto dos Arquivos Nacionais da Torre do Tombo and the Biblioteca da Ajuda in Lisbon, and the Archivio Segretto Vaticano; also to the staff at the Prado Museum in Madrid, the Museu Nacional da Arte Antiga and the Gabinete de Estudos Olisiponenses (both in Lisbon) and Argelía Martínez at Editorial Patria Cultural in Mexico City for helping in my search for illustrations.

While I have made every effort to trace copyright holders for permission to quote, in one case this has proved impossible. Any omissions brought to my attention will be rectified in any future edition.

Ian Rakoff is always a great friend to me through the writing process. This time, however, he has surpassed even his high standards of generosity, reading each chapter as it has come hot off the press and sharing with me the benefit of his many years in the business of making ideas and stories accessible. It has been a remorseless process for both of us. The readability of this book owes more to him than to anyone.

My greatest and most lasting debt, however, must be to my family. Emily, Lily and Flora always bring light and life where before there may be furrowed brows. They were always there for me when I returned from my research trips, and without their love I could never have finished this book.

Glossary

alcázar – fortress
alfaqui – Islamic scholar
aljama – term given to communities of Muslims and Jews in Iberia
alumbrados – term for a religious sect which concentrated on internal devotion rather than ritual. *Alumbrados* became increasingly associated with sexual excesses
auto-da-fé – literally 'trial of faith' – ceremony of the punishment of heretics
beata – secular holy woman living in the community and frequently attracting a large following
burn in statute – the fate of those convicted heretics who had died or escaped – their bones or an effigy were burnt at the stake
calificador – a person charged with assessing the orthodoxy of published books, and whether they should be censored by the Inquisition
canonjía – income from a post in each diocesan cathedral of Spain which was given to the Inquisition and became a crucial part of the institution's funding
commissary – paid official of the Inquisition resident in larger towns
comunero – name given to those who rebelled in Castile against Charles IV in 1521–22
converso/conversa – descendant of Jews who converted to Christianity
convivencia – the centuries of shared Christian, Jewish and Muslim life in Iberia
Cortes – parliament
crypto-Judaism – term for the faith of those who abandoned Catholicism and lived as secret Jews in lands governed by Portugal and Spain, from which the Jews had been expelled
dejado – mystic of the 16th century who held that giving oneself to God was enough for mystical union
edict of faith – pronounced by inquisitors on arriving in a town, giving people 30 days to come forward and confess their lack of orthodoxy or denounce the failings of others
Estado da Índia – zone of Portuguese control in the Indian Ocean, including parts of east Africa, Arabia, India and the Far East
familiar – spy of the Inquisition in towns and villages expected to keep an eye on behaviour and help with arrests and manhunts

germanías – name given to the brotherhoods which led the revolt in Aragon against Charles V 1520–22

limpieza de sangre – cleanliness of blood – the absence of any Jewish or Muslim 'impurities' in lineage

morisco/morisca – descendant of Muslims who converted under duress to Christianity

Old Christian – 'pure' Catholic who had no Jewish or Moorish ancestry

pertinaz – someone who refused to confess their 'crimes' to the inquisitors

potro – form of torture involving strapping victims to a trestle and forcing water down their throats

recogido – mystic of the 16th century who sought to find peace and union with God through contemplation

reconciliado – one who underwent more minor penances at the hands of the Inquisition such as lashing, imprisonment, the galleys and confiscation of goods, and was 'reconciled' to the Church

relajado – literally 'relaxed' – term used by the Inquisition for someone to be transferred to the secular authorities to be put to death, either through burning or by being garrotted and then burnt

Reyes Católicos – the 'Catholic Monarchs', Ferdinand and Isabella, who united the kingdoms of Spain at the end of the 15th century

sanbenitos – garb of a penitent of the Inquisition – usually a white shirt decorated with demons, and worn even after the penitent had been reconciled. *Sanbenitos* were then hung up in the parish church of the penitent as a warning to parishioners and often remained there for centuries

Suprema – supreme council of the Spanish Inquisition

tocado – a form of head covering inherited from the Moors and used in Spain in the 15th century by all and in the 16th century by *moriscas*

trampa – addition to the *potro* – a hole through which a torture victim's legs were swung

tzedakah – charitable giving by Jewish people, regarded as a moral obligation

ultramontane – term used to describe those who support absolute papal authority

Chronology

711 Moors invade and conquer most of the Iberian peninsula.

1085 Christians recapture Toledo.

1236–48 Key cities of Andalusia such as Cordoba (1236), Murcia (1241) and Seville (1248) recaptured by the Christians.

1391 Riots against the Jews of Spain, beginning in Seville and spreading elsewhere in the country; many Jews convert to Christianity.

1449 Riots against the *conversos* of Toledo; the authorities in Toledo issue a statute barring *conversos* from official positions.

1453 Turkish forces capture Constantinople from the Christians.

1474 Henry IV, king of Castile dies; his half-sister Isabella and purported daughter Juana 'la Beltraneja' fight for the crown. Juana is supported by the Portuguese, but the faction behind Isabella wins at the Battle of Toro in 1476.

1478 Sixtus IV issues a papal bull permitting the establishment of the Inquisition in Spain on 1 November.

1480 The first inquisitors of Castile, Miguel de Murillo and Juan de San Martín, are appointed.

1481 First autos-da-fé held in Seville.

1483 Jews expelled from Andalusia.

1484 Torquemada issues the first instructions for the operation of the Spanish Inquisition.

1485 Assassination in Zaragoza of Pedro de Arbues, inquisitor of Aragon; large numbers of autos follow over the next few years.

1492 In January Ferdinand and Isabella conquer the last Moorish kingdom of Spain, Granada. The Jews are expelled from Spain in August, and many of them go to Portugal. Columbus 'discovers' America.

1494 Treaty of Tordesillas divides the world of the discoveries between Spain and Portugal, with Spain responsible for most of America and Portugal for Africa and Asia.

1497 Forcible conversion of the Jews of Portugal.

1502 Expulsion of all Muslims from Granada.

1504 Tribunal of the Spanish Inquisition founded in the Canaries.

1504–6 Inquisitor Lucero sentences hundreds of people to death for Judaizing in Cordoba; riots break out and Lucero is forced to flee.

1506 Approximately 2,000 *conversos* killed by mobs in Lisbon.

1510 Portugal conquers Goa under Afonso de Albuquerque.

1517 On 31 October Martin Luther posts his 95 *Theses* on the door of the castle in Wittenberg.

1520–2 Civil wars in Aragon and Castile led by *comuneros* and *germanías* against the court of Charles V; in Aragon and Valencia the *germanías* forcibly baptize many Muslims.

1522 Charles V of Spain bans *conversos* or *moriscos* from legally emigrating to the New World.

1524 First *alumbrado* arrested by the Spanish Inquisition.

1525 Spanish Inquisition issues first edict of faith regarding *alumbrados*.

1526 Expulsion of all Muslims from the kingdom of Aragon. A meeting in Granada draws up a series of repressive measures to be directed at the cultural practices of *moriscos*.

1528 First auto in the New World: two *conversos* burnt in Mexico City.

1529–36 Purges of the followers of Erasmus by the Inquisition in Spain.

1536 Papacy gives permission for a Portuguese Inquisition with reduced powers.

1540 First auto-da-fé in Lisbon.

1543 First burning ordered under inquisitorial law in Goa.

1547 Papacy gives permission for a Portuguese Inquisition with full powers. A statute of purity of blood is promulgated in the cathedral of Toledo.

1547–66 Fernando de Valdés, inquisitor-general of Spain, pushes through many important reforms of the Inquisition.

1551 Jurisdiction of the Tribunal of Lisbon is expanded to encompass Portugal's Atlantic islands (Azores and Madeira), Angola, Brazil, Cape Verde, Guinea and São Tomé.

1553 Inquisitor-General Valdés introduces the *Concordia*, which standardizes the use of familiars across Spain.

1557 Holy Roman Emperor Charles V retires as king of Spain and is replaced by his son Philip II.

1559 Great autos in Valladolid and Seville. Archbishop Carranza of Toledo is arrested by the Inquisition. The most detailed index of censorship to date is published in Spain.

1560 First inquisitors appointed to Goa by the Portuguese Inquisition.

1561 Inquisitor-General Valdés issues General Instructions which standardize inquisitorial procedures.

1566 The measures drawn up in Granada in 1526 on the *moriscos* are implemented.

1568–70 Uprising of the *moriscos* of Andalusia; after their defeat, most are dispersed throughout the rest of Spain.

1569 Foundation of the Tribunal of the Inquisition in Lima, Peru.

1571 Foundation of the Tribunal of the Inquisition in Mexico City.

1576 Carranza is finally sentenced to abjure in Rome in April, and dies 18 days later.

1580 The crowns of Portugal and Spain are united under Philip II.

1591–5 Inquisitorial officials dispatched to the Azores, Brazil and Madeira from Lisbon to perform trials and receive denunciations.

1609 Foundation of the Tribunal of the Inquisition in Cartagena de las Indias, in modern Colombia.

1609–14 The *moriscos* of Spain are expelled, beginning in Valencia (1609) and ending in Murcia (1614).

1610 Grand auto in Logroño sees the last ever burning of witches by the Inquisition in Spain.

1618, 1627 Further inquisitorial visits to Brazil.

1633 Philip IV of Spain orders the Council of the Inquisition to create two courts, one of which deals solely with handling proofs of genealogy.

1636–49 Portuguese communities throughout Latin America are persecuted by the Inquisition. Great autos in Lima (1639) and Mexico City (1649).

1640 Portugal begins its war of independence against Spain.

1648 Spain recognizes the independence of the Dutch United Provinces.

1650–1700 Decline of Portuguese power in the *Estado da Índia*.

1668 Spain recognizes Portugal's independence.

1680 Grand auto of Madrid, perhaps the most lavish auto in the history of the Inquisition.

1700–46 Reign of Philip V of Spain. Rekindling of the Inquisition, with 54 autos and 79 people 'relaxed'.

1701–14 War of the Spanish Succession.

1713–15 Melchor de Macanaz, minister of state of Philip V of Spain, proposes reforms of the Inquisition; the Inquisition launches a case against him.

1743–4 Trial of Freemasons in Portugal.

1751 Edict issued against Freemasons in Spain.

1755 Great earthquake destroys Lisbon on 1 November.

1756 The works of Diderot, Montesquieu, Rousseau and Voltaire are banned by the Spanish Inquisition.

1759 Jesuits expelled from Portugal.

1761 Last burning of a *relajado* at an inquisitorial auto in Portugal.

1767 Jesuits expelled from Spain.

1773 Decree issued in Portugal removing legal distinctions between Old Christians and *conversos*.

1776–80 Arrest, trial and penance of Pablo de Olavide in Spain.

1789 French Revolution.

1807 Napoleon invades Portugal; the Portuguese royal family flees to Brazil.

1808 Napoleon invades Spain and installs his brother as puppet king. On 4 December the new regime issues a decree abolishing the Inquisition.

1810 Decree permitting freedom of the press is promulgated at Cádiz on 18 October.

1812 Liberal constitution proclaimed at Cádiz on 12 March. The Tribunal of Goa is definitively abolished on 16 June.

1813 A decree abolishing the Spanish Inquisition is approved by the parliament in Cádiz.

1820 Ferdinand VII is forced to accept the liberal constitution after a revolt in Cádiz. On 9 March he passes a decree suppressing the Inquisition in Spain.

1821 Official abolition of the Inquisition in Portugal.

1834 Law abolishing the Inquisition is formally passed in Spain.

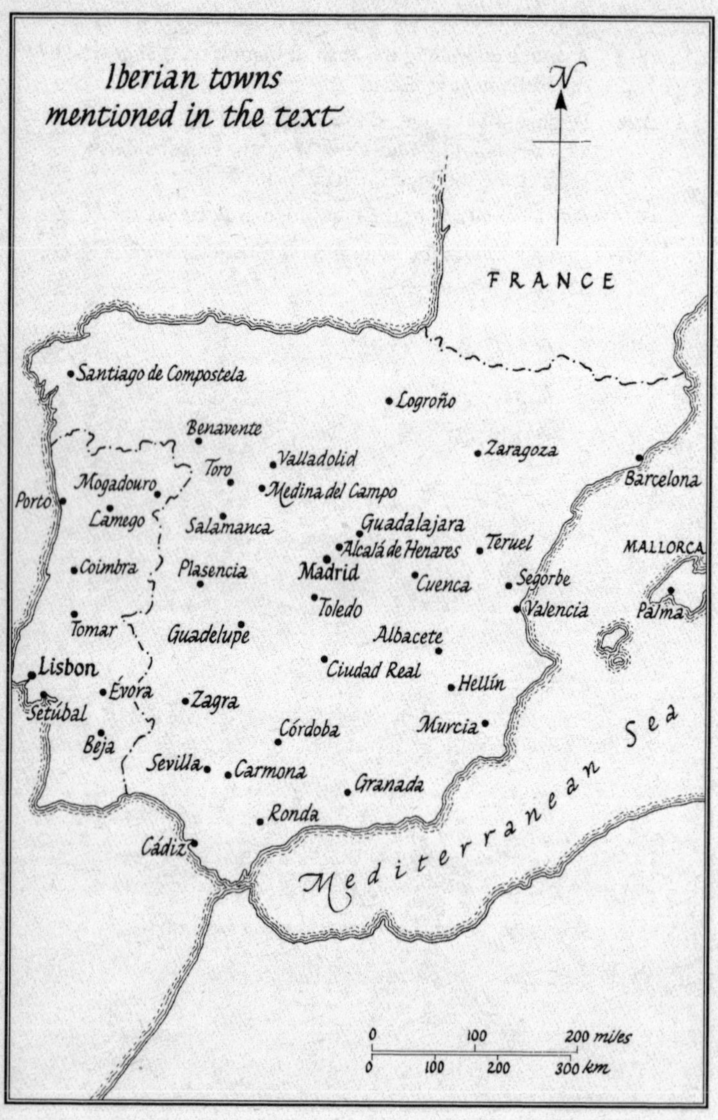
Iberian towns
mentioned in the text
N
FRANCE
Santiago de Compostela
Logroño
Benavente
Zaragoza
Valladolid
Toro
Barcelona
Mogadouro
Medina del Campo
Porto
Lamego
Salamanca
Guadalajara
Alcalá de Henares
Teruel
MALLORCA
Coimbra
Plasencia
Madrid
Cuenca
Segorbe
Toledo
Valencia
Palma
Tomar
Guadelupe
Albacete
Lisbon
Ciudad Real
Hellín
Évora
Setúbal
Zagra
Córdoba
Murcia
Beja
Sevilla
Carmona
Granada
Ronda
Cádiz
Mediterranean Sea
0
100
200 miles
0
100
200
300 km

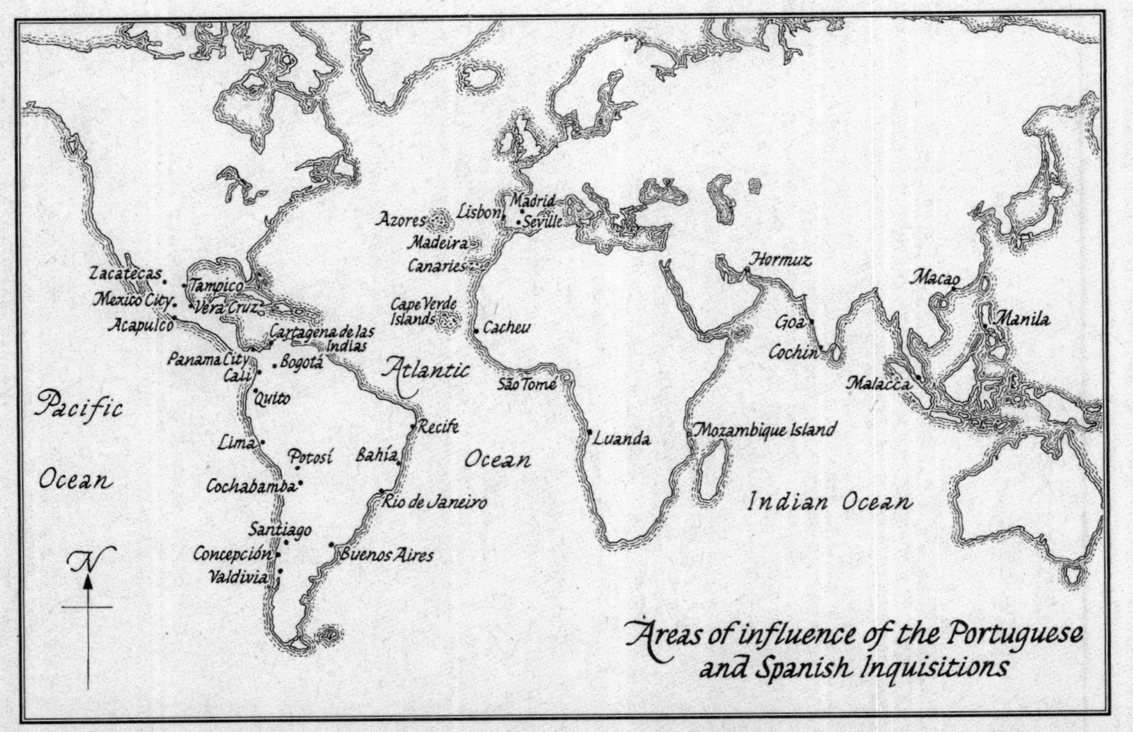
Areas of influence of the Portuguese and Spanish Inquisitions
Pacific Ocean
Atlantic Ocean
Indian Ocean
N
Zacatecas
Tampico
Mexico City
Vera Cruz
Acapulco
Cartagena de las Indias
Panama City
Bogotá
Cali
Quito
Lima
Potosí
Cochabamba
Santiago
Concepción
Valdivia
Bahía
Recife
Rio de Janeiro
Buenos Aires
Azores
Lisbon
Madrid
Seville
Madeira
Canaries
Cape Verde Islands
Cacheu
São Tomé
Luanda
Mozambique Island
Hormuz
Goa
Cochin
Malacca
Macao
Manila

PROLOGUE

Above all were his peaceful procedures.
He always administers justice in the beautiful link of peace.
It could be the heraldry of his canopy –
'Justice and peace have kissed.'

Mexico City 1649

ON MONDAY 11 MARCH 1649 a procession left the headquarters of the Holy Office of the Inquisition in Mexico City. The gala troop swept between the whitewashed houses, enlivened by musicians dressed in silks of different colours playing trumpets, kettledrums and woodwind. The musicians' horses were followed by the ministers of the Holy Office and the noblest gentlemen of the city, the ministers bearing the arms of the Inquisition, which so appropriately mirrored the battle between peace and violence which was at the heart of that curious institution: a cross in the middle, an olive branch to the right and a sword to the left.[1]

The procession, brought up at the rear by Don Juan Aguirre de Soaznava, the chief warden of the Inquisition in Mexico, snaked through the streets of one of the two most important cities in America, announcing amid the din of kettledrums and wind instruments that a grand trial of faith, or autos-da-fé, would be held in a month's time. Notices were published in the buildings of the Holy Office, at the house of the archbishop, in front of the viceroy's palace, in the town council and in various streets in the city.[2]

A month was in truth the absolute minimum necessary to prepare the great theatre for the auto. A stage was built, about 37 metres long and 24 metres wide, around which were placed eight marbled columns grouped in twos. In the keystone of an arch set above the boards was a depiction of a shield with the royal coat of arms, while a pyramid was built and decorated with a shield of the faith. Boys playing trumpets were painted above the doors for entering and leaving the stage, while the prisoners were to be housed in a structure topped by a cupola. The arena was shaded by sails nailed to the tops of forty tree trunks roughly 18 metres high, while thirty stairways were built connecting it to apartments and other buildings so that onlookers could take a rest from the demands of the auto. The whole was lavishly decorated with velvet hangings, carpets and crimson curtains, and the activity was such that 'people were congregating every day and they remained from sun-up to the close of the day . . . they admired everything and felt that they were seeing something that could be perpetuated through the ages'.[3]

On 10 April, after a month's hectic construction work, over 20,000 people filled Mexico City to watch the procession of the green cross which heralded the morrow's auto. The streets between the Inquisition offices and the great arena were dotted with minor stages. People watched from benches, coaches, balconies and windows as Don Juan Aguirre de Soaznavar set out at three thirty in the afternoon, accompanied by a twelve-strong guard, pages and lackeys. The bells of all the churches and monasteries in the city rang out as the procession passed by. The guards were dressed in the green and black of the empire, embellished with gold and silver braiding. The pages wore fine green clothes and capes, while the lackeys were in groups of eight bearing swords of silver and gold. When the procession finally reached the Plaza del Volador, soldiers fired a celebratory salute and twenty Dominican friars walked forward with white candles to welcome the cross, at last, to the stage.[4]

It was seven o'clock. Night had fallen across the city, yet there were so many candles that they 'made the entire theatre appear as if it were day'.[5] The candles themselves were so thick that they would burn for two nights. Prayers were led from the stage, and a vast throng filled the Plaza del Volador. All the seats were taken. Few slept as they imagined the sentences that would be meted out to the condemned.

Yet 'while the city was rampant with all varieties of rumours, the Holy Office . . . proceeded in silence with its labours'.[6] In the offices of the Inquisition, two confessors were sent to the 15 people who had been condemned to die for secretly practising Judaism in spite of being baptized and outwardly professing the Catholic faith. These were the so-called *relajados*, the term used by the Inquisition for those who would be transferred to the secular authorities and put to death. All but one of the *relajados* protested their innocence and claimed to be good Christians. The exception was Tomás Treviño de Sobremonte, an itinerant merchant who admitted to being a Jew.[7] Owing to Sobremonte's refusal to accept the Christian faith he would be burnt to death the following day, while the other fourteen *relajados* would be given the relative clemency of being garrotted and then burnt.

At four in the morning the chief inquisitor of Mexico, Juan de Mañozca, arrived. The cathedral bells began to toll, to remind the populace that the auto was an earthly representation of the Last Judgement. As well as the fifteen *relajados*, the effigies of sixty-seven deceased people had been sculpted, to be burnt in place of their bodies for the heresy that they were no longer alive to exculpate; the effigies went first in this procession, followed by twenty-three boxes of their bones, which were also to be burnt. Then followed those prisoners who had been sentenced to suffer penances such as lashing, imprisonment, the galleys and confiscation of goods – the *reconciliados*. Last of all, the *relajados* were called and given the banners of their condemnation, which 'consisted of *sanbenitos* [the penitential garb of all prisoners] decorated with flames and figures of demons'; these terrifying images also decorated the *corozas*, the conical hats which the prisoners wore as they made their way to the stage.[8]

The procession left the Holy Office at dawn. The *relajados* were given a green cross. Some of them were gagged, including Sobremonte, who 'walked through the streets like a volcano of desperation . . . everyone was shouting at him, trying to persuade him or preaching to him. But he wouldn't listen to anyone, being furious even with himself. He made his own obstinacy a point of honour'.[9] Every *relajado* was accompanied by two confessors, who never let up in their preaching and exhortations to the condemned to repent. Many of the confessors cried as they went, 'which caused copious tears to fill the eyes of all the onlookers on realizing the charitable spirit showed by the ministers and the scarce interest shown by the accused'.[10] The prisoners were followed by the ministers of the Inquisition on horseback, and then by a mule carrying a chest which bore the trial records and sentences of the accused. The head of the mule was adorned with silver plates engraved with gold designs; her neck was hung with silver and gold bells; and the chest with the trial records was mauve-coloured and inscribed with Japanese inlays and elaborate copperplates.[11]

The brilliant piece of theatre brought the entire colony to a standstill. People came from nearly 1,000 miles away to watch, so that 'it appeared that all of New Spain* had been depopulated and brought to Mexico [City]'.[12] The crowd hung from the fences, the scaffolds, carriages and balconies; they sat on 16,000 seats before the stage, shouting and applauding, riveted by the piety of the event and fascinated by the prisoners. As the condemned mounted the stage individually to hear their sentences, the Jesuit friar Mathias de Bocanegra marvelled at the doings of Chief Inquisitor Mañozca, whose 'glorious solemnity, comprehensive capacity, wise intelligence, mature discretion, old experience, zealous integrity, all . . . justified his work'.[13] 'Above all,' as Bocanegra put it, 'were his peaceful procedures. He always administers justice in the beautiful link of peace. It could be the heraldry of his canopy – "Justice and peace have kissed." '[14]

JUSTICE AND PEACE were adjectives ill-suited to describe Mañozca's usual mode of behaviour. The record of this individual reveals a more chequered approach to the art of inquisitorial persecution. In fact, Mañozca's true character had been apparent for forty years, ever since his appointment as one of the first inquisitors of Cartagena, Colombia, in 1609.†

In Cartagena Mañozca and his colleague Mateo de Salcedo had made a habit of hauling market traders before them and seizing whatever took their fancy, throwing them into the inquisitorial jail

---

* The modern republic of Mexico was known as 'Nueva España', or New Spain, in the colonial period. In order to make things clearer, in this book I shall refer to New Spain as Mexico.

† The area known today as Colombia was called the New Kingdom of Granada, 'Nuevo Reino de Granada', in colonial times; for clarity's sake, I shall refer to this as Colombia.

if they did not comply.[15] In January 1624 Mañozca was accused of having routinely smuggled goods in and out of Cartagena and freeing his associates when they were arrested for carrying contraband.[16] He had destroyed rivals of his friends,[17] and appointed a friend of his prior of the Dominican monastery even though his friend could not read Latin.[18] When a butcher whose house adjoined his own made a ruckus by killing a pig, Mañozca arrested the butcher's butler and servants and threw them in the inquisitorial jail.[19] It was also public knowledge that he was having an affair with a married woman in the city.[20]

Perhaps hoping to improve matters, the Supreme Council of the Inquisition in Spain – the *Suprema* – transferred Mañozca from Cartagena to Lima in Peru.[21] In 1625 Mañozca was sent on a commission of inquiry to Quito, Ecuador, where he immediately stood down all the judges except the youngest one, whom he dominated absolutely.[22] An associate of Mañozca's took to parading Quito's streets with an armed gang, occasionally assaulting royal officials in the plaza, and once stabbing an African slave with his sword to see if it was working properly.[23] Mañozca summoned prisoners in chains from Cali, hundreds of miles away in southern Colombia, and kept them in jail for eight months. In all, he and his sidekicks spent over two years racking up huge bills and all but bankrupted the colonial authorities in the province.[24]

It was this sort of corruption that encouraged men like Juan Pérez de Segura, a trader in Peru in the 1580s, to declare that 'inquisitors should be tied to the tail of a horse'.[25] How delicious it would be to see them dragged through the very muck that was their bequest to so many others! But inquisitors were widely seen as above the law. Was it not typical that none of the litany of complaints had prevented Mañozca from being appointed chief inquisitor in Mexico in 1643 and preparing the trials which came to a head with the great auto of 1649?

Yet persecutors do not abide in a vacuum. Mañozca's genius for tyranny took advantage of a time when what was called crypto-Judaism flourished. By 1649, Judaism had been condemned in Spanish dominions for over 150 years, and the religion of the twenty-five congregations of secret Jews in Mexico was a curious hybrid of Catholicism, Judaism and taboo rituals which in Mexico were associated with illicit sex.[26] Although the Inquisition was charged with the extirpation of this heresy in Spanish territories, it had made little progress since its formation in 1478. New cells of these religious rebels were constantly being uncovered. There were even specialists in their detection, men such as Mañozca, who, prior to the events in Mexico in 1649, had been one of the inquisitors who uncovered the 'great plot' of the crypto-Jews in Lima in the late 1630s.[27] It turned out to be impossible to separate entirely the pursuers of heresy from the heretics themselves; on some deep and unconscious level, each seemed to need the other.

The 1649 auto in Mexico was in every sense a grand piece of theatre, yet it is only a minor episode in the story of the Iberian Inquisitions. For the victims of the inquisitors, such as the crypto-Jews of Mexico, resistance punctuated their suffering and music occasionally alleviated their torture. As one of their sabbath prayers put it:

> Whoever sings lessens his pain;
> Whoever cries begets more strain:
> I sing so as to remedy
> The suffering that torments me.[28]

One must begin by acknowledging the sheer vastness of the subject. From 1478 to the mid-18th century the Inquisition was the most powerful institution in Spain and its colonies in the Canaries, Latin America and the Philippines. In neighbouring Portugal and Portugal's colonies in Africa, Asia and Brazil the Inquisition was pre-eminent for 250 years from 1536 onwards. This means that the Inquisition was a significant force in four continents for more than three centuries; we are dealing with a period stretching from the unification of Spain under Ferdinand and Isabella in the 15th century to the Napoleonic Wars.

These vast reaches of time and space are matched by the size of the perceived criminal class. Trials were held of witches in Mexico, bigamists in Brazil, seditious Freemasons, Hindus, Jews, Muslims and Protestants, fornicating priests and sodomizing sailors. In Mexico the Inquisition banned peyote – the hallucinogenic cactus written about by Carlos Castañeda in the 1960s and 70s – in 1620, because it 'has been introduced into these provinces, for the purpose of detecting thefts, of divining other happenings and foretellings'.[29] Neither indigenous cultural practices nor sorcery and superstition were suffered gladly, even though many of the fortune-tellers and sorcerers around were evidently second rate. Should the Inquisition really have bothered with sorcerers such as Isabel Jiménez, denounced in Guatemala in 1609 for 'telling fortunes by reading palms . . . always provided that it was a Friday'?[30]

One of the main structural similarities between the Inquisitions of Portugal and Spain was their interest in places as far-flung as Angola, Brazil, Cape Verde, Goa and Mexico. Only the Iberian Inquisitions had the means to persecute such minor acts of blasphemy and superstition across the world, acts that would simply have raised laughter elsewhere. In Salvador da Bahia,* Brazil, the labourer Manuel de Paredes was denounced by his brother-in-law Gironimo de Bairros in 1591; Bairros was upset at Paredes's jibe that his sister Pauloa had been no more a virgin when she had married him than Mary had been when she had given birth to Jesus (it was the slur on Mary's virginity that made this a case worthy of the Inquisition).[31] A similar idea was expressed by one Domingo Hernández in Valdivia, southern Chile, around 1580: when discussing 'how the women of Valdivia slept with the men, [Hernández] said that Joseph had also slept with Mary'.[32]

Keeping a check on such irreverence was a way of shoring up authority over these gargantuan empires. Power was at the heart of the Inquisition, and thus, inevitably, did religion enter the province of politics. It was no accident that in 1587, just one year before the Spanish Armada set sail for England, Francis Drake's cousin John was tried by the Inquisition in Lima. John Drake had lost his ship on the River Plate and spent fifteen months as a captive of the Guaraní Indians before managing to escape in a canoe and reach the city of Asunción in Paraguay.[33] From here he had been taken to Buenos Aires, before being arrested and transported thousands of miles to the nearest inquisitorial headquarters, in Lima, where he was 'reconciled' in the auto of 1587 and imprisoned in the Franciscan

---

* Known today as Salvador, but in the colonial period more commonly as Bahia, a use I follow in this book.

monastery of the city, still aged just twenty-three.[34] One can but wonder if Francis Drake knew of his cousin's fate and brooded on it in the months running up to the arrival of the Spanish Armada.

The long, sorry history of the Inquisition reveals countless similar examples. There were always, it turned out, others to persecute. But these others could remain dormant for decades, their heresies unapparent, until some political trigger released them for discovery. The challenge for the historian is the hugeness of the subject, something which in recent years has encouraged academic writers to concentrate on one small area or issue rather than on the whole. The intention of this book is to adopt a more overall perspective, to try and see what the significance of the whole ghastly business really was. For the Inquisition provided nothing less than the first seeds of totalitarian government, of institutionalized racial and sexual abuse.

SOONER OR LATER, one turns to numbers. Populations were much lower in the 16th and 17th centuries than today, perhaps one-fifth or one-sixth of current figures, so one needs to bear in mind that any human statistic represents a much higher percentage of the total population than it would now. Moreover, the Inquisition acted in many other ways beyond mere trials, through investigations of the purity of genealogies, preventing descendants of convicted heretics from taking up many jobs or wearing certain types of clothing, and through instilling a culture of secrecy.

The Inquisition was at its most severe in Spain during the first fifty years after its formation in 1478, when it is estimated that 50,000 people were tried, a significant proportion as *relajados* burnt at the stake.[35] In some years, such as 1492, 2,000 people may have been 'relaxed' in person and another 2,000 burnt in effigy.[36] Approximately 700 people were put to death in Seville alone between 1481 and 1488, and another fifty in Ciudad Real 1483–4.[37] Around 10 per cent of the entire population of Toledo was tried by the Inquisition between 1486 and 1499, and 3 per cent 'relaxed' alive or in effigy.[38] In the crown of Aragon, meanwhile, roughly 1,000 people were 'relaxed' between 1485 and 1530.[39]

After this initial fury, the Spanish Inquisition became less bloodthirsty, so that between 1540 and 1700 84,000 people were tried.[40]

In the reign of Philip V (1700–46) there was a rekindling of violence after the War of the Spanish Succession finished in 1714, with 1,463 trials and 111 executions. But thereafter the institution was in decline.[41] In Portugal, meanwhile, where there was a lower population than in Spain, there were approximately 45,000 trials between 1536 and 1767 (including 13,667 in Goa)[42] with at least 1,543 people being relaxed.[43]

There is no doubt that these figures are lower than many have long believed.[44] Removing the first fifty years of inquisitorial history in Portugal and Spain from the equation, the number of deaths is much lower than the number of people killed during the witch-hunts of northern Europe between 1560 and 1680, which is put at a minimum of 40,000.[45] And whereas bloody witch-hunts engulfed Austria, England, France, Germany, Holland, Scotland, Sweden, Switzerland and Transylvania, the Inquisition in Portugal and Spain, while prosecuting 'witches', executed very few of them. These comparisons have led historians – both past and present – to claim that Spain has been the victim of a 'black legend' which paints the violence of its Inquisition and of Spain's conquest of America in the worst light possible whilst skating over similar or worse excesses elsewhere.

The 'black legend' originated in the mid-16th century after the pope freed Alfonso Díaz, a lawyer at the papal court; Díaz had instigated the murder of his own brother Juan because he had become a Protestant whilst studying in Paris.[46] The case became something of a cause célèbre and led to numerous anti-Catholic pamphlets across northern Europe. These were augmented by the publication in the 1560s of a book by an anonymous Spanish fugitive from the Inquisition written under the pseudonym Reinaldo González Montes. Montes had probably been a monk accused of Protestantism in Seville in the 1560s, and he published a graphic and unsympathetic account of the Inquisition after his escape to northern Europe.[47] Such publications were seized on by countries jealous and fearful of Spain's power; they quickly became tools in a propaganda campaign which, there can be no doubt, unfairly demonized the activities of the Inquisition in comparison to other persecutions then occurring both in Europe and elsewhere.[48]

Yet there is a difference between putting the Inquisition in context and excusing its excesses. The Inquisition did not overly persecute witches, but this was principally because, as we shall see, the unique cultural mixture of Portugal and Spain provided other scapegoats to persecute without the need to invent witches.[49] Even more seriously, in the desire to put right the black legend, worrying errors of fact are still being made by some, such as the claim that torture was 'only rarely applied – almost exclusively during the first two decades' (see Chapter Three).[50]

In Spain, many of these revisionist historians were originally trained under the Franco regime, to which the Catholic Church was a formidable ideological prop. The intellectual atmosphere of this era is well expressed by the view of Antonio Sierra Corella, author of a book on censorship under the Inquisition, who declared in 1947, 'Only some wretched author, infected by an anachronistic sense of liberalism, could argue with any conviction against the legal censorship of science and literature, as if this vital social function were an unjust and annoying interference of power.'[51]

The Francoist era was one when people often wrote obliquely about present events by concentrating on an aspect of the past.[52] The growth in revisionist views of the Inquisition under Franco in fact mirrored the attempt to sanitize views of the general's regime and of its impact on Spain.[53] The legacy of these views today should not, therefore, be treated with the respect which in some circles it is still afforded – unless we want to find that the black legend is replaced by a white one, and that the dangers of creating a persecuting state apparatus are not fully appreciated.

WE MUST EXAMINE the Portuguese and Spanish Inquisitions together.[54] The procedure of these institutions was almost identical.[55] The Inquisition spread from Spain to Portugal, and the first papal bull establishing the Inquisition in Portugal was obtained through the pressure of Charles V, the Habsburg ruler of Spain.[56] Moreover, the Inquisition originated in both countries through the persecution of crypto-Jews, and in both it became subordinate to the monarchy.[57] Perhaps most importantly of all – and in contrast to the papal Inquisition and the earlier medieval Inquisition – in each of the two countries the institution spread to the colonies.

Thus, this book does not focus on the medieval and Italian

Inquisitions. While many of the procedures of the Spanish body – such as secrecy in court proceedings – were inherited from the medieval Inquisition,[58]* the crucial difference is that whereas the medieval Inquisition was controlled by the papacy or its representatives, the bishops, the Spanish Inquisition formed in 1478 came directly under the control of the Spanish crown.[59]

It was this which made the Inquisition in Spain, and then Portugal, a new departure. The first inquisitors were installed in royal buildings, and the first inquisitor-general in Spain, Tomás de Torquemada, sacked the medieval inquisitors of Aragon and installed his own replacements.[60] At the first Spanish auto, in Seville on 6 February 1481, six people were burnt in spite of the fact that this sentence was not justified according to previous inquisitorial procedure – these were all warning shots that this new court of faith was going to be different.[61]

Thus one of the best reasons to concentrate on the Portuguese and Spanish Inquisitions is that this is a story of power and the abuse of power, rather than an excuse to reprise the anti-Catholic propaganda of the past. During the formation of the Inquisition in Portugal the papacy was always more benign than the Portuguese crown under John III: where John banned converted Jews from leaving Portugal in 1532, Pope Clement VII issued them a general pardon in 1533; when, after the Inquisition had been founded in 1536, John wanted the bishop of Lamego made the Portuguese inquisitor-general, the papacy refused for fear that he would be too violent; and when Pope Paul III issued the bull *Meditatio Corbis* on 16 July 1547, which at last gave the Portuguese Inquisition the same freedoms as its Spanish counterpart, he did so on condition that for a whole year everyone who wanted to would freely be able to leave Portugal, and so escape persecution.[62] Similarly, when the institution of the Inquisition in Spain led to violent excesses, Pope Sixtus IV tried hard in 1482 to curtail the powers of the new body and complained to the monarchs Ferdinand and Isabella.[63]

The papal role in the Inquisitions of Portugal and Spain was, in

* Founded in the early 13th century in southern France and brought to Aragon – but not Castile – in 1237.

fact, almost always moderate. The papacy was always reluctant to sanction the excesses of the Inquisitions in Iberia, and was routinely bypassed. Leonardo Donato, an Italian traveller, noted in 1573 how the Pope had 'no involvement' in the Spanish Inquisition, and that Pius V had been unable to override it in order to achieve a position for a servant of his.[64] Even the victims of the Inquisition came to recognize the difference between justice in Rome and justice in Iberia, with Juana Roba, a *morisca* (descendant of a converted Muslim), prosecuted in Valencia in 1587 for saying among other things that 'since the pope let everyone live according to their faith in Rome why were things done differently [in Spain]?'[65]

Thus the abuse of inquisitorial power in Iberia was a political rather than a religious abuse of power, and the story of the Iberian Inquisitions need not be an anti-Catholic diatribe.[66] Persecution never was the monopoly of Spaniards, Portuguese or Catholics. It was something of which all peoples were capable.[67]

In 1595, six residents of the small town of Hellín, in the south-eastern Spanish district of Murcia, gave evidence to an inquisitor. During this era inquisitorial visits were supposed to be made on a regular basis to inquire into the orthodoxy of residents of even the smallest villages, and in Hellín a considerable scandal had been caused by the labourer Francisco Maestre.

Maestre had been elected major-domo of the Brotherhood of Our Lady of Rosario. Unfortunately, this election had been held in his absence, and when the insignias, sceptre and standard were taken to his house he was less than pleased and said, 'What manure, shit, what stench or rubbish are you bringing me here?', and having been informed that these were the insignias of Our Lady of Rosario he replied, 'It's just shit and more shit'.[68] This response did not go down well. Maestre was hauled before the inquisitors, excusing himself by explaining that he had been tired and had not taken in the insignias properly when they had arrived.

As this story shows, to understand the nature of the Inquisition there is no need for legends, either black or white. There is in fact a huge archive.[69] Reading through it, there are many times – as with the Maestre case – when laughter is as appropriate a response as sadness. Sometimes, the mirth is caused by the constant examples of people who refused to be cowed by fear; at others, it is tempered by admiration at the wit of prisoners in the face of adversity.

Here I think of the Englishman William Lithgow, who was arrested by the Inquisition in Malaga in 1620 and harangued for being a Protestant. The arrest was unlawful, since there was an agreement at this time between the Spanish and English crowns that the English should not be arrested by the Inquisition. Nevertheless, after being given eight days by a Jesuit confessor to convert or face the consequences, the Jesuit departed Lithgow's cell with the words, 'My Son, behold you deserve to be burnt quick, but by the grace of our Lady of Loretta, whom you have blasphemed, we will save your body and soul'. At a hearing with the inquisitor the next day Lithgow was subjected to a tirade of accusations. Yet instead of showing any fear he replied, 'Reverend Sir, the nature of Charity and Religion does not consist in opprobrious speeches' – whereupon he was kicked in the face by the inquisitor and soon enough tortured.[70]

William Lithgow turned out to be a fortunate man. The English consul in Malaga heard of his case, managed to get the ambassador in Madrid to secure his release, and he was able to write his memoirs twenty years later. Of course few were as lucky as him, and it is in this constant struggle between fear and resilience that the real drama of the Inquisition emerges. Just thirty-two years after the first auto in Seville, the Florentine ambassador Guicciardini wrote in 1513 how the inquisitors, 'confiscating the goods of the guilty and at times burning them, have made everyone afraid'.[71] Fear percolated every layer of society: in 1559 a case was begun against the archbishop of Toledo, Bartolomé Carranza, the primate of all Spain, for 'heresy', which revealed that no one was free from suspicion (see Chapter Five); by the late 16th century, the *moriscos* of Cuenca kept their goods away from their houses, since if they were arrested by the Inquisition these would all be confiscated;[72] and by 1602 *moriscos* lived in such fear of the Inquisition that some fainted at the mere sight of an inquisitorial aide.[73]

This sense of fear was carefully cultivated by the inquisitorial authorities. In 1564 a lawyer wrote to the *Suprema* from Galicia to say that there was a need 'that people nurture fear' there respecting the Inquisition.[74] And in 1578, when Francisco Peña republished

Directorium Inquisitorium – the 14th-century rubric for inquisitorial procedure written by Nicolas Eymerich, an inquisitor of Aragon – he wrote, 'We must remember that the essential aim of the trial and death sentence is not saving the soul of the defendant but furthering the public good and terrorizing the people'.[75]

The Inquisition clearly believed that fear was the best way to achieve political ends. This was, as the French historian Bartolomé Benassar has put it, a 'pedagogy of fear':[76] an entire institutional and political armoury designed to propagate terror in the population whose best interests it supposedly had at heart. The fear was mythologized through the use of torture and burning. It began from the very moment the inquisitors arrived in a town and read their edict of faith, enjoining anyone who had either committed an error of the faith, or knew of someone who had done, to come before the inquisitors within thirty days and confess or denounce.[77] Fear spread through society with the power of the Inquisition to deliver social and financial ruin, ensuring the poverty of its victims by confiscating their goods, banishing them from their home towns and decreeing that their descendants could not fill any official post or wear silks, jewels or any other adornments of prestige.[78] Most of all, fear was ensured by the principle of secrecy, which meant that the accused could not know the names of their accusers.

Yet it was the apparatus of fear which in the end destroyed the whole. As the stories of Lithgow in Malaga and Maestre in Hellín show, resistance was never far away. The inquisitors' attempts to impose their will through force merely inspired rebellion; this in turn created more targets, and so a vicious circle formed. It was impossible to purge society of its enemies, because society – and the Inquisition – was itself creating them.

The essential world view of the Iberian Inquisitions was that anything that was different was a form of rebellion. Their sheer diversity and long time-span, together with their enormous bureaucratic machine, make them unparalleled as institutions through which to examine persecution. This is, in the end, the story of how persecution can arise and how it can be avoided; it is a story whose relevance never vanishes, a warning from the past.[79]

My hope is that the violence of some of what follows is tempered, and transcended, by the ultimate refusal of people in the

Iberian worlds to submit to the reign of fear. The fact that excesses of power always, in the end, destroy their perpetrators is a source of consolation, and a testament to the complex and paradoxical nature of the human condition that emerges from the remarkable stories which fill the archives of the Inquisition in Portugal and Spain. Thus in telling this story I hope to fulfil something of what the great American historian Henry Charles Lea described as his philosophy of history: Lea, whose three-volume history of the Spanish Inquisition remains the standard work on the subject, completed the publication of his book with Macmillan exactly one hundred years ago; it was his hope that the study of the past 'can make us more exigent with the present and more hopeful of the future'.[80]

Chapter One

THE END OF TOLERANCE

Who can doubt that what seems in this tribunal to be severity of justice is in fact a medicine, ordained by mercy for the health of the delinquents?

Teruel and Zaragoza 1484–1486

IN THE HOUSEHOLD OF Juan Garces de Marcilla, hatred coursed its prey. Marcilla was a local noble in the remote Aragonese town of Teruel. Ashamed of his indigence, he had married Brianda, daughter of a powerful local businessman, Jaime Martínez Santángel. Marcilla loathed his in-laws and this was an era in which such workaday odium could be taken to its extreme: he made sure that they would be burnt to death.

The new inquisitor, Juan de Solibera, arrived in Teruel in May 1484. There was no welcoming committee. In fact, the local authorities were appalled. They probably knew that there had been resistance in some parts of Castile to the introduction of the Inquisition there.[1] They determined to follow suit. When there were so many great and elegant cities in the kingdom of Aragon, why had their remote settlement high in the bare hills been selected as the first calling point for the new institution? What were the implications of the sacking of the old inquisitors and the introduction of the new? The town leaders wrote that they feared the Inquisition would bring the same chaos as it had 'in Castile, and that [the inquisitors] would bring the very same heinous procedures that they had used there, in violation of all law'.[2] Yet not everyone was as fearful; some, like Marcilla, sensed an opportunity in the interstices of hatred.

Initially, however, Marcilla was in the minority. The authorities held out. In resisting, they were not merely standing up for local autonomy; they perhaps sensed that the new Inquisition, designed to persecute people who were different, would destroy the delicate cultural fabric which made the town what it was. For the inhabitants of Teruel were a mixed bunch. In addition to the majority Christian population, there was a large community of people descended from Jewish converts to Christianity – *conversos*.* Between 1391 and 1413 there had been many such conversions, some of them voluntary and some of them forced;[3] the children and grandchildren of these converts were mostly sincere Christians, but they maintained some of the cultural practices of their Jewish ancestors. In addition to the *conversos*, Teruel had a large population of converted Muslims who had switched to Christianity along with the Jews after listening to the preaching of St Vincent Ferrer in the early 15th century. These converts – known as *moriscos* – had abandoned Moorish dress and no longer spoke Arabic; they had assimilated fully into society.[4]

The arrival of the inquisitor caused panic. The Inquisition had been created in Spain within the past few years to target alleged bad Christians among the *conversos*, and three years previously the first auto had been staged, in Seville. The combination of fear and local official resistance meant that as soon as he appeared in Teruel Solibera was shut up in a monastery for three weeks and prevented from preaching his inaugural sermon. Eventually he had to move to a nearby hamlet, from which he righteously thundered excommunications at the town officials.[5] They responded with gusto. In open mockery of inquisitorial procedure, they built a great fire with a stake in the middle. Yet instead of this serving as a place for the burning of heretics, they surrounded the fire with stones which were hurled at anyone who came to the town with royal letters or decrees supporting the Inquisition.[6]

Marcilla organized the inquisitor's fightback. First he ensured that Solibera was given an armed guard. Then he used the guard to ensure

---

* Over the long history of the Inquisition, many different terms were used to describe the descendants of converted Jews. For the sake of clarity, I shall describe them as *conversos* throughout this book, although it needs to be remembered that this is a word usually limited to 15th-century Spain, and that the term New Christian (*cristão novo*) was used instead in Portugal; however as in Spain New Christian referred to people of Muslim as well as Jewish descent, I shall stick to *converso*.

that Teruel's rebellious officials were arrested. All of them were sacked. Marcilla was made captain of the town. He was instructed to seize Teruel, appoint new officials and install the new Inquisition.

In March 1485 Marcilla took the town and the Inquisition began work. In August the first auto was held and two *converso* effigies were burnt; in January 1486 there was another auto and nine *conversos* were burnt. The most important of them was Jaime Martínez Santángel, the brother-in-law of one of the officials who had resisted Inquisitor Solibera the year before. Two of Santangel's sons were burnt alive and one was burnt in effigy.[7] Jaime Martínez Santángel, one recalls, was the father-in-law of Marcilla, and his sons were Marcilla's brothers-in-law. Through the Inquisition Marcilla had set about destroying his relatives by marriage.[8] He had also given his support to an institution which the new monarchs of Aragon and Castile, Ferdinand and Isabella – known as the *Reyes Católicos* – had placed at the forefront of their domestic policy. This alone was enough to see him rise through the ranks even as his wife's family was destroyed.

Soon enough, in Zaragoza, the capital of the kingdom of Aragon on the banks of the Ebro river, events in Teruel would be echoed. Zaragoza was renowned for its nobility and the beauty of its women. Just eight years before the Spanish conquest of Granada in 1492, there was still a large Moorish quarter with an oil press and functioning mosque,[9] while travellers often admired its houses of thin red Roman-style bricks and its bevy of churches.[10]

Soon, however, there would be blood. Word of events in Teruel began to reach the town. Anger in the *converso* community grew. It was bad enough that the Inquisition had begun work in Castile, but now who was this Marcilla, to bring down Don Jaime Martínez Santángel of Aragon! Doubtless this doughty champion of the Inquisition had married Brianda for her *converso* money: he despised her, although perhaps her family had slighted him, flaunting their wealth in the face of his much-vaunted but straitened nobility.

Beneath the anger pulsed fear. For what Marcilla had really done was to effect a coup. With the Inquisition, there was the prospect of power.

★

SOLIBERA'S FELLOW inquisitor was Pedro de Arbues. Arbues had been born not far from Zaragoza in 1441.[11] He had studied at Bologna in Italy and risen through the ranks of the Church before being made an inquisitor alongside Solibera in 1484. His attachment to the ideology of the times was revealed by the inaugural speech he made to the Council of the Inquisition in Zaragoza. 'Our purpose,' he said, 'is to watch over the vine of the Church as careful sentries, picking out heresies from the wheat of religion . . . if it is carefully considered, it will be seen that all this, which seems horrible at first glance, is nothing but mercy . . . Who can doubt that what seems in this tribunal to be severity of justice is in fact a medicine, ordained by mercy for the health of the delinquents?'[12]

With Arbues and Solibera, the Inquisition set up shop in Aragon. As edicts of faith were read, people began to follow the initial rebellious example of Teruel. Both Catholics who had no Jewish or Islamic ancestry – the so-called Old Christians – and *conversos* started to murmur against the Inquisition in Zaragoza. The *conversos* were joined by members of the nobility and the richest people of the city, who complained that the new Inquisition acted in violation of the laws of Aragon, confiscating goods and keeping secret the names of witnesses, two things 'most new, and never seen before, and most prejudicial for the kingdom'.[13] By February 1485 the indignation was such that some *conversos* decided to attempt something outrageous: the assassination of the feared Arbues.[14]

The plot was hatched in the house of the leading *converso* Luis de Santángel. A bounty of 500 florins was placed on the head of Arbues, and a team of six assassins was chosen. The team was a mixture of *conversos* – the father of one of them, Juan de Esperandeu, had already been imprisoned by the Inquisition – and Old Christians, including Vidal Duranzo, the Gascon servant of Juan de Abadía, another of the assassins.[15] The idea was that if Arbues was killed, no inquisitor would dare to fill his shoes.[16]

Rumours were rife. The first auto in Zaragoza, with burnings, took place in May. Another followed in June. Indignation rose all the while among the *converso* community. Assuming a conspiracy, Arbues took to wearing a chain-mail undershirt and an iron helmet beneath his hat.[17] One night, Juan de Esperandeu tried to cut away one of the bars of his window while Arbues was asleep in bed but he was discovered and ran off in the dark.[18]

On the night of Wednesday 14 September 1485, the assassins gathered by the cathedral. Three entered by the main entrance, three by the sacristy. They knew that that night Arbues, a Dominican, would come to midnight mass. Towards midnight the cathedral canons assembled in the choir. Arbues entered from the cloisters in his canonical dress, bearing a lantern in his hands, and walked towards them. He knelt next to the pulpit on the left and began to pray. Charging from the shadows, Vidal Duranzo stabbed the inquisitor through the back with such force that he pierced the chain mail and cut his jugular vein; Esperandeu, probably overexcited at the prospect of gaining revenge on his father's nemesis, stabbed weakly and grazed Arbues's arm. Duranzo now struck again, the helmet pitched from Arbues's head and the inquisitor fell to the floor.[19]

Arbues was carried back to his lodgings. He died before dawn. The news spread at once and the cry went up throughout the town: '*A fuego con los conversos!*' – 'To the fire with the *conversos*!' It was only through the intervention of Don Alonso de Aragón, viceroy and archbishop of Aragon, who rode out into the mob to calm them, that the *converso* quarter was saved from being put to the torch.[20] As it was, it was decided that the perpetrators would be punished by the Inquisition instead.

The investigations started at once. The famed inquisitor-general Tomás de Torquemada sent three replacement inquisitors in Arbues's stead, and the prime suspects were interrogated. One of those seized was Duranzo, who confessed after being tortured. Promised mercy if he would disclose the names of his accomplices, he revealed all; on claiming his mercy when he had finished, he was told that, unlike the other conspirators, he would receive the mercy of not having his hands severed before he was hung, drawn and quartered.[21]

So began the fires in Zaragoza. In 1486 there were to be no fewer than fourteen autos there: forty-two people were burnt alive and fourteen in effigy. To increase the public fear and the impressiveness of the autos, Inquisitor-General Torquemada ordered that a fortnight before each auto the event should be proclaimed publicly across the city by a parade of mounted officials.[22] This, for the first time, turned the Inquisition into a genuinely public affair. The terror of the *converso* community was total, and many of them fled. Among the victims were three ancestors of the French philosopher Michel de Montaigne: Juan Fernando López de Villanueva, his son Micer Pablo and their cousin Ramón López; the rest of the family escaped to France, Antwerp and London where the fear was distilled for several generations to come.[23]

In general, following these events in Zaragoza, people's fury at the Inquisition rarely exceeded their fear. Yet even before their anger clouded their judgement, the *conversos* had not been alone in their distrust of the new institution, as the events in Teruel and the initial reactions in Zaragoza had shown.[24] The suspicion and resistance with which the Inquisition had been greeted in Aragon had arisen because this was a new institution which represented a way of treating people which seemed excessive. Yet it would not take long for the excessive to appear normal, and for fear of the new institution to become a way of life.

SPAIN DURING THE REIGN of the *Reyes Católicos* was unique in Europe. The Jews had arrived before the birth of Christ,[25] and with the Moorish invasion of 711 there had been large-scale migration from North Africa. Even after the Christian reconquest, which had its most decisive triumphs in the mid-13th century,* Spain, with its blend of cultures, was more akin to a Muslim society than it was to the rest of Europe. Physical geography may have tied Iberia to the lands north of the Pyrenees but the importance of geographical ideas of space was limited then, and the fact that Spain felt like an Islamic sort of place was much more important:[26] for visitors from northern Europe, the legacy of the *convivencia* – the centuries of shared Christian, Jewish and Muslim life in the peninsula – was a place with what seemed to their eyes to be confused categories.

There was, for instance, the way in which people dressed.

* Under Ferdinand III, Castilian forces took Cordoba (1236), Murcia (1241), Jaén (1246) and Seville (1248).

Whether they were going to a party or doing the housework, women in Spain covered their heads with *tocados*, elaborate headdresses sometimes made of velvet or satin that wound down the neck.[27] For most women's clothing, however, silk was the material of choice, something which went back to the manufacturing traditions of Moorish Andalusia.[28]

Among men, the second half of the 15th century had even seen a growing fashion for Moorish dress. During the reign of Henry IV (1454–74) this was so prevalent that 'whoever imitated [the Moors] the best pleased the king the most'.[29] And in 1497 King Ferdinand no less presented himself with his train of nobles dressed in Moorish style at Burgos to celebrate the betrothal of his son Prince John.[30] Moorish fashion accessories for men included the *sayo*, a bodysuit over which other garments were worn, and two types of hooded cloak, the *albornoz* and the *capellar*.[31]

For other Europeans, then, even Christian Spaniards seemed exotic. The secretary of the Baron de Rosmithal, visiting Burgos in the middle of the 15th century, described a Christian noble's house where the women were all 'richly dressed in the Moorish style, following Moorish customs in their dress, food and drink . . . dancing very beautifully in the Moorish style, all of them dark, with black eyes'.[32] Over seven centuries of Moorish presence – and for much of this time dominance – in Iberia had left deep marks which the conquest of Granada in 1492 would not erase; even the most widely recognizable of all Spanish phrases today, *¡Olé!*, derives from the Arabic *Wa-l-lah* – For God.[33]

Cultural crossovers were many. In Castile Jews often sponsored Christians at their baptisms, while Christians did likewise at Jewish circumcision ceremonies.[34] In the 14th century Christians would bring Muslim friends to mass and even hire Muslim buskers to play music in churches during night vigils.[35] As late as the 15th century Christians and Jews apprenticed their children to live among the other religious group for years[36] while Jews converted to Islam and Muslims converted to Judaism.[37] And although sexual relations between peoples of different faiths were taboo, they were common enough; in 1356 the king of Aragon granted a local monastery jurisdiction over Muslim women caught having sex with Christians in the locality, but the following year had to change this so that women who had had sex with the monks themselves were not included.[38]

Yet in spite of all this sharing in one another's lives, the fault lines between the three faiths were always there, waiting to be exaggerated by extremists. Muslims and Christians used bath houses on different days, for instance, while neither Jews nor Muslims were permitted to convert Christians.[39] By the late 15th century there was considerable pressure to separate Jews and Muslims in cities from Christians. The barriers were coming up.

Thus it was that by the end of the 15th century, when the furore around the Inquisition broke out in Aragon, the three communities performed quite different functions in Spanish society. The Christians were nobles, churchmen and fighters;[40] Jews were craftsmen, financiers and intellectuals; and Muslims were predominantly agriculturalists and craftsmen.[41] This was a society where activity was increasingly defined by faith – something which would have disastrous consequences for Spanish society when two of the faiths were excluded.

In Spain, the militarized nature of Christian society after the reconquest created a national character that was decidedly testy. 'They are proud, and think that no nation can be compared to their own,' wrote one Italian traveller, '. . . they do not like foreigners, and are very surly with them; they are inclined to take up weapons, more so than any other Christian nation, and are extremely good at using them, being agile and very expert, and very quick in moving their arms; they value honour to such a degree that they prefer to give little thought to their own deaths rather than stain it'.[42]

Such characteristics were problematic. The tendency of human societies towards aggression had been exaggerated in Spain by the triumph of the warrior caste in the reconquest. After the whole country but Granada had been won for Christendom, the 15th century saw a series of civil wars. Seville was sacked in 1471 by the rival supporters of the duke of Medina Sidonia and the marquis of Cádiz,[43] and the factionalism spilled out into a civil war which raged across Andalusia for four years.[44] The situation was so bad that, said the chronicler Bernaldez, 'it is impossible to write about the travails of King Henry [IV] at that time'.[45] Towns were destroyed, crown goods stolen, and royal rents plummeted to levels never seen before.[46]

If Spain were to survive, the aggression would have to be directed at some external foe. A target was needed on which all this destructive energy could be spent. In societies ambiguous groups are often thought dangerous and can become the focus of violence at times of pressure.[47] The *conversos* were just such a group, now in the category of Christians, but not long ago belonging to the category of Jews. They would prove to be easy enough to vilify, and destroy.

Toledo 1449

ON 26 JANUARY 1449, Don Álvaro de Luna, King John II of Castile's special constable, passed through Toledo. Luna was a short man with an unusually small face, but he was a great horseman and a talented fighter. He was the most powerful man in Castile.[48]

Luna was en route to fight John II's cause against the Aragonese, who had recently attacked. Crossing the River Tejo and climbing the steep steps away from the yellowing plains up to the Plaza de Zocódover, he demanded one million *maravedís* from Toledo for the campaign. The Toledanos were incensed; suspecting the rich *converso* tax collector Alonso Cota of instigating the tax, a mob gathered the next day, after Luna had departed, and sacked the Magdalena quarter, where the richest *conversos* lived. The targeting of scape-goats had begun.[49]

Luna was hardly a popular figure in Toledo. In justifying the riot to King John, the mayor (*alcalde mayor*) of Toledo, Pero de Sarmiento, described how for the past thirty years Luna had 'tyrannically and dissipatedly devastated and usurped your kingdoms every day . . . seizing for himself the task of ruling and commanding and the glory and power of [the] Crown'.[50] Near Toledo, Sarmiento continued, Luna had destroyed vines and plantations, killed or seized the residents and burnt their houses, 'making war against us as if we were Moors'.[51] Luna's most grievous crime, however, was selling public offices to the highest bidder; he had dealt openly with *conversos*, 'who are mostly infidels and heretics, and have Judaized and Judaize [were secret Jews while outwardly Christian]'.[52]

John II was one of the weakest kings Castile had had for a long time. Tall, blond and pale-faced, he was more interested in reading, hunting in the woods, singing and playing musical instruments than in ruling.[53] He left the daily running of the kingdom's affairs to Luna, and this was the cause of much resentment. Luna was said to be richer than all the nobles and bishops of Spain put together.[54] If there was any town or property near his own he had to have it, and so 'his estate grew like the plague'.[55]

This was, then, the condition of the kingdom when Luna arrived in Toledo early in 1449. Power under John II had become increasingly concentrated; witch-hunts of imaginary enemies took place, and some collaborated to rob others. It was a foretaste of the Inquisition; the feebleness of the king had allowed dangerous precedents to be set.[56]

Having sanctioned the riot against the *conversos* of Toledo, Mayor Sarmiento needed to find some justification for his behaviour. Moreover the attack on Luna's *converso* ally Cota was a thinly veiled attack on the king himself. When John II arrived, Sarmiento refused to allow him in, and instead bombarded the royal party with arrows and stones from the bluster of crags upon which Toledo perched.[57] Sarmiento then threw numerous gentlemen, ladies, monks and nuns out of the city. An excuse for all this had to be found, and, in keeping with the initial riot of 27 January, it was found in the *conversos*.

On 5 June 1449 Sarmiento published his so-called *Sentencia-Estatuto* on behalf of the city. In this he described how the *conversos* slaughtered lambs on Maundy Thursday, eating them and 'making other sorts of Jewish holocausts and sacrifices'.[58] They had recently gathered and plotted to seize the city and destroy the Old Christians. In view of the arbitrary power which they exercised over Christians and the dubiousness of their Christian faith, the *conversos* were banned from all official posts in the city and from acting as witnesses.[59] Only those who could prove their *limpieza de sangre* (the absence of any Jewish ancestry) could hold public office.

The arguments of the rebels in Toledo did not stand up. If Luna was such a tyrant that he appointed *conversos* to tyrannize Old

Christians, it could not be true that the *conversos* were all-powerful in the city (as they answered to Luna); while if the *conversos* were all-powerful, Luna could not be such a tyrant.[60] Moreover the accusation that *conversos* were bloodsucking financiers was a wild generalization, since the vast majority of *conversos* in Toledo and elsewhere in Spain did not work in finance and were artisans.[61] As with the history of scapegoating in general, the activities of a few were extended to the whole.[62]

The inconsistencies of the argument suggest that the religious failings of the *conversos* – the supposed justification for the statute enacted against them – were, if not simply false, exaggerated to promote the rebels' own political agenda.[63] If religion was so important to the outbreak of violence against *conversos*, it is difficult to understand why, after the pogroms of 1391, Jews were able to live in such peace in 15th-century Spain that people migrated there from both Portugal and North Africa to join Jewish communities.[64] Many *conversos* had actually risen to powerful positions in the Church and were unimpeachable Christians; the same accusations could not be made against all of them with a clear conscience.

In fact, one of the crucial differences between Jews and *conversos* was that in the 15th century the Jews were agriculturalists and lived in small towns,[65] whereas the *conversos* tended to congregate in large urban centres where power was increasingly concentrated. Resentment of *conversos* can therefore at least partly be ascribed to animosity towards the new urban concentrations of power.[66]

The 1449 rebels of Toledo put forward several justifications for the attack on the *converso* quarter and the suppression of *converso* rights. Yet these justifications were mutually incompatible, and merely served to show that the assault was driven by a different and more shadowy agenda. In the dusty, frightened and remote towns of medieval Spain, the chain of events which led to the establishment of the Inquisition had begun with the invention of a fictitious threat. Thus emerged the first great lie of so many.

THE VIOLENCE AGAINST *conversos* spread rapidly. Just two weeks after the publication of Sarmiento's statute in Toledo, on 18 June 1449, the *conversos* of the nearby city of Ciudad Real led by Juan Gonçalez, 'knowing that at this time they were sure to be robbed', formed a militia of 300 men and marched through the city, shouting that before they were despoiled they would burn the city to the ground. This desperate action – a foretaste of the events in Zaragoza of 1485 – merely provoked their enemies. Riots broke out on Tuesday 8 July. The *converso* quarter was sacked and looted.[67]

Violence against *conversos* became a feature of Castilian life for the next thirty years.* In 1474 Ciudad Real was again the focus. The riot began on 6 October, when a mob 'poured out of houses and monasteries . . . killing fifteen people, and robbing and sacking all the property of the victims, taking jewels and merchandise . . . neither possession nor store was left which was not robbed, and they stole the cattle from the fields around the city . . . burning many of their stores and homes . . . and when [the *conversos*] retreated to claim asylum in the alcazar (fortress) of the city with the chief magistrate the mob fought and entered the alcazar and knocked down its towers and killed many people . . . and after having killed them they threw their bodies in the caves and the fields for the dogs to eat'.[68] Those *conversos* found were killed, but the hatred was not universal; eight *conversos* sheltered in the house of an Old Christian, Pedro de Torres, who hid them and so saved their lives.[69]

The violence directed at the *conversos* would have been difficult to justify without good arguments. Fortunately for the rioting Old Christian population, the failings of the *conversos* were said to be many. Their enemies painted elaborate pictures of how their customs in the years 'before the Inquisition were no more nor less than those of the stinking Jews themselves'.[70]

Yet if the *conversos* were hated by the Christians, the Jews liked them no better. The rabbis of North Africa repeatedly stated that they were assimilating into Christian life and by the middle of the 15th century saw them as voluntary converts,[71] while in Spain the Jews testified falsely against them when the Inquisition was finally founded.[72] The *conversos* were therefore in the unenviable position of being seen as Jews by the Christians and as Christians by the

* There were attacks in Medina del Campo (1461), Toledo (1467), Jaén (1468), Valladolid (1470) and Cordoba (1473); the latter was perhaps the most serious, as the riots spread throughout the surrounding province.

Jews; each saw them as an ambiguous group and wanted to exclude them.

Everyone hated them, yet it was impossible to generalize about the faith of *conversos*. Families were split down the middle. One widow in 1470 requested in her will that her Christian daughter Margarita and Jewish son Vidal should 'deal with one another in seemly fashion and shall live in peace and unity and love'.[73] In some families the husband would be Jewish and the wife Christian. Some *conversos* would circumcize themselves and keep some of the Jewish fasts but not all, and some of the Christian ones but not all.[74] One satire depicted the *converso* as having the cross at his feet, the Koran at his chest and the Torah at his head, testament to the confusion and ambiguities which their position as outsiders had forced on *conversos*.[75]

The caricature of *converso* life put about by their enemies was therefore far from the truth; there was no evidence of a hidden and subversive Judaizing movement among them in this period,[76] and those *conversos* who did keep Jewish customs often did so more in a cultural than religious fashion.[77] Many of them, we should recall, were the children of people who had converted to Christianity in good faith.* Indeed, where there was evidence of active Judaizing among *conversos*, this appears to have been awoken by their persecution as 'Jews'.[78] Where a softer approach might well have led to genuine assimilation, the very exaggeration of the minority's supposedly seditious behaviour actually created the threatening ideology which the Inquisition was supposedly formed to eradicate.[79]

Seville 1477–1481

CONSIDER THE PIOUS archbishop of Santiago de Compostela, Rodrigo de Luna, who raped a young girl he was supposed to be caring for at a wedding party,[80] or the great flame seen in the sky and the stones that rained upon the plains of Old Castile just before the death of Henry IV in 1474, or the curious behaviour of Henry IV's pet lions – the younger ones ganged up on the dominant beast and

---

* See page 18.

ate him.[81] Portents of evil were everywhere. The faithful set out on processions. They made vows as they sought to stave off the dangers that surrounded them. Yet the signs of doom worsened. On 29 July 1478 came the most terrifying sign of all: a total eclipse of the sun made everything go black, so that the stars appeared in the sky as if it were night. People fled to the churches, and it appeared that Spain was on the brink of a great terror.[82]

There was one source of hope: the reign of the *Reyes Católicos*, who had taken control of Castile in 1476. Ferdinand was of medium build, with a demeanour that swung between gravity and laughter, and was renowned for his lofty thoughts and his love of hunting. Isabella had become queen of Spain following the death of her half-brother Henry IV. She was tall and well-built, and had chosen Ferdinand over all other suitors, apparently out of love. For much of their marriage Isabella would sleep with her maidservants and attendants whenever Ferdinand was away to preserve her reputation for fidelity.[83] She loved wearing *verdugos*, skirts fashioned on a rigid frame and made very wide which scandalized the churchmen of the day for being, as Isabella's own confessor Fernando de Talavera put it in 1477, 'vain and without benefit . . . indecent and shameless because it very easily allows for the feet and legs to be revealed'.[84]

With Ferdinand heir to the Aragonese crown* and Isabella now in control of Castile the hope was that the two would unite Spain and end all divisions. Among some people, however, there were whispers that Isabella trusted her *converso* courtiers more than Old Christians.[85] During the anti-*converso* 1470s this was something that the *Reyes Católicos* would have to address if they were to achieve the universal support of Castilians. It was in Seville that the chance first came their way.

Seville was then on the cusp between Moorish and Christian identities. Challenging the lingering atmosphere of the old medina were the tiny plazas springing up everywhere – over eighty of them – so that 'there [was] not a gentleman in Seville who [did] not have a small square outside his house, nor a church that did not have one

---

* He would become king of Aragon in 1479.

or two'.[86] The city was enclosed by a great wall over four miles long, built by its Muslim Almohad rulers in the 12th century.[87] The wall protected against a sudden rise in the Guadalquivir, but it also separated the urban society inside from the orchards that stretched to fill the river plain. It characterized an embattled mentality.

In 1477, the year after taking power in Castile, Ferdinand and Isabella went to Andalusia to try to resolve the civil wars which had been raging there since 1471. Reaching Seville, they stayed at the old Moorish alcazar, just next to the vast cathedral. Each day the queen would sit on a high platform covered with a gold cloth, while beneath her the bishops and nobility sat on one side of her and the members of her council and court on the other. For two months her secretary would bring her the petitions of plaintiffs, and Isabella would try to resolve them within three days at most. Here, the queen saw at first hand the enmities which had torn the region apart during the wars between the followers of the marquis of Cádiz and the duke of Medina Sidonia.[88]

A visitor arrived from Sicily, subject to the Aragonese crown. Felipe de Barberis was attached to the old medieval Inquisition in Sicily, and he suggested that the *Reyes Católicos* found one in Spain. He was supported by the prior of the Dominicans in Seville, Alonso de Ojeda, who urged action against the *conversos*.[89] The idea of an Inquisition had been circulating at court for some years, following the writings of the Franciscan friar Alonso de Espina in the 1450s.[90] Espina's ideas now found a receptive audience. It is said that the *Reyes Católicos* were shown a panorama of the city one Friday night; none of the chimneys in the *converso* quarter was sending up smoke. Significantly, their religion prohibited Jews from lighting fires on their sabbath running from the eve of Friday to the eve of Saturday.

Ferdinand and Isabella were convinced. They sent embassies to the Vatican to plead their case. On 1 November 1478 Pope Sixtus IV issued the bull *Exigit Sincerae Devotionis Affectus*, the foundational papal bull of the Spanish Inquisition. In keeping with the confusion in Andalusia, the religious and political motivations for the new Inquisition were confused in the bull: 'We are aware that in different cities of your kingdoms of Spain many of those who were regenerated by the sacred baptismal waters of their own free will have returned secretly to the observance of the laws and customs of the

Jewish [faith] . . . because of the crimes of these men and the tolerance of the Holy See towards them civil war, murder and innumerable ills afflict your kingdoms'.[91]

As with Toledo in 1449, the distinct political and religious reasons suggested here for the Inquisition are revealing. It was not simply a matter of Ferdinand's desire to plunder *converso* goods or the papacy's desire to extend its influence to Castile.[92] The modernizing forces driving urbanization, and later the expansion towards America, created social discord and strife which needed to be displaced. The monarchs saw this at first hand in Seville in 1477, and then were presented with a solution: the violence would be displaced and directed at the *conversos* through an Inquisition. This, combined with a renewed assault on the Muslims of Granada, funded in part through the confiscations of goods of the 'Judaizing' *conversos*,[93] would serve to unite Christians and lance the boil of the arguments then dividing them.[94]

Ah, glorious, brave, adventurous Spain! One wanders the whitewashed carcasses of imperial towns from Mexico to Peru, Ecuador to Uruguay, wondering how this arid appendage of the European continent achieved so much in such a short time. Yet it turned out to be a very simple matter: the great power which Spain was to become forged its sense of purpose in part through the invention of an enemy: the persecution of the *conversos* and the recapture of Grenada allowed for a renewed sense of national togetherness and strength in Spain.[95]

THE FIRST CASTILIAN inquisitors were appointed on 27 September 1480. When the two men, Miguel de Murillo and Juan de San Martín, neared Seville, local preachers and members of the nobility came out of the city to meet them. Some went as far as the town of Carmona, a day's ride from the city, to offer them gifts and hospitality.[96] The welcome must have confirmed in the inquisitors' minds that theirs was a popular undertaking. Their power, and the deference which some were prepared to give them on account of it, was something that neither of them can have experienced before. The edict of grace was read in the cathedral of Seville, and the legalized war against the *conversos* began.

As the inquisitors arrived, others fled. Many *conversos* crossed the border into Portugal; others went to Italy and Morocco, and some travelled as far as India.[97] One refugee was Yahuda Ben Verga, who fled to Portugal as soon as the Inquisition was established. Before departing he left three doves in the window of his house in Seville, each with broken wings. On the first, which was plucked and had had its throat slit, was a note saying, 'These are those who left it too late to leave'. On the second, which was plucked but alive, the note said, 'These are those who cut it fine'. On the third, an otherwise healthy bird with all its feathers, the note said, 'These are those who got out first'.[98]

Many shared Ben Verga's feelings. Business slumped as people fled, taking their money with them. The capital flight caused tax receipts to collapse, while creditors of the *conversos* – including many Church institutions and foreign traders – were left with bad debts.[99] The fact that there were also Jews in Andalusia was said to make the heresies of the *conversos* worse, and so the Jews were expelled from Cordoba and Seville in 1483.[100] However, the Inquisition had no powers over Jews or indeed over any non-Christians; it could only prosecute baptized Christians who had committed heresy against the Church.

Some *conversos* wanted to fight. A group gathered at the house of Diego de Susán, one of the most important merchants in Seville, who came from a family that had previously been prominent in Toledo.[101] Among the others involved were Abolafia, 'the scented one', who ran the customs house for the *Reyes Católicos*, Pero Fernández Benadova, among the most senior figures in the cathedral chapter, and the Adalfe family of Triana, who lived in the castle on the far side of the Guadalquivir.[102]

These said to one another: 'Are we going to let them come against us like this! Aren't we the richest people in this city, well-loved by the people? Let's raise a militia! You can get so many people ready; and you can get some more, etc . . . And if they come to get us, with our guards we'll make a disturbance out of the whole thing, and kill them all, and revenge ourselves against our enemies' . . . then an old Jew who was there raised his voice: 'Children, noble people, on my life I think that everything is ready. But where are your souls? I want to see souls!'[103]

The plot was revealed by Susán's daughter, known as the *fermosa fembra* – the beautiful maid – who was a devoted Christian. She appears to have believed that she was doing the soul of her father a good turn.[104] Susán and the others were thrown into the castle at Triana, which was used as the inquisitorial jail, and the sentences of burning began to be pronounced. At the first auto, on 6 February 1481, six people were burnt.[105] The condemned were led forward barefoot, wearing the yellow penitential robe, the *sanbenito*, and holding a candle. Guarded by halberdiers, they were preceded by a Dominican in his black robes holding the green cross of the Inquisition and by officers of the Inquisition marching in twos. The condemned were followed by the inquisitors and the Dominican prior Alonso de Ojeda, who had mooted an Inquisition to the *Reyes Católicos* back in 1477.

Outside the cathedral Ojeda preached the sermon. When he had finished, the condemned were handed over to the secular authorities, for the moral scruples of the inquisitors meant that they were not permitted to burn people themselves. Then the six victims were led out by the crown bailiffs to the *quemadero* – the burning place. This was a scaffold in the fields outside Seville's city walls built for the express purpose of staging autos. The scaffold remained for over 300 years, into the 19th century, with four large statues at the corners known as the 'four prophets'. The statues were hollow, and the condemned would be put inside to die slowly in the flames.[106] In this way, even if the number of burnings was not high, fear could be implanted deep in the heart of society.[107]

After this first purging, another auto followed on 26 March at which seventeen people were burnt. By November, 298 people had been burnt outside the city.[108] Between 1481 and 1488 at least 700 people were burnt at Seville alone, and another 5,000 were reconciled and had their goods seized.[109] Seville had never seen anything like it. Records of the doings of the Inquisition read like something from a satire:

> Sunday, May 2nd 1484: On this day, Sunday, a procession of reconciled *conversos* set out in the morning to go from the church of San Salvador to the monastery of San Pablo, bearing the cross of San Salvador: there were 120 reconciled men and 217 reconciled women, and they all wore their *sanbenitos*; and

> this day the officiating priest Rebelledo was sacked, and condemned to perpetual imprisonment.
>
> May 9th: On this day, Sunday, at the hour of Mass a procession of 94 men and women was taken to be put in the castle in Triana, since they had been condemned to perpetual imprisonment as heretics . . . they were taken to the sound of litanies . . .[110]

The castle could not cope with the numbers of those condemned to 'perpetual imprisonment' and the streets filled with people clad in *sanbenitos*, embossed with crosses on the front and the back, which the reconciled were obliged to wear as testament to their shame even after their appearance in an auto.[111] Seville was thick with litanies and the condemned, a threnody for what Spain had been and for what it was to become. A city in which conflict had until recently been a matter of politics now bore the scars of religious struggles.

The result was increasing polarization and fundamentalism, justified by religion but feeding off something else. When Susán was burnt, he appeared to die a Christian,[112] which suggests that evidence for the Judaizing of his group was extremely thin. What was more, his repentance should have meant that he was spared death in the flames according to previous inquisitorial practice; what the excesses revealed was that religion was an excuse rather than the guiding motivation.

In many ways, when looking at the decision of the *Reyes Católicos* to establish an Inquisition in Seville in 1477, it is difficult to see what choice they had in the matter. Human nature appears prone to creating scapegoats in times of crisis. Had Ferdinand and Isabella not sought to stabilize their kingdoms, they doubtless would have been among the first to suffer from the continuing rebellions.

What was new in their Spanish Inquisition was not persecution, but the institutionalization of persecution. The crisis had been provoked by the modernization of Spanish society in the 15th century, and the Inquisition was the first modern persecuting institution in history.[113] It was the fear and distrust which people felt towards the economic requirements of the new social system which ensured that the *conversos* would be among the first victims of the modern world. And yet it was not the *conversos* alone who suffered; just weeks after the first auto the plague swept across Seville, and among the very first victims was Alonso de Ojeda, the prior who had lobbied so hard for the Inquisition in the first place.

Ciudad Real 1483

By the time the Inquisition began its work in Seville, Ciudad Real, remote and high on the Castillian *meseta*, was waiting to explode. If one strayed onto the plains north towards Toledo or south towards Cordoba, one entered baking, desiccated, hostile territory. It was easy to internalize that hostility and direct it at one's friends and neighbours. In April 1483 the new Inquisition established a court in Ciudad Real; the riots against the *conversos* of 1474 had passed, but this time they would not be allowed to escape.

As soon as the court was established it was flooded with business. The Inquisition office was located in a public area, and if someone was seen entering others would worry about who was being denounced. People knew that if they did not present themselves freely to declare something that was – or ought to have been – on their conscience, they could well end up on the *quemadero*. Thus one denunciation led to another, and the new court was so pressured that their only free days were holy days and those Sundays when no autos were held.[114]

One of the first cases was against Sancho de Çibdad and his wife Mari. They had fled the city two weeks before the arrival of the inquisitors. Sancho was a powerful local figure, a town councillor and tax collector with many enemies. He was accused of acting as a rabbi, keeping Jewish festivals and mocking Jesus; he had been seen praying in Hebrew in a cart, and insisted that people bring him animals alive (presumably so as to kill them according to Jewish ritual); other people came from all over the *converso* quarter to his house to pray in a tower there.[115] Another *converso* religious leader in Ciudad Real was said to be Maria Diaz, 'la Çerera', who had also fled; she was said by many witnesses to keep the Jewish sabbath, lighting a candle on Friday nights, refusing to work on Saturdays, and never going to church.[116]

The truth was that evidence of Judaizing activity among the *conversos* was extremely mixed. There was some proof, such as the Hebrew prayer found in the house of the cobbler Juan Alegre[117] and the Hebrew prayer book found being read by the spice merchant Juan Falcón on the Jewish sabbath.[118] Much of the evidence, however, was stretched to its limits. Many of the depositions against the Çibdad family and la Çerera, for instance, referred to events that had happened at least ten years previously – and in Çibdad's case, some of it was from thirty years before. Another defendant, Juan González Pintado, had paid for an altar and a statue of the Virgin in the church of Santo Domingo, and numerous priests said they had seen him at mass and confessing, and that he ate pork. Tragically for Pintado, however, he had been the secretary of John II and Henry IV, and the political rather than strictly religious nature of the Spanish Inquisition ensured that he was burnt anyway.[119]

So the Inquisition in Ciudad Real, far from only punishing genuine heretics, burnt just as many good Catholics as it did people whose religious outlook was more mixed. As would prove often to be the case, sincere Catholics were among the principal victims of the Inquisition. In fact, what really emerges from the trial records of the city is the envy and family discord at the heart of so many of the cases – emotions that meant that some of the denunciations were sure to be malicious.

In the trial of Sancho and Mari de Çibdad, for instance, one of the witnesses was the couple's daughter Catalina, who gave evidence of her life in the family home as a child many years before and also accused her brother Diego and sister Teresa of Judaizing.[120] In another case, the son of one Catalina de Zamora went to his mother's house when he heard that the Inquisition was to come to Ciudad Real, and said, 'Listen, you old whore: if the inquisitors come here, I'll make sure that you and your sisters are burnt as Jews, and I'll make sure that the bones of your Jewish mother are exhumed and burnt as well'.[121] This sorry excuse for a human being, a friar in the town, clearly believed that his family's blood should not be thicker than water – there should simply be more of it.

Some will find it hard to understand how people could say and do such terrible things. Yet possible motivations are easy to imagine: perhaps Catalina de Zamora's son had always resented being groomed for a career as a celibate in the Church and had keened for revenge; perhaps he felt excluded by the vestiges of Judaizing culture in his family and wanted to punish others for the shame he felt. Certainly, these were unhappy lives, and for some the persecution of the Inquisition, following on from all this bitterness, was the final straw: one prisoner, Juana Gonzalez, committed suicide on 29 November 1483 by drowning herself in a pool by the house where she was kept under guard.[122]

Around fifty people are thought to have been burnt in 1483 and 1484 in Ciudad Real, a significant number for a relatively small, isolated town in medieval Spain.[123] The cases graphically reveal the reasons for the desperation of the *conversos*, who had converted from a desire to assimilate but were rejected by the very people with whom they wished to become one. Many of the trials – such as those of Sancho de Çibdad and Juan González Pintado – were clearly political. In other cases, people who confessed their sins were burnt anyway.[124]

The *conversos* of Ciudad Real were evidently neither all Judaizers nor all Catholics, but occupied various positions in between. With time, they probably would have been assimilated into the wider cultural ambience. Those who really longed to be Jews could have joined the Jewish exodus from Spain in 1492 to lands where they could practise their faith openly. But the *conversos* of Ciudad Real were not allowed this luxury, and the flight of so many people from the city on hearing of the coming of the inquisitors merely reflected the fact that they knew that they would not get a fair trial.

This was certainly the case with Sancho and Mari de Çibdad. The distinguished couple fled the brown heart of Castile for the port of Valencia. Here they hoped to escape to Italy. They set sail and were at sea for five days until headwinds drove them back to port. There they were arrested and taken back to Ciudad Real, before being transferred to Toledo – the Inquisition had moved here from Ciudad Real in 1485 – and the following year Sancho and Mari de Çibdad were the first *conversos* to be burnt to death in an auto in the very city where the anti-*converso* movement had originally begun, on that rocky redoubt above the plains.[125]

*

THEATRE HAS PERHAPS always been the province of religion. At the death of John Paul II in April 2005 and the acclamation of his successor Benedict XVI the seething crowds in St Peter's Square reminded the world of the spectacle that only faith can deliver. Just a week after Benedict XVI's inaugural Sunday mass the possibility of theatre's corruption by power was also apparent. The crowds were still there, as were the newly printed autobiographies of Ratzinger/Benedict on all the stalls around the piazza. Only in the great cathedral itself, with its hanging friezes of sunlight stilled in the haunting nave, did spirituality fully assert itself above publicity and the potential of every spectacle to turn to violence.

The papacy, with its ancient history and keen appreciation of balances of power, was always a moderating influence on the Spanish Inquisition. In 1481, newly confident from the success of the inquisitors in Seville, Ferdinand had replaced the papal inquisitors of Valencia with his own nominees, Cristofor de Gualbes and Joan Orts. Hearing of this and of the violence of the inquisitors in Seville, Pope Sixtus IV – aware that this all represented a radical departure from previous inquisitorial procedure – protested in January 1482.

Hearing repeated reports of outrages and petitioned by *conversos* over injustice, soon the pope went further. On 18 April 1482 he issued a new bull which proposed to clip the wings of the new institution. In this Sixtus IV described how the inquisitors had accepted evidence from the enemies and slaves of the accused, how they had proceeded not out of zeal for the faith but out of greed for material gain, and how the result was a procedure with no legitimacy, a pernicious example and a lachrymose scandal for all to see. Instead, he declared, the new Spanish Inquisition could only proceed with the approval of bishops; it had to reveal the names of accusers and witnesses; it had to suspend cases to hear appeals; and it had to accept any confession as having the effect of absolving the defendant.[126]

Sixtus IV's proposals were hardly severe but, given the fundamentally political motivations of the new tribunal, the *Reyes Católicos* were furious. Ferdinand wrote angrily to the pope arguing that the heresy of the *conversos* was now too widespread to be stemmed except through the institution. Eventually, in October 1482, Sixtus caved in and suspended the norms he had proposed for the Inquisition in Spain.

Soon matters became even worse. In May 1483 the court of appeal for the Inquisition in Castile was moved from Rome into the hands of the archbishop of Seville, Íñigo de Manrique. In July 1485 the *Reyes Católicos* even ordered the Church authorities in Toledo to suspend papal bulls obtained by *conversos* to protect them from the new tribunal.[127] Hereafter the ability of the Inquisition in Spain to act without papal interference was certain.

It was this process that permitted the Inquisition to spread rapidly across Spain. After the tribunal was installed in Seville in 1480, new courts of the Inquisition were founded at Cordoba, Valencia and Zaragoza in 1482, Barcelona in 1484, Llerena and Toledo in 1485, Murcia, Valladolid and Majorca in 1488 and Cuenca in 1489.[128] Autos also occurred where there was no tribunal, such as at Guadalupe in 1485, where fifty-two people were burnt in person, twenty-seven in effigy, and forty-six corpses were dug up and burnt for good measure.[129] The chronicler Hernando de Pulgar – himself a *converso* – said that 2,000 people were burnt across Spain in these years;[130] or, as another chronicler put it 'an infinite number were burnt and condemned and reconciled and imprisoned in every archbishopric of Castile and Aragon. And many of the reconciled reverted to Judaizing and were burnt because of it, in Seville and across Castile'.[131]

This expansion of the Inquisition was pushed through by the zealous Tomás de Torquemada, the first inquisitor-general. Torquemada was a dark man with a healthy complexion. He was a Dominican friar and the confessor of the *Reyes Católicos*; when he tried to tell Isabella that he was only human, she is said to have replied, 'Confessor, I only feel that I am with an angel from heaven when I am with you'.[132]

Torquemada was appointed inquisitor-general on 17 October 1483, and the following year the *Suprema*, or supreme council, was founded under his leadership. He had the power to appoint inquisitors as he saw fit, and in October 1484 all the inquisitors gathered at a council in Seville after which Torquemada issued a set of instructions to guide their judicial practice. He remained at court until 1496, suffering badly from gout in his later years.[133] The rich diet which tends to lead to this condition may also have produced an excess of full-bloodedness which his life as a monk could not satisfy; perhaps this made him peculiarly suited to the demands of his job with the Inquisition, which required, after all, a peculiar mixture of anger, repression and energy.

Under Torquemada's stewardship of the Inquisition, Spain became a very different place. The fires spread from Seville in the south to Zaragoza in the north. Everywhere people were aware that something radically new had begun. By 1488 there were so many prisoners that the jails were full and people had to live under house arrest instead.[134] An atmosphere of extremism developed which meant that the expulsion of the Jews, in 1492, and of the Muslims of Granada in 1502, seemed natural steps. The *convivencia* had gone forever, and by 1526 – after the forced conversion of the Muslims of Aragon – no non-Catholics would be permitted to form part of the Spanish nation. The development of the Inquisition implied that loyalty to the state required adhering to the new militancy; a piece of aggression that had been conceived in political expediency had ended up dismantling a way of life.

IN ZARAGOZA, THE AUTOS rumbled on through the last years of the 15th century. By 1502, at least 116 people had been burnt, with another thirty-two in effigy.[135] The struggles between Ferdinand and the papacy over the new inquisitors, and between Garces de Marcilla and his relatives and the officials in Teruel, had been resolved in fire; there should now have been no question but that the institution was here to stay, but the Aragonese continued to resist it.

Over the next fifty years, appeals were regularly made in Aragon for the reform of inquisitorial procedure. This culminated in 1533, when during the Aragonese Cortes at Monzón a violent protest occurred against the new institution. According to representatives at the Cortes, inquisitors had imprisoned people for crimes outside their jurisdiction; they had tried people where there was no evidence of heresy and just a few blasphemous words had come out in the heat of the moment; they had threatened grocers with the Inquisition when they came with their wares to inquisitorial offices.[136]

One of the main locations of resistance was Sicily, at the time subject to the inquisitorial court of the crown of Aragon. Here in Palermo, sheltered from the world by the great bay and the knife-edged mountains behind the port, over seventy people were killed in autos between June 1511 and January 1516.[137] Thirty-five people were burnt in 1513 alone. The Sicilian parliament protested at the proceedings, 'by which people were taken to the stake shouting out their innocence in vain and that they had only confessed under torture their guilt, which did not in fact exist'.[138] The atmosphere was so highly charged that year that when an unbalanced man, Battista Rizzo, seized the host from a priest's hands on Easter day in Catania he was burnt alive by a mob.[139]

Matters came to a head on news of the death of Ferdinand in 1516 when mobs gathered in the streets of Palermo. The Aragonese viceroy had to flee almost 200 miles across the island to Messina to escape. The mob turned its attentions to the Inquisition, which was located in the viceroy's palace in Palermo. For three days the palace was besieged by the crowd, until eventually the inquisitor, Cervera, fled holding the Eucharist in his hands. Brought in to do God's bidding, one wonders how the inquisitor explained such events to himself: God's judgment? The triumph of the devil? Cervera rushed to the waterside and escaped into the great bay by ship, while the mob sacked the entire palace, burning the Inquisition's archive, freeing its prisoners, and stealing even the windows and the doors.[140]

Such vengeance is particularly striking since both Aragon and Sicily had had inquisitors before under the old medieval institution. The string of revolts from Sicily to Teruel and Zaragoza emphasized the fact that this was a fundamentally new inquisition. Confiscation of goods had not existed previously, and the secrecy of witnesses had been guaranteed only in cases where there were threats against their lives.[141] What is perhaps of most significance in these complaints and rebellions is that neither Aragon nor Sicily had been affected by the civil wars of Castile. There was thus no need for a persecuting institution or scapegoat, even though as in Castile there were large numbers of *conversos*. It is this above all which reveals that the religious grounds for the institution of the Inquisition were a sham and an invention of propaganda.[142]

The resistance of Aragon and the papacy to the new Spanish Inquisition invites us to speculate that those who had lived with the old Inquisition sensed that, under the *Reyes Católicos*, an arbitrariness and cruelty had accompanied the increase in inquisitorial power. These people did not trust the monarchs' stated motivations for their violent conduct. Even if we are to judge the Inquisition according to the standards of the time it is found wanting.

The really important question to ask is how this position could have been prevented in the first place; how the factionalism and the violent hatreds which settled on a sort of racial persecution could have been prevented.[143] Certainly, if Castile had not been riven by conflicts, this reality and the new Inquisition could have been avoided. These conflicts were part of a searching towards a national identity in Spain, something which for linguistic and cultural reasons occurred earlier here than elsewhere in Europe.[144] The factionalism was in part the result of weak kings, but it also resulted from powerful interest groups grasping at power and attempting to strengthen their material position, unaware that by inventing the *converso* enemy and painting it in the worst light possible, all sorts of disastrous consequences would result.

ON THE GROUND FLOOR of the famous Prado museum in Madrid, near the room where the macabre creations of Hieronymus Bosch and Pieter Breughel the Elder hint at some of the darkness that can be involved in being human, is a gallery devoted to the work of Pedro de Berruguete. Berruguete was perhaps the most important artist in the Spain of the *Reyes Católicos*. One of the paintings in the gallery was finished in around 1495; it is called *Auto de Fe*. Berruguete's *Auto de Fe* depicts St Dominic presiding over an auto of Albigensian heretics in the 13th century. The Albigensians had been the first targets of the medieval Inquisition in southern France. The saint is portrayed benevolently, but what is most striking is the air of serenity and justice which envelops the dignitaries around him. The prelates, nobles and monks barely watch the little men beneath them as they are led to the flames. One of the monks is even asleep, his face red with postprandial torpor. Meanwhile, two of the Albigensians are already being licked by the flames, and others are being taken up to join them.

Whenever I visit the Prado, taking a break from the archives of the Inquisition, I go to look at this painting. It is the calmness, indeed the indifference, of the dignitaries to the fates of the condemned which is striking. Groups chosen for sacrifice are always dehumanized by societies, just like the goat offered to Abraham by God in place of the life of his son Isaac. Their suffering is not supposed to be a cause for concern. One suspects that what Berruguete has successfully depicted here is the attitude of many of his contemporaries towards the fate of the *conversos*.

One of the details of this painting relates to the condemned men at the stake. Here, short metal spurs stick out from beneath their genitals; the spurs taper away at the end, as if circumcized. With this oblique reference to the Judaizing *conversos*, there can be no doubt that Berruguete intends his portrait of the past to raise important moral questions about the present. Even today, it speaks to us about the nature of persecution and the forces which can provoke it, which bubble away beneath even the wealthiest and most ordered of societies.

Chapter Two

SPREADING THE FIRES

. . . fearful of the punishment which for [his heresies] he deserved [he] determined to try to kill himself, without waiting for Justice to fulfil its legal obligations towards him . . .

Évora 1490–1545

IN 1474 A WHALE was beached and killed on the Portuguese coast near Setúbal, not far from Lisbon. The waxen monster from the deep had been attacking and devouring fishermen along the coast. As it lay inert upon the sands, a Portuguese rabbi announced that this was the Leviathan of the Old Testament, and that the Messiah was at hand.[1] Just as in Spain, this was a time of omens; the great struggle was near.

Yet the cataclysm stayed away. Even as the inquisitorial flames licked the *quemaderos* of Seville, Ciudad Real and Zaragoza, in Portugal everything was normal. The old king, Afonso V, died in 1481; John II replaced him, and in 1490 John's own son, Crown Prince Affonso, was betrothed to Princess Isabella of Spain. The pattern of alliance, advancement and mutual self-interest continued.

The city of Évora, less than forty miles from Portugal's border with Spain, was chosen to celebrate the royal wedding of Affonso and Isabella. In the days before the Spanish princess's arrival, there was dancing in the palaces. Parties spilled out of noble houses in the crooked streets beneath the Roman aqueduct. Mummers staged farces. Culture revealed its animalism at the bullfights. As the royal chronicler Rui de Pina put it, 'the general excitement really made it seem as if the earth was shaking'.[2]

On 27 November 1490 Princess Isabella entered Évora. All the

African slaves had been expelled from the city for ten days for her arrival, and John II had ordered the most beautiful young girls from the area to be brought in. Local farmers and stockmen brought cows and goats from their pastures, pigs with their piglets and cows with their calves. Five squares in the town were set aside for provisions so that no one would go hungry. The king built a banqueting hall of wood for the occasion. The windows of town houses were filled with boughs from orange and laurel trees and with jewels and tapestries.[3]

So much colour! Muslims were ordered to come from every Moorish community in the country; the best dancers, singers and musicians were demanded, and John II paid for them to have fine clothes and financed their journey. As Princess Isabella entered the town she was greeted by the Moors and the large local Jewish population with farces, dancing and revelry. Soon the farces filled the town. In one pageant John II himself appeared at the head of a great fleet of ships 'portrayed on cloths painted with wild waves, accompanied by an awesome roar of artillery and trumpets and kettledrums, with tremendous shouts and the racket of whistles, and beside him were shipmasters, pilots and sailors dressed in brocade and silk . . . and the awnings of the ships were made of brocade, the sails of white and violet taffeta, the cordage of gold and silk'.[4] In Portugal in 1490, theatricality did not yet imply the autos-da-fé.

As in any masquerade, John II had chosen the image which best characterized his identity. He depicted himself at the helm of a country changing by the month because of its maritime exploits – those exploits which were as terrifying as the noise that accompanied him, but grand and beautiful in their own way. The farces performed by the Jews and Muslims of Évora were also highly symbolic and in keeping with the traditions of court celebrations of the period. But these were among the very last such farces which would be performed in Portugal. Soon such raucous inter-cultural festivities would be decisively in the past. Intolerance was spreading from one part of Iberia to another.

The Inquisition did not move at once from Spain to Portugal. Some fifty-eight years separated the Inquisition's formation in Spain in 1478 and its Portuguese establishment in 1536. But attitudes and fears moved with greater vim and what had been let out could not so easily be contained. Almost sixty years later, as the *converso* Álvaro de Leão festered in the cells of the Inquisition in Évora, he must have wondered what sort of future it was that the world had sleepwalked into; the freedom and spontaneity of the celebrations that had graced that city in 1490 were crumbling husks of memory, buried under a sediment of fear.

ON 10 JANUARY 1545 the prosecutor of the Holy Office of the Inquisition in Évora put forward his case against Álvaro de Leão. Leão was a merchant, born in the frontier town of Mogadouro in north-eastern Portugal near the lush green forests alongside the Douro river. Leão came from a large family of five brothers and one sister; over the course of the next fifty years, the dealings of these people, their children and their grandchildren would encapsulate much of the global history of the Inquisition.

The prosecutor laid out his case with care. Leão, who was around thirty years old, lived in the desolate hills between Mogadouro and the nearby town of Cortiços. It was in Cortiços, the prosecutor alleged, that he 'was seen to keep the law of Moses and its ceremonies, keeping the Jewish fasts by not eating on them until stars could be seen, and giving alms to *conversos* in the Jewish manner, as *tzedakah*'. Álvaro de Leão prayed like a Jew. He gathered with other *conversos* in a sort of synagogue, keeping the Jewish sabbath, lighting candles on Friday nights and refusing to work on Saturdays. Leão was arrested with his wife Lianor de Carvajal on suspicion of Judaizing and they were both remanded in the inquisitorial prison of Évora.[5]

Álvaro denied it all. He worked on Saturdays just as he did during the week, going to local markets and selling his goods. He was known as a good Christian who always went to hear mass on Sundays and holy days, paying for masses to be said throughout the year. He had been baptized at the age of eight days just like the Old Christians were. He was a devoted Christian, and there was no reason to doubt his good faith.[6]

The prosecutor was not convinced. Prisoners often claimed innocence on their arrest; they had to be worn down. The prosecutor was used to a battle of wills; he had learnt to enjoy the struggle to impose his own over the defendants. In Mogadouro and Cortiços, he alleged, it was public knowledge that Leão had committed these crimes. He had refused to pay for the curtains and large sacramental candles for the altar, and even if it was true that 'he kept the Sundays and feasts of the Church it was also true that [Leão] kept and keeps the Jewish rites and ceremonies'.[7]

And then, abruptly, the case was shelved. Leão was sent back to the inquisitorial jail to ponder his crimes and consider repentance. He was to spend more than three years there before his case was resolved.

Leão could have been forgiven for thinking that there was some sort of vendetta against him and his family. His brother Jorge was also in the inquisitorial jail in Évora, along with Jorge's wife Branca. Like Álvaro, Jorge and Branca lived in Cortiços and Jorge was a trader there – the brothers had been arrested together on the same day.[8] Meanwhile, one of Álvaro and Jorge's maternal uncles, Bernardo López, had also been arrested by the Inquisition and was in the same prison.[9] A spell had been cast on these families which it would take centuries to break.

This case was typical of events in Portugal. In the 1480s many *conversos* fleeing the Spanish Inquisition had gone to Portugal, and when the Spanish Jews had been expelled by Ferdinand and Isabella in 1492 the majority had gone to Portugal as well – the 'easy option'.[10] These refugees had settled in towns such as Mogadouro, within spitting distance of the Spanish frontier, where they lived in uneasy coexistence with their neighbours and were blamed for the arrival of plagues which afflicted Portugal in every year between 1477 and 1496.[11]

The *converso* refugees often intermarried to an almost unhealthy degree. Thus Álvaro's sister Catalina was married to Gaspar de Carvajal,[12] who was himself related to Álvaro's own wife Lianor. Both the Carvajal and Leão families were from Mogadouro, and had strong connections to the parts of Spain just across the frontier, which were likely to have been their original stamping ground before the exodus in 1492.[13]

These outsiders were easy targets for a country attempting to come to terms with its own power. Portugal was then a nouveau riche among the nations of Europe. The conquest of Goa and the exploration of the African coast from Senegal to Kongo had given this, the final sliver of Europe before the Atlantic, control of the spice trade to Europe from Asia and of the slave and gold trade to Europe from Africa. Manoel I, John II's successor, had been called 'the fortunate'; John II was known as the 'golden king'.[14] Not everyone was as complimentary, however; Francis I of France, in a foretaste of Napoleon's dismissal of the English as a 'nation of shopkeepers', had described Manoel I as 'the grocer king'.[15]

Unprecedented amounts of money poured into Portugal. Under John II gold from Mina – located in modern Ghana – supplied almost half of the country's entire monetary wealth.[16] With money abundant as never before, the royal court soon became a monster. After Manoel I's death in 1521 the new king John III journeyed up and down the country with a huge train of retainers who wrought havoc wherever they stopped. Among the layabouts who masqueraded as courtiers, gambling and robbery were rife. These *fidalgos* trailed large numbers of servants in their wakes who all demanded sustenance and provisions. Food, horses and carts were stolen. Orchards and woods were laid waste as a sort of entertainment. The *fidalgos* had so many retainers that there was a chronic shortage of farm labour in the countryside. Fields lay fallow – razing others to the ground did not help matters.[17]

Such casual excess was typical of a society which had recently experienced an unprecedented concentration of power. In order to convince oneself that the trappings of success were not mere chimeras, such power had to be wielded in full view of others. This inevitably meant that those less fortunate than the new oligarchy had to suffer. Unlike Spain, Portugal did not have a large Muslim population which could be conquered and subdued, since the Portuguese reconquest had been completed by the middle of the 13th century and the Muslim population easily assimilated.[18] The power would therefore have to be directed elsewhere and fortunately, with the mass immigration of *conversos* and Jews from Spain in the 1480s and in 1492, there was an obvious alternative.

Incarcerated in the inquisitorial jail of Évora, Álvaro de Leão could not, of course, see how his own plight mirrored that of others in Spain and elsewhere, and indeed said something about the spending of power which characterizes aspects of the human experience. What he could do, however, was feel hatred and despair. In January 1546, a year after his first arrest and interrogation, he tried to commit suicide by stabbing himself in the belly button, making a hole four fingers wide. The inquisitorial authorities had little sympathy. Leão, they said, 'fearful of the punishment which for [his heresies] he deserved determined to try to kill himself, without waiting for Justice to fulfil its legal obligations towards him'.[19] Amid the seething religious atmosphere of Portugal at the time, there cannot have been many people who would have awaited these 'legal obligations' if they could have taken matters into their own hands instead. Nonetheless, it was frustrating when prisoners did not wait for the Inquisition to give them the punishment which they deserved.

Lisbon 1497–1506

MANOEL I came to the throne in 1495 aged 26. His predecessor John II had died from an outbreak of plague which had also carried off eight nearer claimants than Manoel, and thus many saw his kingship as preordained. Who if not a chosen one could become king in such circumstances? His birth itself was supposed to have been a miracle, with his mother Dona Beatriz racked by labour for several days until a religious procession passed the doors of her house and raised the host – the boy was born at once.[20]

Manoel was a well-built man with a round head distinguished by a prominent forehead. He had chestnut hair, greenish, mirthful eyes and a melodious voice. Music was perhaps his greatest love, and with Portugal's new wealth he brought singers and musicians from all over Europe to his court. Manoel lunched and dined to musical performances on Sundays and feast days, listening to cornets, harps and tambourines, and to *moriscos* playing lutes. Following Vasco da Gama's discovery of the route to India during his epic voyage of 1497–9, Manoel had five elephants brought back to his kingdom, which went before him whenever he rode through Lisbon, preceded by a rhinoceros.[21]

Manoel's injection of the exotic was a reflection of the country which he inherited in 1495. Lisbon at this time was one of the most cosmopolitan cities in Europe. The size of London or Cologne, it was thronged with foreigners attracted by the new trading routes.[22] Men and women freely shared one another's beds and played cards until dawn. People rode horses with very short stirrups, in the *morisco* style, and some saddles were made of silver or gold.[23] As well as the bustling port and the busy streets running off it, there were olive groves within the city walls until 1500.[24] The city's centrepiece was the Rossio, a large irregular square fringed by hills on two sides and running down towards the banks of the Tejo river; it was by the Rossio that the offices of the Inquisition would be established.

In Lisbon it was obvious that the Portuguese had no intrinsic aversion to the foreign. But just as the country was opening up to influences from outside, there was an inner sense of a need for national definition. Groups, as most people have learnt from their own experience of friendships and professional networks, gain their shape in large part not only from deciding who is to be included, but also from deciding who is to be excluded.[25] As foreign traders and products were being welcomed into the country and the number of African slaves grew, those perceived outsiders already in the country fell under closer scrutiny. This inevitably turned attention towards the Jewish and *converso* population.

At first, Manoel acted charitably towards the Jewish refugees who had arrived from Spain in 1492. Where John II had enslaved many of them after they had failed to depart within one year of being granted sanctuary, one of Manoel's first acts was to free the Jewish slaves. However in 1496 he sought the hand of Isabella, the same daughter of the *Reyes Católicos* who had been married in such lavish circumstances to John II's son Affonso at Évora.* Affonso had died shortly after the wedding and Isabella was now a widow. It was Isabella herself who imposed the condition that she would only agree to the marriage if Manoel expelled all the Jews from Portugal.

Manoel made his decision. On 5 December 1496 he issued a decree giving Jews until the following October to leave Portugal. At first this seemed compassionate in comparison to the expulsion from Spain, where the Jews had been given only four months to leave

---

* See page 45.

and had been unable to take money or jewels with them. Yet things in Portugal were to turn out differently. Manoel was worried; by some estimates the Jews comprised 10 per cent of his population.[26] Since he could not afford to lose them, he decided to prevent them from leaving in the first place.

In April 1497, during Lent, Manoel ordered the forcible baptism of Jewish children under the age of fourteen. These children were to be taken from their parents, sent to live elsewhere and educated in the Christian faith at the king's expense. Many of the Old Christians were moved at the plight of the Jews 'and themselves took the Jewish children into their houses so as not to see them swept up by other hands, and saved them'.[27] Where their children could not be saved, 'huge groans were raised, and the air filled with the lamentations and sobs of the women'.[28]

At last here was a form of cataclysm, but not that imagined by the rabbi who saw the whale on the beach at Setúbal. Some of the Jews drowned their own children rather than see them taken from them. Others committed suicide. Life, good order, law; all had been turned on their heads.

In the end, 20,000 Jews made their way to Lisbon, the only port in the whole country from which Manoel permitted them to depart (they could not of course cross Portugal's land border into Spain). Here the king imprisoned them. The deadline expired. The vast majority of the Jews were baptized and thus kept in the country, though a few did manage to leave for North Africa.[29] Manoel gave his own newly created *conversos* an amnesty of twenty years. During this period there would be no Inquisition and they could learn the Catholic faith. Their only consolation was that many of these poor souls had their children returned to them.[30]

The forced conversion of the Jews of Portugal was widely seen in Christendom as a travesty of Catholic doctrine. Traditional Catholic theology rejected such forced conversions and urged that people should be brought to the faith through teaching and persuasion. Even one of Manoel's chroniclers described the act as 'unjust and iniquitous',[31] and the hypocrisy of the justification of the conversions is summed up by the fact that, according to Manoel's own ordinances, no African slave could be converted without his consent if over ten years old.[32]

In these circumstances one could not expect the Catholicism of people like the parents and grandparents of Álvaro de Leão to be anything other than insincere. It was natural that they would attempt to maintain their cultural and religious identity. And yet, within forty years, the Portuguese Inquisition would declare this a heresy; having created a phenomenon, the Portuguese crown would set about persecuting it.

By 1506 everyone in Portugal was aware of the way in which the Spanish Inquisition dealt with *converso* heretics. Everyone, moreover, was aware that the *conversos* in Portugal were mostly simulating their Christianity. The plague still afflicted Portugal, and someone needed to be blamed. The atmosphere was ripe for a popular auto, sanctioned only by prejudice.

That year, in one of the chapels of the city's Dominican monastery a strange light was seen on one of the crucifixes. Some took it as a miracle. Others were not so sure, and one *converso*, whose common sense was overcome by his honesty, declared that it looked more like a lit candle put next to the image of Christ. Overhearing this, some parishioners grabbed the man by the hair and dragged him into the street, where he was beaten, kicked and then burnt in the Rossio before a large mob.

One of the witnesses to the burning was a friar who began to incite the mob against the *conversos*. Two Dominican friars then came out from the monastery with a crucifix in their hands screaming, 'Heresy, heresy!' In what was clearly a popular version of the autos of Spain, where the Dominicans were the religious order in charge of the Inquisition, a mob of 500 people then ran through the narrow streets of the city, seizing *conversos* wherever they found them, killing them on the spot or dragging them half-dead to bonfires where they were burnt alive. The mayor of Lisbon tried to defend the *conversos* with sixty armed men, but the people turned on him and nothing could be done. The bonfires were stoked by servants and African slaves. There they glittered on the riverbank and in the *Rossio*, and that day 500 people were burnt.

Things worsened. The following day, a crowd of 1,000 broke down the doors of houses where they knew *conversos* were hiding. They pulled men, women and children out of churches, tearing images of Christ and the Virgin from their hands. The victims were dragged through the streets by their legs, crushed against walls and thrown onto the bonfires.

By Tuesday the fury had lessened, although not less than 1,900 people had died in the carnage. Manoel, who was out of the city, trying to avoid the plague, had the friars who had incited the crowd with their crucifixes burnt to death.[33] Probably, his first feeling was anger at the mob taking the law into their own hands; yet what had happened was largely his fault for craving power through his marriage to Isabella and forcing the conversions.

How these actions coexist with Manoel's gracious sensibilities is difficult to grasp. For this was also the musical ruler, the sponsor of fine architecture such as the Jeronymite monastery in Belén, a few miles down the estuary of the Tejo from Lisbon, with its haunting sense of interior space offset by finely detailed embellishments. The solidity of this vast undertaking – fifty years in the making – was such that it was one of the few buildings to withstand the great earthquake that destroyed Lisbon in 1755, and its off-white façade still dominates the Tejo today.

The king's blend of ruthlessness and grace can only be explained by the contradictoriness of human beings. That side of us which craves power would suggest that, though Manoel was pleased by fine art, he was roused more by the possibility of possession; this was why he had to have the widow of his predecessor's son as wife and accepted her demand that he expel the Jews. The insecure pragmatist inside us would suggest instead that Manoel was troubled by the legitimacy of his rule after the death of so many before him in line to the throne, and felt that marriage to the widow of the rightful heir would resolve this.

Thus did the purely personal struggles and vanity of its ruler contribute towards the establishment of Portugal's own Inquisition, which would affect everyone. Yet this tragedy brought its own irony. Manoel's queen, Isabella, the initial trigger of so much bloodshed, died herself in childbirth in 1498, bathed in her own cataracts of blood just one year after the forced conversion of the Jews.

*

Lisbon today is one of the most unhurried cities in Europe. The clanking of the bells from trams mingles with the sound of leather on cobbles as people walk up and down the hills which give the city its shape and definition. In a bowl between the Castle of St George – once home to the inquisitorial jail – and the clubs playing fado and Brazilian music in the Bairro Alto, the old Rossio sprawls around a central fountain.

The sides of the Rossio are lined with genteel pavement cafes, shoeshine boys and newspaper stands. Strong coffee and custard pies – *pasteis de Belén* – are consumed. The atmosphere is at once romantic and decadent, and also shorn of the driving ambition which one can see on the streets of London and New York. It is difficult in this graceful atmosphere to imagine the fires being lit amid the riots of 1506. Yet while the violence has passed on, residues remain.

Though the details were different, the slide in Portugal towards the Inquisition had many similarities to that of its neighbour. In both societies a scapegoat was created out of an anomalous group which the society had no interest in preserving. When institutionalized persecution had begun, it was easier to promote than rein back.

As with Spain, the religious attitudes of the *conversos* in Lisbon were far from being as straightforward as the lynch mob believed. The fact that some of them took shelter in churches and had to be dragged away from Christian icons tells its own story, as does the fact that some Old Christians settled scores by setting the mob on their enemies, claiming them to be *conversos*. Portugal was in the grip of the plague, and of mass hysteria. There had already been minor riots against the *conversos* in 1504 in Lisbon and 1505 in Évora.[34] Following events in Spain, Iberian societies knew where to turn for their escape valve in such times of crisis.

Though the riots of 1506 had nothing to do with the Inquisition per se, their mimicry of inquisitorial autos reveals that the Portuguese were well aware of what was occurring in Spain and were preparing to follow suit. Intolerance, once invented in Spain, had been easily exported; it would only be a matter of time before the Inquisition was established in Portugal as well. Once again, the target of persecution had largely been created by the very society which was to profess so much outrage at the enemy within.

Évora 1545–1548

Once Álvaro de Leão had been rescued from his suicide attempt, two years of stalemate set in. Álvaro's lawyers tried to claim that their man was insane, but the prosecutor rejected the defence. The accused had acted as a man of perfect good sense when it came to his business affairs, and when making his confession. There was nothing insane about him at all, merely something heretical.[35]

There was method in the stringing out of inquisitorial cases. The longer someone spent in prison, the more likely it was either that they would incriminate themselves to their fellow inmates, or that these inmates would themselves become so desperate that they would invent stories about other prisoners. The more cowardly, desperate to gain the favour of their judges, were often only too eager to betray their cellmates.

In Álvaro de Leão's case, a prisoner came forward to claim that Leão had declared that the Messiah would come before the year 1550 and that the Old Christians would repent their maltreatment of the *conversos*. Álvaro was said to show his support of all those prisoners who refused to confess and to be extremely hostile towards those who were compliant with the inquisitorial process. When one prisoner said to him, 'Our Lord and Saviour Jesus Christ will soon take us out of here', Leão was said to have replied, 'You're the only one he'll take' [suggesting 'You're the only one who believes in him'].[36]

Leão denied everything at first. Then he blamed it all on his wife Lianor. It was she, he said, who had Judaized in the family home, while he had been a good Christian all along. Lianor, he said, had kept all the Mosaic practices, while he had been accused by others in Cortiços and Mogadouro simply because he was rich and disliked. Once they heard this, the inquisitors knew that they had their man. Prisoners would often begin by blaming their nearest and dearest, before finally confessing that they had been seditious heretics all along. So it was with Álvaro, who belatedly admitted attending a covert synagogue in Mogadouro and keeping the sabbath. Now, however, he claimed that he was a good Christian, and that he had made a sincere repentance and conversion to the one faith of Portugal.[37]

For the inquisitors, confession was everything. In theological terms it represented the sinner's acceptance of his sin and the possibility of cleansing; in psychological terms it represented the triumph of their will over the prisoner's and the prisoner's acceptance of their own powerlessness. So yes, Álvaro admitted, he was a heretic who with his ideas had been subverting the nation's identity. He was not 'one of us'. He confessed everything that the inquisitors needed and wanted to hear.

Many of the features which become familiar in accounts of the Inquisition are apparent in the case of Álvaro de Leão. We see how family ties became nothing in an inquisitorial hearing, where a man could blame his wife to make himself seem less guilty. The friendships made in inquisitorial cells often trailed ugly motivations in their wake, as prisoners denounced one another for crimes whose theological rationale almost certainly they did not understand. Conversations were started with the intention of drawing others out and with the hope that they could be denounced without the need for exaggeration or plain lying.

Such circumstances reveal the survival instinct in its basest form. Those who were subjected to this sort of treatment reacted in many different ways. Of course there were some who kept their counsel to the end, but many others became bent only on achieving their release at the expense of others. Something of this sordid process could not help but filter out into the society which had turned the *conversos* into victims.

THE DISCOVERY OF the 'heresies' of the Portuguese *conversos* had to wait for the death of Manoel I. After the riots of 1506 Manoel appears to have suffered something of a crisis of conscience. At least he kept his word: in 1512 he extended the period of grace which the *conversos* had from the Inquisition until 1533. However, on Manoel's death in 1521, his successor John III showed less willingness to allow the *conversos* to integrate peacefully into national life and soon the first inquiries began to be made into the religious beliefs of the forced converts.[38]

In 1524 John III, goaded by his Spanish wife Catherine, planted a spy among the Portuguese *conversos* to see what faith they really practised. In Santarém, an old Moorish fortress town perched above the humid plains around the Tejo, he ordered Henrique Nunes to live and eat with the *conversos* of Lisbon. Though Nunes was himself a *converso*, he was someone in whom John III had complete confidence, since he had denounced his own brother to the authorities for Judaizing. Nunes had justified his betrayal to himself because he loved 'God perfectly and the real perfect friend has to be a friend to friends and an enemy to enemies and have no respect for father or mother or brother but only for the truth'.[39]

With his conscience thus sparklingly clear, Nunes reported that the *conversos* of Lisbon kept the Jewish sabbath as best they could, that some of them had Jewish calendars of festivals and others acted as ritual slaughterers. They managed to keep Passover without eating yeast, baking some unleavened bread if they could and eating rice or chestnuts as an alternative. Some even married according to Jewish law and had ovens in which Passover cakes could be cooked. Their rabbi was a tailor called Navarro whose wife had been burnt in Spain. Navarro's daughter knew countless Hebrew prayers by heart, and Navarro had an inordinately long beard which he had sworn not to cut until the Messiah came. Many other *conversos* had fled from Spain, or had had their parents and other close relatives burnt or reconciled there.[40]

His reports did not please the *converso* community and Nunes was murdered. He was rapidly adopted as a martyr, and miracles were said to occur at the place where he was buried. In the same year – 1524 – Jorge Temudo, a parish priest from Lisbon, produced a further report on the practices of the *conversos* which confirmed much of what Nunes had said and added to popular hostility.[41] There was no doubt that the Portuguese *conversos* were stronger in their Judaizing than those in Spain, since many had come there after the expulsion from Spain in 1492 so as to be able to continue as Jews.

John III could now install his own Inquisition secure in the knowledge of full popular support. There were, in fact, precedents. In the 1480s John II had ordered some of the fleeing Spanish *conversos* to be tried by the bishops of Portugal for heresy,[42] and some of these refugees had even been burnt in autos at the time.[43] However, what Portugal lacked was the administrative structure which existed in Spain. It was this which John III really wanted to achieve.

The gathering hostility towards the *conversos* was such that when a severe earthquake struck the Tejo region in January 1531, the friars of Santarém declared that it was a punishment for the people of Portugal for allowing Jews to live among them. Not everyone was convinced however, and Gil Vicente, the greatest Portuguese poet and dramatist of the age, explained to the friars at a public meeting in the Franciscan monastery that an earthquake was in fact a phenomenon of nature.[44]

Vicente's instructive homily had little effect. In December 1531 Pope Clement VII appointed Diogo da Silva the papal inquisitor in Portugal. However, the Portuguese *conversos* sent a one-eyed envoy, Duarte de Paz, to argue their case in Rome, and the bull appointing Silva was suspended the following October. But the prospect of the Inquisition was now very real.

The atmosphere in Portugal was that of gathering for the kill. As soon as news of the first bull was heard in Lamego in 1531, people started to discuss what property they wanted from the *conversos*. Some accused the king of being a coward, and said that he should just put the *conversos* to the sword and not bother with drawn-out trials. Others said that they and all their relatives were ready to act as witnesses right now, and the most moderate held that John III merely intended to burn the *conversos* within three years.[45]

Four years of diplomatic wrangles followed before the all-clear was given by Pope Paul III. The bull permitting a Portuguese tribunal to be established was issued on 23 May 1536 after considerable pressure from Emperor Charles V, ruler of Spain, who was in Rome at the time. Paul III had diluted the powers of the new tribunal by issuing a pardon to *conversos* the year before and ruling that no crimes prior to that date could be tried. Moreover the new Portuguese Inquisition did not have the same absolute power as its Spanish counterpart: the Pope had the power to elect three inquisitors and the king only one, there was no right of secrecy for witnesses, and the new institution did not yet have the same powers of confiscation as the Inquisition in Spain.[46]

The resistance of the papacy to the spread of the Inquisition emphasizes how far the new institutions in Spain and Portugal were political. The hatreds expressed by the people of Lamego on hearing of the publication of the bull revealed – as in Spain – that prejudice needed to be channelled. As in Spain, the *conversos* were the targets, and the papacy, try as it might, could in the end do nothing to protect the scapegoat. A dangerous ideology had created the threat within as a source of unity and power. It was not to be denied.

IN PORTUGAL, the first inquisitor-general was appointed in 1539. Cardinal Henry was John III's brother. Born in Lisbon on 31 January 1512, it had snowed heavily on his first day of life; as this occurred very rarely in Lisbon, it was taken as a sign that the Lord would give him a clear view of things.

Henry was of medium build and very hardy. He was an excellent hunter and horseman, but also very learned. He was proficient in Latin and had studied Greek and Hebrew. He was a very serious person and spoke with asperity, telling things as he saw them. At the age of fourteen he had taken the habit, and was thus, given his character and position, ideally suited to embedding the new Inquisition in Portuguese society.[47]

With a basic administrative structure in place, the Inquisition soon began its work. The first edict of grace was read at Évora in 1536, nine years before Álvaro de Leão was imprisoned there. A tribunal followed in Lisbon in 1537, where the accusations flooded in.[48] During the next few years courts sprang up all over the country, in places such as Tomar – still quite near Lisbon – and Coimbra, Lamego and Porto, all further to the north.[49]

These early years in Portugal were not as terrible as the first years had been in Spain. The dependence on Rome meant that the papal nuncio often intervened to secure a more lenient punishment, and there were comparatively few burnings. The first auto occurred in Lisbon in 1540, but in Coimbra one did not occur until 1567.[50] The moderating influence of the papacy was not what John III wanted, and his ambassadors spent much of the 1540s pressing Pope

Paul III to free the Inquisition from the limitations he had placed on it with the first bull. Eventually, on 16 July 1547, after John III had threatened a break with Rome, Pope Paul III succumbed, but even this was on condition that *conversos* would be able to leave Portugal freely for a whole year.

This condition was of course anathema to John III, who rejected it out of hand. Eventually he accepted papal conditions that no goods could be confiscated during the first ten years after the 1547 bull and that there should be no sentencing of people to burn in the first year.[51] On 10 July 1548, just before the end of the year's grace, a pardon was issued to the *conversos* in the jails of the Inquisition and 1,800 people were released from prison; at the same time, the tribunals of Lamego, Porto and Tomar were abolished and the institution was centralized.[52] This was perhaps an attempt by John III to show the papacy that he had kept his side of the bargain, and in the event the power to confiscate goods would only be granted in 1579, when John's brother Henry, the inquisitor-general, was the elderly king.[53]

One of the beneficiaries of these negotiations was Álvaro de Leão, who would probably have been condemned to the stake at an earlier period in Spain. In Évora, however, he was merely sentenced to abjure (renounce) his errors, and released at the time of this general pardon of 1548.[54] Álvaro had more sense than to remain in a place where he had enemies, and migrated to the great market town of Medina del Campo in Castile. Here traders gathered from all over Europe for the annual fairs, where most of the goods from Spain and the New World changed hands.[55]

Medina del Campo sits on one of the flattest parts of the Castilian plain. Here, in the shadow of the foreboding castle of La Mota, Álvaro would meet other members of his family. His niece Francisca, the daughter of his sister Catalina, had married Francisco Rodríguez de Matos, who traded regularly at the fairs.[56] The couple had a large family and also moved to Medina del Campo, in the 1570s. It was here that the branches of the Leão and Carvajal families gathered. As we have seen, Álvaro's wife was a Carvajal, and his niece Francisca was the daughter of another Carvajal; it was also here that the families would meet Francisca's brother Luis, now doing great things for the Spanish in Mexico.

It is not difficult to imagine the fears and undercurrents which must have cut through even the most minor interactions in families like this. Álvaro de Leão, as we have seen, believed that he had been denounced by his enemies, and *was* denounced by acquaintances in the jail of Évora. He had himself denounced his wife. There was no effective defence against false witnesses, and *converso* contemporaries of Álvaro accused the Inquisition of bribing people to denounce them.[57]

There was, moreover, no defence against abuse of power for someone like Álvaro who had already been reconciled. In Madrid in the 1520s a rich *converso* who had been reconciled saw his four daughters become sexual prey for some friars. One of them, Vicente, was seen with his habit off, romping with the eldest girl in her room, and two other girls were seen at dusk entering the lodgings of Charles V's confessor the bishop of Osma, and not leaving until the dawn had risen.[58]

One must suspect that these girls fell into the laps of these ugly individuals because of the fear of what might happen should they or their father suffer another accusation. There had been a dangerous concentration of power in Iberia and progressive limitation of local rights and freedoms. The results were there for all to see, and for people like Álvaro de Leão to fear. For all too many people, the religious path had become simply an excuse for the exercise of power.

Perhaps it should not be surprising that the Portuguese crown showed little understanding of this process, and of its dangers. Power, and keeping up with their Spanish rivals, were what mattered to the country's monarchs. So while John III and his brother Henry were determinedly lobbying their case before the papacy, they did not pause to consider how, after the initial bloodletting of the 1480s and 1490s, the new Inquisition had been brought to its knees in Spain by a series of scandals that almost led to its abolition.

On the death of Queen Isabella in 1504 the new king of Castile was Philip I, a Habsburg born in the Low Countries. Isabella's widower Ferdinand remained only as king of Aragon. Philip suspended inquisitorial trials in September 1505.[59] As heretics became increasingly difficult to track down tribunals were abolished. Of the seventeen tribunals which had existed under Torquemada, only seven were left by 1506.[60] But in this same year Philip died. His wife, Juana – daughter of the *Reyes Católicos* – took to travelling the country with his corpse and was declared insane. She was incarcerated in a monastery in Tordesillas for the rest of her life, and Ferdinand acted as regent of the couple's infant son Charles, later Charles V. Thus with its greatest champion effectively ruling the country, the Inquisition was saved.

There was nevertheless an increasing awareness in many circles that inquisitorial justice left much to be desired. The city of Granada complained to Charles V in 1526 that the procedures of the Inquisition meant that 'good Christians are more in danger than bad ones of being both imprisoned and condemned even though they are blameless, something which has happened many times'.[61] The secrecy of inquisitorial procedure meant that 'many souls have been condemned to hell . . . since they are able to say what they do secretly, they condemn themselves and give evidence about things they have never seen'.[62]

The complaints from Granada were prompted by the fact that this was the year in which a tribunal was transferred to the city.[63] Nevertheless, they underlined the fact that thinking people were well aware of the abuses that were carried out in the name of inquisitorial justice in Spain. They knew about them, but nothing was done to stop them. That supposed guardians of the faith should commit these crimes was of course horrendous but, as we shall see later, it was nothing out of the ordinary.* In the final analysis, few people were willing to put their own personal security and material wealth on the line provided that the institution did not affect them. By the time it did affect them, it would, of course, be too late to do anything about it.

The troubles of the Spanish Inquisition were common knowledge in Portugal in these years. To see the dangers of the judicial process that they were about to install, all the Portuguese needed to do was to recall the major crisis which had almost brought down

---

* See Chapter Ten.

the Spanish Inquisition in 1506: the terrible torture and abuse of power by the Inquisition in the ancient city of Cordoba. But the Portuguese monarchy evidently cared more for power than for what could truly be called justice.

Chapter Three

TORTURED JUSTICE

... if the prisoner should die or be injured or suffer heavy bleeding or have a limb mutilated during the torture, this will be their fault and responsibility and not ours, because they have refused to tell the truth.

Cordoba 1506

IN 1506 CORDOBA was in the clutches of Inquisitor Diego Rodríguez Lucero. Inquisitor Lucero was known as *'el tenebrero'* – the bringer of darkness.[1] His mode of procedure was summed up by one complaint made about him to the *Suprema*:

> Lucero wanted to make love to the wife of Julian Trigueros, and he took her because they resisted; her husband, who was an Old Christian, went to demand justice from [King Ferdinand] and [Ferdinand] confirmed the justice of his cause and sent [Trigueros] to the archbishop of Seville [Diego Deza, the inquisitor-general], who sent him back to Lucero. [Trigueros] arrived at Cordoba one Wednesday to continue with his case and he was burnt on the Saturday of the following week. Lucero kept his wife as his mistress. [And in another case] as the daughter of Diego Celemín was exceptionally beautiful, her parents and her husband did not want to give her to him, and so Lucero had the three of them burnt and now has a child by her, and he has kept her for a long time in the alcázar as a mistress.[2]

The city's noble families complained. They wrote to the court that Lucero and his minions had invented a terrific lie against many of the most distinguished Christians of the city and the surrounding area. Innocents had been accused of being heretics; prisoners had been forced to give evidence against them. It was not just the nobility who suffered; accusations were levelled at monks and nuns, and at ordinary folk. And what was more all this false and misleading evidence was secured through torture.[3]

In 1507 Cordoba's authorities went further. They wrote to King Ferdinand, noting how the devil had a habit of putting rotten apples among the good. With the Inquisition, where the 'work was most saintly . . . demons dressed in flesh have appeared'.[4] The inquisitor, they said, secured as many witnesses as he felt like from those in his jail. He forced their acquiescence through torture and threats, and withheld rations from those who refused to cooperate. Of his 500 prisoners, claimed the authorities, 150 had resisted the threats: they had been burnt and paraded past Cordoba's great mosque-turned-cathedral with gags in their mouths so that they could not tell the truth of what had happened before being burnt.

The Reverend Inquisitor Lucero was evidently a hawk rather than a dove. His motto was, 'Give me a Jew and I'll give you him burnt'.[5] A former schoolteacher in the desert region of Almería, he had been installed as inquisitor in Granada in 1500, which he had described as 'Judea la Pequenna' – Little Jewry – declaring that the city gates should be shut and all its heretical inhabitants burnt. During his time there approximately eighty people died at the Inquisition's hands in Granada.[6] Lucero had been appointed to Cordoba in 1502 to 'improve' things, with the tribunal at a low ebb following the corruption of Inquisitor Pedro de Guiral, accused in 1499 of taking bribes from the families of defendants.[7]

The first serious historian of the Inquisition, Llorente, who had access to records that have since been lost, said that 2,592 people died in Andalusia during these years, with another 829 burnt in effigy and 32,952 reconciled.* It was not for nothing that Lucero was known as the bringer of darkness.

★

---

* Many historians dismiss Llorente's figures out of hand. During the 19th century he suffered a withering attack from conservative historians such as Marcelino Menéndez y Pelayo, from which his reputation has never entirely recovered. Nevertheless, although

ONE OF THE MOST dubious trials led by Lucero in these years was that of the *converso* Juan de Córdoba Membreque. Membreque had been arrested in 1502 and accused by his slave Mina[8] from the Gold Coast of leading a synagogue which met on Mondays and Thursdays, of keeping all the Jewish fasts and of wearing the appropriate clothing for each of the Jewish holy days. Membreque's sermons to the assembled *converso* faithful were said to include promises that they would all be taken to a promised land where they would find great riches. On the way they would cross a river of milk and another of water, and when they bathed in this they would all return to the age of twenty-five. The prophet Elias would come to lead them forth, and when he came the land would shake and the sun and moon would die and the heavens would open, the sea would run red with blood, the trees would dry out and a great storm of stones would rain down on the earth. Dressed entirely in white the *conversos* would depart, and all Christians would convert to Judaism and join them.

What was curious about Membreque's trial was that at a time when the merest hint of Jewishness in a Spaniard could lead to their being burnt to death, there were ninety-three witnesses to his heretical activities who all came forward to give exactly the same story about his 'secret' synagogue and sermons. Either Membreque was the least secretive person in the world, or he had had some kind of death wish – or there was more (or rather, less) to the evidence of his ninety-three accusers than met the inquisitor's eye. Membreque even proved at his trial that he had been hundreds of miles from Cordoba at the time the 'offences' had been committed. But it didn't matter; he was found guilty and 'relaxed' to the secular arm, burning at the stake in 1504.[9]

Travesties like this revealed just how open to abuse the Inquisition's powers of arrest and interrogation really were. The murmuring in Cordoba swelled. The Bishop of Catania in Sicily sent an official to inquire into the complaints, and some of the witnesses confessed to giving false evidence. Lucero and his officials had asked

there evidently was a large dose of ideology in Llorente's critical history of the Inquisition, Llorente was secretary of the Suprema and had access to many records which were lost during the Napoleonic Wars (partly, it is true, because he himself stole some of them). Where records exist with which to compare his estimates, he is broadly borne out.

them leading questions, they said, and when they refused to testify they had been tortured and subjected to terrifying threats. These prisoners, many of them just children, were then forced to learn the prayers of the Jews by heart. They were taught the prayers by Jewish converts to Christianity to 'prove' that they had been subverted by those they accused. The prisoners said that they had been so terrified by the threats of torture that they had done nothing else in jail except learn these prayers.[10]

Thus the jails that were supposed to safeguard the Catholic faith echoed to the sound of Hebrew. Cordoba's winding streets, touched by the ghosts of their Islamic past, buzzed with the scandal. When Lucero and his officials realized that they had been reported to their superiors, they hurried through a new auto, burning most of those whom they had previously tortured into testifying to the heresies of others.[11]

The inquisitorial investigation into Lucero, when it finally commenced following the Cordoban authorities' complaints, came too late. Although higher authorities were now plainly aware of the way in which torture had been used to secure false information, and of how this information had led to the incineration of numerous innocents, they did nothing to suppress its use by the Inquisition. Torture was, after all, an age-old weapon of the state, and not one it wished to relinquish.

Though the well-documented excesses of inquisitors such as Lucero gave the central inquisitorial council, the *Suprema*, strong evidence of the miscarriages of justice that could result from torture, in the first 150 years of the Inquisition there was never any question of it being deemed incompatible with civilized society, or even plain counter-productive. In medieval Castile and Portugal torture was in daily use by criminal courts so its employment by the Spanish and then Portuguese Inquisitions was not remarkable. Torture was integral to Iberian judicial systems, and even the horror of an auto has to be placed in the context of the punishments of the time; those sentenced to death by the English judicial system in the 16th century could be disembowelled and castrated whilst still alive before being beheaded.[12]

All this has made some authors argue that the evils of torture under the Inquisition have been exaggerated. As well as the fact that torture was simply a feature of the time, it has been said that the Inquisition was 'slow to use torture', that the civil courts were much worse than inquisitorial ones in its application, and even that torture was rarely used after around 1500.[13] It is indeed true that inquisitors could show leniency towards those they were torturing; during the inquisitorial trials of Valencian *moriscos* in 1597 several were spared being 'put to the question' because of their age or infirmity.[14] And of course one must be aware of the curious phenomenon of condemning this aspect of the past through the present's more civilized values. Yet the fact is that inquisitorial torture – as the evidence from Valencia also shows – carried on far beyond 1500, and it *was* more severe than in the civil courts.

Thus in 1596 in Valencia half of all the *moriscos* who confessed were tortured or threatened with torture.[15] In Toledo in 1590 one *morisco*, the cobbler Alonso de Salas, died in the torture chamber.[16] Almost 85 per cent of *moriscos* examined by the Inquisition in Valencia were tortured between 1580 and 1610, and almost 79 per cent of those in Zaragoza.[17] The threat of torture often led to confessions; as in Ciudad Real in 1483,* it also often led to suicides,[18] and one *morisco* declared that 'with torture the inquisitors had made him say what they wanted . . . and that he had more fear before them than in front of all the devils of hell and that God in Heaven did not have as much power as they did'.[19]

In the 16th and 17th centuries it was not, moreover, just the *moriscos* who suffered. Over in Portugal, in Évora, a quarter of all those accused of sodomy were tortured, including a twelve-year-old boy who was raped by his brother-in-law and then tried for his 'crime' and tortured into a confession.[20] Torture was simply an aspect of the judicial process and not one which many people found abhorrent. On the contrary, it was seen as a useful way of getting to the 'truth'.

Nevertheless, contemporaries often did think that the Inquisition's use of torture was worse than that of the secular courts, as the Lucero case and the protests from Cordoba show. The chronicler Hernando de Pulgar, secretary to the *Reyes Católicos*, noted that

---

* See page 38.

torture by the Inquisition was thought particularly cruel.[21] Counsellor to the Inquisition, the theologian and bishop of Zamora Diego de Simancas (died 1564), argued that inquisitors should be more inclined to use torture than other judges as the crime of heresy was hidden and difficult to prove.[22] In 1578 Francisco Peña* noted that torture was frequently used straight away by inquisitors without awaiting other proofs, even though it had traditionally been used differently;[23] others noted that whereas in the old medieval Inquisition two pieces of evidence were needed before proceeding to torture, in Spain 'torture was entirely arbitrary, the judges being able to order it whenever they want to'.[24]

Moreover, it was not just the philosophy and use of torture that was different in the Inquisition. Whereas a civil judge was punished if he tortured someone until they lost a limb or died, this was not the case with inquisitors;[25] this may explain why civil judges sometimes chose not to apply the harshest penalties to the accused.[26] Torture was indeed used earlier in inquisitorial trials than in civil trials,[27] and there were more forms of torture open to inquisitors;[28] it was, in every way, an essential weapon of the inquisitorial armoury at least into the early part of the 17th century.

When used according to the Inquisition's rules – and not arbitrarily in the manner of Lucero – torture was inflicted on victims in precise circumstances. When the evidence was strong but not decisive, and it was suspected that a confession was not complete, prisoners were given the chance of 'purging' the evidence. Torture was thus often used against those who had already confessed their own guilt but were suspected of withholding the names of accomplices. Once one name was extracted, this was evidence that others might be lurking, and so the torture could go on, and on.

There were two main instruments of torture – pulleys and water – with many variations. For the pulleys, the prisoner's hands were tied behind their back. Hoisted from the floor, they were kept suspended at the inquisitors' pleasure like slaughtered rabbits hung up to dry. Occasionally they were let fall a short distance. If the 'right' answers were not forthcoming, weights were sometimes

* See pages 13–14.

attached to make the joint pain more intense and the abrasions of the cords chafing at mangled wrists even more severe. The use of water was more common. The prisoner was placed on a *potro*, a trestle table, with the head lower than the feet, the throat and forehead held fast by a metal strap. The limbs were tied to the *potro* with ropes which bit into the flesh while others were twisted around them like tourniquets. The mouth was then forced open and water poured down the prisoner's throat. Unable to breathe because of the water in their throats and with their bellies horribly bloated, their victims gasped for life as the inquisitors patiently admonished them to tell the 'truth'.

With time, methods of torture evolved. By the early 17th century a refinement had been added to the *potro* known as the *trampa*, in which the prisoner's legs swung through a gap in the table to which they had been tied down; another wooden bar with a hard edge was placed below the gap, and the legs were dragged through this tiny opening with a rope fastened to the toes and the ankle. Each time the rope was given a turn about the ankle and pulled tight, the prisoner was dragged further through the gap. Five turns were thought to be severe, but in Latin America seven or even eight turns were not unknown and some *moriscos* were subjected to ten or more.[29]

Pablo García, secretary of the *Suprema* in Madrid, wrote detailed instructions in 1591 as to how inquisitors were to proceed when torturing someone. The prisoner, García wrote, should receive a warning, advising them that they were suspected of not having told the whole truth and that the evidence of their case had been shown to learned people with clear consciences who felt that they should be tortured. Torture, it was believed, would lead to their confession.

García then instructed that the inquisitors should recite the following prayer before the torment began:

> *Christi Nomine Invocato*:
>
> Having paid attention to the evidence and merits of this case, we have grounds to suspect the prisoner, and so have found that we must condemn them to be put to the interrogation of torture, in which we order that the prisoner should spend as much time as we see fit, so that they should tell us

> the truth about the accusations made against them. And in addition we declare that if the prisoner should die or be injured or suffer heavy bleeding or have a limb mutilated during the torture, this will be their fault and responsibility and not ours, because they have refused to tell the truth.

Having thereby cleansed their consciences, the inquisitors would order the prisoner to be taken to the torture chamber. There they would be arraigned in the instrument of torture by the torturer, who would be disguised by a mask which showed only their eyes. Light was usually provided with lanterns, and the inquisitors sat in their chairs and prepared to interrogate. Again the prisoner was urged to tell the truth, and, said García, the inquisitors should remind them that they did not want to see such suffering, even though it was usually 'necessary' to proceed.

García ordered the inquisitors to pay particular attention to ensure that everything was recorded with scrupulous accuracy: 'how the prisoner was stripped naked, and how his arms were tied and how the ropes were tied around him, and how he was ordered to be placed in the *potro* with his legs, head and arms tied, and how it was ordered that the garrottes should be put onto him and how they were tightened, stating whether to the leg, muscle, spine or arms, etcetera, and what was said to him at each of these stages . . . so that everything which happens will be written down without exception'.[30]

This attention to detail was in the eyes of the inquisitors an exercise in transparency before God, yet it also reveals an unmentionable truth: the minutiae of torture were to be written down with such lurid precision because the officials and perpetrators were themselves compelled by it. This was surely one of the reasons why the authorities sought to ensure that every aspect of each process of torture should be recorded. In a religion where the iconography of torture was apparent on a daily basis through images of the cross, fascination with pain could be exorcised through turning the iconography into reality.

It is disturbing to think how rapidly such horrendous proceedings became a part of 'civilized' society. One thinks back to the great auto of 1649 in Mexico City and the chronicler Bocanegra's eulogy of the peaceful proceedings of Inquisitor Mañozca.* Bocanegra saw such goings-on as normal; after over 150 years of these events, they had come to seem so. Indeed, inquisitorial torture had long been a routine occurrence in Mexico. When Francisca de Carvajal, the niece of Álvaro de Leão of Mogadouro,† was ordered to the torture chamber in 1589, she cried out, 'Kill me! Garrotte me as soon as you can. But don't strip me naked, don't affront me'. Then her wit got the better of her fear, and she added, 'I'm an honest woman and widow, I can't put up with this in the world, and not in a place where there is so much saintliness!' The inquisitors of course ignored her, stripping her so that Carvajal tried to cover up her breasts. 'Everything is wicked! Everything is wicked!' she wailed. 'This horror must count as remission for my sins.'[31]

Inquisitors were trained to be impervious to such appeals and in spite of Bocanegra's views were clearly not men of peace. In torturing their prisoners to further their ideals and vanquish their perceived enemies, they revealed their own lack of humanity. The use of torture to secure the fantasy of a desired end became a mirror which society could hold up to itself, in order to grasp the extent of its growing disease.

The Canary Islands 1587

IN THE MID-ATLANTIC dust mountains reared out of the ocean to reveal a very different world to Europe. In the late 16th century the wild slopes of Tenerife's volcano offered a lookout across the Atlantic. Below the mountain in the sky and its desert slopes the soil allowed fields of wheat, vines and sugar to grow. The sugar plantations were worked by Berber and Wolof slaves brought from the Sahara and Senegal, hacking at the canes with their machetes, piling up the stalks ready to be processed and then shipped back to Spain.

The Spanish had conquered the islands from the indigenous

---

* See page 4.

† The Portuguese *converso* whose fate we followed in the last chapter.

Guanche population between 1478 and 1496, with Tenerife the last to fall. By 1500 the Spanish way of life was established, if hardly decorous, in the Canaries. Prostitution was everywhere, and first Gran Canaria and then Tenerife decided to run brothels as public services, with the profits going back to the community.[32] The atmosphere suited some; the chronicler Abreu Galindo recounted the story of Juan Camacho, who died on Lanzarote in 1591, reputedly at the age of 146. 'I knew him and talked with him many times,' wrote Galindo. 'Even though so old he was not hunch-backed, but walked upright, and two years before he died he married a young woman of twenty and had a child with her.'[33]

By this time the Inquisition had long been established in the Canaries. Founded in 1504, as with the other Spanish tribunals its initial focus had been the *conversos*, and there had been eight *relajados* in 1526.[34] By the time of Camacho's dotage, however, a new enemy had appeared on the horizon, and the foreign threat was no longer provided by apostate Judaizers but by English Protestants. In 1587 matters came to a head, and several of them were thrown into the Inquisition's jail on the island of La Palma.

Devout Catholics on the Canaries well knew the damage that Lutherans had done to their faith. As one witness to the trial of the Englishmen put it when asked if he knew what Lutherans were, 'being a Lutheran involves not hearing Mass and stealing';[35] or, as an inquisitor put it to Hugh Wingfield, from Rotherham, when interrogating him in October 1592, 'the church in England is not a church but the devil's synagogue'.[36] And, it was true, the Catholics of the islands had been subjected to sore provocation by one of the prisoners, John Smith from Bristol, who had said that 'it would be better if the friars married rather than going with one woman today and then another tomorrow'.[37]

Smith had been arrested by the Inquisition together with John Gold, Michael James and John Ware. The men claimed to have been on a fishing expedition off the African coast when their ship had been captured by French pirates and they had been set adrift in a skiff. They had made for the Canaries and, on nearing Fuerteventura, had been attacked again by the French and dumped on the island with nothing but the clothes on their backs.[38]

Gold also came from Bristol, while James came from Cornwall

and Ware from Swanage. Their arrests came as the tensions between Phillip II of Spain and Queen Elizabeth of England were about to reach their height, just a year before the Armada was dispatched. The inquisitors clearly smelt blood, so although Ware confessed that he had stopped eating meat during Lent not because he thought it was holy but because he had been ordered to by the Queen, he was sentenced to torture. He had not told the whole truth, and needed to purge his evidence.[39]

Ware was clearly someone whose Protestant faith did not extend as far as the *potro*. Once in the torture chamber, with his arms tied and the torturer looming, he began to talk. In fact, he admitted, it was the justice and compassion of the Holy Office which had encouraged him to return to being a proper Christian; only after being thrown into prison by the Inquisition had he seen the light and returned to the Holy Mother Church! He begged forgiveness, and admitted that he had not told the truth because the devil had tricked him. The inquisitors decided not to torture him, but instead sentenced him to be a galley slave – which was often tantamount to a death sentence. Ware managed to escape and his effigy was burnt in an auto on 1 May 1591.[40]

Ware's reaction to the threat of torture was not uncommon. Faced with the almost unimaginable physical pain which the inquisitors could inflict, many people invented their evidence. Faced with the remarkable coincidence that people under torture suddenly started to confess and denounce others,[41] inquisitors did not conclude that their victims were frequently terrified into lying and providing useless and/or misleading evidence. On the contrary, they were seen as people who until now had hidden the truth – a somewhat elastic concept that bore an uncanny relationship to the predilections of the interrogator.

The dogma of torture was therefore simple and irrefutable: the inquisitors knew what the truth was, and they would carry on until it was revealed. So even though inquisitors were repeatedly confronted with evidence that torture had precisely the opposite effect of its aim, promoting lies and not truth, they ignored this. Belatedly, in 1774 the Portuguese Inquisition's final code of practice (*regimento*) would recognize that 'torture is a most cruel manner of investigating crimes, entirely foreign to the pious and merciful sentiments of the

Mother Church, the surest way of punishing a weak innocent and saving a stubborn malefactor, and for extorting lies from both of them'.[42]

For much of the period prior to this realization, those who pointed out the evils or shortcomings of torture were themselves accused of heresy. Thus in Portugal in 1605 Alejandre de Abrinhosa was denounced by Francisco Rodrigues, a prior, for claiming that almost all those taken by the Inquisition in Lisbon were innocent, and that 'of 150 prisoners only five were not Christians'. Abrinhosa had himself been a prisoner of the tribunal, and said that it was well known that proof of heresy was secured by torture. Even very young girls were tortured, and Abrinhosa said that he had been jailed near the torture chamber and had heard 'the cruelty with which the torture was given and the confessions and cries of those being tortured and the scandalous mockery which the priests and inquisitors directed at their victims'. Those being tortured simply denounced anyone who came to mind, he said, 'just to be free of the torture and so that they would not be tortured again'. One prisoner had asked another who Muhammad was, just so that she could confess to believing in him, having heard that this was a standard accusation of the torturers.[43]

This sort of revelation was of course far from welcome. But what really angered Prior Rodrigues about Abrinhosa's views was perhaps something else. When Rodrigues said to Abrinhosa that the priest Francisco Pereira had told him, with what one can surmise was a straight face, how much rectitude, justice, legitimacy and charity was involved in the process of torture, Abrinhosa had replied, 'That priest!' wishing to libel him and imply that the ministers of the Holy Office proceeded with passion and hatred.[44]

Few perhaps could afford to acknowledge the psychological drives which impelled the torturers to inflict pain on others in their search to spread peace. Such realities did not belong within the grand beneficent project in which the empires of Portugal and Spain were said to be engaged. They were too close to the bone.

The real effects of the inquisitors' procedures is apparent in many trials. In Cartagena, Colombia, Antonio Rodrigues Ferrerín was put in the *potro* in 1635, and 'the rope was tied and as the first turn of the rope was made around his leg he fainted and gave off a cold sweat and said nothing more, and even when the rope was tightened he did not complain or answer and the torture had to be suspended'.[45] In 1639 in Lima, Peru, Juan de Azevedo came sobbing to the inquisitors during the trial of Manuel Bautista Pérez to admit that 'he did not have the courage or strength to withstand the torture and so he had told a lot of lies in the torture chamber . . . and if he was returned to the torture chamber he would tell more lies because of his weakness and despair'.[46]

The cases of victims such as Azevedo and Ferrerín show that the actions of the inquisitors went far beyond the sphere of spirituality into the realm of collective fear. Indeed, while the 'evidence' collected by the inquisitors through torture was deeply flawed, this mattered far less to the authorities than the development of such fear. Even in the second half of the 17th century, when the use of torture by the Inquisition declined considerably, this was not the public perception; by then, as we shall see, an attitude of fearful deference had successfully been implanted.

Fear is of course a wonderful tool for consolidating the power of an increasingly authoritarian state. Successfully embedded, this fear can always be invoked, in the name of the war of good against evil, against targets that pose an economic or political challenge.

AS THE INQUISITION would discover, inventing enemies was the easy part; it was resolving the problems which arose afterwards that proved impossible. People who had been loyal Catholics became enemies of the Church after their incarceration in inquisitorial cells, as Isabel Lopes, a prisoner of the Inquisition of Évora, made clear in 1594: 'My husband and I are innocent,' she told the priest Manoel Luis. 'We never were Jews but we confessed that we were under torture and the threat of death . . . some people come into these cells as Christians and when they leave they are Jews, and all because of the lies and torture which the inquisitors have subjected them to.'[47]

The Inquisition was securing the exact opposite of its intention: instead of reconciling apostates to the Church, it was turning loyal Catholics into apostates. And if anything was likely to transform loyal citizens of a state into rebels who sought the destabilization of its government, it was the legal process of the persecuting institution. For here was a system of justice in which truth came a poor third to prejudice and power.

This legal process had first been set out by the Aragonese inquisitor Nicolás de Eymeric in the 14th century. In his handbook for inquisitors Eymeric had noted how inquisitorial judges were privileged 'as they are not obliged to follow the judicial order, and so the omission of a legal formality does not render the procedure illegitimate'.[48] In other words, the procedure was at the whim of the inquisitor.

The handbook continued in the same vein. The evidence of those convicted of heresy was only accepted if they accused someone, not if they testified in their favour, since 'when a heretic declares in favour of the accused, it can be supposed that he does it out of hatred for the Church ... but this presumption disappears when the same heretic declares against the accused'.[49] Relatives, servants, children and spouses were only accepted if they denounced the accused, not if they spoke in their favour.[50] The general attitude towards the prisoner was summed up by Eymeric's view that death in the torture chamber was a form of spiteful sorcery designed to frustrate the inquisitor: 'not even torture is a safe way of getting at the truth ... there are some who, through their sorcery, will become almost insensible and would die rather than confess'.[51]

Although these astonishing guidelines was modified somewhat by the *Instrucciones* decreed by Tomás de Torquemada in 1484 as a code of practice for the Spanish Inquisition, they were key in the shaping of his ordinances.[52] To begin with, prisoners of the Inquisition were not actually told what the evidence was against them, nor who had accused them. Instead, at their first hearing they would be asked who their parents and grandparents were, and then whether they had any personal enemies who might have denounced them maliciously. This was often an especially harrowing part of a trial, with the defendant desperate to cast doubt on the evidence of anyone who might have accused them, and reeling off lists of names of people who were said to be their 'deadly enemies'. Many of these people were probably not enemies at all, but family members, friends or acquaintances who the prisoner suspected of being in the same situation as them.

So, at his trial in Cartagena in 1637, Luis Fernández Suarez accused ten people of being his personal enemies, only for witnesses to come forward soon afterwards to say that until his arrest Fernandez Suarez had been business partners with many of them.[53] Arrested at the same time, Luis Gómez Barreto claimed to have several enemies; with one he had disputed over a shipment of slaves to Panama in 1627, and to another he had had problems repaying a debt.[54] Later, in the torture chamber and with the ropes twisting around them in the *potro*, prisoners would cry out that this or that person was the enemy of their uncle or father-in-law;[55] that another person owed them a great sum and wanted to see them ruined.

It was the anonymity of accusers which fomented such an atmosphere of suspicion. As we have already seen, the Aragonese saw the new judicial practice of the Inquisition as excessive, and not knowing the identity of witnesses in particular troubled them.* Indeed as late as 1521 the Aragonese were still demanding the publication of names of witnesses, even though such demands had been routinely ignored.[56] As the historian Juan de Mariana put it in his history of Spain, written in 1592, 'In the beginning [the Inquisition] appeared very onerous to the [Spaniards]. What amazed them above all was that the children paid for the sins of the parents, and that the accused did not know and were not told who had accused them, that the accuser was not confronted with the prisoner and that there was never publication of the witnesses. All of this was to the contrary of what had formerly been done in the other courts'.[57]

Again, one is struck by how inquisitorial excesses did *not* seem normal and were *not* acceptable by the standards of the times, at first. The judicial practice of the new Inquisition was initially seen as a gross violation of ordinary legal proceedings. However, defenders such as Mariana argued that society had to change according to the demands of the time.[58] Once people believed themselves to be surrounded by enemies, they would acquiesce in the use of extraordinary methods of interrogation.

The anonymity of witnesses was of course carte blanche for the venting of jealousy and vendettas. It also meant that the Inquisition could not be held to account for the justice of its actions. Unsurpris-

---

* See page 20.

ingly, the principle of secrecy was jealously guarded, and those who violated it were severely punished. In Murcia in 1563 Gregorio Ardid was sentenced to be a galley slave for six years and given 100 lashes for breaking the secrecy of the Inquisition, and Cristóbal de Arnedo was given 200 lashes and sent to the galleys for eight years for the same offence.[59] Yet at the same time officials of the Inquisition were quite capable of acting with supreme hypocrisy by letting it be known when a certain person was about to be arrested, if it suited them.[60] They were keen for others to be troubled by scruples. They tested victims, and were prepared to torture them, to ensure that they reacted appropriately. Yet such rules did not design for them their own moral canvass in life.

THE MOST PERNICIOUS effect of this code of secrecy on society was, as Mariana noted, the cultivation of wariness and dissimulation.[61] The practice encouraged general suspicion of society and the invention of stories in an attempt to avoid torture.

At the first hearing, on top of being asked whether they had any personal enemies, the prisoner would also be asked if they knew or suspected why they had been called to the tribunal, and if they had done anything which might be against the tenets of the Church. If they replied that they had no idea why they were there, they would be dispatched to the cells, with the implication that they had better think harder.

Trials then entered a period of cat and mouse. The inquisitors tried to tease out the truth as they already knew it to be; the accused tried to confess as little as possible (if guilty) or loudly to protest their innocence. After the early years in Spain when cases were dispatched summarily, this period of the trial often dragged on for years. One prisoner in Peru, Manuel Henriques, spent twenty-nine years in Lima's jails before being burnt at the stake in 1664.[62] Defendants lay festering in the cells, called for questioning at the whim of their tormentors to be told that the inquisitors had 'evidence from reliable people' that they were concealing the truth.

If the secrecy of proceedings was guaranteed to foster mutual distrust and injustice, then the lawyers chosen for the task of the prisoner's defence were little better. After the first fifty years of the tribunal in Spain, during which time defendants were able to choose their lawyers,[63] defence counsel were chosen at the discretion of the inquisitors from a panel which they appointed. These hand-picked advocates were to make no suggestions to their client except to confess; the lawyer's sole duty was to abandon someone considered a *pertinaz* or stubborn heretic – that is, someone who would not confess – and admonish a Christian to tell the truth. Prisoners were expected to pay for the privilege of counsel out of their own pockets, unless they were too poor to be able to do so.[64]

To be fair to the lawyers, their advice was the best option for the accused. Those who confessed fully and professed sincere repentance, denouncing all their 'accomplices' as a sign of contrition, were reconciled to the Church. Although they were forced to wear a *sanbenito* as a public sign of their humiliation, their goods were most often confiscated by the Inquisition and the names of their descendants permanently tarnished by their public shame, at least they did not have the fear that they might be 'relaxed'.*

With all the cards stacked against the prisoners, inquisitorial jails could be fractious places. Although conditions varied and in some places were lax enough for prisoners to wander the streets by day or be allowed to serve out their terms at home,[65] things were often more severe. As late as the 1770s suicides were such a serious problem in Portugal and Goa that the codes of practice for the Inquisition in both places had chapters dedicated to those who killed themselves in jail.[66] The famous Jesuit preacher from Brazil António Vieira described the inquisitorial cells of the mid-17th century in sombre terms: 'There are usually four or five men, and sometimes more, in the cells . . . each one is given a pitcher of water to last eight days (if it runs out before then, they have to be patient) and a bedpan, as well as a container for defecation which is also emptied every eight days . . . the cells are usually full of rats, and the stench is such that it is a mercy for the prisoners to leave the cells alive.'[67]

Often, the atmosphere boiled over. One night in 1631 Jorge

---

* Although the number of relaxations declined in the late-16th and 17th centuries, this was not the common perception. Many prisoners believed that they would be burnt right up until the day of the auto, since it was only then that their sentence would be revealed to them. This is made clear by Dellon's (1815) account of his sentencing in Goa in the late 17th century.

Rebello, a prisoner in Lisbon, was challenged by a warder for making too much noise with his cellmates. Rebello shouted back that 'the prisoners were much more honourable than the warders', and when the warder told him to shut up if he did not want to be gagged, Jorge Rebello took out a knife and started brandishing it violently, saying that 'he swore by the Holy Sacrament that any son of a bitch who wanted to come into the cell would first have to nail him down if he did not want to be killed'. The warder went to fetch some guards, but when they broke into the cell and tried to take the knife Rebello sank his teeth into one of the guard's hands and left permanent marks there.[68]

Reading records of inquisitorial trials, it becomes clear that, far more than the burnings at the stake (which became more a punctuation than a regular feature of trials), it was the relentless injustice of the system that created fear among prisoners. Those arrested were not only destroyed economically, physically and psychologically, they were forced to subsidize their own humiliation. William Collins from Oxford had to pay the muleteer who brought him as a prisoner to the Inquisition in Mexico City in 1572, where he would eventually be convicted as a Lutheran and sentenced to ten years in the galleys.[69] Meanwhile, it was those who were sentenced to be lashed that had to pay the person who lacerated them, not the Inquisition.[70]

It was therefore not for nothing that, having himself been through this judicial system in Goa, the Frenchman Charles Dellon noted at the end of the 17th century that 'the judges [of the Inquisition] execute a system of jurisprudence unknown to other tribunals'.[71] The legal system was such that mere suspicion could be enough to satisfy the authorities of a person's guilt, as was graphically revealed when the 'threat' of the Freemasons appeared in Spain in the 18th century. In 1751 Francisco Rávago, the confessor of Ferdinand VI, urged the king to take action, since 'in matters of this gravity, suspicion alone – and one which is not at all implausible – is enough to prevent the damage, without awaiting certainty or evidence'.[72]

Such stagnant and paranoid thinking was in many ways a reprise of what Eymeric had said in the 14th century: 'If an accusation appears stripped of all appearance of truth, the inquisitor should not strike it from his book because of this; for what is not uncovered at one moment, may well be uncovered at another'.[73]

MADRID'S *Archivo Histórico Nacional* is an elegant building adorned with marble stairways which conceal a cool, shaded courtyard where researchers can rest from their labours. Documents are conveyed to a large, rectangular room, where historians pore over the gently disintegrating ledgers of Spanish and Latin American history. Sunlight flows in from outside, occasionally illuminating the records of torture and mutilation. Here in the present, the past is relived.

One summer's day I read the trial of Manuel Álvarez Prieto, a *converso* accused of Judaizing and imprisoned in Cartagena in 1636. Álvarez Prieto first confessed to his crime, and then retracted his confession, saying he had been mad when he made it. He was taken to the *potro*, where he spent three hours and withstood seven turns of the rope without confessing. At this point the torturers suspended his agony and Álvarez Prieto was noted to be in a perilous state of health: both his arms were broken and so mangled that the surgeon said that he was in peril of his life.

Álvarez Prieto died two days later. The inquisitors declared that this was his fault. Having asked for water in his cell he had spat it out over his wounds and made them worse. He had wanted to die. The inquisitors declared him guilty as charged and ordered that his bones be burnt, his goods confiscated and the names of his descendants besmirched forever.[74]

This pleasant room, filled with humane and pleasant people reading about inhumane and terrible events, took on a different light as I read of the inquisitors' refusal to accept responsibility in this case of death by torture. For in pondering inquisitorial justice, one returns so often to the question of torture. This declined in use from the middle of the 17th century onward but was still not unheard of in 1700.[75] Yet for all torture's long inquisitorial history, records are mute when it comes to the torturers themselves. What did the inquisitors think as their victims writhed in the *potro*? How did they feel at the prospect of scarring people for life in the name of God?

Clearly, in Álvarez Prieto's case, the inquisitors had given such questions little thought. Yet one would like to imagine that occasionally some of them might have questioned their own motives and asked why they were so compelled by the suffering of others. The documents are mute on this subject. In the archive the pain is studied in silence, and the silence is returned. One comes to suspect that it was only because inquisitors were certain of the absolute justice of their cause that they were able to torture their prisoners with such a pitiless sense of purpose.

Mexico City 1594–1596

In November 1594 evidence began to be received by the Inquisition in Mexico City of the crypto-Judaizing activites of Luis's de Carvajal *el mozo* – Luis the Younger. Arrested and imprisoned for the second time by the Inquisition, he had already been reconciled for Judaizing in 1589 and had done four years' penance in a monastery.

Soon the evidence began to build up from both within and outside the jail. One of the key witnesses was Luis's cellmate Luis Diaz, who had told him that he wanted to convert to Judaism. Diaz was in fact an inquisitorial spy, and the evidence he secured was confirmed by the notary and secretary of the Mexican tribunal. These functionaries of justice had crept through the jail's secret passageways by candlelight to a hidden door to the cell. There they had written down everything they heard exchanged between Carvajal and Diaz.

The prisoner remained oblivious to such machinations, believing himself to be protected by his God. Discovering that his sister Leonor was also in the jail, on 13 May 1595 Luis asked his jailer to send her some fruit from him. At first he sent a melon. When the jailer looked inside the melon he found an avocado stone wrapped up in a piece of purple cloth; Luis was using the fruit as an elaborate postal service – he had carved the words 'the patience of Job' into the stone. The next day he asked the jailer to give Leonor a banana. Again, he had taken out the fruit and replaced it with an avocado stone on which he had written a message to his sister. These messages, filled with references to Jewish prophets, were the final pieces of evidence. The inquisitors allowed them to pass for some days, until on 17 May Luis sent a bowl of fruit containing another telltale banana whose fruit had been taken out. This time he had sewn up the skin so that no one should be able to tell what he had done.[76]

Such stories of ingenuity are not as rare as might be thought. At the final hearing of his trial in Lima in 1638 Francisco Maldonado da Silva – who had been arrested in Concepción, Chile eleven years before – produced two books each more than one hundred pages long. Da Silva had cobbled together the books from scraps of paper which he had managed to accumulate, and written down his thoughts in an ink made from charcoal. He wrote using pens which he had cut out of eggshells with a knife made from a nail. It was an extraordinary feat, and Da Silva said that the books were a full discharge of his conscience. The inquisitors sentenced him to be relaxed the following year.[77]

Luis's case was not so dissimilar. With the evidence mounting up, on Monday, 6 February 1596, the inquisitors voted to torture him. Hearing the sentence, the prisoner protested. He had already admitted that his mother had Judaized. 'She is the thing that he loved most in the world, and he would much more easily have denounced anyone else he knew of than her. And so if there is evidence against him that he has information on other people who he has not mentioned these witnesses do not deserve to be believed.' After all, as Luis pointed out, such witnesses 'do not know the way in which the reverend inquisitors desire that people should not tell lies, [so they] say more than they ought to because they are afraid that they will be tortured'.

Perhaps sensing the barbs of irony, the inquisitors proceeded with the torture. The process began on the Wednesday at 9.30 in the morning. Luis said:

'God give me strength to burst rather than tell a lie.'

> And with this he was ordered to enter the torture chamber and he went in with the torturer who was ordered to strip him. And standing naked in the flesh . . . he was again urged to take steps so that the torture did not proceed. And he said: That he had told the truth and that God would not desire him to bear

> witness against anyone. At this, his arms were tied loosely and he was urged to tell the truth. And he replied: seeing that he was in this state, he wanted to tell the truth.

Luis was taken out of the *potro* and proceeded to denounce his entire family and their Judaic activities, in particular his mother Francisca and his sisters Isabel, Leonor and Mariana. However, even this confession did not satisfy the inquisitors.

> And urged to tell the truth, he said: that he had nothing more to say. And with that he was ordered back into the *potro* and entered with the torturer, and was urged to tell the truth. He was given one turn of the rope and he said: 'Ay! Oh Lord, forgive me Lord, let this be a payment for my abominations'. Urged to tell the truth, he was given a second turn of the rope, and he gave a huge shout: 'Ay! Ay! Ay!' And he said: that it was true that his little sister Anica kept the law that God gave to Moses, and that he had told the truth, and that the inquisitors should not revenge themselves on him. And he said all this crying, and was then urged to tell the truth, and was given a third turn of the rope, and he shouted again: 'God, Lord of Israel, I am being forced to lie, Lord the one God take pity on me! Woe is me! How sad to have to lie'. And then he said that he had already told the truth and he filled the air with his complaints.[78]

Twisted in the *potro*, Luis proceeded to incriminate more people, some of them distant relatives and passing acquaintances. This victim of the torture chamber was the great-nephew of Alvaro de Leão from Mogadouro, tried by the Inquisition in Évora almost fifty years before. He proceeded to denounce Álvaro de Leão's three brothers, Duarte, Francisco and Jorge, all great-uncles of his whom he had never met and who had been instrumental in his travelling to Mexico in the first place.

Some of the accusations probably were accurate; some probably were not. Given the inquisitorial justice system, it is difficult to be sure of anything except the reality of suspicion. For inquisitorial procedure used mallets to crack acorns. Its practitioners were actors in a system of jurisprudence which prosecuted the innocent as well as the guilty and fomented a hatred of the system itself. Such a code excelled at securing convictions but also undermined the society which it had supposedly been designed to defend.

Chapter Four

ESCAPE

. . . if the corrupted boy did not denounce what had happened within a day of being raped, he would be burnt for it.

Cape Verde 1548–1563

SOME TIME AROUND April 1548 Luis de Carvajal y la Cueva arrived from Portugal on the Cape Verde Islands off the west coast of Africa.*[1] He was then only nine years old.[2] To many of the islanders Luis's arrival would have seemed odd. This rosary of mountains rising sheer from the sea was not a place for boys. What was he doing there? Surely he would be one of the first to fall victim to Cape Verde's annual round of fevers.

Thousands of miles away from Europe, life on the islands was tough. The main island of Santiago lay 300 miles west of the coast of Africa; its capital, Ribeira Grande, was 'richer in money than in virtue', as the Bishop of Bahia put it four years later.[3] Ribeira Grande was a notorious breeding ground for fevers.† Some blamed this on the Africans for 'corrupting the air as it is [corrupted] in their land'.[4] Each year, the rainy season between August and October would claim the lives of many settlers, so that as the Italian traveller Francesco Carletti put it some years later, 'the Portuguese men and women always appear to be staggering through the streets at each step, and have a colour so pallid or, to say it better so yellow, that

* This Luis was the uncle of the Luis the Younger we met in the previous chapter, and was called in Mexico Luis the Elder. However as he is a young man in this chapter I will simply call him Luis to avoid confusion.

† Today, however, malaria has been almost entirely eradicated from the islands.

they seem more dead than alive'.[5] And yet this was to be the Carvajal child's new home: the major African slaving port throughout the 16th century, where ships were 'constantly arriving with goods from many countries' to exchange for the black ivory[6] and where the sea was always a brilliant guard, the walls of the island prison withdrawing into its blue impenetrability.

In fact there was a simple explanation for Luis's presence. For he was the son of Gaspar de Carvajal and Catalina de Leão, and the nephew of Álvaro and Jorge de Leão, who were still languishing then in the inquisitorial jails in Évora.* The young boy was on the run. He had had a tortuous journey.

With his uncles' incarceration in Évora hanging over the family, Luis had been taken by his father from Portugal to Spain. It cannot have been a coincidence that this took place in the second half of 1547, just after Pope Paul III had granted full powers to the Portuguese Inquisition.† Fearing that the first years of the Portuguese Inquisition would visit the same excesses on the *conversos* as they had experienced after the installation of the Inquisition in Spain, Gaspar de Carvajal was looking for a secure future for his young son.

First they had travelled to Sahagún, in Spain. Here they had visited the abbot of the monastery, who was a relative of theirs. But then Gaspar had fallen ill in Salamanca and Luis had tended to him. Gaspar had tried to get back to Portugal, but he had died in Benavente before reaching the border.[7]

The young Luis was now in serious danger. His father was dead and his mother's family were incarcerated in Évora. Unaware that Álvaro and Jorge de Leão would be released by the Inquisition as part of the general amnesty, Luis's relatives must have feared that their imprisonment would lead to a chain of arrests that would destroy the family. Luis's uncle, Duarte de Leão – the brother of Álvaro and Jorge – was the factor of the Casa da Guiné in Lisbon, the major administrative body dealing with Portugal's African trade. This meant that he was in charge of buying and selling slaves and

---

* See Chapter Two. This was prior to their release as part of the general pardon in July of that year.

† See page 61.

for the accounts. Duarte had spent time in Guiné and knew many people there.[8] He came to Benavente to collect the orphan Luis and took him to Lisbon.[9]

Lisbon was then the most African city in Europe. It was the perfect introduction to the sort of life to be found in Cape Verde, for in 1551 it was estimated that there were 9,950 slaves in the city, one in ten of the population.[10] African slaves were auctioned at the Pelourinho Velho – the old pillory – a square where criminals were punished.[11] The luckier slaves were bought by masters who fitted them out in livery and sent them to spend their days wandering the narrow cobbled streets attending to household business; those who were less fortunate had to carry their owners in litters up and down the cluster of hills overlooking the Tejo river and the flatlands on the south side of the estuary.[12]

The Casa da Guiné where Duarte de Leão worked was located on the waterfront, near the Mina stores, which were piled high with North African cloths, carpets, copper saucepans, trays and rosaries made of glass which would be taken to Africa to trade for gold and slaves.[13] Just round the corner was the slave house.[14] It was here that the Africans who had recently arrived on slave ships were kept in two large rooms and fed a daily ration of rice, biscuit and olive oil as they waited to be auctioned off.[15] If they died in the slave house their bodies were carried to a pit by St Catherine's Gate and dumped there in a mass grave. This was a harsh fate, but better than being left to rot where they had fallen, which had been the practice until 1515.[16]

In contrast to the manacled slaves were the many Africans to be found nearby at the docks, working as stevedores handling the sacks of charcoal and straw which were brought to the city, the charcoal being used for fires and the straw for bedding, floors and stables.[17] African women, meanwhile, tended to be found elsewhere in the city, working as water carriers or washerwomen. Some of them sold rice pudding, couscous and chickpeas in the squares and by the dockside from pots which they carried on their heads; but the less fortunate cleared rubbish and excrement from the wealthier homes of the city, carrying away the excrement in *canastras*, wicker baskets with lids concealing basins inside.[18]

Luis spent three months in Lisbon. At this time there were relatively few Africans living in the remote towns of Portugal's interior which he knew, places such as Mogadouro, so this was his introduction to the people and customs that he would meet in Cape Verde.[19] Duarte had big plans for his young nephew, for once Luis had arrived in Ribeira Grande he would be trained up by his uncle so that later he could be installed as treasurer and accountant.[20] First, however, Luis had to experience at first hand the reality of slavery in order to see how the business operated.

By the 1540s, the slave trade was already a moral circle constantly in the process of being squared. Ships sailed from the Cape Verde Islands to the coast of Senegal with horses; they sold the horses to the Serer people of the coast and returned with slaves in the very same ships, the first step in the process whereby humans became equated with animals.[21] From Cape Verde the ships sailed to America or Lisbon, where the slaves were met by people like Luis, who quickly learnt how to continue the process of degradation. Under his uncle's tutelage the young Luis learnt to log the slaves and check their health before registering them for sale, accompanying the administrators out to the ships to examine teeth and limbs and forcing the slaves to perform physical exercises, noting down any deformities or unusual markings so that the slaves could be identified.[22]

Such dehumanizing on arrival set the tone for much of the African experience in Portugal. In 1576 the Inquisition would receive a denunciation from Domingos Gomez, a black resident of Lisbon, of two of his fellows, Fernão Callado and Antonio Rodrigues. Gomez had seen them both naked with Callado carrying a cross on his back and Rodrigues whipping it.[23] Slavery created abuses which human beings might redirect through new outbursts of aggression, and such an atmosphere would not be irrelevant to the world of Luis.

With the inquisitorial cloud hanging over his uncles and the death of his father, fear was a condition of this child's existence. In Lisbon Luis learnt to see how this condition might be transferred to others. This was a process of some urgency, for Luis's relatives knew that for decades the people they lived among had received psychological conditioning for unleashing persecution on *conversos* like them.

For Duarte de Leão, his status in the Casa da Guiné offered a breathing space. Moreover, for *conversos* such as Leão and his nephew Luis a whole new continent of possibilities had been opened up by Columbus. Threatened by the Inquisition in a place they had called home for centuries, many *conversos* felt they had no option but to flee into the unknown.

Columbus's first voyage to the New World had in fact involved at least five *conversos*.[24] One of them, Rodrigo de Triana, had been the first sailor to spy land, and another, Luis de Torres, the first to set foot in America.[25] The emerald waters of the Caribbean were soon cluttered with Spanish ships bringing settlers, seedlings, livestock. The rich equatorial earth smelled of even more life, and death, than usual. Tempers frayed; scapegoats were needed. As early as 1506 the bishop of Puerto Rico complained that 'Hebrew' merchants were flooding the island.[26] The complaint was repeated by his counterpart in Cuba in 1510, and by then the proctors of the Spanish colonists were complaining that Jewish teachings were corrupting the natives.[27] Certainly, the name of the main port of Cuba might have given rise to suspicion, as the three consonants of Habana, if transliterated into Hebrew, produced הבנ – Ha B'Nei – the tribe.

This *converso* diaspora was rapidly to encompass the whole world. The Inquisition and forced conversions created dangers in Iberia, but there were other places in which to seek sanctuary. Looking to the east, there were many *conversos* in Goa, Ceylon and India by 1520.[28] In America the story was the same. By around 1550 roughly one in five of the European population of Mexico City was *converso*.[29] By 1570 there was twice the proportion of *conversos* to Old Christians in Peru as there was in Spain,[30] and they were so numerous in Brazil that they occupied many of the official posts in spite of royal prohibitions.[31] One *converso* from the important Aboab family,[32] Francisco de Vitoria, was even made the first bishop of Tucumán in Argentina in 1581,[33] and they were generally well represented in the Spanish American Church,[34] making a mockery of the supposed heresy for which they had been persecuted in Portugal and Spain.

It is tempting to see this *converso* flight across the Atlantic as a romantic escape, but this was a brutal episode in history. In the Caribbean the military force which had accomplished the reconquest of Spain and the installation of the Inquisition was now directed at a new target: the Amerindians. Caribbean women were routinely raped by overseers while their husbands dug for gold in the mines. Newborn children were stripped from their mothers' arms and smashed against rocks or thrown to be eaten by dogs. Men tied hand and foot lay under the beds on which Spaniards slept with their wives. The hands, noses, tongues and breasts of the Amerindians were frequently mutilated or simply hacked off.[35]

One of the major currents running through history is fear, something about which historical documents – and historians – tend to remain silent, since few people are brave enough to write about their fears. Yet persecutions tend to arise from a constellation of different currents of fear. *Conversos* had been subjected to the Inquisition and forced conversion; in the New World the dangers which faced them in Iberia might be transferred to others. As 'whites' in an environment where persecution was becoming racially directed they could be emancipated. While it is disturbing that this was a condition of the lessening of their persecution, it is only human that they should have escaped to a place where there were readier targets than they for aggression;[36] possibly more disquieting is the realization that both the aggression channelled through the Inquisition and the sudden expansion of empire to America were two sides of the same coin.

For Portuguese *conversos* such as Duarte de Leão and his young nephew, these undercurrents shaped their behaviour. The adventures of Luis de Carvajal would be paradigmatic of the sorts of extraordinary escape which many *conversos* managed to carry off in these years. With the army of heretics which the authorities believed to be at large in Portugal and the Inquisition only recently installed, it was difficult to imagine the persecuting institution being exported to somewhere as remote as Cape Verde.

Surely everything was in their favour. Duarte de Leão, with his control over many of the administrative posts in Ribeira Grande, could try to ensure that rabble-rousers were kept away, while Luis could at last begin to rebuild his life, his childhood. Here he would be free from persecution, and could grow up in an atmosphere of some security. Fear no longer needed to be the first reflex. This, at any rate, was the plan.

A closer look, however, might have disabused Luis of his sense of safety. The harbour of Ribeira Grande was narrow, guarded by rocks to the east. On a clear day the anchorages revealed the summit of Fogo, the neighbouring island, an active volcanic cone sitting like a fiery medieval God, judging his wayward flock. At times the clouds of ash drifting from Fogo across the ocean concealed the brilliant tropical sun, intimating in their fire and darkness the sadness of what was to follow.

CAPE VERDE IN 1548 was at the peak of its wealth.[37] There were 500 households in Ribeira Grande, with many of the homes built of stone and whitewashed in Portuguese style.[38] With the continuing settlement of the New World, the demand for slaves was growing all the time and most of the ships came to Cape Verde. Of the 252 ships which legally exported slaves across the Atlantic between 1544 and 1550, 247 went to the Cape Verde Islands.[39] The slaves were brought down from the cool highlands of Santiago, where they had been taught the rudiments of Christianity in the villas of their rich owners,[40] and sold from the stone pillory in the main square of Ribeira Grande. Free blacks rowed the unfortunates out to sea and the ocean-going prisons that awaited them; here the women were often put on deck and the men in the hold, so that the women did not goad the men into rebellion.[41]

Such a history is difficult to imagine today. Ribeira Grande is known as Cidade Velha – the old city – and is a sleepy village of beach bars and sandy streets drifting up towards the rocky valley. The river which brought the settlement here in the first place has dried up, but the valley retains sweeps of green beneath the ochre desert above. The cathedral stands in ruins, pored over by archaeologists from the nearby modern capital, Praia. But the slave pillory remains in the oblique square by the beach, a reminder of what went before and a memento of the world that Luis knew.

Luis's experiences in Lisbon had prepared him for some of what he saw when he arrived at Ribeira Grande. Yet whereas Africans in Lisbon were but a sizeable minority, in Cape Verde it was Europeans who were few and far between. Most people had adopted African customs, and the Portuguese settlers married African women by preference.[42] Some sent slaves away from the city, inland along the valley whose sides were covered with groves of orange, lime, lemon and fig trees.[43] The slaves made for the bone-dry plateau that rose up towards the mountains and their collars of cloud. Here they caught monkeys, who were taught how to dance and perform tricks. Said the Italian Carletti, 'I have seen some of [the monkeys] learn to stay on a corner of the table at which people eat, each with a candle in its hand, giving light to the people eating and showing a certain extraordinary shrewdness in not letting drops fall on the table'.[44]

As in Lisbon, Luis's role in Ribeira Grande revolved around the slave trade. As he became older, he took on greater responsibilities. The houses of the so-called factory were near the pillory on the square. There, once he had learned to be accountant and royal treasurer, it was Luis's task to charge the appropriate taxes to merchants taking slaves across the Atlantic. Luis and the ships' captains signed a joint declaration as to the numbers of slaves being shipped and their origins: whether they had come straight from the African mainland, been purchased by the factory itself for the king of Portugal or come from the interior of Santiago.[45]

Once the slaves had been bought, they were kept in two rooms, one for the men and one for the women.

> Many of the males showed a certain delicacy of their own, tying up the member with a ribbon or other grassy threads and pulling it back between their thighs, thus concealing it so that one could not tell whether they were males or females. And others covered it up by putting it into the horn of some animal or a seashell. Still others so filled it with rings of bone or of woven grass that it was both covered and decorated. And others painted it or, to say it better, daubed it with some mixture so as to make it red or yellow or green.[46]

Though Luis had been sent thousands of miles from home for a better life, he was not alone. Another uncle of his, Francisco Jorge – like Álvaro and Jorge de Leão a brother of Duarte de Leão and of Luis's mother Catalina – had taken the same option. Francisco Jorge was the factor on the African mainland and had a house in the settlement of Buguendo on the River São Domingos (in the modern country of Guinea-Bissau).[47] Here Jorge traded with the African peoples for slaves, who were then shipped over to Santiago to be exported to the New World. Other relatives of Luis and Jorge were also brought over to Africa through Leão, so that the family as a whole could benefit from the new opportunity.[48] For this close-knit group from a distant corner of the Portuguese hills, west Africa had become a refuge from the Inquisition.

Buguendo and Cape Verde may have seemed remote, but already the Inquisition was beginning to export its idea of persecution. In 1546, two years before Luis's arrival in Cape Verde, complaints had reached Portugal urging the installation of a tribunal in this outpost of the empire. Members of the elite in Santiago had written to the Inquisition in Évora claiming 'the Holy Inquisition has so much to do in this little corner of earth that it would be immoral to delay installing it'.[49] They denounced the customs house in Ribeira Grande as a hotbed of heretics, claiming that its officials had granted safe passage to a fugitive from the Inquisition whose father and brother had been burnt in Lisbon. When things had got too hot for the refugee in Ribeira Grande, the officials had sent him to the African coast for safety.[50] What was worse, they said, was that for as long as twenty years up to 200 *conversos* had been living on the African coast, performing the Mosaic rites and also the religious rituals of the cultures of Guiné.[51]

Five years later the Portuguese Inquisition finally took note of the complaints. In 1551 the Tribunal of Lisbon was extended to cover Portugal's Atlantic colonies, taking responsibility for the islands of the Azores, Madeira, Cape Verde and São Tomé, for Angola and Guiné on the African mainland, and for Brazil.[52] The decree reveals the inquisitorial turn of mind in its coming-of-age. The fully fledged Portuguese Inquisition was still just four years' old and the fact that an office on Lisbon's *Rossio* was seen as the best place to oversee the religious belief of colonies in Africa and America shows just how rampant the fantasies of control had become.

Nonetheless, the decree had immediate effects in Cape Verde. The inquisitors nominated a visitor to investigate the *conversos* on the islands that same year.[53] In the 150 years that followed the

Inquisition would never be entirely absent. By 1700 a total of 442 denunciations had been sent from the two main Cape Verdean islands of Santiago and Fogo.[54] This works out at roughly three per year, which in such a remote place where the population did not exceed 10,000 (of whom at most around 800 were ever European)[55] shows how enduring and pervasive the Inquisition became. Even these desolate specks of rock in the Atlantic – so remote that as João Rodriguez Freire, one of the accused, put it in 1629, they 'are not even found on *mapa mundi*'[56] – were not passed over. And even if the Inquisition could not actually bring home the heretics from Africa, it kept a watchful eye. As late as 1672 the inquisitor-general sent officials to wait at the port of Lisbon for two men from Cape Verde known to inquisitors, who were seized before they could land and thrown into the inquisitorial jail.[57]

THE SPREAD OF the Inquisition to the Cape Verde islands in the 1550s was not a first for Iberian colonies. A few decades earlier the well-known presence of *conversos* in the New World had led to some forays by the Inquisition as early as the 1520s into the highlands of Mexico. Here, two *converso* conquistadors, Hernando de Alonso and Gonzalo de Morales, had been burnt at the stake in Mexico City in 1528, the first victims of the Inquisition in America.[58]

It may seem strange that representatives of inquisitorial authority should have given so much thought to the actions of *conversos* in Mexico at this time. Vicious factional power struggles were convulsing the conquistadors and the Amerindian population was dying in the mines. But the moral justification of the conquest was religious, and thus preserving the purity of the faith was essential.

In Mexico persecution had spread rapidly from the *conversos* to the Amerindians. By 1530 cases were being mounted against Amerindians in Mexico for worshipping idols, killing hens every twenty days and spraying their blood in the fire, and permitting marriages according to pre-Hispanic rites.[59] This process culminated in a trial presided over by the episcopal inquisitor bishop Juan de Zumárraga of Mexico against Don Carlos Chichimecatecuhtli, the chief of Texcoco, an important town near Mexico City. Chichimecatecuhtli was tried and burnt in 1539 for promoting local religions;[60] however, of equal relevance was his hostility to the Spanish conquest, as he was reported to have said, 'I will have you know that my father and my grandfathers were both great prophets and they could see many things in the past and those yet to come and they never said anything about this . . . Who are these people who undo and perturb us, and live off us and break our backs?'[61]

Chichimecatecuhtli's burning at the stake was intended as exemplary, but considering the atrocities inflicted on the Amerindians in those years its impact may not have been as severe as all that. Moreover, the local authorities felt that it was an overly harsh way to treat the Indians, whose status was still being decided in Spanish law, and this case eventually led to Zumárraga being stood down as chief inquisitor in 1543.

In spite of Zumárraga's fate, these events had shown the Portuguese inquisitors how readily the institution could be transferred. With the dispatch of the inquisitorial visitor to the islands in 1551, it became clear that Cape Verde was one of the testing grounds for such a transfer. In these early years the Inquisition was perhaps seen by some as of special relevance because of the islands' role in the slave trade. Here the authorities followed Aristotle and Thomas Aquinas in asserting that one part of mankind had been set aside by nature to be slaves in the service of masters, and that such slaves depended on their masters to exercise choices for them.[62] There were natural slaves and natural masters; the condition of slavery benefited both.

With the moral justifications for the slave trade founded on such painfully thin ideas, the purity of the faith was particularly acute somewhere like Cape Verde. But Luis was of course up to his neck in this world, and as the 1550s progressed and he became an active player in the system, such justifications of man's inhumanity to man doubtless appealed. They allowed wealth and power to come with the sanction of God. The ideology was winning, and in Cape Verde, where the role of the *conversos* in Portugal had been transferred to others, Luis felt that he was on the right side. But the ideology went with the Inquisition, and this would, in the long run, be his undoing.

TROUBLE BEGAN IN 1562. On Christmas Eve some young *conversos* gathered at the house of Luis's uncle Francisco Jorge in Buguendo.

They wore masks and costumes and sent word round the town for people to come and watch. Buguendo was a large African town with around forty-five resident Europeans.[63] When Jorge's house was full, a 'very ugly' *converso* called Mestre Diogo appeared. The scandal had begun.[64]

Diogo was dressed as a woman. Cloths were piled up on his head as if he were about to go to the well to draw water. He squatted down on his haunches on the earthen floor of the house and began to cry out that his name was Mary and that he was in the throes of labour. The farce gathered pace, with some calling out, 'Mary's given birth! Mary's given birth!' Some people asked if she had really given birth, and others replied that indeed she had, to 'our Saviour who is going to save us'. 'Is it a boy or a girl?' 'A boy, a boy!' 'Where did she give birth?' 'In Bethlehem!' 'No, right here in Guinea, in Buguendo'.[65]

Their experiences in Spain and Portugal meant that mockery of Christian doctrines was commonplace among many *conversos*, particularly once they escaped Iberia. Nonetheless, mockery was rarely as brazen or as provocative as this nativity scene in Buguendo, and anywhere other than Africa the *conversos* would have expected to pay dearly.

In addition to theological sedition, the farce of Mestre Diogo posed another challenge to the Inquisition: transvestism also broke taboos in a way which was highly threatening. Cross-dressing was a feature of life in the 16th century, and not infrequently people appeared before the Inquisition because of it. In 1581 Manoel Pires confessed in Évora that a few months before he had met a person dressed in woman's clothes who seemed like a woman. It was dark and he did not ask too many questions, especially when she began to make advances. As they were about to make love the woman took his penis and proposed anal sex instead; it was only when Pires persisted with his original plan and she resisted strongly that he realized that the woman was in fact a man.[66] As a loyal Christian Pires had come to confess, since the 'evil sin of sodomy' as it was known was punished by the Inquisition, in extreme cases with burning at the stake.*

* For more discussion of the treatment of sodomy by the Inquisition, see Chapter Twelve.

Occasionally, transvestites themselves were punished by inquisitors. In 1556, just a few years before these events in Buguendo, a slave called Antonio had arrived in the islands of the Azores from Benin, a powerful city-state in what is now Nigeria. Refusing to wear the clothes given him by his master Paulo Manriques, Antonio took to dressing like a woman, wearing a white waistcoat buttoned at the front and tightly wrapped cloths on his head. He was then placed among the female slaves, working as a prostitute called Vitoria. Antonio/Vitoria paraded making knowing winks like a woman, while removing his hat and bowing like a man. The combination was a great success, and queues of seven or eight men could sometimes be seen waiting to visit him. But the public scandal could not be contained and he was denounced to the Inquisition and shipped back from the Azores to Lisbon. Here Antonio/Vitoria informed the inquisitors that he was in fact a woman with a vagina. Antonio was inspected; no vagina was found, and he was sent to be a galley slave.[67]

The view which the Inquisition took of this 'sin' was a complex one. Homosexual sex was usually an act of mutual consent, but in Africa and the New World things were often more murky, with masters and members of religious orders frequently abusing their male slaves as soon as they had bought them.[68] This did not prevent the Inquisition from seeking to try those who had been abused in this way; when an Angolan slave called Joseph was raped by his master João Carvalho de Barros in Bahia (Brazil) in 1703, he was then tried by the Inquisition, convicted, whipped and sentenced to five years in the galleys.[69]

In inquisitorial jurisprudence the guilt of homosexuality was shared between the partners, even if force was involved.[70] People were 'relaxed' for being the passive partners in Valencia in 1574[71] and Goa in 1612.[72] While active partners often received the more severe punishment, the attitudes of some in the inquisitorial hierarchy towards homosexuality is illustrated by Diego de Simancas's views on the matter in his autobiography: 'I was told in Rome that it was now impossible to remedy or punish the wicked sin [of sodomy] in Italy. I replied that it didn't seem like that to me, if it was provided (and executed) that if the corrupted boy did not denounce what had happened within a day of being raped, he would be burnt for it'.[73]

Mestre Diogo's performance in Buguendo was therefore doubly provocative, sexually and doctrinally. Taboos may exist to be broken, but mocking them at will is a dangerous game. The *conversos* thought they could get away with it in Africa, but they had reckoned without the bishop of Cape Verde, Francisco da Cruz.

Once rumours of the scandal reached Santiago, Cruz set about gathering witnesses. This was easy, as 'many people had seen the event and all of them thought it was bad'.[74] Mestre Diogo was arrested, taken by ship back to Cape Verde and thrown into the jail in Ribeira Grande. He did not even bother to deny that the event had taken place. He claimed rather that they had merely been 'dancing' to honour the birth of Christ.[75] This was a weak excuse, and Diogo knew it. Soon enough he was on a boat back to Lisbon, where, like Antonio from Benin before him, he was locked up in the jail of the Inquisition.[76]

Things soon began to look bleak for Francisco Jorge and his relations. Back in Lisbon Diogo stated that it was Jorge who had called him to his house that Christmas Eve and asked the *conversos* if they had prepared anything for that night. He said that during the performance that had given such scandal one of those involved had been Antonio Fernandes, Jorge's nephew (and probably a cousin of Luis).[77] In Cape Verde it had also emerged that another of those involved in the show, Antonio Duarte, was also related to Jorge.[78] Meanwhile, Francisco da Cruz had mentioned in his dispatch to the inquisitors in Lisbon that Jorge was himself just as suspect of Jewish rites as those mentioned in the accusations.[79]

While Mestre Diogo was in a very dangerous position, for Luis de Carvajal and the rest of the Jorge circle matters were not yet desperate. But Cape Verde was no longer the safe haven that it once had been. Luis left the islands in 1563[80] – just as the material for the trial was being put together – as did his uncle Francisco. While Jorge fled to Mexico and became a monk, Luis returned to Europe and moved to Seville.[81] It was time to settle down and marry; it was time to escape the inquisitorial shadow of fear that had been following him ever since childhood.

Veracruz 1568

They sailed out on the white seas
Breaking apart a turbulent wave;
They felt the air's stiffening breeze
Billowing out their sails concave;
The ocean was sealed with white foam,
And the ship's prows went a-breaking
Those holy maritime waters
Which their Protean force had cut open.[82]

Camões, the poet of the Portuguese discoveries, captured the elation and the terror of the seas for a whole generation. The ocean was a great horror, but also an opportunity. When things went wrong, as they frequently did, passengers had to face their ends as best they could. Robert Thomson, an English merchant from Andover, described the near shipwreck of his vessel off the Mexican coast in 1555, shortly before Luis de Carvajal returned to Iberia:

> Our ship being old and weake was so tossed, that she opened at the sterne a [fathom] under water . . . and for feare of sinking we threw and lightned into the sea all the goods we had or could come by: but that would not serve. Then we cut our maine mast and threw all our ordinance into the sea saving one piece . . . [soon] we thought there was no hope of life. And then we began to embrace one another, every man his friend, every wife her husband, and the children their fathers and mothers, committing our soules to Almighty God, thinking never to escape alive . . .[83]

Thomson and his fellows were rescued by a passing ship, but not everyone was so lucky. Even if the weather did not set about you, there was always the possibility that your enemies would. The traveller Jean de Léry described a French attack on a Spanish ship in 1555. The French sailors 'did not leave a piece of biscuit or any provisions at all to the poor souls, and what was worse, destroyed their sails and stole their lifeboat . . . so that it would have been better to cast them into the deep than leave them in such a miserable state'.[84]

Even without pirates, voyages were painfully uncomfortable. During the rainy season sailors' skin would seethe with boils and sores. Rainstorms would rot the ship's biscuits. In the dry season the drinking water would fill with maggots so that people had to pinch their noses to drink it.[85] It was not for nothing that the sea was often represented as Satan's domain.[86]

The danger of capture by French pirates was particularly acute near the waters off Cape Verde, which Luis travelled through as he returned to Spain.[87] Yet having passed through all these dangers and escaped the approaching investigations by the Inquisition into his circles in Cape Verde, Luis felt blessed. For the next few years after reaching Seville he led a life of ease.

Seville was capital of the booming trade to and from the New World, and here, in around 1566, Luis married Guiomar de Rivera. Rivera's father was Miguel Núñez, the factor of slaves for the Portuguese crown on the Caribbean island of Santo Domingo.[88] Luis had probably dealt with Núñez from Cape Verde, and the contacts of his father-in-law set him up in life. Luis soon undertook a range of tasks, from shipping wheat to taking command of a fleet off the Dutch coast in the years running up to the rebellion of the United Provinces against Spain.[89] But by 1568, around five years after his return from Cape Verde, his eyes were turning towards what was now the great prize for ambitious people in the new global empire: America.

For a *converso* like Luis, emigration to the Indies was supposed to be impossible. In 1522 Charles V of Spain had banned the emigration of converted Muslims and Jews to the New World without his express permission.[90] The decree had little effect, as the law had to be renewed in 1539, 1552, 1559 and 1566.[91] Though people seeking passage to the New World were supposed to present proof that their ancestry was not tainted by Muslim or Jewish blood at the Casa de Contratación in Seville by providing certificates of 'cleanliness',* in practice they got round this through bribery and forgery.

Though ancestry could not be altered in fact, corruption could alter it in appearance. In 1591, twenty-five years after Carvajal first

* See Chapter Eight for a full discussion of this idea.

went to the New World, the inquisitorial official Melchior Cano* penned a long complaint to the Inquisition of Toledo that 'many investigations have been made here for people going to the Indies, proving that these people are clean when they are not, and even when some of them are grandchildren of people who have been burnt or punished the witnesses have sworn to the contrary'.[92] Long into the 17th century the problem would continue, with members of well-known *converso* families like the Gramaxos of Lisbon 'proving' their cleanliness in the halls of power in Seville.[93]

Amid all these strangling regulations, the authorities also turned a blind eye to a few favourites. There were some families who were so powerful that no one dared testify against them,[94] and Luis de Carvajal had maneouvred himself into just such a position. Though his uncle Duarte de Leão was coming under increasing attack, accused of smuggling and tax avoidance in places as far afield as Colombia, Mexico, Puerto Rico and Santo Domingo, Leão controlled the lucrative (for the Portuguese crown) contract for supplying slaves to the Indies through the 1560s and was difficult to touch.[95] Meanwhile, the illustrious role of Luis's father-in-law Miguel Núñez in the Spanish colonies meant that he had a secure position in Spain. The fate of his uncles and the problems of Cape Verde seemed a distant memory, and Luis was part of the emerging oligarchy of imperial trade.

So it was that in July 1568, at the age of thirty, Luis de Carvajal was invited to be an admiral in a fleet of eleven ships sailing for the New World with the new viceroy of New Spain (Mexico), Martín de Enríquez.[96] He would sail without his wife, Guiomar, something common for men trying to make their fortunes in America at this time. These expeditions were ostentatious affairs, the flagships replete with insignias of office and ornate chests containing royal orders. The decks heaved with ambition, vanity and anticipation. Carvajal's arrival in such a fleet meant that he would be instantly guaranteed an illustrious position in the New World that most *conversos* could not imagine for themselves.

Nevertheless, Carvajal's position brought its own pressures too.

---

* This is not the Melchior Cano who was an enemy of Archbishop Carranza of Toledo – see pages 130–140.

As the fleet reached the first Caribbean islands and made for Veracruz on the coast of Mexico, three ragged ships were sighted off the coast of Jamaica. The ships turned tail, and Carvajal ordered that they give chase. They turned out to be English pirate ships which had been illegally trading in hides, and Carvajal sent the men and their cargoes to the Spanish governor.[97] But soon even greater adventures were at hand: arriving at Veracruz, it was discovered that the English adventurer John Hawkins had taken control of its port and was fortifying it against the viceroy's fleet. The empire was being challenged by upstarts from its own backyard.

VERACRUZ WAS a beautiful place. Situated on a river a few miles inland from the Atlantic coast, it was surrounded by forest and orchards of orange, lemon and guava trees. The arbours teemed with parrots, some of them with tails as big as pheasants.[98] The town itself had about 300 households. A humid, tropical settlement, in the years before Carvajal arrived it ate up the lives of many of those who arrived there. Usually these were people who did not look after themselves, and 'would commonly go in the Sunne in the heat of the day, & did eat fruit of the countrey with much disorder, and especially gave themselves to womens company at their first coming; whereupon they were cast into a burning ague [malaria], of the which few escaped'.[99] By the 1560s, however, people were only living in Veracruz from the end of August to April, retiring to the lush green hills around Jalapa for the rainy season.[100]

Veracruz was served by the port of San Juan de Ulúa, about twenty miles down the coast.* The beach between the two was littered with mighty trees, roots and all, uprooted by hurricanes in Florida and washed down the Gulf of Mexico.[101] San Juan itself was a fortified island sheltering a good harbour where ships tied up and 150 African slaves helped to maintain the facility.[102] It was this port that Hawkins had captured and which would now lead to Carvajal's first showdown in Mexico.

This was Hawkins's third visit to the Caribbean. He was a successful privateer largely because his bravado and audacity outstripped his integrity. His usual practice had been to seize slaves in

* San Juan de Ulúa lies on the outskirts of the modern city of Veracruz.

Africa by burning a village here and there, and then trade them in the Caribbean for gold and sugar, claiming to the local authorities that he had to sell the slaves in order to repair his ship after storm damage.[103] If this third voyage was unusual, it was only because this time he had bought the slaves rather than kidnapping them.[104]

While the Portuguese and Spanish authorities deeply resented Hawkins's intrusion on their domains, local plantation owners and prospectors had less trouble squaring their consciences; African slaves were in high demand for the mines and plantations. On this third visit Hawkins had merrily cut deals with the local authorities in Santa Marta and Cartagena on the Colombian coast, selling slaves and commandeering provisions from farms but leaving some cloth as a sort of payment.[105] He had begun his return trip to England on 8 August 1568, with unsold slaves, gold, silver and pearls stowed aboard his flagship, the *Jesus of Lubeck*. On 12 August, however, a violent hurricane had lashed the ship between Florida and the tip of Cuba, and Hawkins had been forced to return for repairs. En route he had taken three Spanish ships, and placed them at the head of his fleet to make them look like the new viceroy's flotilla. Arriving at San Juan de Ulúa, Hawkins had been told by the captured Spanish pilots to respond in kind to the firing of a salute so that the ruse was not given away. A welcome party of small sailing ships and boats put out into the harbour, and was staggered to find Hawkins the pirate sailing towards them and taking control of one of the two most important ports in the whole of America.[106]

This was on 16 September, and the fleet carrying Enríquez and Carvajal arrived the following day. There followed a week of tense negotiations over the windswept island. Hawkins wanted to repair his fleet at minimum cost and demanded the right to trade, something considered illegal by the Spanish. Viceroy Enríquez pretended to agree, and then reneged at the first opportunity, routing Hawkins and his fleet comprehensively so that the only pirate leaders to escape were he and Francis Drake. But the two were separated, and Hawkins was forced to cram all the survivors on board his one remaining ship, HMS *Minion*, to attempt the 3,000-mile voyage home.[107]

Soon it became clear that there were not enough provisions to go round. On 8 October the ship touched land near Tampico, 200 miles north of Veracruz. Many of the sailors, realizing that if they all stayed they would end by eating one another, asked to be set ashore to try their luck among the Amerindians. Hawkins agreed, but as the men were about to leave the *Minion*, wrote one of them, Miles Philips, 'it was a world to see how suddenly mens minds were altered'. They all begged to stay. Hawkins would have none of it, and they were forced overboard in stormy seas amid a 'pitifull mone'. When one of the rowing boats could not make land amid the high waves, the bosun John Sanders threw the castaways out into the sea and they swam to shore, two of them drowning.

Over one hundred sailors were left to fend for themselves in the humid coastlands of Mexico. Here the indigenous settlements which once had dotted the terrain had vanished into oblivion. The land was overgrown with forests and creepers. Brutalized Indian refugees from the Spanish empire attacked and killed six of the castaways. The party separated, and one group, led by Anthony Goddard, made its way towards Tampico.[108]

It was here that Carvajal made his biggest impression. After the excitement of the arrival and the battle with Hawkins, he had been appointed mayor of Tampico. Although many of the Spanish settlers and African slaves were reluctant, Carvajal raised a militia and rounded up the group of seventy-eight men led by Goddard. Acting as magistrate, Carvajal seized all the gold and jewels they had left, took the captives' testimony, and after three days sent them on the long road through the jungle, cresting barren passes on the old Aztec route into the uplands, until they reached Mexico City in the lee of the smoking volcano Popocatepetl.[109]

Carvajal had shown himself to be a man swift to act and quickly became a busy colonial figure. As mayor, he was employed in the Tampico area 'pacifying' the local Indians. He was also sent by Viceroy Enríquez to the endless vistas of the desert north. He passed the mines of Zacatecas where silver ran beneath the dusty sierra and the bones of those who sought it. He moved on into the emptiness where the nomadic Chichimec Indians lived among the mesquite and the coyotes.[110] He built flyblown camps, sheltering beneath the hides of dead animals in the arid wastes of his yearning.

It is fair to assume that in all these adventures he gave little thought to the English captives. Perhaps, though, he came upon some of the ex-pirates among the chancers of the mining towns, where the more adventurous of Hawkins's castaways had gone to seek their fortunes. Six years later he certainly would have heard that these foreigners, once cast upon his mercy, had been rounded up by the inquisitors in Mexico City. He would have known that they had been tortured and convicted of being Lutherans in a large auto there in 1574.*[111]

As he heard this news, he must have felt a flicker re-emerge of that fear of the Inquisition which he had tried to bury ever since the events of the 1540s in Évora and the 1560s in Cape Verde. But the good news for him seemed to be that it was Protestants who were being targeted. The inquisitorial net was casting wider: in Spain it was the Lutherans and *moriscos* who were now the main targets, as the Inquisition found itself besieged by increasing numbers of the enemy within.

* For a description of these events, see page 144.

Chapter Five

THE ENEMY WITHIN

Why does it bother your Excellency whether he is burnt there or here, since in the end he has got to die?

IT WAS IN SPAIN that fear first began to touch all corners of society. To the north of Seville, where the new Inquisition had originated, lay the baking plains of Extremadura. Here stood settlements of clustered stone houses, angry in their clannish isolation. And it was in Extremadura, in the last days of May 1574, that a remarkable thing happened near the town of Zafra.

The event was widely seen as something of a warning. The most terrible and horrifying snake 'ever seen in Spain' appeared. About twenty reliable eyewitnesses declared that they had seen this beast roaming the pastures three miles from the town with 'its head as big as a bullock and its eyes huge and terrifying, its face thick and twisted, the tail as thick and long as a tree-trunk, the chest high and risen above the earth'. The appetite of this monster was such that it devoured two cows daily yet, curiously, when the whole town of Zafra marched out in search of it together with many people from neighbouring villages, it never emerged except in isolation to one person or two. This terrible portent was taken as an omen 'and a very timely one'. Twenty days later an inquisitor arrived from Llerena to make inquiries in the town. He stayed for four months, providing tenebrous fuel for the townspeople's imagination. After his arrival, no one ever saw the beast again.[1]

It does not take the most unreconstructed cynic to suppose that Zafra's terror at knowledge of the approaching inquisitorial visit had been displaced onto the story of the serpent. Once the inquisitor, Montoya, arrived, fear of the serpent was transferred to its original and truest target, the figure of the officer of the Inquisition. For in Spain, almost a century after the Inquisition's formation, the officials of this institution were increasingly the subject of such feelings. It was not hard to see why.

Back in Seville in the 1550s the bishop and first inquisitor of Tarragona walked out one day with his retinue to enjoy himself in the gardens on the banks of the Guadalquivir. Here were brilliant flowers, circling swifts in the sky, views of a city in its pomp. Yet power grabbed at the coat-tails of such elegance.

A son of one of the keepers of the garden, a toddler of two or three, happened to be sitting beside the ornamental pond, playing with a reed. One of the inquisitor's pages snatched the reed out of the child's hands. Seeing his son burst into tears, the gardener tried to take the page to task. Could he not see that this was the boy's toy? What right did he have to behave so selfishly? An argument ensued, and the inquisitor, tiring of this intrusion into his peaceful perambulations, arrested the gardener, who was kept imprisoned for nine months with heavy fetters around his ankles.[2]

Such stories reveal an institution in which abuse of power came all too easily to its functionaries. The fear of the people of Zafra and the casual punishment of the slightest challenge to an inquisitor's authority were related. Tensions had not disappeared following the targeting of the *conversos*. As these victims were burnt, or escaped to Portugal, America and the New World, different targets had to be found. Thus it was that in Spain a new hidden enemy was identified, an enemy which meant that fear would penetrate to the heart of Spanish society.

Valencia 1535–1539

Valencia is situated in a beautiful plain irrigated by rivers and springs. In the 16th century it was an important port city and by some accounts the destination of the ship taken by Jonah before his encounter with the whale.* Valencia was a delight, its gardens filled with fruit trees and shaded by the leaves of orange trees.[3]

Here, the Inquisition had not been idle. In the 1480s the *Reyes Católicos* had replaced the previous papal inquisitors,† and when the German traveller Hieronymus Münzer had visited in the mid-1490s he came across the son of a *converso* in the madhouse, 'naked, locked in a cage and chained up. Our companions threw him a few coins for him to pray; but he began to do so in Hebrew and to throw down terrible blasphemies on all Christians, as is the custom of the Jews, for he was the son of a very rich *converso*, who had brought him up secretly to be a Jew; but the father had been given away through the madness of the son, and burnt for it'.[4] After a series of autos in the first years of the 16th century which saw the deaths of some of the *converso* relatives of the great humanist philosopher Joan-Lluis Vives, the Valenciano Inquisition began to move on from the *conversos* to other heretics.

Thus on 23 September 1535 depositions were collected in the small town of Cinctorres, skulking in the hills north of Valencia. Accusations had been received concerning one Miguel Costa. Costa had been the schoolteacher in Cinctorres for about a year and a half, and before that had lived in Italy. However his activities were seriously disturbing the villagers, some of whom had given evidence to the Inquisition about this stranger in their midst.[5]

The first witness was the farm labourer Anthony Gueron, who claimed that Costa said that Martin Luther 'did not say bad things but good ones'. When a monk had spoken of the bulls issued by the pope, Costa had said, 'Let the monk and the bulls go to the devil! The money should stay here and the bulls can go to the devil!' Then, when one Pere Valles had come to give alms to the Virgin Mary and light a candle for St Anthony, Costa had exclaimed how St Anthony himself would not care for the offering.

Soon the evidence mounted. Anthony Gueron's brother Mikel

---

* Tarshish is thought to have been the biblical name for Spain, and the destination of Jonah's ship suspected to be on the eastern coast in the region of Valencia.

† See page 39.

said that Costa did not cross himself when he entered the church and had said that there was no need to confess. The inquisitorial authorities had heard enough. Costa was arrested and charged with these crimes as well as others: he had claimed that there was no need to say the Ave Maria and that when the soul left the body it already belonged to God or the devil, implying that there was no such thing as purgatory. Costa was indignant. He claimed never to have read any works by Luther – he didn't even know who Luther was! He was the victim of calumnies and lies. In spite of the inquisitorial code of secrecy, he correctly guessed that his two main accusers were the Gueron brothers. These ingrates were, he said, mortal enemies, since one of their sisters had fallen out with him. Languishing in the inquisitorial jail, Costa wrote moving epistles in Latin of his dedication to the Catholic faith.

There is, even more than in most inquisitorial cases, a terrible pathos to the crumbling parchment which contains the details of Costa's tragedy. The hand of Costa is firm and upright in its explication of his belief in the principles of the true faith. Yet this steadfastness is marred by his terror; as soon as he heard rumours circulating of his 'heresies' in the village of Morella, he jumped onto a horse and rode through the rain to Cinctorres, arriving at nine o'clock in the evening to the astonishment of his friend Antonio Valles. Costa had clearly seen the necessity of scotching the gossip. Rightly, he had feared the consequences of failure. Yet the inquisitors continued with their interrogations, seeing his tongue as 'a sharp knife, exploding with heretical and blasphemous words, and also with insanity'. But they could not get him to confess his sins. He was, as the inquisitorial phrase put it, relaxed to the secular authorities to be burnt in 1539.

Costa's death was a terrible waste. Born in Cinctorres in around 1502, he had spent the first ten years of his life there before studying in Valencia and then Aragon. He had been talented enough to be selected to accompany Pope Adrian to Rome in 1522. From Rome he had travelled to Lombardy, where he had spent five or six years before being captured by the king of France. After spending three or four years as a prisoner of the French he had gone to Flanders before returning to Spain.

Spanish villages were in general enormously suspicious of outsiders in these years.[6] Costa's main crime appears to have been that, after his foreign experiences, he seemed different. Thus in getting Costa put to death the gossipers of Cinctorres were repeating the attacks previously directed at the *conversos*. When that ambiguous group had been purged, a new one had been required. 'Lutherans' such as Costa were emblematic of the sort of misfit who could easily be turned on, as the realization dawned of how numerous and perilous the enemy within really was.

These fifth columns were extraordinary resourceful. Something of how their wiles and infernal stratagems had embedded them in Spanish society was revealed twenty years later in a letter written by the inquisitor-general of Spain, Fernando de Valdés, on 14 May 1558. This letter can stand as testament to the terrible events soon to unfold. Valdés explained that he had left Valladolid intending to go to Seville, where he was the archbishop, but that no sooner had he reached Salamanca than problems had overtaken him. Large numbers of Lutheran books had been discovered, and he had received a letter on the problems of the *moriscos* of Granada. Then the *moriscos* of Aragon and Castile had petitioned him for edicts of grace. And soon things were to get even worse.

'Together with this, and at the same time, the law of Moses – which had been thought to be extinguished in these kingdoms – began to renew itself in Murcia, where many guilty people were found, some of whom were punished in a public auto.' And then the machinations of the enemy accelerated, as large conspiracies of Lutherans were discovered among some of the nobility of Seville and Valladolid. The threats were too great, and Valdés was unable to continue with his journey.[7] It can be seen that he did not see himself as short of enemies; on the contrary, they were everywhere: *moriscos*, Judaizers, Protestants . . .

In these years, it was to be 'Lutherans' such as Costa who would emerge as most dangerous. What was especially sinister was that these heretics were not 'foreign' like the *conversos*, but people difficult to distinguish from law-abiding Old Christians.[8] They were agitators who came from the very heart of Spanish society. Thus it was that nobody could any longer be deemed free of suspicion.

*

ON 31 OCTOBER 1517 Martin Luther posted his 95 *Theses* on the door of the castle in Wittenberg and a revolution took hold of Christendom. Luther challenged the authority of the pope and the merits of the monastic life, and maintained that the individual's connection to God was of more significance than the rituals of the Catholic Church conducted by its priests. When on 10 December 1520 Luther burnt the papal bull *Exsurge Domine* in Wittenberg, the die was cast for a split in the Church.

In Spain the challenge posted by Luther was particularly serious. While, as we have seen, the aims of the new Inquisition – though couched in religious terms – had had definite political ends, its effect, combined with the expulsion of the Jews in 1492 and the Moors of Granada in 1502, had been to turn the Catholic faith into the unifying national force in Spain. This meant that political and religious interests had become one and the same; thus Luther's threat to the Catholic Church was taken as an implicit threat to the Spanish nation and the monarchy itself.

For the Inquisition, however, Luther was an opportunity for an institution reeling from scandal. The excesses of inquisitor Lucero in Cordoba* had contributed to a strong anti-inquisitorial movement.[9] The complaints had led to a council being held in Burgos in the summer of 1508 which had decided that the evidence against many of those condemned by Lucero in Cordoba had been insufficient. Lucero had been released in 1511 after three years in prison and barred from any further inquisitorial activity.[10]

Lucero's judge was the inquisitor-general of Spain, Cardinal Jiménez de Cisneros. Cisneros was a man of extraordinary influence, provincial of the Franciscan order, founder of the university at Alcalá de Henares near Madrid and champion of a movement that propagated the publication of devotional literature in Castilian as well as in Latin.[11] His belief in spiritual renewal however was married to rabid extremism. When he arrived in Granada in 1499, seven years after the fall of the Moorish Kingdom, he ordered unconverted Muslims to be thrown into jail where they were treated with such cruelty by one of his chaplains – nicknamed the lion – that they came forward within four or five days to beg for baptism.[12] Then

---

* See pages 65–68.

Cisneros ordered the imams to bring him their books of Islamic theology, which he proceeded to burn publicly in spite of their extraordinary beauty and lavishness.[13] Later, as inquisitor-general, he persuaded the newly installed king of Spain Charles V not to listen to petitions that witnesses' names be published in inquisitorial trials.[14]

Cisneros was, then, a good shepherd for the Inquisition. He dampened down the furore over the Lucero affair by ensuring that final judgement was delayed until 1517. Yet all the same the affair had cast a shadow.[15] After forty years of persecution the *conversos* had been cowed, and many thought that the persecuting institution should go. They needed to be persuaded to think differently, and with curious good fortune Luther began his heretical activities in the same year. Just two years later the first cases of the new threat surfaced in Spain.

The problems began in Guadalajara, to the north-east of Madrid. Here in 1519 information was received by inquisitors about groups of people who had developed a philosophy which was termed *alumbrado*, or illuminist. The sect was associated with many scandalous doctrines by the Inquisition: members were accused of holding that prayer should be mental (interior) and not verbal (ritual); of saying that hell did not exist; of having contempt for the cult of the saints and for papal bulls; of showing no deference to the sacrament or to images of saints or the Virgin; and of holding that the ceremonies and fasts of the Church were onerous bonds (*ataduras*).[16]

One of its leaders was Pedro Ruiz de Alcaraz.[17] The grandson of a scribe and the son of a bread merchant, Alcaraz was an accountant and owned a vineyard in Guadalajara.[18] He travelled widely around Castile on the business of his patrons, and this gave him the opportunity to meet like-minded people in his search for a new spirituality. One of these was Isabel de la Cruz, attached to the Franciscan order as a tertiary but not living in a nunnery; another was María de Cazalla, whose brother Juan was a bishop and chaplain to Cardinal Cisneros.[19]

As was so often the case, the interest of the Inquisition originated in jealousy. On 13 May 1519 a secular holy woman – called a *beata* in Spain* – by the name of Mari Núñez, together with her maid and the priest Hernando Díaz, came forward to denounce Alcaraz, Cazalla and Cruz. Mari Núñez was afraid. While she was a holy *beata*, she was not wholly discreet. Her nickname for Hernando Díaz was 'the ladies' priest'. She had also been the mistress of a powerful noble, Bernardo Suárez de Figueroa, but desire had trumped tact and intelligence, and she had taunted him with impotence. Alcaraz frowned on this sort of behaviour and he had threatened to destroy Núñez's reputation for holiness. He and his friends began to gather information against her which they planned to give to the religious authorities. Thus it was that Núñez decided to get her accusation in first.[20]

At first the Inquisition paid little attention. Alcaraz continued to travel and preach widely, while Isabel de la Cruz gained new followers. It was only after news of the Lutheran rebellion became more alarming that officials re-examined the evidence and decided that the *alumbrado* sect could prove dangerous. While there was no question of the *alumbrados* being influenced by Luther – the sect appears to have originated around 1512 – they shared many ideas in common, in particular the notion of the importance of mental prayer, and their mockery of religious institutions. In the spring of 1524 Alcaraz was arrested. During his long trial he was tortured and eventually sentenced in 1529. He and Isabel de la Cruz were flogged and paraded through the streets of the towns where they had preached; Alcaraz remained in prison until 1537, de la Cruz until 1538.[21]

Stepping back from the case and thinking about the world which it reveals, one touches a reality that is both familiar and strange. Here on the baking plains of the Castilian plateau, people were earnestly visiting one another's homes, discussing theology and thinking fervidly about the mysteries of prayer and devotion. All this can seem remote and yet violent disagreements about religion and the customs of daily life are not without a certain resonance.

One of the problems for the Inquisition in dealing with the *alumbrado* group was that it was not exactly sure what sort of heresy this was. But this did not have to be too much of a problem as

---

* For a full discussion of *beatas*, see Chapter Twelve.

prurience and sexual frisson could fan the desire to censure. When María de Cazalla was arrested in 1532 she was accused of saying that 'she was closer to God having sex with her husband than if she had been performing the most high-minded prayer in the world',[22] while a *beata* and *alumbrada* of Salamanca, Francisca Hernández, engaged in an unusual type of religious experience with the priest Antonio Medrano, where it was held that 'male and female devotees could embrace one another naked as well as clothed'.[23]

The reality was that confusion over the new heresy developed because there *was* no overarching heretical movement of *alumbrados*. *Alumbrados* themselves could be divided into two groups, *recogidos*, who sought to find peace and union with God through contemplation, and *dejados* like Francisca Hernández, who held that no thoughts should be refused as giving oneself to God was enough for mystical union.[24] The philosophy of *alumbramiento* in fact was first fully articulated by the Inquisition itself, in its edict of faith of 23 September 1525, and was never discussed in these terms by any of its supposed adepts.[25] As such, this was a philosophical schema which, like the 'Judaizing' of the *conversos*, had substantially been invented by the Inquisition. Similarly, there had been no network of *alumbrado* fifth columnists until the Inquisition had identified it. Though ideas had been circulating which were not orthodox, these had not taken on the characteristics of a movement until the Inquisition had labelled it and started to prosecute it.

Indeed in many ways the perception of heresy in the *alumbrados* owed much to the perception of the *conversos*. Alcaraz, Cazalla and Cruz all came from *converso* families, and some of their relatives had been punished by the Inquisition.[26] At first Alcaraz was himself portrayed as a Judaizing *converso*, being accused of supporting *dejamiento* as a way of bringing Castile to the Mosaic law.[27] When Alcaraz showed himself utterly ignorant of Judaism, the inquisitors decided that this new movement had more in common with Lutheranism. But even though the shape of the accusations changed, some inquisitors stated that the danger was exacerbated because *alumbrados* were all *conversos*.[28]

Thus the old way of conceptualizing heresy became a bridge to the new. When many *conversos* at the court of Charles V turned to the reformist ideas of Erasmus of Rotterdam, they were labelled by their enemies *alumbrados*.[29] Here was another convenient catch-all phrase, a name which would stick. Such labelling, it turned out, was a prelude to destroying the followers of these new ideas.

From his base in the Low Countries, with its huge skies and burgeoning wool industry, Desiderius Erasmus had produced a string of works which urged the recasting of Christian faith in Europe. Erasmus's influence had spread rapidly. During the 1520s a veritable fever struck the nobility in Spain as everyone sought to become acquainted with his works. One of his Spanish admirers wrote on 1 September 1526 that the inquisitors had ordered that no one should write against him, and that:

> Your enemies went to the houses of the noble ladies, and to those of their daughters of confession, and to the nunneries, persuading them that they should not listen to anyone who has read Erasmus, or even picked up any of his works . . . but as forbidden fruit is a great stimulus to appetite, they managed to use every trick they could to understand Erasmus, looking for people to interpret him, which meant that his works soon became very well known in noble houses and in the nunneries.[30]

In 1525 Erasmus's principal works in Latin were published at the University of Alcalá, and in 1527 a conference organized by Inquisitor-General Alonso de Manrique at Valladolid discussed his ideas. The following years saw the publication of numerous translations of his works.[31] This early admiration owed much to Flemish influence in the court of Spain's Habsburg King Charles V, many of whose retinue were personal friends of Erasmus. But there was too a resonance in Erasmus's emphasis on spiritual renewal and intimacy with God for a nation which, with the defeat of the Moors and the discovery of America, saw itself as burdened with a historic purpose.[32] The universalist tendencies of Erasmian thought perfectly suited the universalist ambitions of Spanish rule and its sense of imperial destiny.[33]

Here one should feel some sympathy for Spain. In the space of fifty years it had moved from a state of permanent civil war to leading the fightback against the Muslims following the fall of

Constantinople in 1453, and discovering and beginning to settle an entirely new continent. According to the ideas of the time, some sense of religious destiny was inevitable.

In these circumstances, there was ideological ferment. The friars in particular loathed Erasmus and his challenges to monasticism. When Inquisitor-General Manrique confronted the friars in 1527 and ordered them to obey his commands and to stop burning Erasmus's books, they replied that the wickedness was such that divine authority superseded that of human beings.[34] This was a sign of things to come; when Charles V's court eventually departed Spain for Bologna, where Charles received the imperial crown from Pope Clement VII on 24 February 1530, the anti-Erasmus faction set to work.[35]

First of all, in 1529 Inquisitor-General Alonso de Manrique was himself sidelined to Seville, where he spent most of the rest of his life in his archbishopric until he died alone and ignored in 1538.[36] Then accusations were levelled at some of the Erasmian figureheads in court circles. In 1530 Juan de Vergara, the secretary of Alonso de Fonseca, archbishop of Toledo, was accused of Lutheranism, and an inquisitorial case against him began in July 1533. The Erasmian Mateo Pascual was arrested by the Inquisition in June 1533, and Alonso de Virúes, who had spoken in favour of Erasmus at the 1527 conference at Valladolid, was arrested in 1535. One of Inquisitor-General Manrique's friends, Juan del Castillo, was burnt to death, and four other friars followed.[37] Other cases were pursued; in 1536 Miguel Mezquita, who, like Miguel Costa of Cinctorres, had travelled in Italy, was burnt in Valencia for holding Lutheran opinions which merely derived from the study of Erasmus.[38]

This was a veritable witch-hunt. Most of these people survived the inquisitorial trials, but their careers were ruined; those who could escape, did so.[39] Whether they were genuine Protestants or merely Catholics attracted to the ideas of Erasmus became an increasingly moot point, because both groups were targeted. The Inquisition, having begun its work on *converso alumbrados*, was now shifting its attention.

Yet the old categories of prejudice persisted. As the 16th century progressed mystical writers increasingly became targets of the inquisitorial authorities. With its mania for bureaucratic legalese, the

Inquisition was bound to be hostile to any sense of internal spiritual enlightenment such as was promised by some of the great Spanish mystics of the age.[40] Moreover, just as with the *alumbrados*, many of these writers were themselves of *converso* lineage. As the Inquisition toyed with investigating Juan de Ávila and Teresa de Ávila – later beatified – and cast Luis de León into its cells for five years in the 1570s, it was taking issue with the ideas of a whole range of *converso* descendants.[41]

This was not because *conversos* were innately heretical. The fact that so many of them developed complex Christian theological ideas shows that for many their original conversion had been voluntary. The predominance of *conversos* among *alumbrados* and the controversial theologians of the time was, rather, because the dramatic nature of their turn to Christianity pushed many *conversos* towards both a more intense and a more personalized sense of Christianity.[42] This led to a profound search for meaning, and all too often towards doctrines which were out of step with the orthodoxy. Thus in trying to clamp down on one ideology perceived as dangerous, the Inquisition had created and codified another which it would come to see in the same way.

Murcia 1552–62

THE NUMBER OF ERASMIAN *alumbrados* and Lutherans tried in the mid-16th century was small. Their significance for the Inquisition lay in the fact that their prosecution opened the way towards an ideology in which repression could move beyond the *conversos* and become universalized. Yet in order to persuade the population that the enemy could be everywhere and anywhere, it was also sometimes necessary to remind them of the continuing danger of the old enemy. Thus while the notion of the expanding Protestant threat was feeding into Spanish society a terrible crypto-Jewish conspiracy was – as Inquisitor-General Valdés noted in his abovementioned letter of 1558* – uncovered in the region of Murcia.

The problems began in 1552 with Inquisitor Sánchez. This

* See page 113.

individual may have been in Murcia to enforce conformity on the faithful, but there was little that was faithful about him. Sánchez had propositioned a married woman who had gone to him for advice about a civil court case, saying that if she would submit to his desire he would get the case dropped.[43] Indeed, Inquisitor Sánchez seemed particularly attracted to married women. He had developed a 'close friendship' with the wife of one of his inquisitorial prisoners, 'closing himself in with her day and night'. When a married woman whose husband was away went to see him regarding an inquisitorial matter, he propositioned her and ordered her to come back to his apartments later on. He had also slept with a married *converso* woman and had got a young girl pregnant when she had come to ask him for advice. While secrecy was the cornerstone of inquisitorial procedure, Sánchez was so lacking in this faculty that he left the doors of his house open all night for prostitutes to come in and out at their leisure; there they lowered inquisitorial apparel without lowering inquisitorial zeal.

Sánchez's demands were mirrored by those of his staff. One official, Diego de Valdés, a relative of Inquisitor-General Fernando de Valdés, was accused in 1551 of seeing through his posting in Murcia with his mistress, with whom he had several children.[44] Meanwhile, one of Sánchez's messengers, Blas de Vega, was a drunkard who spent his time in brothels and bars and could not read or write. On one of his inquisitorial errands he took a girlfriend with him, who he slept with publicly. All this was the cause of great scandal and not inconsiderable irony, since one of the blasphemies which the Inquisition began to prosecute at the time was the statement, 'Simple [unmarried] fornication is not a sin'.[45]

Believing that discretion was the better part of amour, the *Suprema* replaced Sánchez with a new inquisitor, Dr Cristóbal de Salazar, who had previously been the inquisitor of Granada. But Salazar was not the sort of person who would necessarily make things better. The notary of the Inquisition, Diego de Herrera, wrote a letter on 6 October 1553, noting that in Granada Salazar had a reputation as 'a man who was a great fan of women'; already in Murcia, he had begun a relationship with Catalina Lopez, the daughter of a widow who lived opposite his apartments.[46] Unlike his predecessor, however, Salazar was a determined inquisitor as well as a determined libertine, and he quickly began to interrogate the *moriscos* of Murcia in such a terrifying manner that they rapidly agreed to all of his insinuations. When some of the notaries protested that charges had been invented, Salazar threatened to throw his colleagues into a cell and clap fetters on them, and they all backed off.

Soon after Salazar's arrival in Murcia, the *morisco* Juan de Spuche was arrested for continuing to perform Islamic rites. This was based on the fact that he had been seen washing his face and hands in a fountain.* Spuche confessed that he had committed this dastardly act after coming back from chopping wood in the fields. Such a clear sign of heresy required interrogation. Spuche was tortured. He denounced many people but revoked his confession as soon as he was out of the torture chamber. This merely intensified his suspiciousness in Salazar's eyes, and Spuche was tortured again. This time his hands were damaged so badly that he was unable to dress himself. He died soon afterwards, and his corpse was burnt in statute in an auto.

Thus it was not for nothing that Salazar was described by Herrera as 'terrible in appearance and . . . excessively rigorous in his procedure and his judgments'. Salazar's general modus operandi is summed up by the case of a fisherman who did not give as much of his catch to the inquisitor's page as Salazar had wanted, since the catch that day had been a poor one and there would not otherwise have been enough to satisfy everyone; the fisherman was hauled before Salazar and spent the whole day being interrogated.

Herrera's accounts of Salazar's methods came too late to the *Suprema*. Two months before, Salazar himself had protested about Herrera, who had been stripped of office on 14 August 1553.[47] But the accuracy of Herrera's reports was soon to be amply demonstrated. By 1558 Salazar had become involved in a series of running disputes with the civil authorities of Murcia.[48] These people, Salazar complained in a letter of 14 June 1558 to the *Suprema*, were inspired by those 'who bear ill will to this Holy Office' and were his enemies. In a revealing phrase which the 'crypto-Jews' of Murcia would soon

---

* For a more detailed account of the relationship of washing and crypto-Islam, see pages 200–201.

come to understand all too clearly, Salazar declared that he esteemed his honour 'more highly than a thousand lives'.

That same summer the plague descended on Murcia. The devotion of the inquisitorial team did not extend as far as putting their own lives at risk for the sake of the truth; they fled the city and descended on the small town of Hellín. Salazar lodged with one Miguel Mateo, who lived with his thirty-year-old widowed daughter Catalina. Salazar quickly insinuated himself into their company, and ensured that he did not have to go hungry; a typical lunch consisted of a leg of bacon, six seasoned chickens followed by twelve roast chickens garnished with bacon, a roast goat, two medium-sized dishes of blancmange, cherries, apricots, all washed down with both white and red wine.[49]

Such repasts were hardly designed to cool passions, and Salazar rapidly struck up an intimate relationship with the widow Catalina.[50] Tongues began to wag, and one resident, Lope Chinchilla, became particularly suspicious of the relationship. Catalina had been seen publicly with Salazar at the window of the building where the inquisitorial court was held, watching bullfights, and Chinchilla let slip his thoughts one evening as Salazar was devoutly playing a game of cards.

On 16 January 1559 Lope de Chinchilla was arrested by the Inquisition on a charge of crypto-Judaism. He had been 'accused' by a 'Jewish friend' of Juan de Valibrera, and by Juan de Ávila and his wife, who had all been arrested on charges of crypto-Judaism by Salazar. The accuracy of this testimony can be judged by the fact that Salazar went 'alone on feast days and by night to the jails and persuaded people to testify against others, and got third parties to do the same and even went alone without any companion or pretence of a legal hearing to torture them'. Yet in spite of all this evidence and Salazar's history, Lope de Chinchilla was burnt on 8 September 1560, largely because he had spoken out about an appalling abuse of power.

The next few years saw a conflagration in Murcia. Numbers are not known in full because of the loss of records but in 1562 nineteen Judaizers and two *moriscos* were burnt,[51] and the following year four more Judaizers.[52] In 1569 the people of Murcia complained to Rome that more than 500 people had been burnt, screaming their Catholic faith to the end; when envoys protested to the *Suprema* at the beginning of the clampdown, they were arrested on their return to Murcia and thrown into the inquisitorial jail, and when a visitor from the *Suprema* attempted to free some prisoners he was censured by Inquisitor-General Valdés and told never to do this sort of thing again.[53]

In this ghastly tale of venality and paranoia there is of course more than an echo of the doings of Lucero in Cordoba fifty years before. Yet it is a mark of the changing times that, whereas in Cordoba the city's protests led to the council at Burgos* and a decline in the prestige of the Inquisition, the complaints from Murcia passed more or less unnoticed. Questioning the integrity of the Inquisition was now just not done, and whereas Lucero's paranoia had been challenged, Salazar's was in vogue.

WE SHOULD NOW RETURN to this letter of Inquisitor-General Valdés from 1558, and the numerous threats to the faith which he mentioned in it. Among those had been that posed by the converted Muslims, the *moriscos*,† who as we have just seen had been particular targets of Inquisitor Salazar during his early years in Murcia. The *morisco* problem was one which by the end of the 16th century would be centre stage in Spain.

These *moriscos* were the descendants of the Moors who had been forced to convert to Christianity in Granada in 1502, and in Aragon and Valencia in the 1520s. The problems posed by the two groups were distinct: in Granada, the *moriscos* were descended from the population of the last Moorish kingdom of Spain, but in Aragon and Valencia they had been living under Christian rule for centuries, which meant that they ought to have been much easier to assimilate.

However, the way in which the Aragonese and Valenciano *moriscos* had been converted had got things off to a bad start. Between 1520 and 1522 a civil war had raged across the region. This took the form of a popular rising against the nobility and was led by brotherhoods known as *germanías*. Since the Muslims of Aragon

---

* See page 114.

† See page 113.

were overwhelmingly agricultural labourers who worked for the great lords, they were an easy target for the rebels. The Moors constituted a large part of the army of the duke of Segorbe at the battles against the *germanías* at Oropesa and Almenara in July 1521, and a third of the infantry of Viceroy Mendoza at Gandía on 25 July; in targeting them, the *germanías* could both defeat their enemies and salve their consciences by claiming a pseudo-religious motivation.[54]

Thus as the revolt swept eastern Spain in 1521, the Muslims were driven to the fonts and murdered. Some 40,000 people died in the battles, not to mention many others through hunger and epidemics.[55] The *germanía* fighters looked for Muslims wherever they could find them, killing all those who refused to be baptized.[56] Mosques were consecrated as churches and mass was said in them.[57] In Gandía baptisms were performed by using wet brooms and branches which had been dipped in a spring. In Polop the Moors took refuge in the castle for several days and only emerged when the *germanía* forces promised to spare them if they would be baptized – 'and as soon as the baptisms were over they slit the throats of 600 of them, ignoring their promise and saying that this was a way of sending souls into heaven and coins into their pockets'.[58]

The revolt was finally crushed by the end of 1522. At once Inquisitor Churruca of Valencia demanded powers over the former Muslims, seeking lists of those who had been converted. The problem was that the forced conversions had been so random and disordered that no one knew who had been baptized and who had not. The only solution was seen to be to complete the job in hand, and in February 1524 Churruca was given powers by the *Suprema* to investigate apostate *moriscos*. An extraordinary meeting of the *Suprema* was convoked in Madrid the following spring, and on 11 April Inquisitor-General Manrique ruled that all Muslims were thereafter to be deemed Christians.[59] As the congregation put it, 'since in the conversion and baptism there was not any absolute violence or force, those that were baptized must be compelled to keep the [Catholic] faith';[60] clearly they had decided that, if the conversion had not been forced under the *germanías*, they needed to ensure that it was so now.

The order for the *moriscos* to convert or leave was accompanied by a set of provisions which actually made it impossible for them to do anything but remain in the country as 'Christians'. A series of letters from Aragon made it clear that they were essential to the prosperity of the kingdom, and on 22 December 1525 Charles V issued a decree simply banning them from leaving Aragon. Thus, as the king himself had written to the pope on 14 December 1525, 'the conversion which was made was not at all voluntary for many of them, and since then they have not been instructed and taught about our Catholic faith'.[61]

The result of all this was of course that the *moriscos* had little love for their new 'faith'. As the Venetian ambassador Andrea Navajero put it in the same year, 'the *moriscos* speak their own language and very few of them want to learn Spanish; they are Christians by force and very poorly instructed in our faith, since no effort is made in this direction';[62] they kept their old style of dress and dyed their hair black, and were either secret Muslims or atheists, according to Navajero.[63]

The complete absence of Christian instruction did not prevent the Inquisition from setting to work examining the orthodoxy of the new converts, however. Though on 6 January 1526 an edict was issued stating that the *moriscos* should have forty years free of inquisitorial investigation, this was modified a few months later. In Valencia a series of autos between 1533 and 1540 saw fifty people burn at the stake.[64] Only in 1542 did Charles V finally order a sixteen-year moratorium on the investigation of *moriscos* by the Inquisition. This was on the petition of Friar Antonio Ramírez de Haro, who was given the task of instructing the *moriscos*. Something of the situation at the time was revealed in his first set of ordinances, in which he commanded that *moriscos* had to inform their priests on giving birth so that the child could be baptized. Clearly, this was not common, and even at this late stage there were *moriscos* who were never baptized and could not properly be called Christians.[65]

Such, then, was the sorry condition of the *moriscos* in much of Spain by the 1550s. After the violence of their first conversion, they had been subjected to a series of bloody autos before belatedly evangelization began. Yet they still retained their customs and were clearly a community apart. As the *conversos* had found in the 15th century, this was a dangerous situation in Iberia, and by 1558, as Inquisitor-General Valdés considered their petition for a pardon in Salamanca and recounted his dilemmas in his letter, danger loomed again for the *moriscos*.

This had been evident for a few years. When the Count of Tendilla tried in 1555 to secure a brief from the papacy absolving and returning any confiscated property to all *moriscos* who confessed their crimes, he was blocked by Valdés, who suggested that Tendilla himself should be arrested for daring to come up with such a plan.[66] Throughout the 1550s the Turks had been making conquests at the expense of the Spaniards in North Africa, and the *moriscos* were increasingly seen as an Islamic fifth column.[67] The scene was set for their persecution as the second half of the 16th century unwound; but before this could begin, Inquisitor-General Valdés would have to deal with the most dangerous enemy of all, one mentioned in his letter, which had struck right at the heart of the Spanish court, at Valladolid.

Valladolid 1558–9

ON 6 JUNE 1554 Charles V drew up his will in Brussels. His reign over the Holy Roman Empire had become bogged down in wars in Germany and the Low Countries with Protestant rebels, and he sensed that he would not be able to maintain his grip on his vast dominions for much longer. His son Philip was already ruling Spain, and was soon to become Philip II. Many issues preoccupied Charles in these his last years, but foremost among them was the imperative to see off the Protestant threat. Thus, as he put it in his will:

> Because of the great paternal love that I have for my dearest and beloved son, the serene Prince Philip, and because I desire an even greater increase in his virtues and the saving of his soul . . . I order and request him affectionately that, as a very Catholic prince fearful of God's commandments, he should be always mindful of matters pertaining to his honour and service, and obey the commandments of the Holy Mother Church. In

> particular I request that he favours and makes others favour the Holy Office of the Inquisition.[68]

Philip had been born in May 1527. He had large blue eyes with thick eyebrows, a prominent lower lip, and was held to resemble his father Charles, in particular at the point of his chin. Philip followed a carnivorous diet, refusing to eat fish 'or any other thing that was not nutritious', liked to dress elegantly, usually wearing feathers in his cap, and had a very sweet tooth. In spite of the sobriety which he would attempt to impose on Spanish society, as a young man he was attracted to women and liked to wander about disguised by night even in the midst of the most serious affairs of state.[69] When his father Charles retired to a monastery at Yuste in Extremadura, early in 1557, Philip II was ready to take on the mantle of defender of the faith; in the two years that followed, opportunities rapidly came his way to win his spurs as a champion of the Inquisition against the Protestant threat.

On 31 May of that year Cardinal Silíceo, archbishop of Toledo and primate of Spain, died and the most important see in Spain became vacant. Philip II, then in Flanders, decided to nominate the Dominican monk, preacher and theologian Bartolomé de Carranza for the post. This was one of the most significant acts he had made since the retirement of his father. Philip had got to know Carranza well in England as the husband of Mary Tudor; Carranza had been one of his main Spanish allies among the Protestant English.[70]

Carranza had been chosen for the mission in England in part because of his long inquisitorial experience. For thirty years he had undertaken numerous inquisitorial commissions and, in his own words, had 'constantly persecuted heretics'.[71] In England Carranza insisted on the burning of the Protestant Archbishop Cranmer of Canterbury in 1556; over 30,000 people fled the country in fear.[72] Carranza visited Oxford in 1556 and Cambridge in 1557, and in Cambridge ordered the public burning of heretical books and Bibles in English.[73] Such was Carranza's zeal that the English soon came to know him as the 'black monk',[74] and there were many assassination attempts.[75]

This pious Dominican, who preferred to believe everything he was told rather than doubt people, who was a byword for modesty, with his large bald head, his eyebrows set close together like Philip II and his hirsute face, was surely one of the least likely targets imaginable for the Inquisition.[76] But such was the obsession with hidden enemies, and such the fears coming to convulse Spanish society, that none of his zealous activity against Protestants would be sufficient to protect him.

Carranza's problems were to begin because of the rivalry which existed between him and Inquisitor-General Fernando Valdés. Valdés was something of a talisman for the Inquisition, without question the most important inquisitor-general in the history of the institution after Torquemada. His was not a will that was easily checked, and the election of his rival Carranza to the see of Toledo was not something he was prepared to observe with equanimity from his inquisitorial eyrie.

Valdés was not without skeletons in his closet, having fathered an illegitimate child as a young man.[77] This had not prevented him joining the court of Cisneros in 1516, aged 33. From here his rise had been smooth, appointed to the *Suprema* by Inquisitor-General Manrique in 1524, before being made president of the chancellery of Valladolid in 1535, archbishop of Seville in 1546 and inquisitor-general in 1547.[78] Yet such consummate political and networking skills did not accompany softness and piety of temperament. Valdés was impressively ahead of his time in dismissing stories of witchcraft as fantasies,[79] but this in itself may well have been because he had no need of imaginary demons, being quite capable of inventing them among his own adversaries.

As soon as Valdés became inquisitor-general, he made a series of appointments. His nephew Menendo was made inquisitor of Valladolid; other relatives, Diego de Valdés and Diego Meléndez, were appointed to posts in the Inquisitions of Murcia and Granada. One of his closest confidants, Hartuno de Ibargüen, was made secretary of the *Suprema*, and Ibargüen's brother Juan appointed receiver of confiscated goods for Asturias, Castile and Galicia. He also promoted his nephew Juan, who by the time of Valdés's death in 1566 was inquisitor of Zaragoza.[80] This manipulation of the inquisitorial bureaucracy was to occupy so much of Valdés's time that he only spent fourteen months in his see of Seville during the twenty years during which he was its archbishop;[81] something which was to be one of the principal sources of his hatred for Carranza.

Prior to being made archbishop of Toledo Carranza had declared that it was the duty of bishops to reside in their dioceses, and that they should not be made presidents of royal courts (*audiencias*). Valdés was never in Seville and was the president of several *audiencias* so was unlikely to be pleased by such opinions.[82] Valdés saw little difference between the private and the public, as his nepotism after his appointment revealed, and was widely regarded as a person of passions and hatreds.[83] Well able to make use of the enormous power that he wielded, Valdés determined to bring down the primate of Spain through the Inquisition.

WHAT OF THE MOOD in central Spain at this crucial moment? In Valladolid, home of the Spanish court, the *Suprema* sat in its palace, increasingly isolated by its embattled mentality from the orchards and plains beyond the city walls. From Valladolid the plateau swept south and then crested the forested slopes of the Gredos mountains. Beyond the hills lay more of the plateau, stretching its aridity out towards the province of the new archbishop, Carranza. The very proximity of the territories of the two adversaries added drama to their conflict.

On accepting his appointment to the see of Toledo, Carranza at once made for Spain. At the same time, however, he published in Antwerp in 1558 his *Commentaries on the Christian Catechism*,* a book designed to remedy the ignorance of the clergy in the Netherlands and to put a halt to the spread of Protestant teachings in England.[84] In spite of these noble Catholic aims, however, it was this very same book which was to prove his undoing.

Hearing of the book, Valdés wondered if it was not his chance to ruin the new archbishop, who had not yet even arrived in the country. Although copies were rare in Spain, he obtained one and began to consult it in his apartments. One day the Dominican theologian Melchor Cano entered Valdés's lodgings and saw Carranza's *Catechism* on the table.[85] Cano was a longstanding enemy of Carranza, as numerous witnesses were to attest in subsequent

---

* *Comentarios del Catecismo Cristiano.*

proceedings;[86] Carranza was the elder, the humbler and indisputably the more successful. Cano, aware that the inquisitor-general had no love for the new archbishop either, sensed his chance. Seeing the book lying there, Cano said to Valdés, 'In that book there are lots of things which people should not be allowed to read'. Valdés was delighted, asked Cano to show him which things these were and decided there and then to give the book to Cano for a definitive view as to its orthodoxy.[87]

Prior to coming across the work in Valdés's apartments, Cano had searched high and low for a copy. So desperate was he to sniff out its heresy and feel righteously appalled by it that he had even broken into the cell of a friar in the monastery of St Paul one night and confiscated a chest containing a copy of the book.[88] This desperation was married to his preconceived certainty that the book was heretical. Indeed, as he had told one of Carranza's friends, Antonio de Salazar, 'since [Carranza] had not wanted to write in his [Cano's] favour to the general of the order and the pope, he had read his [Catechism] with a great deal of curiosity and attention'.[89]

One could not expect such a person to provide an objective opinion. But this did not trouble Valdés, who quickly numbered Cano among his confidants. Cano soon took a trip to the town of Laguna on one of Valdés's mules, with one of his servants and with his expenses covered by the *Suprema*.[90]

By the time Carranza arrived in Valladolid from the Low Countries in August 1558, he knew a storm was brewing. Twice he wrote to Valdés offering to follow the inquisitor-general's advice in making any corrections that were perceived necessary to his *Catechism*. Twice, he was ignored. Carranza then continued his journey south through the northern hills of Extremadura, towards Yuste, where Charles V was entering the last days of his life. On 13 September he met Melchor Cano in the town of San Leonardo de Alba; Cano was en route to Valladolid to begin his censorship of the *Catechism*. When Carranza asked Cano about the interest which the Inquisition had taken in him, Cano piously replied that he could tell him nothing owing to the secrecy of the Holy Office.[91]

Eight days later, on 21 September 1558, Charles V died at Yuste. Carranza was present and was said by his companion the friar Diego de Ximenes to have had a perfect comportment.[92] However during his presence at Yuste he had given Charles's confessor Juan de Regla short shrift, and thus in December Regla travelled to Valladolid and declared that Carranza had uttered 'Lutheran-sounding' phrases at the emperor's deathbed.[93] The reality was that in the state to which Spain had descended, *any* phrase was capable of sounding Lutheran if sufficiently twisted.

Personal enmity and paranoia were thus the twin vectors of Carranza's fall from grace and eventual destruction. While the Inquisition in Valladolid was patiently gathering the evidence, Melchor Cano was hard at work censoring Carranza's *Catechism*. His conclusion was that 'many expressions [in the book] are Lutheran, even though this is not the author's intention'.[94] He cited 141 propositions within the book deserving of censure.[95] Carranza's view that 'faith and knowledge of Christ the redeemer are the key to the Christian edifice' had a 'Lutheran flavour if not Lutheran meaning', and Cano proceeded to interpret the *Catechism* in such a tendentious manner that he qualified some of Carranza's views as Lutheran even though they came verbatim from the Gospels.[96] Every phrase, and every person, could be open to manipulation.

Cano's judgement was music to Valdés's ears; he had told him what he wanted to hear. When other theologians issued opinions saying that there was nothing wrong with the *Catechism*, he ignored them.[97] When one, Juan de la Peña, pointed out that St Augustine himself had said that faith alone could save mankind, and that on this ground alone one could not convict Carranza of heresy, he himself became an object of suspicion, so that his cell was broken into and his papers seized.[98] And when in May 1559 Valdés heard that the theologians of the University of Alcalá were planning unanimously to approve the *Catechism*, he ordered the commissary (local representative) of the Inquisition in Alcalá to decree that no member of the university could publish a theological opinion on any book whatsoever.[99]

Valdés's quarry was not going to escape his clutches. While Cano was protesting to Carranza that he could tell him nothing because of the secrecy of the Inquisition, Valdés was happily breaking the very same code of secrecy, preparing the public atmosphere for this most sensational arrest.[100] One could accuse others of hypocrisy, but this did not mean that one had to forego hypocrisy entirely, particularly if it could aid the inquisitorial process.

In the midst of this double-dealing, Valdés's agents were lobbying hard in Rome for a papal brief which would permit the Inquisition to proceed against bishops. The fact that suspicion was now enough to demonstrate guilt was revealed when one of them said in the curia, 'Why does it bother your Excellency whether he is burnt there or here, since in the end he has got to die?'[101] On 9 January 1559 the pope gave the desired brief, and, as one of Valdés's servants put it, 'the whole house celebrated as if [Valdés] had been made a cardinal'.[102]

Carranza did his best to continue work. Ignoring the rumours, he reached his see and began his duties as archbishop. According to his biographer, during the ten months and nine days which he spent there he disbursed over 80,000 ducats on dowries for orphans, sustaining widows, pensions for poor students and alleviating conditions in hospitals and prisons.[103] The implacable zeal which he devoted to his activities was testament to a man whose condition meant that he had plenty of spare energy. Yet in spite of the transparency of his good works, on 6 May 1559 the prosecutor of the Inquisition in Valladolid issued a warrant for his arrest, accusing him of propagating Lutheran errors;[104] on 26 June this was confirmed by Philip II.[105]

Discussions began as to how to bring Carranza to Valladolid. Early in August the archbishop, who was in the university town of Alcalá, received a letter from the regent Doña Juana, requesting his presence in Valladolid for the arrival of Philip II from Flanders.[106] Meanwhile, the Inquisition sent Don Rodrigo de Castro, a future archbishop of Seville, to be his companion and keep an eye on him, though ostensibly he was his friend.[107]

Castro arrived in Alcalá on 9 August. He and Carranza left there on the 18th to tour the archbishop's diocese en route to Valladolid. Soon, in the town of Fuente de Sal, Carranza met his friend Felipe de Meneses, who told him that it was public knowledge in Valladolid that the Inquisition was going to arrest him.[108] On Sunday, 20 August 1559 the archbishop came to the small town of Torrelaguna and the scene was set for the denouement.

Two days after Carranza and Castro arrived in Torrelaguna, the inquisitor of Valladolid, Diego Ramírez, reached a spot just two miles outside the town. He was accompanied by a hundred men who hid in the woods on the banks of the River Malacuera. Castro came to consult Ramírez and it was decided to arrest Carranza that evening. For two nights Castro had been plotting with the bailiff of the Inquisition, Hernando Berzosa, who had been in Torrelaguna for four days in disguise; Castro and Berzosa had made twelve residents of the town familiars of the Inquisition (local officials who helped with arrests and collecting evidence), and they were prepared to act.[109]

That night Ramírez entered Torrelaguna and went to Carranza's lodgings. Guards were placed at the doors and on the stairs, and Ramírez, Castro and Berzosa went up with around ten armed familiars and hammered on the door to Carranza's chamber. His page, the monk Antonio Sánchez, called out, 'Who's there?' Those outside responded, 'Open up for the Inquisition!' The archbishop hurriedly closed the curtain. His head was resting on his pillow as his enemies burst in and seized him in the candlelight.[110]

From Torrelaguna there would be no escape; Carranza would be taken under armed guard to Valladolid, there to confront his great enemy Fernando de Valdés in one of the most controversial trials which the Inquisition ever prosecuted.

A CURIOUS consonance developed. Valladolid, home to the royal court, was also the focal point of threats to the Spanish empire. The ruling elite was under attack! Everywhere one turned, there the enemy was. Such was its versatility, could one be surprised if the devil himself was seen dressed in the clothes of these wretched *conversos*, *moriscos* and Lutherans? In spite of the difficulties caused by *moriscos* and the crypto-Jews of Murcia, the real threat came from the Protestants. It had after all always been apparent that Jews and Muslims were dubious, but the Protestant threat came from the very heart of Christianity, and was sewing dangerous discord among the peoples of the Low Countries and Germany.

Matters were increasingly grave. In 1557 the Jeronymite monks of the monastery of San Isidro in Seville had been suspected of Protestantism and had fled to Germany, though eight of them were arrested by the Inquisition in Seville. Then, in the spring of 1558, it was discovered that Lutheran errors were being preached throughout Castile. Moreover, these heresies, as Inquisitor-General Valdés wrote to Pope Paul IV on 9 September 1558, had 'taken the form of sedition and mutiny among important nobles, clerics and property owners'. This, Valdés said to the pope, meant that the Inquisition could not use the benign procedures which had hitherto been its wont in dealing with the crypto-Jews and the *moriscos*.[111]

The letter showed how inquisitorial circles were thinking their way towards bonfires. It must of course be borne in mind that around this time a terrible purging occurred of Protestants in England under Queen Mary and in France under Henry II, where more Protestants probably died in England and France than in Spain in the years after 1558.[112] Nevertheless, Valdés's marshalling of evidence and destruction of victims provides a sobering preview of the way in which persecuting institutions would so often prove capable of securing the convictions which they desired.

While fifth-columnist Lutherans became apparent in Seville in 1557, in Valladolid the first signs of the conspiracy emerged at the same time. One evening the wife of the silversmith Juan García rose discreetly after she had gone to bed and followed her husband, aware that it was his practice to go out after she had retired. She saw him enter a house. Suspecting adultery she followed him inside, hiding herself behind the door of the room where he could be heard talking. Soon she heard the conversation turn to what seemed to her to be Lutheranism. This was enough for her delicate ears.

Perhaps, indeed, in those sensitive times adultery was almost as bearable as heresy. No doubt she had felt for some time that her marriage was nearing a crisis, and heresy was the final straw. She determined to turn her back on their shared lives and on any sense of mutual responsibility. She left, and the following day went to denounce him to the Inquisition. Two years later, García the silversmith was relaxed to the secular arm.[113]

Quickly, the chain of denunciations reached the nobility. In April 1558 Ana Enríquez – known as the 'beautiful maid' – the daughter of the marquess of Alcañices, told Inquisitor Gulielmo that the Dominican friar Domingo de Rojas had brought her a book in her mother's orchard written by Luther and declared his doctrines to be holy. Rojas had also convinced the nuns of the convent of Belén, and they had begun to read Luther's works. The marquis of Alcañices's servant Cristóbal de Padilla was said to be another important dogmatist, as was the Italian Carlos de Seso. The canon of Salamanca, Agustín de Cazalla, was said to be behind the spread of Lutheran doctrines, and the Lutheran conventicle met in the house of Cazalla's mother Leonor de Vibero. Another noble involved was Francisca de Zúñiga, the daughter of the royal accountant Alonso de Baeza.[114]

Here was an ever-growing web of connections, contacts, sedition. All the heretics were communicating with one another. The conspiracy was much greater than had ever been dreamt possible. By 1558 the inquisitorial jails were heaving with prisoners, and Inquisitor-General Valdés noted how 'each day new witnesses arrive . . . some suspects have not been seized, since there are no cells to keep them in'.[115]

Terror roasted in Valladolid. The Dominican Domingo de Rojas, accused by 'the beautiful maid' and then by others of saying that there was no hell and that it was impossible for a baptized person to sin, asked advice from Francisco de Tordesillas, a fellow friar at the monastery of St Paul in Valladolid: 'Father, if I am accused before the Inquisition of things which I have said in error and of other errors which I have never committed, what remedy can I have?' Tordesillas replied that he should simply go and confess everything to the inquisitors. 'And if it is proved that I have said things that I never have said, and I cannot touch the witnesses who have deposed against me, will I have no remedy?' Tordesillas replied that in such a case there was nothing for it but to die for the truth. As Rojas put it, 'realizing the lies and truths that were being said about me, I felt lost'. He tried to flee to Flanders, but was arrested, with his attempted flight taken as an indication of guilt rather than fear.[116]

The case of the Italian Carlos de Seso was if anything more pathetic. Seso had been born in Verona and by 1554 was the chief magistrate of the town of Toro. There was no question that Seso had picked up some controversial ideas in Italy and had begun to talk about them to a small circle of his intimates; yet this did not mean that he was a Lutheran. Seso was sentenced to burn in the auto of 8 October 1559, and the night before his death he made a declaration, stating, 'I believe that which the Apostles believed and the doctrine of the Holy Mother Catholic and Apostolic Church'. He was, he stated, dying because he had said that 'Jesus Christ our Lord had saved his chosen ones through his passion and death and that he was the only one to make peace between God and ourselves'. The story goes that the following day, as he was dragged through the streets of Valladolid in the auto, he saw Philip II and asked him how he could let him be burnt, to which the king replied, 'I would bring wood to burn my own son if he was as bad as you'.[117]

There were two autos in Valladolid in 1559, in which twenty-five Lutherans were relaxed. They were given this sentence in spite of their confessions and penitence – contrary to the usual procedure of the Inquisition – after special papal dispensation requested by Valdés.[118] Eight days before the first auto, on 21 May, a preacher declared that everyone should attend the ceremony, and people flocked from all over Spain so that over 100,000 crammed into the squares, peering from windows and specially erected stages at the macabre spectacle.[119] So great was the audience that two days before the auto it was impossible to walk the streets, and when the fourteen condemned prisoners were taken out of the city to be executed they had to be guarded by four hundred troops.[120] At the auto of 8 October there were said to be 300,000 people in attendance – all the townsfolk for forty leagues (*c.* 125 miles) around had come to Valladolid. This was indeed a 'spectacle as strange as ever had been seen'.[121]

In Seville, meanwhile, thirty-two Lutherans were relaxed in 1559 and 1560.[122] A further eighteen were relaxed in 1562 (when three *moriscos* perished as well), with another sixteen burnt in statute.[123] Six more died in 1563[124] and another six in 1564.[125] As late as 1577 three people were relaxed, two of them being English, while seven of the nine Lutherans tried that year were tortured.

Something of the atmosphere of permanent threat that coursed through Spain during these years is revealed by the list of prisoners in the inquisitorial jail of Seville in 1580:

> Englishmen, accused of a plot – 19.
> Scotsmen, accused of a plot – 23.
> *Moriscos*, accused of a plot – 6.

Moriscos, accused of another plot – 12.
Moriscos, accused of still another plot – 3.
Moriscos, accused of a still further plot – 3.
Moriscos, accused of one more plot – 2.
Cases of prisoners accused of no plot – 32.[126]

THE LANGUAGE IS that of a society which perceives threats everywhere.

The concentration of terror in the years 1558 and 1559 was no accident; Philip II, the new king, needed to show that there was no power vacuum and that he was an adequate successor to his father.[127] There is no question that some of the people imprisoned or executed did profess beliefs anomalous to Catholic doctrine, but at the same time there can be little doubt that these differences were exaggerated by the inquisitorial procedure – as the evidence of Domingo de Rojas attests. In fact much of what these people held to be true was little different from old Erasmian beliefs.[128]. Moreover, far from eradicating heresy, the fires of the Inquisition often encouraged it. Many people forced to flee from Seville in the 1560s to northern Europe survived by becoming proselytizing Protestants and circulating terrible stories of Catholic Spain.[129] Paranoid Catholicism therefore created targets of which it could genuinely be afraid.

The greatest proof of this creation of the enemy within came from Portugal, where there was no reason for there to be any less infiltration by Lutheranism than in Spain. Yet here there were very few Lutheran trials at this time, apart from one or two show trials like that of the royal chronicler Damião de Goes.[130] This was not because that there was any greater danger of Protestantism in Spain than in Portugal, but rather because in Portugal, where the Inquisition had only just been founded, persecution was still being channelled towards the first major targets, *conversos*. There was no need to create a Lutheran threat when the original *converso* enemy was still being dealt with.

CARRANZA'S ARREST, so carefully orchestrated by Valdés, was intimately related to the events in Valladolid. At some time in the 1550s Carranza appears to have had one meeting with the prisoner Carlos de Seso, during which he had tried hard to convince Seso of the error of his beliefs, but he had not denounced Seso to the Inquisition.[131] This was taken as a sign of guilt by the inquisitorial prosecutor even though Carranza, with his long experience of the Inquisition, would have known if a denunciation had been appropriate. Moreover, the hapless Domingo de Rojas who had once been Carranza's servant, arraigned in the torture chamber on 10 April 1559 and casting around desperately for some means of survival, claimed that Carranza had subscribed to some of the ideas which he was said to have propagated.[132] These connections were crucial to Carranza's arrest.

Not surprisingly, the archbishop of Toledo plunged into depression once he was incarcerated in Valladolid. He suffered from chronic insomnia and did not sleep for nineteen days.[133] Then he set about proving that Inquisitor-General Valdés was his enemy and could not be relied on to judge him objectively. In this at least he was successful, and Valdés was removed from responsibility for the case. But none of this sped the trial along.

Carranza spent his years in prison in Spain in terrible conditions. He occupied a cell so cut off from the outside world that when a fire devastated Valladolid on 21 September 1561, burning over 400 houses and lasting for a day and a half, he knew nothing about it and did not find out until years later when he was in Rome.[134] His cell had no ventilation and he and his servants had to perform their bodily functions there, which meant that they all fell ill. It was so dark that Carranza sometimes had to light candles at nine in the morning. His jailer, moreover, was Inquisitor Diego González, who had arrested him in Torrelaguna. González humiliated him by bringing his food on broken plates and fruit on the covers of books, and by forcing the archbishop to use his sheets as a tablecloth.[135]

After over seven years in the jail in Valladolid Carranza was transferred to Rome on the insistence of the new pope, Pius V. Here vast numbers of court papers had to be translated into Italian before the case could proceed, which was not completed until 1570. Even then Carranza's ordeal was not over. Pius V died and his successor, Gregory XIII, came under intense pressure from Philip II to declare Carranza guilty. On 14 April 1576, almost seventeen years after his first arrest, Carranza was sentenced to abjure heresy and sixteen Lutheran propositions of which he was deemed suspected.[136]

As his sentence was read in the Vatican, the archbishop shed floods of tears. He died eighteen days later, unable to pass water.[137] The repression had come full circle.

There may be some who, remembering Carranza's zeal in burning the Protestants of England, find it difficult to feel sympathy for such a man. Yet it must be remembered that this was a time of religious warfare in Europe. What his case reveals is not so much a righting of wrongs as the way in which power had adopted an agenda which was utterly its own. Valdés had used hypocrisy, lies and torture to ruin a man who, by the standards of his time and country, was a holy person. If the primate of all Spain could be convicted of heresy, no one could be thought free of suspicion.[138] Fear could reap its bitter crop among all the classes of Spain.

The mentality that triumphed in these conditions was conservative, hierarchical and dogmatic, afraid of all novelty. Melchor Cano, who preached at the auto of 21 May 1559 in Valladolid to consolidate his position in the new order, held that the great dangers of translating the scriptures out of Latin could be seen 'among women and idiots'.[139] The secrets of faith were only safe with wise men, people rather like Cano, in fact.

Yet isolation and persecution of the enemy within was not a contradiction to the golden age in Spain; it was in many ways of a piece with the country's imperial destiny, the counterpoint at home to the global power exerted by Spain in the 16th century. Enemies were focuses for unity as well as violence in both America and Europe, and while the targets were the easily identifiable 'others', the crypto-Jews and the *moriscos*, the tactic worked brilliantly and Spain continued to advance. But the crackdown on the Protestant enemy within marked a turning point. When Philip II continued his father's policy of imposing the Inquisition on the Low Countries, where there was no Jewish or Moorish 'problem', this precipitated rebellion. The Dutch United Provinces seceded from the empire, and came to present one of the major challenges to Spanish power in the late 16th and early 17th centuries.[140]

Thus in overreaching itself and stretching the concept of the enemy so that it had the potential to cover everyone, the Inquisition and the inquisitorial state of mind helped to sew the seeds of the rebellions which ate away at Spanish power and its role in the world. Yet the institution failed to appreciate the self-destructiveness which was a necessary condition of its existence. Even as the Dutch were launching their first rebellion against the Spanish in the late 1560s, the decision was taken to export the Inquisition to America. With fear pursued – but never vanquished – on all sides at home, it was perhaps inevitable that it would come to be pursued in the same way abroad.

Chapter Six

TERROR ENVELOPS THE WORLD

. . . he swore that if she did not return to God and the Virgin, he would kill her himself . . .

Mexico 1568–1583

ON 12 SEPTEMBER 1572 the ten members of the newly inaugurated Tribunal of the Inquisition of Mexico arrived on the coast at Veracruz. Chief among them was Inquisitor Pedro Moya de Contreras. As soon as he arrived Contreras appointed the members of the inquisitorial infrastructure. He established commissaries in every town where there was a bishop, not only in Mexico but also in Guatemala, Honduras and Nicaragua. By 1600 no important settlement of the captaincy of Guatemala would be without its inquisitorial commissary.[1]

Already in 1572 the first cases were pending; it was as if some had been itching for the opportunity to condemn. The Genoese Niccolo Boeto was in jail in Nicaragua for erroneously interpreting what God had prohibited to Adam in paradise. And in León in northern Mexico Hernando Sánchez was arrested for declaring that 'simple fornication was not a sin, provided that you paid for it'.[2] Criticism and opprobrium were so much easier to develop than love. Thus the export of the Inquisition's peculiar brand of terror and hypocrisy had begun.

Though the Inquisition had been active in Mexico before, this had been under the auspices of the bishops – the old episcopal Inquisition – and without the infrastructure and powers of the new tribunals which had spread across Spain after 1478. On top of the cases of the Amerindians,* some foreign Protestants had been tried by these earlier authorities. One of the biggest cases had been in 1559, when the Englishman Robert Thomson had been arrested for Lutheranism and forced to do penance in the cathedral of Mexico City with an Italian.

The ceremony had been held in the presence of five or six thousand people, some of whom had come from a hundred miles away to see them, cresting the passes that led to the city and seeing the whitewashed glare of the colonial city below. The audience had come having been told, as Thomson said, that 'wee were hereticques, infidels, and people that did despise God, and his workes, and that wee had bene more like devils than men'.[3] Strangely, though, when Thomson and the Italian entered the church, 'the women and children beganne to cry out, and made such a noise that it was strange to see and heare, saying, that they never saw goodlier men in all their lives, and that it was not possible that there could be in us so much evill as was reported'.[4] Cases like that of Thomson made the authorities feel that a growing threat was posed by Protestant enemies ('pirates') in the New World. This feeling, combined with the atmosphere that had accompanied the autos in Valladolid and Seville in 1559, led to the foundation of the tribunals in Lima, Peru in 1569 and Mexico in 1571.

Reaching Mexico City, the inquisitorial staff found several thousand Spanish households and 300,000 Indians in the suburbs.[5] On arrival, Contreras and his assistants concentrated on the Protestants. Inquisitor Contreras knew all about the castaways of the pirate Hawkins who had been captured by Luis de Carvajal and sent to Mexico City in chains in 1568.† Some of them had been arrested on the authority of the Inquisition even before Contreras's arrival and one, Robert Barrett, had been sent back to Seville where he was burnt at an auto in 1573.[6] These Englishmen made a very easy first target, particularly since, as one of them, Miles Phillips, pointed out, the inquisitors 'had perfect knowledge and intelligence that many of us were become very rich'.[7]

Within a few months of the tribunal's installation, the English

* See pages 97–98.

† See page 107.

who had settled throughout Mexico after their abandonment by Hawkins were summoned to Mexico City. Dozens were arrested and thrown into jail in solitary confinement, where they stayed for 18 months. All of them were tortured three months before the final judgements were pronounced.[8] The night before the auto, Phillips said, '[the inquisitorial authorities] were so busied in putting on their coats [*sanbenitos*] about us, and bringing us out into a large yard, and placing and pointing us in what order we should go to the scaffold or place of judgment upon the morrow, that they did not suffer us to sleep the whole night long'.[9]

The auto began early. Each morning twenty to thirty canoes would enter the city on a canal bringing apples, pears, pomegranates, quinces and tortillas, fodder for the horses, lime and brick for building, and coal and wood for fires.[10] Today, however, there were no canoes. The motionless crowd lent drama and legitimacy to the ritual of punishment and condemnation.

At the auto a small number of prisoners were executed and the rest lashed before beginning their penances of imprisonment or the galleys.* Phillips was one of those sentenced to imprisonment in a monastery, and here he found the monks very courteous, as 'many of the Spaniards and Friers themselves do utterly abhorre and mislike of that cruell Inquisition, and would as they durst bewaile our miseries and comfort us the best they could, although they stood in such feare of that divelish Inquisition, that they durst not let the left hand know what the right doth'.[11]

Miles Phillips's sense of general opposition in Mexico to the Inquisition is confirmed by the account of the earlier arrest of his compatriot Thomson, who had said that many of the Spaniards who lived in the New World were opposed to the new body.[12] Unlike in Spain, people in Mexico had not been brought up to respect the Inquisition. They feared the control which it might come to exert over their daily activities. There was a general sense that this oppressive institution was an enemy of the freedom which was taken as a birthright in America.

---

* It is difficult to be precise about numbers; Miles Phillips said three died, but the trial records reveal only one execution – (Conway (ed.) (1927: 158) – but as this is one of the three mentioned by Phillips, the likelihood is that the figure of three may be accurate.

The nature of the justice wielded by the new institution in Mexico was shown by these first trials of English Protestants. One prisoner, William Collins from Oxford, explained how he had planned to become a priest before the destruction of the Catholic churches and monasteries under Henry VIII, and that after the death of Mary Tudor and the accession of Elizabeth he had been arrested as a Catholic sympathizer in London.[13] Collins described in detail the lack of Catholic ritual in England and the hatred of the pope, holding that mass, communion and confession were 'so abominable . . . that he dared not recount them'.[14] It was apparent from his statements that he had no fondness for the Protestant religion yet the inquisitorial prosecutor then used Collins's own confession to formulate sixty-eight charges against him, many of which did not refer to Collins himself but to events in England which he had been forced to witness. Collins was lashed and sentenced to ten years in the galleys.[15]

Another of those tried at this time was David Alexander from South Looe in Cornwall. Alexander was only nineteen in 1573, and had been just thirteen when he set sail with Hawkins for Africa and the New World. Something of the extraordinary shock that awaited him on this voyage is revealed by his declaration that when he embarked he had thought 'that the Protestant faith of England was believed and kept throughout the whole world' and that 'he [did not] know that there was any other faith [in existence]'.[16] As he travelled through Africa and America, such naivety must have given way to the feeling that he was entering something like a dream, where the unimaginable was true and all that was certain slipped away.

Like the other English castaways, Alexander was punished in the auto. He spent three years in a monastery before being released in 1577, when he was told not to leave Mexico without the permission of the Inquisition. When, in February 1585, he tried to set sail for China from Acapulco, he was arrested and brought to the Inquisition wearing 'iridescent shoes of taffeta with silk and gold straps that seemed to have been made through alchemy (*sic*), a hat with feathers, a rifle and a sword, and a flask'. Alexander, still only thirty years old, said that he thought that as he was going to serve God and Philip II the punishment could be waived. The inquisitors thought differently; they stripped him of his finery and ordered him never to leave the kingdom again.[17]

This export of the Inquisition to Mexico (and Peru) represented an attempt by Philip II to turn the Spanish institution into a power across the world. It was a decision that would change life for some in Mexico, but in order for the institution to develop the same reputation as its counterpart in Spain, a case of similar proportions was needed to that of Archbishop Carranza – one which would make it clear that no one was free from suspicion and would feed the culture of fear. Such a case was not long in coming.

WHILE THE INQUISITION was establishing itself in America, an old friend was busy making his fortune. The dramatic events which had accompanied Luis de Carvajal's arrival in the colony had made him a close confidant of the most powerful man in Mexico.* He was Viceroy Martín Enríquez's trusted tamer of the north. Few among the Spaniards knew what this fastness was really like, but Carvajal had begun to reduce it. It was no longer such a fearful emptiness. It would be brought under control.

In 1576 Enríquez delegated Luis to crush the Indians of Huasteca in the north. The expedition was successful, and the kingdom of Nuevo León was founded. In 1578 Luis returned to Spain for his wife and family, and also to seek some sort of reward. Who would inflict such suffering on themselves in so many penurious expeditions, without the prospect of some recompense for burning desire? On the recommendation of Viceroy Enríquez, Philip II decided to make Carvajal the kingdom's first governor. The decree was signed on 14 June 1579.[18]

Carvajal's transformation from inquisitorial fugitive to colonial governor is unique in the history of the New World. He must have been an attractive personality to others in power. One cannot doubt that at the same time he was a ruthless enemy to those who crossed him. The two attributes went together in lawless spaces like Nuevo León, in the crowded ships crossing the Atlantic and in the vegetation that entombed the ruins among the jungles of the Mexican coast.

Thus when Carvajal arrived with the other colonists in Nuevo León, kindness and sympathy were not qualities to the fore. He and

---

* See pages 105–108.

the other colonists hunted the Indians 'like hares'. As if in reflection of his life in west Africa, Carvajal sent them on as slaves to Mexico City and mining centres.[19] The doomed men were chained together in groups of up to a thousand, and once in the mines were forced to work without pay on starvation rations.[20] Punishments meted out to the powerless in Mexico included castration, the dropping of pork fat or pitch melted over a candle onto the victim's skin, cutting off an ear, hand or leg, and hanging.[21] The transference of persecution that Luis had learnt in Lisbon and Cape Verde would be continued in Mexico.

Once chosen as the first governor of Nuevo León in Spain, Luis had set about finding colonists for his new fiefdom. He travelled to Medina del Campo and the home of his sister Francisca, whose husband Francisco Rodríguez de Matos traded at the great fairs. Francisca had nine children, the sisters Anica, Catalina, Isabel, Leonor and Mariana, and the brothers Balthasar, Gaspar, Miguelico and Luis, who would become known as Luis the Younger to distinguish him from his uncle.*[22] Luis promised that Luis the Younger would succeed him in Nuevo León and that Balthasar could be the treasurer there, and the family decided to leave with their illustrious relation for the New World.[23]

The Carvajals left Medina del Campo and after twenty days reached Seville, where they stayed at the house of Luis and his wife Doña Guiomar. Like many wives of adventurers in America, Guiomar had stayed in Spain while her husband made his fortune in the New World. However, she had decided not to come with him this time either, for while Luis was a devoted Catholic, Guiomar kept some of the ancestral Jewish rites. In Seville she taught these to Isabel, the sister of Luis the Younger, and asked her to tell Luis in Mexico to keep the Mosaic laws. 'I don't dare say that to him', Guiomar told Isabel, 'because I'm afraid that he would kill me'.[24]

The new colonists crossed the ocean. Most of the Carvajals fell ill on the Atlantic, and Luis the Younger was almost dead when they reached Veracruz.[25] The governor took them to Tampico to recuperate. The whole family was still accustoming itself to the different climate and atmosphere of America and, struggling to

* See pages 84–86 for an account of Luis the Younger.

accommodate themselves to the new, they fell back on the family tradition of Judaism.

On the voyage from Seville the Carvajals had been befriended by a Portuguese doctor, Antonio de Morales, whose father-in-law had been burnt by the Inquisition in Lisbon for Judaizing. Morales and his wife Blanca had discussed Jewish rites with Luis's sister Francisca and with Isabel. This came to seem providential when, shortly after reaching Tampico, Balthasar and Luis the Younger were caught out in a hurricane. The two brothers were sleeping in a shack. Worried it would be destroyed they got out just before the building was blown to pieces. The rain was so thick that they could not see the path in front of them. Lightning illuminated the darkness in flashes, confusing them even more. But somehow the brothers made their way back to the house where the rest of the family were staying. Believing that this 'miracle' confirmed that they had made the right religious choice, the family began concertedly to Judaize.[26]

Already, before leaving for Mexico, Francisco Rodríguez de Matos had taught his wife Francisca and their oldest son Balthasar to Judaize. In Tampico Isabel joined them, and Francisco later taught Luis the Younger to Judaize in Mexico City.[27] The family kept many of the Jewish festivals and the sabbath.[28] When one of the children, Leonor, married the rich mine owner Jorge de Almeida, Francisca and her children Isabel, Balthasar and Luis the Younger all went to join them. They kept the Jewish rites there,[29] praying fervently in an orchard on the Jewish Sabbath, preventing their servants from working on Saturdays and trying to convert them as well.[30]

Yet there was one man who did not fit into this picture of ideological sedition: the veteran of Cape Verde and Mexico, the governor himself. After arriving in Tampico Isabel had followed the instructions of Luis's wife Guiomar. One afternoon she invited her uncle to come with her into a room as she wished to ask him a great favour. Once they were alone, she got him to swear that he would never repeat what was said there. Then she told him that he was making an error in keeping the law of Christ. The governor rose in a fury 'covering his ears, and told her that she was a disgrace to her whole family, and when she asked him to listen, he swore that if she did not return to God and the Virgin, he would kill her himself'.[31] He rushed out of the room and went to tell his sister Francisca that she should kill or strangle her daughter. Francisca replied that Isabel had only been trying to help him.[32]

The governor did not want this sort of help. He disowned the family but adopted Luis the Younger, who had yet to be converted by his father in Mexico City. Uncle and nephew toured the towns of the north. They enslaved Indians and set up those flyblown camps smelling of dead animals in the desert. One day, in 1583, the governor said to his nephew, 'Do you realize that your father lives in the Law of Moses?' and Luis the Younger burst into tears and said, 'It's a great sin'. Having spent his entire life escaping from the Inquisition, the governor was pleased by this answer. He had yet to realize that it was this very nephew who would prove the most intractable heretic of all when confronted by the inquisitors of Mexico.

Cartagena, Goa, Lima and Mexico 1543–1609

IN 1994, AS THE Mozambique civil war came to an end, Mozambique Island offered an unexpected window onto the past. The island is a sliver of land barely a mile wide by a few hundred metres across. Here the houses press close together in the manner of a medina. History runs deep. The Islamic heritage of this furthest reach of the Swahili coast was evident in the only building of any height, the mosque with its tower and green domes. A few hundred metres away was the cathedral, in the heart of a warren of lanes. To the side of the cathedral a small sign for the Museu de Arte Antiga brought one up to an old sacristy where priceless relics of the Portuguese empire were found. Here lay tapestries and icons from Goa, images of devotion that had somehow survived the crossing of the Indian Ocean and the years of civil war. Now all was abandonment. The objects were left almost uncared for in this reliquary of an empire and a dream that had died.

Few visitors would have expected to find these connections between Goa and Mozambique, hinting at the vast reach that Portuguese power had once had. Yet in the heyday of the Inquisition in the middle of the 16th century the Portuguese had developed an extraordinary web of international influence. In Africa they had important trading settlements in Cape Verde and Guiné, Sierra Leone, Kongo, São Tomé and along the coasts of modern Mozambique, Tanzania and Kenya; they controlled trading posts at Hormuz in Arabia, at Goa and in many parts of western India, at Macao in China, and in the Malacca Islands, from where they traded with China and Japan. Spain, meanwhile, had at least nominal control of most of Central and South America, with the exception of the Brazilian coast, which was also in Portuguese hands; the Spanish had also established a trading station at Manila in the Philippines.

The Iberian countries were thus the first to have anything like what could be called global empires. Little of this was visible on Mozambique Island in 1994, amid the ruins of the old fort, pockmarked with explosions and overgrown by elephant grass. The only hotel was a relic of the 20th-century Portuguese colonial regime, full of grand rooms where doors banged in the wind and the plumbing system had packed up. Seawater served to flush the toilets, and the swimming pool was full of algae. The sea itself stretched out in a drab grey back to the mainland, where two fishermen said that they had been unable to catch anything for three days; during the cold war the Russians had come with industrial trawlers and fished the seas empty. A sense of desolation gripped what had once been a centre for trade and imperial power; the way in which that power had spread across the world before being eroded to nothingness was difficult to grasp.

Naturally, the rapid rise of Iberian power in the 16th century had not been achieved through kind words. Where violence had begun at home, it did not take long for it to find its way abroad. In the Spanish takeover of America violence was integral to the process of conquest but in Asia, where Portugal established centres of power but did not conquer large areas, a different outlet was required for the violence which in the late 15th century had been targeted at the *conversos*. Thus the organized spread of the Inquisition to the overseas colonies of Spain and Portugal began not in America, but in India; Philip II's establishment of the Inquisition in America was a development of an existing Portuguese structure.

Goa had been conquered for Portugal in 1510 by Afonso de Albuquerque, who took advantage of local divisions and resentment of the shah of Bijapur to gain control of this port on the west coast of India.[33] Goa's importance lay in the fact that it was a centre for the import of horses into the region. With the new strongholds in Sofala in Mozambique, Hormuz and Cochin in south India, a chain of forts had thus been created which would make the Portuguese vital middlemen in the trade of the Indian Ocean, where their zone of control was known as the *Estado da Índia*.[34]

Goa became the seat of the Portuguese viceroys in Asia in 1530. Here the pepper trade was controlled, and there were links to Portuguese factories in other parts of India such as Bengal, Coromandel and Gujarat, as well as to places further afield.[35] From Goa, Portuguese traders conducted operations in Macao and Nagasaki, acting as middlemen between China and Japan; Macao was made a town in its own right in 1583, and traded with the Philippines and Japan, meaning that Portuguese enterprise and settlement now straddled Asia.[36]

The way in which this isolated fringe of the European continent achieved global influence in the space of less than a century is one of the stranger stories in history. Portugal had never shown any sign of such ambition before in its brief trajectory as a nation, and had been defined most by its struggles to achieve independence from Spain. But once the last in a succession of conflicts with the Castilians was won by King John I in 1385, Portugal's achievement was to project its violence outward in its explorations rather than inward through factionalism. The first stage was John I's conquest of Ceuta in Morocco in 1415; this led to further exploration along the African coast under John's son Henry the Navigator, and eventually to the entrepôts of Asia.

Goa was central to Portugal's expansion and by the early 17th century a city of extraordinary wealth. The viceroy resided in an elaborate palace with two large patios: from the first a stone stairway led to a large room, where murals were painted on the walls of all the fleets which had ever sailed from Portugal to Goa, giving the names of the ships and their captains, and even recording those ships which had been lost at sea. Beyond the palace was the town, filled with a bewildering number of craftsmen: carpenters, Masons, blacksmiths and shipbuilders, all working in houses built of oyster shells and sand.

Goa was renowned as an extraordinarily cosmopolitan city. The Portuguese were undisputed masters and the nobility would usually deign to be seen only on horseback, the harnesses of their mounts made of silk inlaid with gold, silver and pearls, and imported from Bengal, China and Persia. The wealth of the city, said the French traveller Pyrard de Laval, came largely from the work of the slaves, many of whom were brought from Mozambique and other parts of Africa.[37] In these exchanges lay the origins of those tapestries which one could see so many years later in east Africa.

Such rapid growth could only be achieved by working with the local people. Having exploited divisions between Hindus and Muslims to capture Goa in the first place, the Portuguese maintained the indigenous system of labour organization and taxation until the end of the 16th century. Soldiers from Goa and Malabar served in the Portuguese army across the *Estado da Índia* to 1600, and Hindu mercenary captains were well known and respected until the middle of the 16th century.[38] In this process of interdependence, bigotry could have little place. However as the home of the viceroyalty, Goa was also to become the centre of missionary operations in Asia; its role as the 'Rome of the Orient' was to map out a future for it where the Inquisition would play a part.[39]

Gradually, intolerance grew. On 30 June 1541 an order was issued to destroy all Hindu temples on Goa, and the following year the property of those temples was transferred into the hands of the religious orders.[40] By the end of the decade a special tax was being levied on mosques in the towns of Bardes and Salsette. Between 1558 and 1561, under Viceroy Constantino de Bragança, roughly 900 temples were destroyed. By this time around one-fifth of Goa's population had converted to Christianity, as Christians were preferred to Hindus for all the best jobs. The exclusion of these new others was gathering pace, in parallel with the exclusion of the recognized others at home, the *conversos*. Thus it did not take long before steps were taken to establish the Inquisition.[41]

The first inquisitorial punishment in Goa occurred as early as 1543, just seven years after the initial establishment of the Inquisition in Portugal, when the *converso* Jeronimo Dias was burnt alive.[42] As yet, however, there was no official tribunal, and the Jesuit missionaries, then spreading through Asia under their charismatic head

Francis Xavier, felt this to be a conspicuous lack. During the ten years he spent in the Orient from 1542 to 1552 Xavier baptized a minimum of 30,000 people and travelled to China, Japan, Cochin and Malacca preaching the gospel; in the midst of such zeal the presence of *conversos* and *moriscos* – in spite of various decrees banning New Christians from going to Asia from Portugal – seemed a considerable handicap.[43]

Thus in April 1545 and May 1546 Francis, who would later be made a saint, wrote to King John III and urged the establishment of an Inquisition in Goa.[44] Eventually, in April 1560, its first inquisitors, Aleixo Dias Falcão and Francisco Marques Botelho, set sail from Portugal.[45] Crucial in this extension of the inquisitorial remit from Europe to Asia was that the new king of Portugal, Sebastian, was just three years old when he inherited the throne in 1557; the regent was John III's brother Henry, the inquisitor-general of Portugal.

With the introduction of the Inquisition, Goa changed. The number of churches grew so that by the early 17th century there was 'not a square or crossroads where one cannot be seen'.[46] All of them were sumptuously built and furnished with reliquaries of silver, gold and pearls.[47] The Inquisition was said to be worse here than in Portugal;[48] while the number of trials in Goa would be similar to those conducted by the Portuguese tribunals, the Catholic population was far smaller.[49] As in Portugal, the Inquisition concentrated at first on *conversos*, with a curious correlation being noticed between the wealth of a *converso* and the fact of their arrest by the inquisitors.[50] Burnings were frequent: seven died in 1574, and four more in 1585.[51] In the nine autos between 1571 and 1580, not fewer than sixty-five people died,[52] although the burnings became more sporadic in the years to follow.

The *converso* population of Goa dispersed. Many fled to China, Malacca and Cochin, where they could live in greater freedom,[53] yet even there they were not always safe. Five were captured in Cochin in 1575.[54] Residents from Malacca and Mozambique were also arrested.[55] Several inquisitorial visits were made to Cochin in the 16th century, and in 1613 the Portuguese King Phillip II* asked the inquisitors of Goa to investigate the mines of Munhumutapa in

* Phillip III of Spain.

modern Zimbabwe.[56] By the end of the 16th century there were commissaries of the Inquisition in such far-flung places as Macau and Timor.[57]

One should not pretend that all or even the majority of people were affected in these outposts. But nor should one deny that this undoubtedly represents the first global spread of a persecuting institution. This was a mournful legacy to set alongside the heroics of the Portuguese navigators of the deep.

ONE NEEDS TO STOP to consider the enormity of this process. In 1492 Spain was still a divided nation with enemies at home, while Portuguese navigators had yet to round the Cape of Good Hope. With the loss of Constantinople, the world beyond the North African coast had become a spectral silence for Christians. And then, within the lifetime of a single human being, all had changed: the world had been explored and persecution had kept pace, the violent flipside to the wonder of discovery.

By the 1570s there were courts of the Inquisition in Goa, Mexico and Peru. In 1609 another tribunal would be added at Cartagena de las Indias in Colombia. Just as the inquisitors in Goa and Mexico set to work as soon as they arrived, in Peru the jail was so full by 1575 – just six years after the tribunal was founded – that there was nowhere to put the prisoners.[58] Cases followed in areas which had no tribunal, such as Buenos Aires. Here the old conquistador of Chile Francisco de Aguirre was tried between 1571 and 1575 for blasphemies and lack of reverence for the Church.[59] Just as in Spain, anyone could be a target in the Spanish colonies. Early cases in Peru concentrated on issues such as the bigamy of Old Christians and not the faithlessness of *conversos* or *moriscos*.[60]

Unlike the Inquisition in Goa, which was the bloodiest and most prolific of all the Portuguese tribunals, the Inquisition in America was more moderate than its counterpart in Spain. Only around 100 people would be 'relaxed' throughout its existence, and the vast bulk of its cases would consist of soliciting priests, bigamists and the like.[61] The total number of cases in the American tribunals probably did not exceed 3,000, a small number in comparison to Iberia and Goa.[62] Yet though trials may have been comparatively few, one must bear in mind that there was a tiny population of Spaniards and their African slaves who fell under inquisitorial jurisdiction; Mexico City, the capital of the viceroyalty, had only a few thousand households of Spaniards in the late 16th century.

In fact, the reach of the Inquisition in the Spanish empire was considerable. In the viceroyalty of Peru people were arrested in towns thousands of miles from Lima, such as Santa Cruz de la Sierra[63] and Potosí[64] in Bolivia, and Quito[65] in Ecuador. Before the foundation of the tribunal of Cartagena in 1609 defendants were even brought from Bogotá to Lima to be tried.[66] After the foundation of the Cartagena Inquisition, people were regularly arrested and taken there from Panama.[67] Meanwhile, attempts were made to found a tribunal in Buenos Aires in the 1620s,[68] and the tribunal of Mexico even tried defendants from the distant Philippines across the Pacific Ocean[69] – for which it was responsible – and corresponded with Portuguese inquisitors about the people it had arrested in Manila.[70]

The reality was that every town in Spanish America was affected by the foundation of the Inquisition. Inquisitorial familiars and commissaries lived even in places far from the centres of the tribunal.[71] They were known to keep watch and to be capable of exerting their influence on a whim. Thus although arrest and punishment did not always take place, surveillance existed.

The fundamental difference between Spain and the New World for the Inquisition was that a different form of social control needed to be exerted. In Spain the dominance of the traditional faith was not in question, and perceived internal blemishes on its purity by *conversos*, *moriscos* and Protestants were therefore the most worrying threats. In the New World an entirely novel society was being built, and the Inquisition intended to ensure that, to a broad degree, this conformed to its values. The problem was not just the mixture of European and Amerindian, but also the influx of Africans, who in Lima claimed that they could uncover criminals on 'Mondays, Wednesdays and Fridays'[72] and in Cartagena openly admitted to having sex with the devil and revelling in his warm semen.[73] In this situation the Inquisition was there not only as a bulwark against heresy but as a standard of correct values in a sea of perceived devilry.[74]

The difficulty with the Inquisition's project was that the success of the Iberian powers in their empire-building had come about in part because of their origins as countries of mixed faiths. This cosmopolitanism had given the Iberians a considerable advantage in dealing with peoples in Africa, America and Asia, and contributed to their achievements as both conquerors and middlemen. By destroying this cosmopolitanism and what passed for tolerance at home through the Inquisition, Spain and Portugal stifled the ability of their representatives to act across borders; thus, over time, the mindset of the Inquisition and its export to the empire would hamper the ability of that empire to engage with different peoples and realities, and contribute to its collapse.

Mexico City 1589–1596

THE PROSECUTOR OF the Inquisition in Mexico was a man with an appropriate name. On 18 April 1589 Dr Lobo Guerrero – Doctor Wolf Warrior – issued an order for the arrest of Luis the Younger. The governor of Nuevo León, Luis's uncle Luis de Carvajal y la Cueva, had already sensationally been arrested and thrown into the inquisitorial jail.

Typically, there was not a little that was political in these arrests. Governor Luis was an enemy of the viceroy of Mexico, Don Luis Suárez de Mendoza. On discovering that Carvajal was of *converso* blood, Mendoza sensed that this could provide the opportunity to snare him.[75] At the same time the arrest of such an important figure would emphasize that no one was above the Inquisition, as the Carranza case had shown in Spain.

The evidence against the family dated back to Christmas 1587 when Luis the Younger's sister Isabel had talked with a certain Phelipe Núñez from Lisbon, and said clearly that the Christian faith was no good. When Núñez became cross, Isabel told him how her father had said that 'some ministers would persecute them in this world . . . these are the inquisitors'.[76] Then she laughed and said that she had just been testing out the strength of his faith. Núñez was not convinced: on 7 March 1589 he denounced her, and she was arrested on 13 March. The evidence against the family was now all prepared, and Inquisitors Bonilla and Sanctos García were ready to strike.

First, however, Luis the Younger had to be tracked down. He worked with his brother Balthasar as an itinerant trader, roaming the broken hills of the colony selling shoes, cloth, raisins and jam. The two of them had determined to raise enough money to return to Europe to live with the Jews of Italy, and were calling in all their debts before they set sail.[77] They must have been a striking sight as they criss-crossed the mule tracks of the empty sierras. The brothers even looked quite similar: Balthasar with his white face and blond beard, wearing a wide-brimmed black hat to shade his long head; Luis the Younger wearing similar shoes and clothes to his brother, with a long face and the beginnings of a beard.

That April Luis the Younger was on his way from his brother-in-law Jorge Almeida's mines in Tasco to Mexico City. Hearing that his uncle the governor had been arrested by the Inquisition, he went into hiding in Mexico City with Balthasar. The brothers pondered their future. In the colony the outlook was bleak. They determined to try to flee to Cuba, where there was no inquisitorial court. Leaving in disguise, they got as far as the coast at Veracruz, but there their scruples defeated their instincts. They decided that one of them would have to return as their mother Francisca was alone in Mexico City at the mercy of the inquisitors.[78]

On Monday, 8 May Luis the Younger returned to Mexico City. The colonial capital crouched in the lee of the smoking volcano Popocatepetl, which provided a constant reminder of the violence that underpinned the city's very existence. Arriving at the house of Francisca, Luis the Younger dined with his mother and sisters. The following evening, the secretary of the Mexican Inquisition Ariás Valdés and the chief bailiff Pedro de Villegas came and hammered at the door of the Carvajal home. Bursting in, they searched the house, and found Luis hiding in a small kitchen; he was bound and some silver coins were confiscated from his pockets, to be used to pay for his rations while he was a prisoner.[79]

As was usually the case, the inquisitorial trial reached an impasse. The prosecutor summoned Luis the Younger and made accusations against him. These were all denied. But finally, on 7 August, Luis asked for an audience and came in on his knees, beating himself on the chest, and shouting, 'I have sinned, mercy, mercy! Give mercy to this sinner!' He was ordered to stand up. He then informed the inquisitors that God had inspired him to confess, and that he had had to fight the devil, who had constantly attempted to dissuade him from telling the truth. Now, with his conscience saved, he freely confessed that his whole family were Judaizers.[80]

This was of course exactly what the inquisitors wanted to hear and enough to ruin Governor Luis, the new viceroy's enemy. Although there was no question that the governor was a good Catholic, as Isabel and Luis the Younger made clear in their testimony, it was also clear that he had known of the heresies of his family and had not informed the Inquisition about them. This in itself was a crime, as everyone was obliged to come forward with such information. With this evidence, the inquisitors would be able to get their man.

Governor Luis of course mounted a vigorous defence. He protested that he had not had time to travel the long distance to Mexico City to make the denunciation of his family as he had been involved in the wars against the Indians. He pointed to all his good deeds: his battle campaigns, the towns he had founded, the mines he had discovered, the churches he had built. He refused all contact with his relatives, and asked his nephews Luis the Younger and Balthasar to repay a quantity of salt and wine that he had once lent them.[81] None of this was enough to save him.

Towards the end of 1589 the inquisitors settled on their sentences. Governor Luis de Carvajal y la Cueva was to be reconciled and exiled from the Indies for six years. Luis the younger, Francisca and Isabel were sentenced to four years penance in a monastery; Mariana had to do two years penance, Catalina and Leonor only one year each. Balthasar, who was still in hiding in Mexico City, and Francisca's dead husband Francisco Rodríguez de Matos – the children's father – were to be burnt in effigy in the auto of 25 February 1590.[82]

For the real heretics, Francisca and her children, this represented suffering but not unusual punishment in a world where the Inquisition was so powerful. For Governor Carvajal it was an unbearable humiliation. This man had carved out his own piece of empire. He had spent his life in flight from the fear which the Inquisition had brought to his uncles in Portugal and then Cape Verde. He had attached himself to the forces of the Spanish empire as a means of self-preservation and had prospered, but the empire could always turn its powers of destruction inward, and had destroyed him.

He died shortly after the auto in his prison cell, awaiting exile from the New World in which he had thought to find sanctuary.

WHILE THE INQUISITION was making inroads in Spanish America, things were different for the slice of Portuguese ambition on that continent, Brazil. In Brazil visitors often felt as if they were in some kind of 'earthly paradise'.[83] The sun had the most golden rays of anywhere on earth; the stars were the happiest in the heavens.[84] Europeans described it as 'the best province for human life in the whole of America, fresh and incredibly fertile, delightful and pleasurable to the human eye'.[85] Everything was covered 'in a very high and thick forest, watered by streams in the many beautiful valleys', and there were enough fish in the rivers and the sea to sustain people without meat at all.[86] Such a bountiful place was this Brazil that the indigenous Tupinamba often lived to be 100 or 120 years old.[87] Habitually naked and with their lower lip pierced with bone, often seen carrying maracas and with their bodies richly painted, they were thought to be carefree.[88] And in beautiful Brazil, unlike Goa and the Spanish tribunals of Cartagena, Lima and Mexico, no official inquisitorial tribunal was ever set up under the Portuguese.

At first this seems anomalous. There are well-documented cases of Judaizing *conversos* in Brazil from the 1540s onward,[89] and by 1553 people who had been accused by the Inquisition had fled to Brazil.[90] It was classic territory for an inquisitorial tribunal. However, the reason for this absence was straightforward and cut to the heart of the political function of the Inquisition.

Unlike the great civilizations of the Aztecs in Mexico and the Incas in Peru, Brazil did not offer the Portuguese a hierarchically organized society with the structures already in place for domination. There were, moreover, no great gold and silver mines, unlike in Mexico and Peru. Thus throughout the 16th century the Portuguese empire derived its wealth from the spice trade in Asia, and Brazil was of minor importance.[91] It was only as profits from the sugar plantations of Brazil grew that the Portuguese crown turned its attention to its colony in America. In July 1621 the inquisitor-general of Portugal would write to the king that owing to the growing population of Brazil it would be a good idea to have resident officers of the Inquisition there.[92] But by then it was too late; the Iberian powers were increasingly under threat from the Dutch and the English, and Portugal would never again have the economic muscle to establish a new tribunal. A policy of realpolitik was required which recognized that arresting wealthy *conversos* in the Americas was likely to do more harm than good.

The absence of a permanent tribunal in Brazil reveals the extent to which the Inquisition was driven by imperatives in opposition to its supposed purpose. The Inquisition often ran at a loss, which acted as a drain on royal resources;[93] this meant that it needed to concentrate its activities where the greatest profits were to be derived. This was why the Spanish were so keen to establish tribunals in America but ignored the Philippines, and why the Portuguese looked first to Goa and ignored Brazil. Thus the Inquisition was prey to the very material values for which it pretended such disdain; in its tortured way it helped to foster them.

However, when the Portuguese authorities realized the potential importance of their Brazilian colony, their attitude began to change. In 1591 the inquisitorial visitor Heitor Furtado de Mendonça was dispatched from Lisbon to the capital of the colony, Bahia, with a wide remit to inquire into the faith there and in Pernambuco. Over the course of the next four years, Mendonça would deal with 285 cases in Bahia and 271 in Pernambuco.[94] In Olinda, the capital of Pernambuco, Mendonça even conducted two autos under powers which he had brought from Portugal.[95] However his efforts almost bankrupted the Inquisition in Portugal and he was ordered to cut his visit short and not to bother visiting the outposts in Africa which had also been within his remit when he left Lisbon in 1591;[96] again, financial worries came to the fore in dealing with heresy.

None of the above, however, should be taken as implying that the impact of the Inquisition was negligible in Brazil. After Mendonça's visit in 1591 hundreds of *conversos* were denounced for Judaizing through to the middle of the 17th century.[97] Although economic problems in Portugal meant that official visits were only made again in 1618 and 1627,[98] the Inquisition could rely on its network of commissaries and familiars to supply information and make arrests. It was the *conversos* in the higher strata of society who tended to be taken, the ones who married into the Portuguese nobility; the poorer *conversos*, who tended to marry Africans and Indians, were often ignored.[99] By the end of the 17th and beginning of the 18th century, when the discovery of gold in Minas Gerais had made the south of Brazil richer than the north, the Inquisition had transferred most of its attention to the area around Rio de Janeiro;[100] Judaizers continued to be sent to Lisbon to be burnt long into the 18th century.[101]

The extraordinary geographical reach which the Portuguese and Spanish Inquisitions had achieved by the end of the 16th century marks out the Inquisition as different from other waves of persecution which preceded it. Moreover, many of the practices which it was censuring by 1600 were unconnected with its founding purposes, which derived from the mainly imagined organized heresy of the *conversos* in 15th-century Spain. What had been exported so successfully, and had grown so rapidly, was an idea: the idea of intolerance.

THE AUTO OF 1590 had achieved all the desired results: Governor Carvajal had been humiliated and had died shortly afterwards, and the Judaizers in his family had confessed their crimes against the faith. After Francisca de Carvajal had served her penance she asked if her son Luis the Younger could be brought to a monastery nearer to the family's home in the suburb of Tlatelolco. Tlatelolco was largely occupied by Indians, and Francisca said that there was a need for a man in the house. She made her request through Friar Pedro de Oroz, whom the Inquisition had asked to watch over the family. The request was granted, and Luis was transferred to a school for 'noble Indians', where he was employed to teach them Latin. He slept at his mother's house, which was almost opposite.[102]

As far as Pedro de Oroz was concerned, the Carvajals were model converts and their reconciliation to the Church genuine. They heard mass daily. They confessed and took communion regularly. They wore the appropriate rosaries and scapularies above their *sanbenitos*. Images of the Virgin with the baby Jesus were kept in a special room in the house, and before them were placed fresh flowers. The Carvajals prayed fervently in keeping with their supposed Christian faith.[103]

Yet this was all an elaborate performance for the benefit of Oroz and for the friars who ran the school in Tlatelolco. Their residence in an Indian neighbourhood made it easier for the Carvajals to perform Jewish rituals unobserved. They kept the Passover of 1592 all together, inviting other crypto-Jews of Mexico City to celebrate it with them. Luis believed fervently that the Messiah would come to earth in 1600 and preach to the whole world.[104] Their apparent conversion to Christianity was a fabrication to buy time from the Inquisition before the great day of redemption came.

The devotion of the Carvajals to the Jewish faith shows just how far the Inquisition had been counterproductive. Of course some of these crypto-Jews would have felt genuine attachment to their ancestral religion without the persecution which they and their relatives experienced, but the Inquisition was also a significant factor. Where the *conversos* of Spain had had the potential for genuine integration into Christian life, their marginalization and persecution fed an atmosphere in which heresy was more likely. The same was true in Portugal, where the pogroms of 1506 and the establishment of the Inquisition ensured that many potential genuine converts to Christianity recoiled.

Far from eradicating heresy, persecution was playing a key role in creating it, and ensured that many *conversos* in Portugal had a genuine attachment to Judaism by the end of the 16th century. It was from these people that the Jewish community in Amsterdam was founded in the late 16th and early 17th centuries, the community from which Jews moved to England in the time of Cromwell. Just as some have argued that the collective identity of African-Americans derives from their shared heritage of slavery,[105] so, among the *conversos*, it was perhaps the shared experience of the Inquisition which made them into a cohesive group and pushed many of them towards re-embracing Judaism over a century after some of their ancestors had tried to accept Christianity.

For the Carvajals, however, the double life could not last. In November 1595 the Inquisition began to receive more information about the family. Manuel de Lucena deposed that he had seen Carvajal the Younger, Francisca and Isabel observing the Jewish sabbath and praying in the direction of Jerusalem, as the Jewish faith recommended.[106] Luis was again thrown into the inquisitorial jail, but this time the threat was far greater than in 1589. There was no illustrious relative for the Inquisition to crush. If Luis and his siblings were found guilty they were liable to be 'relaxed'.

At first Luis denied everything, but then his messianic faith got the better of him. He confided to his cellmate, the priest Luis Diaz, his faith in Judaism; Diaz was an inquisitorial spy and the conversations were recorded by inquisitorial officials as evidence against him in February 1596;[107] then he began to send messages carved into avocado stones which were uncovered by his jailer and led to his self-incrimination before the inquisitors.* This time there was to be no way back. After gruesome torture Luis was sentenced to be 'relaxed'. He would be joined in his fate by his sisters Isabel and Leonor.

The auto took place on 8 December 1596. The three siblings were paraded through the streets of Mexico City on a horse. Of Luis it was said 'en route he showed signs of having converted and took a crucifix in his hands'.[108] This was enough to spare him the ultimate penalty of being burnt to death, and, together with his sisters, he was garrotted before being burnt in front of the crowds.[109]

The fate of the siblings seems a long way from the imprisonment of their great-uncles Alvaro and Jorge in Évora; the connections were the fear that permeated life under the Inquisition and the Governor Luis. Yet where his uncle had been an unpleasant man, Luis the Younger was more innocent. He suffered from sexual frustration into his twenties, experiencing wet dreams at night which he exculpated by performing Jewish rites.[110] His belief in the holy destiny of his family and that he was living through the 'last time' before the coming of the saviour were perhaps redirections of this thwarted and dangerous energy. Yet they were also testament to an era of desperation among a social group that rightly saw itself as persecuted by those more powerful.

In the whitewashed streets of Mexico City demonization had been sanctioned by morality. Yet in the end all that had been created by pursuit of the 'enemy' was a vein of fundamentalism which conceived nothing but hatred for the codes of those among whom the pursued had been born.

---

* See pages 84–85.

Chapter Seven

THE ISLAMIC THREAT

What do you want me to say, do you want me to say that I have been a Muslim? I know nothing . . . I admit that the truth is whatever your graces say.

Teruel, 1581

AT THE END OF the 16th century the story of the Inquisition describes a circle. In Spain, the peak of the *converso* and Lutheran threat was past.* For a moment, though, we should remember the *conversos* of the 15th century, these miserable souls thought of as Jews by the Christians and believed Christians by the Jews. A hundred years later it was the turn of the *moriscos*, the descendants of the converted Muslims, to be seen as the greatest threat to national security in Spain. A category was ready and waiting for them: the Old Christians in Spain thought them Muslims: many of the Muslims of North Africa considered them Christians.

What of the Christian opinion of this fated remnant of Iberia's Muslim civilization? The bishop of Segorbe in the kingdom of Valencia compiled a report in 1587 summarizing the general view. The *moriscos* never confessed their sins. They married as many women as they could support. They believed that if they killed a Christian they would be saved. They circumcized themselves. They observed the Muslim fasts such as Ramadan and ignored all the Christian fasts. They never ate pork or drank wine.[1] They were not Christians.

---

* This was not the case in Portugal, however, where the *conversos* remained the principal target of the Inquisition.

Other reports of the time were just as scathing. The *moriscos* had to be dragged by bailiffs to church. Once inside they always wore their worst clothes with filthy collars. They sat with their backs to the altar. They covered their ears with their hands when sermons were preached. They made obscene gestures when the priest raised the host. Many of them ploughed their fields and sewed their crops on Sundays and Christian feast days.[2]

Many prominent churchmen had seen at first hand how the *moriscos* retained their faith in Islam. When the bishop of Tortosa visited the *morisco* settlement of Vall de Artos in Aragon in 1568 the *moriscos* angrily told him that Philip II oppressed them by forcing them to be Christians. When the bishop jokingly replied, 'Are you telling me you're all Moors?' some of them replied, 'Yes we are!' and when he asked them, 'Are you speaking just for yourselves?' they answered, 'We all say the same'. At that the whole town erupted and yelled with the few outspoken ones, 'We all say the same!'[3]

As we shall see, attempts at evangelizing these folk had been worse than useless. They had been abandoned to their lot in the hills. Here the more rotund emissaries of the national religion preferred not to tread, so there had been few wholehearted attempts to integrate these new sheep in the larger flock. Thus it was that the Islamic threat had been ignored until it was time to turn on it as evidence of the perils of this world.

TYPICAL OF THE WAY in which the new fear of *moriscos* manifested itself were events in Teruel. It had been here, we may recall, that the Inquisition had first come to Aragon in 1484, when Juan Garces de Marcilla's personal hatred of his in-laws had brought him to play his part in the institution's history.* Now once again this small town high in the hinterland between the Mediterranean coast and the Castilian steppe proved to be a bellwether for the forces at work in Spain; almost one hundred years after Marcilla's purge of his enemies, there would be little to suggest that the motivations of the participants in the inquisitorial dance of resentment and revenge had changed.

In Teruel much of the original Muslim population had converted

---

* See pages 17–19.

to Christianity and adopted Christian customs voluntarily in the 1400s.[4] This process had continued in the early 16th century when again Muslims in the town had converted voluntarily,[5] and long before the violent forced conversions of the 1520s. These events made it clear that *moriscos* in Teruel had initially come freely to Christianity. Such was their sincerity that they were even known by all as Old Christians.[6]

There can therefore be no doubt that these converts should have been welcomed by the church, yet the problem for the *moriscos* was to be the same as that the *conversos* had faced the century before: conversion turned them into an ambiguous social group which could easily be targeted at times of unease. Thus the sincerity of the conversions in Teruel did not prevent the Inquisition from bearing down in the 1580s and investigating the town's *moriscos*. No one had previously doubted that these people were Christians; the task was to discover how it was that such apparently genuine converts had been led back towards Muslim apostasy. Could it be the case that none of this *morisco* class could be trusted, and that all of them bore the seeds of heresy in their hearts?

In June 1581 evidence began to be received in Teruel against one Diego de Arcos. Arcos lived in the neighbourhood of San Bernardo along with the other *moriscos* whose families had converted voluntarily over 150 years before.[7] Arcos's sister Luisa Caminera came to tell the inquisitors that 'she had always had the fantasy [*sic*] and intention to come to discharge her conscience before the inquisitors but had not dared to come before for fear of the *moriscos* of the street'. Almost all the residents of San Bernardo, she said, lived as Muslims. The *moriscos* of Teruel had two *aljamas* (communities), one for those who were single and one for those who were married. Arcos prayed in the Muslim fashion and fasted during Ramadan.

The following year another of Diego de Arcos's siblings, his somewhat ironically named brother Joan de Arcos,* denounced him. By now Diego had been arrested, and Joan said that he had told his brother many times before his capture that he should convert properly to the Christian faith and leave Islam, since 'this was the

* Joan being the Catalan variant of the Castilian name Juan.

true path to save his soul and his property' – of the latter, at least, there could be no doubt.

Slowly, the evidence built. Joan announced that the entire community lived as Muslims and that they had all sworn to one another to deny it even if they were seized by the inquisitorial authorities. Then Gil Pérez of the town of Gea de Albarracín described how in 1577 large numbers of *moriscos* had come from Teruel to celebrate a wedding at Gea. There they had eaten turnovers and honey and figs and raisins, and listened to an *alfaqui* (Islamic scholar) from Teruel give high praise to Islam.

With such clear evidence of this Muslim conspiracy further delay would have been dangerous. The authorities arrested the renegade *moriscos* and threw them into the inquisitorial jail in Valencia. Now investigations could proceed apace, and evidence of the conspiracy be collected.

However, when they investigated Diego de Arcos, the inquisitors had a bit of a shock. Arcos declared himself to be an Old Christian; indeed, he said that all the people of Teruel were Old Christians. He was able to cross himself. He could say the paternoster and the Ave Maria in Latin. He clearly came from the group of converts in Teruel who were seen as Old Christians, and had a decent knowledge of Christianity.

None of this, however, discouraged the inquisitorial prosecutor, who formulated fifteen charges against Arcos. He had consulted an *alfaqui* in Gea de Albarracín. He was renowned as the most dangerous Muslim of Teruel. He alone was responsible for the fact that many of the *moriscos* of the town were not good Christians. He used halal butchers and had plotted to kill another *morisco* who had made denunciations to the Inquisition. He kept the fast of Ramadan and dressed smartly for Muslim festivals. He mocked *moriscos* who had become devoted Christians. Last of all, although he was a *morisco* he had the temerity to claim that he was an Old Christian.

It might be expected that such a terrible apostate would show little sign of Christian grace. Arcos denied everything and was tortured. Put into the *potro*, he was given an extraordinary twelve turns of the rope as his leg was dragged through the gap in the rungs of the table. But in spite of appalling agonies, Arcos repeatedly protested his innocence: 'He said: he is a Christian and has lived as a Christian and does not know anything more'. Asked to tell the truth so that the torture would not continue, he said: 'I have already told it, Illustrious Gentlemen'. He said: 'I will say everything which you tell me to'. He said: 'I am already dead and I will say everything you want me to'. and 'I will condemn myself to whatever you want'. As the jars of water were poured down his throat, he said, 'What do you want me to say, do you want me to say that I have been a Muslim? I know nothing . . . I admit that the truth is whatever your graces say'. Eventually he said, 'Ay, I am dying here'.

As the torture continued, the inquisitorial officials probed the extent of Arcos's knowledge of Arabic. This consisted of one word which he had overheard two *moriscos* mention in Teruel. Here was proof of his origins in the Old Christian community, since Arabic was the common language of the overwhelming majority of *moriscos* who had converted in the 1520s. But of course in the agonies of the *potro* Arcos eventually did confess. He said that he had been converted to Islam by his wife; yet this confession of his secret apostasy was littered with phrases such as 'By the body of the Christian God!'

The Inquisition burnt him as a dogmatizing Muslim heretic in an auto in Valencia.

A careful reading of the inquisitorial cases against *moriscos* in Aragon and Valencia during these years reveals a disturbing picture. As in the case of Diego de Arcos, *morisco* heretics often confessed to their sins only after they had been tortured.[8] The precise number tortured into confessing what they had never done, or who after being mistreated determined to turn to the Islamic faith, can never be known, but was surely considerable. Thus, as with the *conversos* in the 15th century, the Inquisition began by torturing false confessions out of some and pretending that some cases of secret apostasy were akin to a movement.

Arcos's case was one among many of the supposedly sincere Islamic converts to Christianity in these years. In Teruel, if some of these old converts had reconverted to Islam, it was not owing to their inherent seditiousness but rather the hostile atmosphere in Spain. They were pushed towards rebellion and rebellion was then held up as evidence against them.

In creating an enemy to destroy, the fantasies of the villagers of

Spain were crucial. We should not forget that Diego de Arcos's sister Luisa de Caminera had said that 'she had always had the fantasy' of denouncing the *moriscos* of Teruel, and her brother, to the inquisitors. Minor squabbles during play in the dusty streets of this remote town could be dramatized on a grand religious stage. In this theatre of the imagination that which was insignificant appeared of lasting importance. Those who knew their Bible and the story of Cain and Abel, or of Esau and Isaac, knew that family rivalries had always shaped the religious history of the peoples of the Book. It was one of the social roles of the Inquisition to breathe life into this sad human tradition, and to give the petty and the unjust a veneer of righteousness and justice.

IN 1566 A CONGREGATION of churchmen met in Valencia to discuss the condition of the *moriscos* in Spain. Forty years had passed since the decree had been finalized that all remaining Muslims should convert to Christianity. Nevertheless, as the evidence from the Congregation showed, progress in evangelizing the new *morisco* flock had been, to say the least, halting.

The Congregation noted that since 1526 the *moriscos* 'have not been taught any Christian doctrine either publicly or privately, they have not been visited or punished by the bishops or by the ministers of the Inquisition'.[9] This absence of inquisitorial attention derived from the amnesty granted by Charles V in 1542,* but also from a general lack of interest by the Church hierarchy in its *morisco* charges.[10] While in the first years after the general conversion 213 mosques were consecrated as churches in Valencia, and many others in the Aragonese districts of Tortosa and Orihuela, enthusiasm soon waned. There were few preachers who spoke Arabic and could communicate with the *moriscos*. The new rectories in the *morisco* settlements soon fell into debt. The abysmal state of the evangelizing effort was confirmed by the Cortes of Aragon in 1564, which demanded that mosques be converted into churches and that the Korans, trumpets and Muslim ritual objects be taken away forty years after Islam had supposedly been abolished in Spain.[11]

Meanwhile, even those mosques which had been made into

* See page 126.

churches were falling into disuse by 1566. The Congregation of Valencia admitted that 'in many cases it will be necessary to build new churches and in others to repair them, and in all places there is a great need for ornaments and communion cups and crosses'.[12] There were many *moriscos* who had simply not been baptized.[13] Most could only speak Arabic and lived in remote mountainous places where the bishops and preachers and inquisitorial commissaries were hardly ever seen.[14]

Moreover, the few priests who did live among the *moriscos* set a terrible example.[15] These shepherds were so suspicious of their flocks that, as the Spanish ambassador to Paris Francés de Álava noted, in the Alpujarra mountains near Granada they would often turn around suddenly when raising the host to the communion cup to see if the *moriscos* were on their knees and then let rip 'horrendous, vituperative and arrogant words'. These priests lived in the towns disposing of 'absolute power and arrogance over the *moriscos*, continually picking quarrels'.[16]

Thus many *moriscos* knew little or nothing about Christian practice, while those that did know something often learnt to hate it. Typically, *moriscos* did not know how to cross themselves and could not recite any Christian prayers.[17] Yet such ignorance was not, at least in the early years, necessarily a matter of choice.

In 1570 the *moriscos* of Valencia repeatedly petitioned the local authorities to be taught Christian doctrines. They wanted to be given priests and have churches built for them. Otherwise, as they quite reasonably pointed out, '[we] will never be good Christians'.[18] In the village of Altzira, for instance, the *moriscos* demanded visitors and people to teach them the articles of the faith.[19] How could they possibly adhere to Christianity if no one deigned to teach them its principles?

That after the Church's abject failure to evangelize or impart doctrine these 'Christian' converts should be subjected to an Inquisition into their religious practices seems obscene. What becomes apparent is that there were many among the priestly hierarchy who, perhaps unconsciously, had no desire to see the *moriscos* join the faithful. Humiliation and distrust do not encourage others to share your beliefs – as Francés de Álava moderately put it 'this certainly seemed to me a bad way of teaching them Christian doctrine'[20] –

and yet this was the recipe concocted by the priests 'of bad example' who went among the *moriscos*.

The reality was that nations, like all clubs, defined themselves by excluding others as well as through more affirmative means. Now that the 'Jewish' *conversos* had been dealt with, the role of sacrificial lamb was to be assumed, with perhaps even more suffering, by the seditious, dangerous, heretical *moriscos*.

Granada 1566–70

HERE WERE THE LAST remnants of one of the great civilizations of the medieval period. The Alhambra burnt red nightly in the gloaming. The city's 200 mosques, still active in the first years after the Spanish conquest,[21] were naked of their original adornments. Reconsecrated, a new sacral language echoed in the empty buildings.

Moorish Granada had not lasted long after the conquest of 1492. Following the intolerant behaviour of Cisneros in 1500,* in 1502 the Muslims had been forced to convert or leave. While at first there was no inquisitorial tribunal in Granada, by the time of the forced conversions in Aragon and Valencia in the 1520s attitudes were changing. A tribunal was established in Granada in 1526, and that same year a religious Congregation met and adopted a series of repressive measures against the *moriscos*: they were prohibited from speaking Arabic; their bath houses had to be run by Old Christians; they were not to practise circumcision or marry under Muslim rites; they were not allowed to bear arms or kill animals according to Muslim ritual.[22]

The 1526 Congregation of Granada was effectively a declaration of assimilation by force. These foreigners within the national body would have to learn to speak like 'us', behave like 'us', and become like 'us'. And yet such demands, backed up by force, revealed a searing tension in the minds of policymakers between the desire to assimilate and the desire to exclude. Something of the state of mind among even those who were supposedly the most enlightened members of the Congregation is revealed by the friar Antonio de

---

* See pages 114–115.

Guevara, who was a famous writer and humanist thinker: Guevara wanted personally to shear off the hair of the *morisco* women living in the land of the marquess of Cenete, and to scrape off their henna with his bare hands.[23]

The desire to inflict such physical humiliation revealed the passions which were disguised in the blueprint for the spiritual transformation of the *moriscos*. Here, in all its fear and guilt-ridden contradictoriness, was the tortured psychology of these holy men, who wished others to submit (to conversion), and yet at the same time could not escape the desire for that submission to come by force; the incompatibility of logic and desire would mean that the most refined theological and political thought was always undone.

The sole respite for the *moriscos* of Granada in the decrees of the 1526 Congregation was that they managed to forestall their implementation, paying 80,000 ducats in return for a forty-year postponement. While this protected them for a time, there was a steady erosion of their freedom to live as they had always done. Gaspar de Ávalos, archbishop of Granada from 1529 to 1542, banned them from performing their traditional dances, the *zambras*.[24] By 1560 the Inquisition was renewing its interest in them: seven *moriscos* were burnt in two autos in 1560, two more in 1562 and again in 1566, while over seventy *moriscos* were being reconciled each year in these autos.[25] Then on 1 January 1567 the 1526 Congregation of Granada was enforced, in spite of renewed appeals from the *moriscos*.[26] Again, the Inquisition was a key arm of the state in enforcing the new policy, and in the auto of 2 February 1567 in Granada four *moriscos* were burnt alive and sixty reconciled.[27] The stage was quite naturally set for rebellion.

The Alpujarra mountains had long been a centre for cultural resistance. On Christmas Eve 1568 the *moriscos* of these beautiful mountains rose against their Christian masters. At first the rebellion was restricted to a few isolated spots, but gradually it spread throughout Andalusia. Contingents of supporters came to help the *moriscos* from North Africa.[28] By the end of 1569 there were 20,000 Spanish troops fighting 26,000 rebels, and more reinforcements were needed as the *moriscos* attempted to gain revenge for seventy years of suffering:

> They robbed, burnt and destroyed the churches, stoned the images of veneration, destroyed the altars, and grabbed hold of the priests of Christ . . . dragging them naked down the streets and through the squares to great public scandal. They knifed some and burnt others alive, and made many suffer a range of martyrdom. They were equally as cruel to the lay Old Christians who lived in these places, and there was no respect from neighbour to neighbour, fellow godparent to fellow godparent, friend to friend . . . they looted their houses, and those who took refuge in towers and forts were trapped inside and surrounded by a ring of fire.[29]

These violent assaults naturally confirmed the Old Christians in their belief that the *moriscos* were dangerous foes. A new internal enemy was at hand, and needed to be dealt with in the same manner as the Lutherans of Valladolid and Seville. Yet the reality was that the Islamic credentials of this rebellion were at best partial. For while the rebels destroyed the churches and recited some Muslim prayers, they also engaged in activity which was hardly consonant with Muslim practice and ritual:

> The married women stripped off and exhibited their breasts, and the virgins their heads; and with their hair falling around their shoulders they danced publicly in the streets, embracing the men as young boys pranced before them waving their handkerchiefs in the air, shouting loudly that now the time of innocence had arrived.[30]

There was no belief here in the need for women to cover their heads and conceal their flesh. What existed was hatred of their humiliators and a desire to cast off decades of cultural and sexual repression. The violence with which they murdered their priests was a mirror to the violence which had originally been directed at them. In effect, the persecution of the 'Muslim' fifth column had fomented the revolt.

The Alpujarra insurgency marked a turning point in the history of the *moriscos* of Spain. Some 80,000 troops were assembled to extinguish the rebellion.[31] After their final defeat in 1570, 80,000 *moriscos* were expelled from the region and dispersed throughout the rest of Spain, leaving just 10,000–15,000 in the old capital of Moorish

Spain.[32] Just as the Jews had been expelled from Andalusia in 1483, so now it was the turn of the *moriscos*. Purge and purify; in Iberia the past returned inexorably, together with the errors of the past.

The expulsion created more problems than it solved. The *moriscos* of Granada were not – unlike their counterparts in Aragon and Valencia – Hispanicized.[33] The refugees had no intention of being amenable in the land of their breaking. Their new neighbours started making scandalized depositions to inquisitors about *moriscos* who declared papal bulls to be 'not glory but shit',[34] or about *morisca* widows who dug up the bodies of their husbands after their Christian burials so as to bury them with Islamic rites.[35] Thus the solution to the *morisco* problem of Granada exacerbated tensions in Castile and further divided the *moriscos* who lived there from the Old Christians.[36]

Of course the Inquisition was not the sole cause of these problems. It was not the Inquisition which enforced the expulsion of *moriscos* from Granada or defeated the Alpujarra revolt of 1568–70. Nor was it the Inquisition which came up with the original proposals of the Congregation of Granada. The Inquisition was, rather, an enforcer, the agent of ideological repression in what was then the most powerful country in the world. And thus it was to the Inquisition that Philip II turned as the atmosphere hardened against the *moriscos* in the late 1550s. It was the Inquisition which seized all the weapons of the *moriscos* in organized searches in Aragon (1563) and Granada (1565).[37] And it was the Inquisition which the *moriscos* would come to blame for their misfortunes.

Valencia 1587

With the dispersal of the *moriscos* of Granada, attitudes began to harden nationwide. The courts of the Inquisitions of Valencia and Zaragoza – now the areas with the largest numbers of *moriscos* in the country – were thick with denunciations leading to torture, reconciliation and 'relaxation'. A curious relationship developed between the year of the Islamic heresy and the actual spread of that heresy itself: just as with the theoretical implications for physics of

Schrödinger's cat, so in history and politics – the perception of danger and enemies contributed decisively to the reality.

In the hinterland of Valencia the *morisco* surgeon Damián Acen Dobber was arrested by the Inquisition in 1572 and reconciled for being a crypto-Muslim. In 1587, as the atmosphere of hostility sharpened, Dobber was arrested again. Five witnesses came forward to say that it was public knowledge in the town of Buñol that Dobber was an *alfaqui*. On many Friday nights the men and women of the *morisco* community of Buñol would gather at his house in their finest clothes, which led to gossip among the other residents of the town. One Friday night the five witnesses decided to catch the heretics red-handed.[38]

That night the main door of Dobber's house was locked but the five good citizens of Buñol found another door in the side of the house. Bursting in, they came upon Dobber seated with a lute in his hands and without his shoes, reading and chanting from a book which another *morisco* had opened before him. Dobber was surrounded by about fifty *moriscos* in an open courtyard encircled by four pillars. On each side there was a stone bench which functioned as a sort of altar, on which were large shells filled with water and a blue cloth. The courtyard, the witnesses said, was reminiscent of the mosques which they had seen in the kingdom of Granada. The women were sitting on clothes and pillows with the men around them on stone benches.[39]

For the Inquisition this was the equivalent of a smoking gun. Here was Dobber caught by five upstanding citizens leading Islamic prayers. However, Dobber denied the charges. The *moriscos* of the town had come to him because he was the public scribe and accountant. There was nothing Islamic about the meeting at all.[40] Indeed, when one thinks about what the witnesses had actually seen, doubts surface as to what had gone on. Dobber had been seen playing a musical instrument and reading a book; there had been shells with blue cloths and water which the witnesses saw as 'altars'. But there is little notably Islamic about these objects, which could have been decorative. The building 'looked like the mosques of Granada', but it was natural for the architectural heritage of Islamic Spain to live on in the aesthetic choices of the *moriscos*. There were fifty *moriscos* at the meeting, but a large gathering of friends is not necessarily a sign of heresy.

The Old Christians of Buñol would probably have been suspicious whatever they had found. Dobber was one of the richest *moriscos* of the town, and this in itself marked him out as a leader of the community. Thus perception and preconception played its part in the denunciations that were made against him. Of course, it is possible that there was some substance in the accusations, but the lack of clear evidence shows just how far the atmosphere made it difficult to distinguish between fantasy and reality.

Dobber, for one, knew that it would be impossible to get a fair trial so while he was incarcerated in the inquisitorial prison of Valencia he attempted to escape. He broke open his window and tried to jump to freedom using a rope strung together from his bed sheets. The sheets became unknotted and he fell to the street, breaking his leg. At this, the Inquisition proceeded apace with his trial. He was tortured. He continued to deny everything. Unable to break him down, the Inquisition sentenced him to 400 lashes and ten years in the galleys.[41]

In many ways the Dobber case epitomizes the condition of the *moriscos* in Valencia and Aragon as the 16th century came to an end. The fear and suspicion felt by Old Christians was matched by the prejudices of the *moriscos*: any meeting of *moriscos* was seen as Islamic and Dobber was ready to risk his life escaping rather than continue his incarceration.

By the end of the 16th century the Inquisition had become the most effective means of repressing the *moriscos*.[42] Between 1545 and 1621, a total of 232 *moriscos* were 'relaxed' across Spain, with the greatest concentration in Zaragoza.[43] By the late 1580s there were so many *moriscos* under arrest in Cordoba that they could not all fit into the inquisitorial jail.[44] *Moriscos* constituted three-quarters of the inquisitorial caseload in Valencia between 1570 and 1614, and 56 per cent of the caseload in Zaragoza.[45] Their arrest and potential 'relaxation' fostered fear, but even more central to the dissemination of hatred among the *moriscos* was the Inquisition's use of torture, which became completely routine in these years.

Reading through the cases of *moriscos* in the inquisitorial courts of Valencia and Zaragoza of the time, it is sobering to see that of the majority it is said 'diligences [of torture] were made'. Frequently, it was only in the torture chamber that a *morisco* would confess 'to having been a Muslim all their lives'. Not infrequently, these 'Muslims' would revoke their confessions once out of the *potro*;[46] however, this was a mistake since a retraction could often lead to their being tortured again.[47] Of course, as we saw in Chapter Three, some *moriscos* were spared torture because of their physical condition or age, but nevertheless the fact that most *moriscos* arrested by the Inquisition at this period were tortured speaks for itself. Although the Inquisition could not deal with the vast number of apostate *moriscos* which they believed to exist[48] and was only capable of trying a small proportion of the total, the indiscriminate use of torture was decisive in creating hatred of the Inquisition among all *moriscos*.[49]

To this use of torture was allied a sort of routine humiliation. When Beatriz Padilla, wife of Francisco Maestro, a basketmaker from Arcos, brought her husband in the inquisitorial jail of Cuenca a clean shirt, she was put on a donkey and paraded naked from the waist up through Arcos with a preacher crying out her crime, before being given one hundred lashes.[50] And when in 1579 the convicted *morisco* of Murcia, Martin Varuni, broke his sentence of banishment to come back and see his wife and children, the Inquisition ordered him to begin his enforced exile all over again.[51]

Cases such as Varuni's reveal that the Inquisition did not merely torture and 'relax'; it broke up families even with relatively minor penances, shattering the community.[52] Often entire villages would be destroyed when the Inquisition descended, as at Cuenca in 1585, when thirteen of the twenty-one prisoners came from the small settlement of Socuéllamos, and Valencia in 1589, when eighty-three *moriscos* from Mislata were punished.[53] Such events inspired fear and hatred, and indeed one came directly from the other; as the chronicler Pedro de Valencia wrote around 1607, the *moriscos* were worse enemies than the Moors of North Africa 'as they fear that they will be seized by the Spanish Inquisition which will burn them and confiscate their goods . . . [the *moriscos*] know that they live with these risks, and that if they were uncovered as Muslims they would suffer these things, and so they hate us just as they would people who want to kill them'.[54]

It was, therefore, fear of the Inquisition brought about by the Inquisition's own actions which was recognized by Valencia as the source of the hatred. This fear was so intense among *moriscos* that they would not intermarry with Old Christians in case this led to denunciations.[55] *Moriscos* suspected of having denounced someone were sometimes murdered.[56] Instead of seeing punishment by the Inquisition as a shameful thing, *moriscos* took to viewing it as a badge of honour, applauding those who were forced to go through the theatre of a public auto and the *sanbenitos*.[57] The macabre ballet of fear and hatred thus reached its zenith in the relationship between the *moriscos* and the Inquisition.[58] This Muslim 'fifth column' was terrified of 'being deprived of our lives, property and children, and that in a moment we can be plunged into a dark cell . . . there to spend many years using up our property and seeing our little children being taken away to be raised by others'.[59]

Yet the attempt to squeeze rebellion out of the Muslims through cruelty and overwhelming force again had the opposite effect. The *moriscos* were more drawn towards heresy than before. They learnt to scorn the Inquisition that symbolized their oppression. Far from achieving its aim of crushing opposition, the use of the Inquisition against the perceived Muslim enemy only made matters worse; while it did not 'relax' as many *moriscos* as it had done *conversos* in the 15th century, the Inquisition was crucial in building up the hatreds which led inexorably to the great *morisco* tragedy.

THERE WAS, INDEED, a cruelty and a pleasure in the Old Christian treatment of the *moriscos*, rather like a cat breaking off the wing of a bird and playing with it before biting its head off.

The story moves to the Ebro valley in Aragon, where in the mid-1580s there were repeated clashes between Old Christians and *moriscos*. Following several violent stand-offs with *morisco* militias, in 1585 some Old Christians decided to murder a *morisco* in revenge. They apparently believed that murdering a *morisco* would be pleasing to God, and that if they died in the process they would gain eternal salvation.[60] This belief in the glory of martyrdom derived directly from the ideology of the crusades in the 11th and 12th centuries. It was as old, and as (dis)reputable, as the hills and it was not surprising that the authorities found it difficult to put down the violence. The skirmishes lasted for three years, and in one assault by Old Christians, on the village of Pina, perhaps 700 *morisco* men, women and children were killed.[61]

With events such as this increasingly commonplace, communities of *moriscos* and Old Christians had become almost entirely separated. One Dutch traveller with the party of Philip II in Aragon in 1585 noted that in the small town of Moel, where there was a thriving ceramics industry, there were only three Old Christians in the whole place. The *moriscos* ate no pork. They drank no wine. The church was almost always empty. When the royal party left the town they broke the plates they had used in disgust.[62]

The mutual loathing of *moriscos* and Old Christians had become so deep that they mocked one another openly in the inquisitorial jail of Cuenca rather than find some fellowship in their shared fate. The Old Christian prisoners cooked bacon ostentatiously in front of the *moriscos*, tossing it around in frying pans greased with lard, while the *moriscos* made crosses from straw and proceeded to stamp on them.[63] Outside the inquisitorial jail it was commonplace for Old Christians to offer *moriscos* plates of pork, knowing full well that this was both a threat (if they declined they could be denounced to the Inquisition) and a humiliation (through the power of the Old Christians to possess such a threat).[64]

The chasms in the community were becoming impossible to bridge. The Muslims of North Africa resented, as Pedro de Valencia put it, 'that a large number of their own kind are – as they see it – oppressed and tyrannized into servitude in Spain, with dishonour and disdain, forced by violence to leave the Mohammedan faith, and for this reason imprisoned and deprived of their property and of their lives, whipped and burnt, as they hear every day from the accounts of those very same Spanish *moriscos*'.[65] This chronicler had a lofty position in the court of Philip III; there is no reason to doubt his account of the daily humiliations visited on Spain's *moriscos*.

Communication broke down. The first rule of *morisco* life was when among the Old Christians to say nothing, since a word out of place would all too easily lead to the Inquisition. With silence came distrust, and with distrust mutual loathing could only grow.[66] The real tragedy of the developing ghettoization was that it did not have to happen. The Portuguese had often found that their colonists became Muslims. In 1585 the inquisitors of Goa complained about the Old Christians who had gone to live among the Moors and converted.[67] In 1623 Amador Lozado, the captain of the fort at Arguim off the Mauritanian coast, was accused of being a secret Muslim, living with Muslim concubines and oppressing all the Christians in the fortress.[68] These were not isolated cases; the archives of the Portuguese Inquisition are filled with stories of people living in North Africa who apostatized.

In Spain, too, it was not unknown in the 16th century for Old Christians to be attracted to Islam. Several Old Christians were penanced by the Inquisition for becoming *moriscos* in the 1560s[69] and in one case an *alfaqui* managed to convert some friars to Islam.[70] Though such stories continue to be found in the 1580s,[71] they are somewhat rarer, something which reveals the growing separation between the two communities. There was little dialogue any longer. Propaganda was winning. Where people still lived among one another there was some mutual respect, but where they existed in mutual isolation they all too easily came to despise each other.

This separation allowed increasingly fantastical stories of the other community to gain currency. There was nothing to stop all manner of idiocies being believed. Thus soon even reasonable Christians believed in the archetype of the seditious crypto-Muslim and came to believe that these fanatics had to be stopped before they could succeed in their plan of destroying the nation and its way of life.

How did one distinguish these seditious, dangerous people? In his treatise on the *moriscos* Pedro de Valencia let slip a remarkable fact about the objects of his study: 'One must consider,' he wrote, 'that all these *moriscos*, as far as their natural complexion is concerned . . . are just as Spanish as the rest of the people who live in Spain'.[72]

There was no racial distinction between the *moriscos* and the rest of the Spanish population.[73] Indeed, after they were expelled from Spain, many *moriscos* returned to Aragon, Murcia and Granada, and were concealed by members of the local population. Those who returned to Granada often sought out new villages to live in, and they were such proficient speakers of Spanish (and so indistinguishable from the rest of the population) that they were easily able to pass themselves off as Old Christians.[74] It would therefore have been very easy to integrate the *morisco* population into the Spanish nation.[75]

In fact, the principal differences between the *moriscos* and the rest of the population were cultural. Yet Old Christian culture itself was an extraordinary mixture of the Christian and the Muslim,* which ought to have meant that fusion with the *moriscos* was possible. The difference in the 16th century was the new culture of intolerance, of which the Inquisition was both the symbol and the spearhead; thus it was that customs which were purely cultural and not religious came to be seen as Muslim and as indicators of heresy.

This cultural intolerance began slowly. In the first years after the conquest of Granada, although Cisneros burnt Islamic books, habits such as taking baths and the wearing of distinctive clothes were not seen as Islamic practices.[76] This approach hardened, and by the time of the Congregation of Granada in 1526 it was proposed that the use of Arabic and the wearing of certain styles of clothing should be banned as indicators of Muslim apostasy.

However, the intolerance of the Congregation of 1526 was not as yet universal. In the same year Charles V agreed with a petition from the Moors of Valencia which noted that some recent converts to Christianity would not know how to 'depart from some *morisco* ceremonies which they will keep more out of habit than because they wish to be Muslims or to offend the Christian faith'.[77] The good sense of this view is shown by the fact that the *moriscos* themselves did not view their clothes as something Muslim, but rather as a regional costume.[78]

The *moriscos* therefore saw themselves as a population with a distinctive culture just as culture within Christian Spain varied from, say, Galicia to Extremadura. There was no racial difference between them and the Old Christians, and in Aragon and Valencia their ancestors had lived peaceably under Christian rule for centuries. The enmity which existed by the end of the 16th century had therefore

* See pages 22–24.

had to be created, and in order to do this a stereotype had been required of the 'Muslim enemy'. Stereotypes of the enemy are fed by paranoia, and following the bonfires of Valladolid and Seville of 1559 there was no shortage of this in Spain.

Thus in August 1582 the archbishop of Toledo wrote to Philip II with a notable piece of advice. As the venerable archbishop pointed out, if the Turkish navy were to take advantage of the fact that it could pick up 50,000 *morisco* infantrymen in Valencia alone the kingdom would be in serious peril, especially if such a force were to join forces with the Huguenots and other heretics. This was clearly intelligence of a considerable threat and moreover it was not an isolated piece of information. Five months earlier the inquisitors of Zaragoza had written with certain knowledge that the plot was for the duke of Orange and Philip II's rival to the Portuguese crown Dom Antonio to join forces with the Muslims of Morocco through the good offices of Portuguese traders (usually crypto-Jews) and *moriscos*, and that meanwhile the *moriscos* of Aragon would link up with the prince of Berne while those of Valencia awaited the Turkish navy, and the French were planning to smuggle gunpowder to them so that they could destroy the Spanish fleet.[79]

Intelligence of new plots was always being received. The danger was, as the evidence clearly showed, mounting all the time. The extraordinary acuity of the enemy knew no bounds; the plots against Spain were such that no longer was your enemy's enemy your friend – your enemy's enemy was also, by some strange quirk of mutual complicity and loathing of the Spanish, their friend as well.

In such circumstances *moriscos* ceased to be seen as individuals. They were a generalized mass, 'the enemy',[80] a stereotyped evil which had to be destroyed.[81] By the 1580s it was assumed that all *moriscos* were, without exception, secret Muslims.[82] Old Christians would often denounce entire villages for the same crime, as if there could be no nuance to behaviour.[83] In Mislata in the region of Valencia the labourer Francisco Corzo was denounced in part because 'it was generally said that all the people of Mislata were Moors'.[84] Juan de Ribera, an archbishop of Valencia later declared a saint, wrote to Philip III early in the 17th century that 'the hatred and obstinacy [of the *moriscos*] against the Catholic faith is as one in all of them [*uno en todos*]'[85] – it may take someone who cannot differentiate individuals among their enemy to perceive this trait in others.[86]

In actual fact, however, the situation was complex. Just as some Old Christians had been attracted to Islam in the 16th century, there were innumerable cases of *moriscos* who genuinely wanted to be Christians. Christian members of *morisco* families would frequently denounce their relatives for Islamic practices, which alone shows that *moriscos* had widely differing approaches to Christianity.[87] That assimilation was possible was revealed by cases such as that of Juan de Soria, denounced in Toledo in 1596 by his twenty-year-old daughter for expressing doubts regarding Christianity which she, as a good Christian, found deeply offensive.[88] The way in which religious practice was anything but uniform across *morisco* families was revealed in 1602, when the wife of Miguel Arapel denounced him for Islamic behaviour; all was clearly not rosy in their marital home, since she professed shock and scandal at his apostasy in spite of the fact that he was circumcized.[89]

Such a litany of cases of family members denouncing one another to the Inquisition feels wretched. The Inquisition is, after all, a better ossuary of memory than most institutions to the interdependency of love and hatred. The ministers of the Inquisition professed love for their prisoners; they treated them with hatred. One intense emotion was, after all, so easily transformed into another.

Segorbe 1608

IN THIS ANCIENT TOWN on the plain of the Palancia river tensions had always run high between the *morisco* community and Old Christians. The great port of Valencia – and the tribunal of the Inquisition – were not too far distant, while the town lay between two sierras dotted with isolated *morisco* communities. It was inevitable that as tensions grew, they would break out in Segorbe, for there was little time left before the terrible decision taken by Philip III to expel all *moriscos* from Spain.

In 1608 the widow Maria Xaramfa, a *morisca* of about forty years old, was denounced to the Inquisition in Valencia.[90] Her accuser was a fellow *morisco* who had already confessed to crypto-Islam to the inquisitors of Barcelona and was seeking to give evidence of the sincerity of his reconciliation to the Catholic Church. Beyond all the cant and sparkling consciences, motivations could never be entirely pure in the most vengeful court in the land.

Maria Xaramfa's large and comfortable house, the witness said, was used by the *moriscos* of Segorbe as a mosque. Various *alfaquis* met there. It was here that they preached to the *moriscos*, reading from the Koran which was placed on a bench before them. The oldest and most learned among them wore head-coverings (*tocados*) fringed with gold and silk, and held staffs in their hands as if they were bishops. They taught the *moriscos* how to perform their ritual ablutions, how to pray and which festivals they should keep. And as they read aloud, the gathered *moriscos* would respond, in the manner of a priest and his congregation.

The anonymous witness was able to give such a graphic description since he himself had attended these prayers in Segorbe on several occasions. Xaramfa, he said, derived great personal benefit from these events. The community of Segorbe paid her thirty ducats to hire her home. They provided her with three poor women to help with cleaning and whitewashing it for the four major festivals of the year. Xaramfa had also been given some mats woven in black and white which had been blessed by the *alfaqui*, and Islamic symbols had been painted upon them.

Maria Xaramfa, naturally, denied all the charges. While it was true that numbers of *moriscos* did come to her house, there was nothing Islamic about this. The accuser was merely trying to gain the favour of the inquisitors. The inquisitors gave her defence short shrift, however. With the gathering evidence against her entire community, they clearly could do nothing but accept the evidence of large numbers of *moriscos* attending her 'mosque' each Friday, having performed their ablutions in their homes. After eighty years of what they saw as sincere attempts at evangelization, there was a despair at the recalcitrance of the Muslims and at their refusal to integrate with the national culture.

By this time there was no doubt that increasing numbers of *moriscos* were indeed actively turning to Islam. In the village of Buñol, the priest Damián de Fonseca wrote just four years later that if twenty children were born in a short space of time the parents would get together and choose one of them to be baptized twenty times, switching his name each time with the priest unable to do anything about it.[91] Meanwhile, Fonseca claimed, there were many *moriscos* condemned to be 'relaxed' by the Inquisition who refused to accept Christian confession so that they could be garrotted before being burnt: 'and as soon as they declared [in the auto] "You are all witnesses that I die in the law of Muhammad" the executioner leapt off the stairs in two bounds and covered himself up, for fear of being stoned to death [by the mob, along with the *morisco*]'.[92]

On top of resistance to Christian rites, Fonseca wrote, there was an active Islamizing movement. Many *moriscos* kept Ramadan, wandering about for the month-long fast 'thin and pale, hardly able to stand up, trying to divine the heavens without being astrologers, and looking longingly up at the sky until they caught sight of the first star in the evenings, at which they all disappeared as one from the squares and streets'.[93] Circumcision was routine,[94] as was the use of Muslim funerary rites, with corpses being wrapped in clean linen with silk headdresses decorated with gold thread and black silk.[95] At weddings people danced and prayed and ate as Muslims.[96]

This was an intolerable situation for Spanish society, which defined itself through its adherence to the Catholic religion. The bishop of Segorbe – where Maria Xaramfa kept her mosque – held in 1595 that the '*moriscos* are apostates and live according to the Muhammadan law'.[97] This was not something that Spain and the Inquisition could countenance, and nor was the growing physical aggression displayed by *moriscos*. In Belchite in Aragon *moriscos* attacked ministers of the Inquisition with swords, lances and guns whenever they arrived to try to arrest someone.[98] In 1591 the *moriscos* of Gea de Albarracín – one of the haunts of Diego de Arcos of Teruel – attacked the jail of the Inquisition, wounding some inquisitorial officers and helping one of their friends to escape.[99] In 1608 the investigator Gregorio López Madera found eighty-three corpses in the region of Hornachos killed by local *moriscos* for denouncing them or collaborating with the Inquisition.[100]

The situation had become grave. The Turks continued their activities in the western Mediterranean, threatening Spanish shipping and supplies, while in Spain they had a contingent of allies, all of whom would jump at the chance to destroy the state. In April 1609 the Spanish crown took the decision that it had no alternative but to expel all *moriscos* from Spain.

Valencia 1609

> And [the *moriscos*] came out of their houses and made to embark . . . and along the way they sold and gave away everything they had, selling wheat at two or three *reales* a bundle, which is an incredibly low price [in Valencia] . . .
>
> And many were found dead in the hills, some of hunger after they had surrendered, others having killed themselves voluntarily [*sic*] so that they did not have to leave . . .
>
> Many people have been led to extremes in their desire to stay, offering their throats to a knife rather than leave . . . others have hid and fled so as not to leave, making vigorous demonstrations of their Christianity and choosing rather the condition of slavery than departure from Spain . . .
>
> There was one fifteen-year-old girl in particular who made great efforts to stay . . . and God was served in giving her a serious illness which could save her, as, seeing herself threatened by the illness she called a Christian who was passing her home and asked him to bring her a confessor, as she wanted to die as a good Christian, and this was done so that the girl was able to confess and give her soul to God . . ..[101]

THE DECISION TO EXPEL the *moriscos* was a political one, taken by the crown and not by the Inquisition, yet the Inquisition provided critical support to the decision through its databank of trial evidence which 'proved' the universal apostasy of the *moriscos*[102] and its fomentation of the hatred which the *moriscos* felt towards the rest of society. It was also a popular decision. When the edict of expulsion was published on 22 August 1609 'such was the crowd of ordinary people that came to hear the pronouncement, that people knocked one another down amid the general applause and happiness'.[103]

This banishment of a significant part of the population had been gestating for decades. It had first been mooted at the Council of Lisbon in 1582 when virtually the entire ecclesiastical hierarchy had favoured it.[104] Thereafter it had been raised as a possibility by various inquisitors and royal councils until a council of January 1602 led by Philip III's chief minister the duke of Lerma planned virtually every detail of the expulsion.[105] The final push came out of fear: the Council of State wrote in April 1609 that 'the fear of the Moors . . . is considerable, and even the duke of Lerma believes that they might be able to conquer Spain'.[106]

What had gestated with the political will to expel the *moriscos* was the psychological conditioning of the population. The Old Christians now felt essentially different from people who were physically identical to themselves. Under the rigid ideology of the Inquisition the mass of Spanish people had been indoctrinated into believing that signs of cultural difference were signs of treachery and of a desire to destroy them. Numerous chroniclers created stereotypes of *moriscos* as ugly, abnormal, different.[107] Slowly, people had come to see the residues of Spain's Muslim population in this light. Slowly, the groundwork had been laid for the enemy's destruction.

The final decree of expulsion was nothing if not pragmatic. The *moriscos* of Valencia were dealt with first, in 1609. Six in every one hundred *morisco* households were ordered to remain to instruct incomers to their lands on agricultural techniques of which they were the masters. Fixed *morisco* property was to be given to their feudal lords in order to compensate them for the loss of their workforce. The *moriscos* were given only three days to leave their homes and clear all their goods.[108] These were people who were no longer deemed worthy of consideration.

Once the Valenciano *moriscos* had been dispatched, it was the turn of the Aragonese. In the spring of 1610 the *moriscos* there had 'stopped all their dealings and labour in the land and [had] sold everything that they owned, right down to beds, plates and bowls'.[109] On 16 April Miguel Santos de San Pedras, inquisitor of Zaragoza, declared that what little the Aragonese *moriscos* had left would be gone in a few days and that 'famine and epidemics are bound to come among them . . . and seeing themselves starving they are bound to rob and kill Christians and commit atrocious crimes'.[110] Philip III signed the expulsion order on 29 May 1610, precipitating a free-for-all between the moneylenders and the feudal lords of the

Aragonese *moriscos*, who suddenly found themselves without any rents with which to pay off their debts.[111] Chaos and stagnation loomed.

In total, perhaps something over 300,000 *moriscos* were forced from Spain between 1609 and 1614.[112] Most went to North Africa. In Oran (modern Algeria) over 116,000 arrived between 2 October and December 1609. Many were robbed and assaulted by bandits, as were many of those who went to Tremecen and Fez in Morocco.[113] While in Tunisia the 50,000 *moriscos* who arrived were treated well, the rest suffered misery, poverty and death. They were frequently suspected of being renegade Christians by the Muslims of North Africa.[114]

Maybe it was in anticipation of this miserable fate that the banished were so reluctant to depart a country which had come to hate them. When the expulsion order was issued 'the lamentations were such that in all the *morisco* settlements one could hear nothing but sobs and tears'.[115] The processions of people down to the chosen ports of exile were as something out of biblical times, 'exhausted with pain and tears . . . the men loaded down with their wives and children, and by those who were ailing, and old, and young, full of dust, sweating . . . some on foot, broken and badly dressed, shod with one shoe and one sandal . . . all of them greeting those who watched them, or met them, saying to them: "May the Lord watch over you . . . Gentlemen, may the Lord keep you." '[116]

Thus it was that the last vestiges of the Islamic population which had lived in Spain for 900 years departed, 'tired, filled with pain, lost, oppressed, sad, confused, chased, furious, corrupted, annoyed, bored, thirsty and hungry'.[117]

IT IS DIFFICULT to erase the memory of a great civilization. The conquistadors tried this in Mexico, destroying the temples of the Aztecs, burning the idols which they found, complicit in destroying precious libraries of Aztec codices. Even today, however, ruined temples which have lain undetected for centuries re-emerge from five centuries of sleeping sediment; when part of the subway system of Mexico City was being built in the 1960s the great temple of the Aztecs at Tenochtitlan emerged into the tunnels of the modern underground.

And when the Spanish came to build the churches which would replace the temples of Mesoamerica in Mexico, a notable thing happened. In Tlaxcala, for instance, a church was built which can still be seen today, with a precious wooden ceiling in the *mudejar* style which Spain had inherited from its Islamic past via Muslim craftsmen. The official ideology which went with imperial expansion averred that there was only one path which could be followed, yet that path was itself a mixture of Christian, Jewish and Muslim traditions.

What, finally, is one to make of a society which makes every effort to destroy a part of itself and to impose unity of belief when so much of its strength and power had come from its diversity? It seems like an exercise in self-mutilation, even an unconscious form of self-hatred.

Where paranoia triumphs, every fact can confirm the paranoiac's prejudices. There were, it was true, strong geopolitical reasons for the Spanish to be wary of Muslim sympathizers: there had been repeated battles between the Spanish and the Turks in the 1570s which emphasized the potential dangers of a Muslim enemy.[118] Yet as we have seen the marginalization of the 'fifth column' at home merely made it more aggressive and impossible to assimilate.

While the Inquisition was not directly responsible for the tragedy of the *morisco* expulsion, it was the enforcer of pariah status for *moriscos* in the late 16th century. Far from effecting a reconciliation between *moriscos* and Old Christians, it merely promoted extremism on both sides. The Muslims, or *mudejares*, who lived in Spain before 1492 had been Hispanicized and acculturated;[119] they ought therefore to have been on the road to assimilation and integration. With its torture, its taxes on every *morisco* in Aragon and Valencia and its punishments, the Inquisition, far from ensuring their conversion to the fold, merely made them obstinate and more ready to turn to Islam.[120]

Just as with the *conversos* in the 15th century, therefore, the Inquisition's activities provoked the very heresy which it claimed to be attempting to extirpate.[121] Whereas in Portugal, after the reconquest of the 13th century the Moorish population integrated thoroughly into society,[122] in Spain in the 16th century the Inquisition made this an impossibility.

At last! All the marginalized and ambiguous groups in Spanish society had been dealt with. But victory was temporary, bitter, a harbinger of failure. With all its obvious enemies destroyed, the hunt for the enemy would become increasingly difficult to sustain and increasingly fractious.

¡Ay, los moriscos! Seen as Muslims by the Christians and as Christians by the Muslims, theirs was indeed a miserable fate. Neither Catholic Spain nor Muslim North Africa could countenance this ambiguous and potentially seditious group in their midst.[123] In spite of everything that had happened to them, many preserved their Christian faith in the most trying of circumstances in exile. By 1613 news had reached Minorca that rich *moriscos* were living as Christians in Algiers.[124] Some dived off the ships where they worked and swam ashore so that they could return to Spain and live openly as Christians.[125]

The *moriscos* were not, and had never been, all Christians or all Muslims. Just like the *conversos* individuals among them professed a wide range of beliefs. But nuances of belief were not something the Inquisition could understand. Thus was it one of the principal forces in their obliteration.

In Seville departing Christian *moriscos* made offerings to churches and one of them gave 4,000 ducats to the Virgin of Iniestra. Others left bequests so that prayers could be said for their souls in the churches where they had always worshipped and attempted to find solace on their troubled voyage towards God.[126] Their tragedy ebbed out of their lives along with the ballad which they sang as they left the banks of the Guadalquivir:

And the *morisca* women
Wringing their whitened hands
Raising their eyes to the heavens
Crying out through their tears:
Ay, Sevilla, my home!
Ay, Church of San Pablo
San Andrés, Santa Marina
San Julián and San Marcos! . . .
Crying out for the help
Of the Virgin of the Rosary
And of the Virgin of Bethlehem:

Let her protect us
As much with her feelings
As she does the babes in arms
Whom she raised at her breasts,
And with her milk brought them lamentation.[127]

Chapter Eight

PURITY AT ALL COSTS

Squarely opposed to religious concepts which had dominated Christian thinking for centuries . . .

Cinctorres (Valencia) 1705

ONE OF THE FEW consolations for the persecuted ought, perhaps, to be that their travails can come to an end *with* their end; there would appear to be little suffering that can be meted out to someone once their flesh has melded into smoke and ashes. And yet, while descent from a convicted heretic had long been social death in Iberia, the absence of 'heretical classes' following the expulsion of the *moriscos* gave the question of ancestry a new importance in Spain.

From this point on, the impact of the Inquisition was to be most visible on a social level, in a different register to the great persecutions of the late 15th and the 16th centuries. One of the principal arenas for this was the obsession with what was called *limpieza de sangre* – purity of blood. This fixation spread also to Portugal, making Iberia a unique case of a society with racialist legislation in early modern Europe. Yet the new laws did not foster feelings of well-being; instead, a sense of decline set in accompanied by the increasing vigilance over the descendants of the *conversos* and the *moriscos*.

And so, back to Cinctorres. Earlier we saw how, in this remote town in the Valenciano hinterland in the 1530s, the teacher Miguel Costa was accused of Lutheranism and burnt to death at an auto in Valencia.* In the early 1700s Costa's distant descendants, or alleged

* See pages 111–113.

descendants, found that they could not be rid of their ancestor. He plagued them like a recurring bout of ague.

In 1705 an extraordinary legal petition was made by one Antonio Costa in an attempt to rid himself of this disease. Costa described in desperate terms the problems which he was facing in Cinctorres:

> Many years ago his father [also called] Antonio Costa applied to become a familiar of the Inquisition of Valencia. And with the Inquisition having ordered inquiries to be made regarding the purity of his ancestry, he died before having achieved his aim. And even though since his father's death Antonio Costa [the younger] has several times written to the Tribunal [of the Inquisition], offering to pay whatever costs might be necessary to conclude this inquiry . . . he has never received a reply; the result has been that such scandal and defamation has fallen upon his family, which used to be among the noblest of the district [of Cinctorres], that they have become unmarriageable, as two of his children are finding to their cost today.[1]

The more one examines the case, the more surreal it seems. Antonio Costa the Elder* had submitted his original petition to become an inquisitorial official on 4 February 1671, fully thirty-four years before his son's protest. The problems which he had run into derived from the widespread suspicion that he was descended from the Miguel Costa 'relaxed' by the Inquisition in 1536. Thus the problems of Antonio Costa the Younger stemmed directly from one dubious case of Lutheranism brought 170 years before.

It is worth trying to imagine the atmosphere in the Costa household of the early 18th century. Spain was in decline and increasingly cut off. In the middle of the 17th century goods had still been being taken to Madrid on donkeys and mules, rather than by cart as in France.[2] In rural areas many villages had been abandoned; other were isolated and underpopulated, often over a day's journey from one another.[3] Yet the growing hardships did not prevent a reputation for arrogance, as there was 'no one [in Spain] who does not think themselves to be a hundred times more important than they are'.[4]

---

* As I shall call him to distinguish him from his son.

In the Costa household such arrogance was of course tempered by the bad reputation which the family bloodline possessed. The Costas must have hated their wretched namesakes who had been punished by the Inquisition so many years before. The family entered a world of isolation and suspicion, and all for the sake of people whom they would never meet, who had been dead for almost two centuries and who may or may not have been ancestors of theirs.

The Cinctorres case dragged on. The archives of the Inquisition of Valencia were mined and the trial of Miguel Costa from 1536 was appended to the petition of Antonio the Elder. Expense sheets from the Tribunal of Valencia were produced from 1533, 1536, 1544, 1572, 1606 and 1666. The problem that Costa faced was that many of the witnesses in the initial inquiry into his lineage declared that he was descended from *conversos*. Eventually, after twelve years of bureaucratic yo-yos, he wrote a letter on 20 April 1684 saying that he suspected that some witnesses thought him descended from the brothers Bartolomé and Miguel whose *sanbenitos* hung in the church of Morella.

Antonio the Elder was nothing if not methodical. In order to prove that he was not descended from these Lutheran heretics, he included in his deposition the marriage vows of those whom he claimed as his ancestors. He denied he was related to Bartolomé and Miguel at all. What a ridiculous suggestion! Instead, he was descended from Antonio Costa, the son of Vicente Costa and Barbara Moliner, who had married in 1533. Antonio had been born in 1539, and had married Barbara Polo of Cinctorres in 1572. The marriage certificates of these ancestors were also included in an exhaustive legal deposition which ran to several hundred pages.

This sort of bureaucratic farrago was normal by the second half of the 17th century. It was vital for everyone from the greatest lord to his poorest peasant to be able to prove their ancestry going back six, seven, eight generations and more, so that they and their family would not become pariahs. If pure ancestry could not be proved, then it would have to be invented. But even when people went to the sort of trouble and expense that Antonio the Elder had in 1684, success was not guaranteed; twenty-one years later, as we have seen from the petition of his son, the matter had not been resolved, and the final ruling was not issued until 1713, 176 years after Miguel Costa had been 'relaxed' at an auto in the noble and elegant city of Valencia.

Purity of ancestry was one of the murkier faces of the Inquisition's hydra. It was not something that caused death directly but, just like the minor penances which we observed in the last chapter, it could ruin families. The obsession with *limpieza de sangre* became a way of isolating members of society. Once the *moriscos* had been expelled, this became a highly effective way of continuing to punish invented enemies from an increasingly distant and legendary past.

The legacy of the doctrine of purity of blood for Iberian society remains controversial. But holding the almost 800 carefully handwritten pages of the purity investigations of Antonio the Younger in one's hands, it is clear that this was an idea, a mania, which came to obsess individuals and the social kaleidoscope of which they were a part. Under this doctrine, children paid for the sins of their fathers in this generation, the next and the next. Not for nothing have some historians seen *limpieza de sangre* as the seed of the modern idea of racism.[5]

WHAT WAS THE MENTALITY from which these ideas sprang? Iberia in the 15th century feels under siege: towns are barricaded within their walls; the streets are narrow and closed off to all but a sliver of blue sky above. From the urban strongholds the world beyond is unseen. This world has been won from the Muslim enemy only after years of struggle and loss. The yellowing countryside is a zone of fear.

The resident of 15th-century Iberia asks: How can these fears of ours be managed before they destroy us? The answer is to project them onto others. Rationalizations of these fears look for qualities which separate and qualities which unite. Those *conversos* are different because of their Jewish forebears, their bloodline. Thus a race is invented where this faith had always been a religion, where the great Jewish sage born in medieval Iberia, Maimonides, had once written that people of all nations were able to be Jews.[6] A pathology of race is devised – something which modern scientists tell us does not exist, even though we must all behave as if it does.[7] And it is precisely because this is an irrational pathology that it has the capacity to endure for so long.

The idea of purity of blood had emerged during the riots against the *conversos* in Toledo in 1449. In those febrile days the *conversos* were accused by the ringleader of the violence, Pero de Sarmiento, of maintaining Jewish rites and of oppressing Christians. Thenceforth in Toledo no one was to be able to hold public office if they could not prove their cleanliness of blood – that is, an absence of Jewish ancestry.* Thus it was that the religious failings of the *conversos* were first carried over into a racialist doctrine.[8]

That this idea of inherent racial impurity was radically new is shown by the fact that the Toledano statute of purity of blood was attacked at once. Pope Nicholas V issued a bull in 1451 condemning the statute and ordering that all genuine Christians, whether descended from Gentiles or Jews, be allowed to hold official posts.[9] The bishop of Cuenca, Lope de Barrientos, wrote a condemnation and several important theologians issued rebuttals of the principles of the statute.[10] The reality was that, as one leading scholar has put it, the statute of Toledo was 'squarely opposed to religious concepts which had dominated Christian thinking for centuries'.[11]

Yet all the same the idea managed to gain a toehold from which it could expand over the coming centuries. Pope Nicholas V's bull was ignored. In 1473 the Old Christians of Cordoba formed a brotherhood banning those of 'impure' lineage.[12] In 1482 the stonemasons of Toledo banned the discussion of trade secrets with any *conversos*, and the town of Guipúzcoa banned *conversos* from living and marrying among them.[13]

Soon, the toehold had become a foothold. In 1486 a statute of purity was adopted by the Jeronymite religious order.[14] In 1489 the Dominicans followed suit. So, in 1525, did the Franciscans.[15] Then in 1547 the archbishop of Toledo, Juan Martínez Silíceo, pushed through a statute barring all *conversos* from membership of the council of Toledo's cathedral. This was highly controversial and provoked condemnations from the University of Alcalá and the archdeacons of Guadalajara and Talavera. It was initially resisted by

---

* See pages 25–27.

Philip II – then regent, not king of Spain – but in 1555 a statute was passed confirming purity of blood as essential for entry to any office in Spain, and the following year the statute of Toledo's cathedral was confirmed.[16]

It is worth pausing, amid this headlong rush towards a pathology, to consider the language with which these statutes were introduced. In his enthusiastic championing of the statute in Toledo's cathedral Archbishop Silíceo compared *conversos* to horses:

> If the horse trader is offered an imperfect horse, even as a gift, he won't accept it in his herd, because what is most important to him is the race of the animal. This is his principal preoccupation, even if he thinks that the horse is of a noble race. However, when one deals with the dark race of the *conversos*, there are those who wish to admit them into the best posts of the Church even when their lips are still wet with the perversions of their ancestors.[17]

Here are some of the characteristic tactics of modern racism, which first began to develop in the 16th century along with the Atlantic slave trade.[18] There is the dehumanization of the *conversos* by associating them with animals, and the idea of an innate flaw in their make-up which can be transmitted from generation to generation.[19] Thus had the end of tolerance which had accompanied the rise of the Inquisition also helped to usher in a new form of intolerance.

As we can see, prejudice based on racial notions developed rapidly in Spain alongside the rise of the Inquisition in the late 15th century. This was no coincidence. While the Inquisition attempted to prove the incompatibility of *conversos* with the Christian religion, the racialist statutes of purity represented an attempt to show the incompatibility of the *conversos* with the emerging Spanish nation. These were different and mutually contradictory projects, since religion had never had anything to do with race. Yet this would not prevent the Inquisition from adopting the new discriminatory doctrine.

By the end of the 16th century the statutes had touched every aspect of life in Spain. The last religious order to impose a statute of purity was the Jesuits, who delayed until 1593.[20] This tardiness occurred because many key figures in the early history of the order were themselves *conversos*, including the second Jesuit general, Diego Laínez.[21] Yet when in 1622 the Italian Jesuit Francesco Sacchini wrote a history of the order and mentioned Laínez's Jewish ancestry, he was staggered to find opposition in Spain. The Jesuits demanded the removal of the offending paragraph. Why was it, Sacchini wrote, that descent from Jews was a stain only in Spain?[22]

As this example shows, over the phenomenon's long history the concern with purity of blood was to remain purely Iberian and had nothing to do with Catholicism. The Inquisition's adoption of some of the policies and language of this ideology in Portugal and Spain was therefore, fundamentally in contravention of Catholic doctrine. It was proof, again, that these were institutions whose persecution originated in political and social forces and not in the religious ideals of the Catholic Church.[23]

So, although from a theological perspective the Inquisition ought to have had no truck with the idea of purity of blood, the institution did not see it like that. After its inauguration in Spain in the 1480s the Inquisition encouraged the ideal of purity by excluding from public office and individual authority anyone who had been condemned as a *converso*.[24] In the 16th and 17th centuries the Inquisitions of Portugal and Spain were the key public institutions consolidating the concept of purity of blood.[25] When in 1586 the Jesuits had still not instituted their statute of purity, Inquisitors Pablo Hernández and Doctor Salcedo wrote to the Jesuit General Claudio Acquaviva to express their disquiet at the number of *conversos* in the order.[26]

The pivotal role of the Inquisition in propagating the idea of purity by this time is revealed by the trial records of Toledo. Thus in 1587 alone the tribunal of Toledo convicted eight people for falsifying genealogical information in inquiries on purity of blood.[27] In one of these cases the archives of the Inquisition were used to prove that the lawyer Antonio de Olvera was the great-grandson of someone who had been reconciled by the Inquisition in Toledo. In another Gerónimo de Villareal, who was trying to place his daughter in a convent where there was a requirement of purity of blood, was found to be the great-great grandson of four people who had been 'relaxed'.[28]

Thus while it had not been the Inquisition which had imposed the idea of purity at first, it was quick to adopt it and profit from it.[29] Here, in these cases from Toledo, we see another reason why the Inquisition was so hated and feared. Even distant descendants of penitents were barred simply from trying to enter convents (and be good Christians), or from becoming public notaries.[30] Moreover, as the generations passed and family connections grew ever more complex, so did the possibility of the discovery of some tenuous connection with an earlier heretic. There was no one who could be sure that they could not be ruined by an inquiry into their purity of blood.

The Inquisitions of both Portugal and Spain were central in the fostering of this social condition. On 3 February 1548 Cardinal Henry, brother of John III and the first inquisitor-general of Portugal, wrote a letter in which he cited St Paul's dictum, '*Modicum fermenti totam massam corrumpit*' – A tiny drop can corrupt the whole – and, wrote Henry, this would be enough not only 'to corrupt the *conversos* . . . but also many of the Old Christians'.[31] The same quotation would be cited in a book on purity of blood written by Juan Escobar de Corro in 1632.[32] That such ideas had themselves thoroughly stained the inquisitorial hierarchy was revealed by a letter of the Spanish inquisitor-general Gaspar de Quiroga dated 1577, in which he cited the adage '*Commixti sont inter gentes, et didicerunt opera ejus*' – If people are mixed their works collapse[33] – a view which in itself reveals the hypocrisy and self-deception of the doctrine since Quiroga himself probably had *converso* great-grandparents.[34]

The feelings of the Church hierarchy rapidly became those of the wider population. A Portuguese saying of the 17th century had it that 'Blood without guilt is enough, and guilt itself is in the blood'.[35] This obsession with the sins of past generations was not merely an early manifestation of modern racist mentality,[36] it also symbolized a coming psychological crisis in Iberian society. A disproportionate obsession with purity is seen by some as symptomatic of dangerous psychological or social conflicts.[37] The desire was to wash out bloodstains which had become invisible to all but those who were unable to forget them, and their own guilt in their creation.

*

WHILE PSYCHOLOGICALLY Iberian society was proud to think of itself as becoming cleaner and cleaner, physically the reality was somewhat different. From Madrid to Lisbon and Murcia to Coimbra, in order to be known as a good Catholic it was important to stink.

One witness gave a detailed description of the Islamic conduct of the *morisca* Maria de Mendoza in the region of Cuenca:

> One workday, after the evening mealtime, this witness saw the said Maria de Mendoça collect a pitcher of water from the fountain in the orchard . . . and take it up to the highest rooms in the house near the chimneypots, since that day they had prepared jams up there and left a lantern. And after seeing her carry up this pitcher of water, about an hour later this witness went up to the space near the chimneypots and found the door of the room closed; thereupon the witness opened it and put their head round the door and saw that the said Maria was as stark naked as her mother had been the day she was born, and that she was barefoot even though it was summertime, in June or July, and that she was kneeling down and washing her hair.[38]

One may read this passage many times, struggling to locate the heresy, unless one knows that, incredible as it seems today, washing was indeed seen as heretical. In a society governed by doctrines of purity, *moriscos* were frequently denounced for washing. This was seen as suspicious because of the ritual ablutions prescribed by the Islamic faith. When challenged their defence was that they had 'only' been cleaning themselves.[39]

Ablutions and simple bodily cleanliness rapidly became indistinguishable; one could not, after all, smell the difference. A *morisco* of Granada, Bermúdez de Pedraza, was denounced for washing 'even though it was December'.[40] In Valencia in 1603 the *morisco* Francisco Mançana confessed to having moistened a piece of cloth and washed his face, neck and genitals with it, but denied that this was a ceremony.[41] The extent of Iberia's stench was revealed by the denunciation of a scandalized Old Christian of San Clemente near Cuenca, who recounted how 'it was not only the *morisco* custom to wash themselves when they got married and when they died but also many times during the year'.[42] One must of course recall that washing was a much rarer phenomenon in 16th century Europe than it is today, but even then the consequences of such views of cleanliness were unusually fetid.

Thus the emphasis on purity, on cleanliness of blood, was purely metaphorical. Its status as an irrational obsession is surely revealed by this curious dichotomy between an ideology of cleanliness and the pong of reality. The fear of genuine cleanliness – and perhaps the unconscious awareness that the ideal was a fantasy – was perfectly expressed by the horror of washing and by the fact that this extended to the smallest social gesture. The French cleric Bartolomé Joly noted in the early 17th century that people never washed their hands in Spain before eating.[43]

Just as the heresies of its *converso* and *morisco* enemies had been largely invented, so of course was this myth of the impurity of their blood. It was in fact precisely in the 16th century, after most *conversos* had disappeared from Spain, that the obsession with impurity exploded.[44] For a time it found expression also through concerns with the *moriscos*, with the children of *moriscos* and Old Christians treated as impure.[45] But after the expulsion of the *moriscos*, the persecution of impure blood was increasingly the persecution of something that, like the windmills of Don Quixote, existed only in a fevered imagination.

AS THIS HOSTILITY towards bodily cleanliness shows, there are many different types and styles of purity. For some *moriscos* the Old Christian concept of purity probably seemed strange, given the emphasis of the Islamic faith on ritual ablutions. And while in Spain pathologies concerning purity of blood were directed at both the Jewish and the Muslim 'stain', in Portugal it was just the descendants of the *conversos* who were associated with impurity. Unlike Spain, Portugal had never had a *morisco* 'problem'. This, combined with the later onslaught of the Inquisition, meant that the *conversos* remained there the target of both the Portuguese Inquisition and of the new racialist doctrines.

This important difference between Portugal and Spain was a source of tension, since in 1580 Philip II of Spain had assumed the crown of Portugal as well; such was the inbreeding among the Iberian royal families that he was the next in line to the throne.[46] Between 1580 and 1640 Portugal and Spain were ruled by what was known as the dual monarchy, although Spain always had the upper hand. The fact that the Portuguese Inquisition was still dealing with the *conversos* meant that the Portuguese became stereotyped in Spain as Jews. As the saying had it, 'The Portuguese was born of the Jew's fart'.[47] This meant that in Portugal the Inquisition became increasingly concerned with ridding itself of this image, and thus with preserving the purity of the Old Christian population.

By the early 17th century, as in Spain, notions of purity had run through Portuguese society like a virus. In 1604, Portugal's *conversos* had bought a general pardon for any religious failings, but this would only prove a temporary respite and did not lessen their marginalization. While in the late 1580s there had still been attempts by *conversos* to prevent statutes of purity from becoming generalized, by 1630 those who were 'unclean' had been officially barred from academic life, judicial and treasury posts, and the religious and military orders.[48]

In Portugal, however, *conversos* were less easy to bar from positions of social prestige than they had been in Spain. They represented an important part of the urban and educated population, and the administration could not function efficiently without them. As over the installation of the Inquisition in Brazil, the Portuguese crown practised realpolitik. Thus in spite of royal decrees passed six times between 1600 and 1640 barring them from public service, 'people of the Hebrew nation' were constantly turning up in the most influential of positions.[49]

So the language of exclusion was pushed further. In 1640, in a published code of inquisitorial practice, the Portuguese Inquisition demanded that its officials be of pure blood.[50] Just as in Spain, paranoia spread with the idea of impurity. Anyone with a drop of impure blood was now seen as a New rather than an Old Christian. One inquisitorial document of 1624 referred to 200,000 New Christian families in Portugal, whereas in fact there were only 6,000 New Christians left in the whole country whose ancestors had not intermarried with Old Christians.[51] At a council in Tomar in 1628 it was even suggested that the *conversos* of Portugal, like the *moriscos* before them in Spain, should be expelled.[52]

The obsession with purity of blood was not something that would disappear easily from Portuguese society. If one walks through the streets of downtown Lisbon today, it comes across as one of the most cosmopolitan cities in Europe, with the streets off the great Rossio and the trams to and from Belén filled with immigrants from Brazil and Portugal's former colonies in Africa. Yet in the Portuguese empire in Africa in the 20th century the residues of these ideas of purity had lived on, and those with lighter ('purer') skins advanced more quickly up the ranks in the colonies of Cape Verde and Guinea-Bissau.

If you were to have walked down the streets of Lisbon back in the late 16th and early 17th centuries, when the spread of the ideology of purity began, it would have appeared a very different place. People were not allowed to move from one parish to another in the city without the approval of the local priest.[53] There were frequent shortages of bread and meat. Lack of fresh water was a constant problem.[54] Fantasists bandied wild superstitions about the place; in 1579, shortly after the death of King Sebastian in Morocco, one visionary declared that he would be reborn as a star in the night sky.[55] Royal decrees were shouted by town criers from various points throughout the city.[56] On the days of the grand autos, people ran to the streets where the *conversos* lived and stoned their houses.[57]

It was in such circumstances of publicly tolerated violence directed at a minority community that persecution and the neurotic idea of cleanliness flourished. Inquisitorial documents began to note down whether a witness or defendant was a half, a quarter, an eighth or even a sixteenth *converso*.[58] In Goa in 1632 the inquisitorial familiar Francisco Pereira was prevented from marrying because his fiancée had Moorish blood;[59] this followed the passing of a law in Portugal three years earlier which limited the dowries of *converso* brides in an attempt to discourage mixed marriages between Old and New Christians.[60] All this was accompanied by the severest persecutions of *conversos* by the Inquisition yet. There were so many trials in the district of Coimbra in the early 1620s that in some towns every single *converso* was arrested.[61] Further south, the region around Beja was also devastated; eight people were burnt there in 1619 alone,[62] while 240 more were 'relaxed' across Portugal between 1620 and 1640 and almost 5,000 were tried.[63]

The Inquisition's interest in purity of blood and its targeting of the minority were therefore two sides of the same coin. Persecution tended to precede this guilt complex of purity. Yet as the numbers of genuine members of the minority groups fell, persecution would return to haunt the descendants of the very people who had applauded it when it had begun, those who were tainted merely in one-quarter, one-eighth or one-sixteenth of their bloodline.

Cartagena de las Indias 1664

On 11 April 1664 an investigation of purity of blood was launched by the tribunal of the Inquisition in Cartagena de las Indias. It was a legal obligation for all the functionaries of the Inquisition to provide proof of their purity. Yet this investigation by the Colombian tribunal was not into some petitioner for an inquisitorial post, but into the lineage of a certain Ana Salgado de Castro who merely wanted to marry Joseph Deza Calderón, the notary of the Inquisition of Cartagena.[64]

Salgado de Castro's family was not, it transpired, one to which inquisitorial jurisprudence was unknown. Her father had been a familiar of the Inquisition in Cartagena, and in order to secure this post inquiries into his ancestry had been made in his home territory of Bayonne – in modern south-west France. Further inquiries had had to be made by the inquisitorial tribunals of Cordoba, Galicia, Seville and Toledo. Each of these inquiries had required separate investigations made in villages of the relevant district, a process which often took years. While Seville had returned its inquiry to the *Suprema* on 10 September 1647, the information from Galicia had not been received until six years later, on 29 October 1653.

Moreover, this was not the only bureaucratic exercise which Ana Salgado de Castro's family had precipitated. Her maternal uncle had also been a familiar of the Inquisition in Cartagena, and so had also had to prove his purity of blood. This had merely required investigation in three inquisitorial districts, Cordoba, Seville and Toledo. Bearing in mind the enormous distance which separates Colombia from Spain and the many months which were required for communications to cross the Atlantic, attempting to prove the purity of one's ancestry was an endeavour which could – as Antonio de Costa the Elder had found even in the parochial environment of Cinctorres – consume a lifetime.

Given that Ana Salgado de Castro's lineage had already been shown to be pure in both her father's and her mother's branches of the family, one might have thought that no further paperwork would be necessary for her merely to marry an official of the Inquisition. This would have been the rational view. But the Inquisition in Portugal and Spain and in their colonies was an organization which imposed a veneer of rationality upon irrational passions. The investigation into Salgado de Castro's ancestry proceeded implacably. A list of thirteen questions was compiled by the tribunal of Cartagena to be put to witnesses in the districts of Galicia and Seville. Years passed. The whole sorry process had to be revisited again and again if the stains were to be well and truly wrung out, even somewhere as distant from the heart of empire as Cartagena.

By the middle of the 17th century, then, as the use of torture declined in dungeons of inquisitorial jails, it was sublimated in the paperwork which every citizen required to confirm the honour of their lineage. The investigation of one's ancestry by a clutch of inquisitorial tribunals had become completely normal. When the grandiloquently named Alonso de Medina Merina y Cortés attempted to become a familiar of the Inquisition in Cartagena de las Indias in 1662 investigations were made in Llerena, Seville and Toledo.[65] And when Alonso Sánchez Espinosa y Luna applied to be a familiar in Quito in 1670 the purity of both he and his wife Feliciana had to be investigated in the regions of Valladolid and Toledo, and the whole process took a staggering eighteen years.[66]

The records of this last case betray one of the main reasons both for the growing mania of the Inquisition for purity of blood and why such investigations took so long. After keeping him waiting for eighteen years the inquisitors trespassed further on the patience of Sánchez Espinosa y Luna. He was expected to pay for the tribunal's ink and paper. Purity of blood was, it turned out, a neat mechanism for ensuring the purity of the finances of the Inquisition.

Mexico 1709

At the height of the War of the Spanish Succession, as Britain, France and the Netherlands fought over the corpse of Spanish imperialism and ambition, the friar Antonio Medrano applied to be a *calificador* of the Inquisition in Mexico – one of the people who assessed the orthodoxy of published books and whether or not they ought to be censored by the Inquisition.

The itemized bill which Medrano had to pay following the requisite investigation into his purity of blood included the following:

- Paying for the letter received in Mexico from the *Suprema* with communications about his genealogy.
- Paying for a letter from the district of Cuenca, in Spain, regarding his genealogy.
- Paying for the official deed which was written to confirm his genealogy.
- Paying for the costs of making a copy of the trial regarding his purity.
- Paying for the time and work of officials in the town of Villarobledo in La Mancha for inquiring into his ancestry.
- Paying for the work of the inquisitorial notary in exhaustively compiling all of this information.
- Paying for the costs of the Inquisition's paper.

And, most cunningly of all:

- Paying for the costs of calculating the bill which was issued when the whole process was completed.[67]

Such itemized bills were commonplace in these investigations. They reveal the methodical processes of the Inquisition. For example there was a charge per witness interrogated by an inquisitorial official in these proofs of purity (in 1629 it was four *reales*[68]). Of course, for the people mired in this belief system such procedures were standard practice and entirely normal. The very fact that from an external standpoint they seem insane reveals that no amount of internal coherency in a belief system can make it objectively true or valid.

Just as some modern law firms derive great profits from their photocopying charges, so the Inquisition could pay a substantial part of its day-to-day costs by fostering this ideology of purity. *Probanzas* of purity – as they were known – continued long into the 18th century[69] and were a crucial source of the Inquisition's financial stability, although eventually they did begin to decline in importance.[70]

This is of course a different thing from saying that the Inquisition was entirely motivated by greed.[71] As passion can so often get the better of cold rationality, the Inquisition was frequently in economic difficulties. After the expulsion of the *moriscos*, one of its main sources of funds in Aragon and Valencia – confiscations and the tax paid by *moriscos* to the Inquisition – evaporated. In general the Inquisition, as an organ of the state, suffered the same economic vicissitudes as the Spanish crown.[72] As decline set in during the 17th century, new sources of income were required, such as charges for increasingly complex investigations of purity.

The problem was that this meant that the Inquisition now sustained itself through meaningless bureaucratic exercises. Although there were various attempts to reform the system, these were stymied. Thus Philip II died before he could implement his idea of only investigating the past hundred years of a person's ancestry, which was mooted in a panel of inquiry which first convened in 1596.[73] A reform of 1623 begun by Philip IV was however accepted: this held that after three positive inquiries no further investigations should be permitted,[74] but sixteen years later he had to reiterate the terms of this condition to the Inquisition.[75] Attempts to ease purity requirements were ignored by the Inquisition, as is revealed by Philip IV's letter to the *Suprema* in 1627 in which he repeated the conditions of 1623 and added that he wanted them to be 'executed and complied with as they are written, and without your own interpretations'.[76]

The way in which the idea of purity had come to dominate the institution was shown when in 1633 Philip IV ordered the Council of the Inquisition to create two courts: one for its affairs and another simply for the handling of proofs of genealogy.[77] The effect of inquiries into bloodlines had been summarized in Philip IV's letter to the *Suprema* of 1627, where he reminded the officials that 'the best interests of God and my person consist in acting justly, and remedying the costs, annoyances and vexations of my vassals, so that you should look for ways of obtaining information in places which do not foment enmities, factions and force the perjury of witnesses'.[78]

A chasm was yawning in front of Spanish society, and yet it pressed blindly on, proving the purity of what could not be proven. People argued over who was or was not clean but it all came down to influence, rumour, bitterness. Far from ensuring the integrity of society, the obsession with purity of blood had merely begun the process of dividing it. This would, in the long run, have terrible consequences.

Lima 1675

Concerns have been raised concerning the purity of the ancestry of a certain Andrés de Angulo, applicant for a post in the Inquisition. Extremely serious discoveries have been made regarding his ancestry. Is it not the case that the great-great-great-great-grandfather of Angulo, Fernando Alonsso, was 'relaxed' by the Inquisition? Was not the heretic Alonsso nothing less than the great-great-grandfather of Angulo's grandmother? To put it plainly, Angulo is the 'grandson of Maria de Nalda Garçon . . . who was the daughter of Pedro de Nalda Garçon, and of Isavvel Martinez de Avenzana and Francisca Gonzalez de Higuera whose parents were Sancho Martinez de Avenzana and Catalina Martinez . . .'[79]

Plain speaking he may not have been, but the prosecutor was nothing if not rigorous. In order to prove poor Angulo's lack of purity, he had prised from the Inquisition's archives an extract of the accusation made against Angulo's great-great-great-great grandfather Diego Saenz, and included in his deposition an extraordinarily detailed family tree which can still be read today in the reading room of the Archivo Histórico Nacional, where the genealogies of Angulo's maternal great-grandparents, and of Angulo's grandpaternal great-great grandparents, and of the grandparents and great-uncles and great-aunts of Angulo's great-great grandmother can all be examined in the archive's fastidious quiet by those given to such studies.

Surely it was clear from such a laborious investigation that the said Andrés de Angulo was irreparably stained, entirely unsuited to an official post, and deserving of the severest humiliation? Yet when investigations were made in Lardero, and in Navarrete, and in

Nalda, all witnesses declared the Angulo family to be beyond reproach. The righteous outrage was an invention. The prosecutor's elaborate paper trail was declared a fiction, and Angulo was awarded his coveted post.

While Andrés de Angulo's ancestry was being libelled, in Ciudad Real* Luis de Aguilera, who had applied to be a commissary of the Inquisition, was undergoing a similar experience. In 1669, using his expert knowledge of bloodlines the prosecutor traced Aguilera's ancestry as far back as 1531 to show that he was not pure of blood; to this was appended a decree of the *Reyes Católicos* from the 15th century related to some supposed *converso* ancestors of Aguilera's, the Loazas.[80]

Family trees were examined. One was included in the trial records – which ran to 500 pages merely on the question of this comparatively minor official's ancestry – which proved that seven generations previously one of Aguilera's ancestors had married a woman of *converso* descent. As the prosecutor declared, the failure to declare 'such close' relationships as those of his 'maternal ancestors to the sixth generation' revealed an insupportable impurity.

The case dragged on for ten years. Further inquiries were made in Ciudad Real. Thirty-seven witnesses declared that Aguilera was of pure blood. Eight said that he was not. The Tribunal of the Inquisition of Toledo decided that this was sufficient to bar him from the post, and Aguilera's life was ruined by the poor marriage allegedly made by his great-great-great-great-grandparents.

There was nothing new about such difficulties. Fifty years earlier, in Ronda, the Inquisition investigated the purity of blood of Don Rodrigo de Ovalle from this hilltop town in Andalusia, where just over three centuries later Franco's forces would execute Republicans daily during the Spanish Civil War. The inquisitors had little time to consider the terrible abyss beneath Ronda's crags or the cultivated valleys below. After all, as they said, Rodrigo de Ovalle's lineage would indeed be 'of very bad quality if it derived from Ysavel Hernandez the wife of Hernando Diaz of Toledo, the public notary of royal income [in Seville]'. Was it not the case that the terrible Ysavel Hernandez had been reconciled by the Holy Office

* The first centre, it will be recalled, of inquisitorial activity in Castile – see pages 36–38.

of the Inquisition the small matter of 123 years before, in 1502?[81] Had not her parents Alonso Hernández and Francisca Sánchez been burnt in statute?

Such damage to the nation's purity could not be allowed! Was it not a reminder of the fusion of cultures and peoples which lay at the heart of Spanish society?

A RUNDOWN HOTEL in Buenos Aires in 1996: the ageing receptionist embarks upon a political discussion. The good thing about the rule of Pinochet in Chile was that he tidied up the country, getting rid of the rabble-rousers and the no-good do-gooders: *limpió* – he cleaned it up. It is a shame that the military rulers of Argentina had not shown similar skills in *limpieza*.

The idea of cleanliness had become a form of purging. In 20th-century South Africa schoolchildren had combs passed through their hair to check for any curls which might betray African ancestors.[82] In the southern United States in the 19th century, in that region so close to the Hispanic influence of Mexico, the 'one-drop' rule marginalized those thought to have any African slave ancestry at all, even if to the naked eye they appeared white.[83] In 17th-century Iberia the evidence of 'one-drop' impurity of Jewish or Muslim ancestors lay in the bowels of the Inquisition's bureaucracy.

Thus did societies learn that the mask of a pure body could be superimposed on an impure soul. Cases of *limpieza* pursue endless chains across the archives of the Inquisition.[84] This is only logical. If the slightest stain going back any number of generations is deemed pernicious, then the greater the number of generations to be checked, the more detailed the investigations must be. The Inquisition was, then, only logical. But its logic was one that strangled with bureaucracy the society which it claimed to be attempting to preserve. The ideology of purity meant that the possibility of heresy did not end with death. Indeed at times even the lineages of dead applicants for official posts were investigated;[85] if purity could be proven it was of benefit to their relatives, while if it could not this was something which every citizen needed to know.

What had begun life as the persecution of one caste, the *conversos*, eventually came to mean that any impurity of ancestry was social death.[86] This was true of heretics and even those whose

Christian faith was unimpeachable and who had only one distant *converso* or *morisco* ancestor. As the distance from the first heretics grew, so did the numbers of those whose lives could be ruined. The way in which all social groups were eventually affected is clear in the petition of Antonio de Costa the Younger of Cinctorres. As the last code of practice for the Inquisition of Goa put it, 'mere imprisonment in the inquisitorial jail for any crime whatsoever has come to imply an ineradicable infamy on the person of the imprisoned and on their descendants, even after fulfilling the punishment and penance imposed'.[87]

Portugal and Spain were of course not unique in their approach to people they considered impure. As the anthropologist Mary Douglas has shown, every society has its ideas about what is or is not clean, and develops techniques for dealing with what it perceives as anomalous. Yet at the same time one of the signs of a healthy society is the failure of such ideas to dominate. Where cleanliness is the principal obsession, neurosis may follow.[88] Pity breaks through. For do not the audience of *Macbeth* feel a stab of compassion for the madness of the cursed king's wife, condemned to an eternity of guilt as she washes out stains which are for her eyes only?

Chapter Nine

EVERY ASPECT OF LIFE

. . . they are observed in their works and their ways of life with such attention that, even if they prevaricate in the smallest Christian rite, they are seen as suspicious of heresy and punished . . .

IN THIS CURIOUS story of violence and fetid emotion, the most obvious questions of all can be difficult to answer. We have just explored a series of protracted inquiries in small villages as to the ancestry of minor officials. In such cases how could inquisitors know that the information they received was accurate? The answer must be through the trust they had in the capacity of villagers to keep watch on one another and to know intimate details of one another's distant ancestry – or at least pretend to know such details. Iberia had become a society of spies.

For a moment, turn back to the messianic ambience of the Carvajal household in Mexico City in the 1590s. Here was a house in the Indian neighbourhood of Tlatelolco where fear had for a time been defeated by longing. After Luis the Younger's reconciliation in 1590, they were inspected by a Franciscan friar, Pedro de Oroz, who noted with approval the religious images which the Carvajals had placed in their home as evidence of their sincere attachment to the Catholic Church.*

Yet not all of the neighbours of the Carvajals were as convinced. One was a Portuguese woman called Susan Galván.[1] Galván was fifty years old and, one can surmise, bored with her lot. She liked nothing better than to meddle in the affairs of others and then

* See page 161.

gossip as to what she had found. To have a family of reconciled heretics living nearby was therefore a welcome distraction.

Galván soon befriended the Carvajals' servant, a Chichimec Indian from the northern Mexican deserts. She asked her what the Carvajals drank and what they ate. She was told that none of the them ate pork or bacon, and that they used olive oil or butter rather than lard when they cooked. These practices were seen in Iberian societies as proof that a person or family was not a Catholic but a crypto-Jew or a crypto-Muslim, neither faith permitting the eating of pork. Excited by this information, Galván nosed her way into the kitchen of the Carvajal household so that she could see with her own eyes what sort of fat was used to grease the saucepans.

When the second trial of family members began, Galván gave evidence. She declared that she had always suspected that the Carvajals still lived as Jews. On top of her culinary evidence, she had been told by the Chichimec servant that the Carvajals dressed in clean clothes on Friday nights, and that they wore their best clothes on Saturdays as if it were a festival. Indeed, one Saturday had Galván herself not seen Luis the Younger's sister Leonor sitting on a cushion doing nothing, wearing a dress of black velvet? When she had seen this idleness on an ordinary workday – which just happened to be the Jewish sabbath – Galván had been suitably scandalized, her thrill disguised by a mask of moral censure.

Reading through the case records, it becomes plain that Galván spent much of her time acting as an unpaid spy for the Inquisition. She noted the sort of clothes that the Carvajals wore and the days on which they wore them. She pried into their cooking arrangements. Thus, for the bored, the gossips and the acid-tongued, the Inquisition provided a notable social service: it was now not only legitimate to watch one's neighbours, it was a social duty, as the edicts of grace, with their admonitions for citizens to report anything that seemed contrary to the faith, made clear.

The way in which every aspect of life was affected in Mexico was summed up just a few years after the auto of 1596 in which Luis the Younger and his sisters Isabel and Leonor had died. In 1604 Antonia Machado, the granddaughter of a *relajado*, was prosecuted for wearing silk clothes with a golden fringe,[2] something forbidden to someone with this sort of blood tie to a convicted heretic.* One can imagine the righteous scandal as this was observed in the whitewashed streets of Mexico, which were kept clean by African slaves and what remained of the Aztec population after the epidemics: one was not shocked by the genocide where up to 95 per cent of the indigenous population had been lost in the preceding century;[3] nor by the scarred faces of those Indians who had survived the disease; nor by the torture in the mines and the slavery of the miners – no, one was disgusted, affronted and scandalized by this descendant of a *relajado* having the temerity to wear silk!

It is difficult to maintain a sense of proportion. By focusing on one or two minor anomalies, bigger anomalies and evils could be overlooked. The Inquisition, defining conformity in religious terms as always, was keen to prosecute all religious deviants. Yet at the same time conformity and normality were increasingly defined in racial terms; thus the descendants of deviants had to be punished as well.

These twin vectors of marginalization were ideologically incompatible, and revealed the contradiction in Iberian psychology between a conservative and almost medieval world view, which concentrated on religious deviance, and the emerging modern world view which saw differences in racial terms. But, as we have seen, the Inquisition was able to straddle these two positions. The extraordinary adaptability of the persecuting mentality meant that it was able to switch horses with all the panache and killer instinct of a champion jockey offered a prize ride. Yet concern with conformity could only thrive if some groups could be shown to be nonconformist. Thus, as the 16th century turned into the 17th and the obsession with purity intensified, every aspect of daily life was chewed over in the search for what was deemed abnormal.

WHILE THESE PARTICULAR Mexican cases concerned details of daily life such as those which preoccupied the Inquisition in Portugal and Spain, in general the Inquisition in the overseas colonies was most concerned with imposing a different type of conformity: the acceptance of broader European ideals.

---

* See page 228.

For the Portuguese Inquisition in Goa and Africa, failure to wear Portuguese-style of clothing was enough for people to be prosecuted. In 1585 the General Council of the Inquisition in Portugal ordered the inquisitors in Goa to 'proceed against Christians who live in the land of the infidels and dress in the manner of the infidels as if they were apostates and separated from our Holy Faith, even if there is no proof of them performing the rites and ceremonies of the infidels' – the proof of apostasy resided in their 'adopting their style of dress, which is different to that of the Christians'.[4] Then in 1619 Manoel da Silva was thrown into jail in the town of Cacheu in modern Guinea-Bissau under inquisitorial law. The sole evidence against Silva was that, although he claimed to be a Christian, he had been observed in the town of Buguendo* and in neighbouring Bichangor† dressed 'like a local black' in a *boubou* (kaftan) and with rings through his nostrils. Da Silva, who had been born in Malacca, was sent from Cacheu to the jail in Ribeira Grande in Cape Verde, where the future governor of Nuevo León Luis de Carvajal had once lived, and was then deported to Angola.[5]

Clearly such accusations could only occur if the members of a society were encouraged to watch out for this sort of thing, even in places as distant from Portugal as Goa and Guinea-Bissau. While Portuguese authority waned significantly in the *Estado da Índia* in the latter 17th century[6] – as Portugal fought its long war of independence against Spain between 1640 and 1668 – the power of the Inquisition there remained significant. One of the main crimes it tried in Goa, particularly from the mid-17th century onwards, was the 'sorcery' of crypto-Hindus who were supposed to have converted to Christianity. Successfully identifying this crime required detailed observation of daily life to pick up on heretical practices. This was the territory in which, as the French traveller Pyrard de Laval had written in 1619, the Inquisition was 'much more severe than in Portugal'.[7]

In Brazil, as in Goa, the Portuguese Inquisition was particularly concerned with sorcery. Denunciations of superstitious practices

* It was here that the provocative farce performed by Mestre Diogo, and witnessed by Luis de Carvajal's uncle Francisco Jorge, had been performed in 1562. See above, page 199.

† The modern town of Ziguinchor, in the Casamance region of southern Senegal.

again required detailed observation of behaviour. They became particularly common in the early 18th century, when a common charm found in Brazil was the *bolsa de mandinga*. These bags often contained pieces of marble, or six-pointed stars, or pieces of paper covered with Kabbalistic signs. They were highly prized by those who carried them and were said to protect the wearer against injury by knives or bullets.[8] They were also used by Brazilian slaves living in Lisbon, and three inquisitorial cases centred on them in 1730–1.[9]

There was an extraordinary degree of superstition and non-Catholic practice in the patchwork world of the colonies. In Brazil in the early 18th century one African slave, Joana, used to lace the food of men she desired with the second batch of water with which she had washed her vagina.[10] Another slave, Marcelina Maria, cooked an egg, slept with it between her legs and gave it to the man that she desired; she had also been taught that when she had sex with a man she should wet her finger in her vagina and then make the sign of the cross upon each of her eyes so that the man would never leave her.[11] In Mexico powders were ground up by slave women and thrown over men so that they would desire them; some carried earth taken from a graveyard and others special herbs, all intended to achieve the same end of sex with a desired man.[12] In Brazil slaves were sent to touch objects of desire with charms so that they would fall under the sway of the slave's master or mistress.[13] There was no shortage of obsession with sex, superstition about sex and attempts to induce others to have sex; in this atmosphere and in the sultry afternoons of the tropics one suspects that, in spite of the best efforts of the Inquisition, there was no shortage of actual sex either.

Such, then, was the 'tropic of sins', as one scholar has put it,[14] a world alien to the climate, ideologies and social requirements of Iberia. Many of those whose lives and approaches to reality were picked over in such detail by the Inquisition were slaves who had been brought to the New World from Africa and had maintained some of their ancestral beliefs.[15] Yet although this meant that slaves were therefore subjected to inquisitorial attention, it is not a little solace that they themselves often became quite adept at using the Inquisition in their own interests.

Cartagena de las Indias 1648–50

IN 1648, THE SLAVE Manuel Bran* was arrested in Cartagena de las Indias, accused of spitting on crosses and denying the existence of God.[16] When one considers his life history, this attitude towards the religious faith of his oppressors is hardly surprising.

Manuel had been born in Cape Verde and went as a babe in arms along with his mother who was taken to be a slave in the Azores. In the Azores he served as a page to an archdeacon, cultivating his master's vines and doing whatever was asked of him. When he grew into adulthood he married a Spaniard called Leonor de Sossa, a servant of his master, and had a child with her. The child died at the age of four. Then his master the archdeacon ordered him to sail in the service of the brothers Don Diego de Lobo and Don Rodrigo de Lobo. They took him to Brazil and then to Cartagena, where Rodrigo de Lobo sold him as a slave. He never saw his wife again.[17]

In such circumstances the hostility of slaves towards the religion of their masters is no surprise. The hierarchy of values was expressed by one case from Brazil, in 1737, where the plantation owner Pedro Pais Machado killed two slaves for allegedly injuring one of his oxen; one of the slaves was murdered by being hung by his testicles until he was dead.[18] Only a few years later one of the wealthiest residents of Bahia in Brazil, Garcia de Avila Pereira Aragão, had a three-year-old slave girl brought to him, and held her face over a fire of hot coals. He then fanned the fire with his other hand. Aragão also tortured a six-year-old slave boy by dripping hot candle wax on him, laughing with glee as the boy screamed in pain.[19]

Such pornographic details exploit the tragedies of these human beings, who were exploited enough in life. But if these cases help us to grasp something of the impossible ocean of desire and the insatiable demand for satisfaction opened up by the power relations within the New World, thinking about them today may not be

* In the Iberian colonies of Africa and Latin America, slaves usually took the surname of their ethnicity, Bran being then a common term for an ethnic group found in modern Guinea-Bissau.

entirely lacking in merit. What we glimpse in these terrible sadists are, perhaps, emotions analogous to those which we have seen in some of the most lubricious inquisitors, the Luceros and Salazars and Mañozcas of the world.

In such an environment one is heartened that slaves often renounced God when they were being whipped, or put in fetters;[20] their real meaning was, of course, 'I renounce *your* God'. This was not only an expression of rebellion but also a means of escape; if the blasphemy was reported to the Inquisition, they might be incarcerated in the inquisitorial jail for a year or more and thereby escape further beatings at the hands of their masters. Some fabricated visions and pacts with the devil and then, once in the inquisitorial jail, confessed that their masters had treated them so badly that they preferred to be prisoners of the Inquisition.[21] In 1650 in Mexico the slave Juan de Morga decided to take his chances. He blasphemed at the drop of a hat, accused himself of bigamy and then declared that he had entered into a demonic pact; Morga finished his confession by explaining, 'I serve a very cruel man in [the mining centre of] Zacatecas, and as long as they keep me here I shall continue to live by this law and to deny God'.[22]

The fact that the Inquisition was a better option for many slaves than their daily life says much about the horror of their existence in the New World. Yet one should not conclude that the Inquisition was therefore entirely benign towards them. The Inquisition was charged with handling the mistreatment of slaves in Mexico, for instance, but although this was a daily occurrence only three cases were brought between 1570 and 1620.[23] The 'deviant' cultural practices of slaves were moreover part of a panoply of difference which was anathema to an institution like the Inquisition, which desired – or pretended to desire – uniformity of practice and belief. Such were the realities and the different peoples in the colonies that the Inquisition was always fighting a losing battle there. It was only by being vigilant over so many aspects of slaves' daily lives and devilish predilections that a modicum of 'normality' could be imposed.

Tomás de Torquemada, the first inquisitor-general of Spain, who presided over the expansion of the Spanish Inquisition and developed rules stigmatizing the descendants of heretics.

The Castle of Triana, headquarters of the Inquisition in Seville. When the first autos-da-fé of the Spanish Inquisition began here in 1481, there were so many prisoners that they would not all fit into the castle.

A Spanish auto-da-fé of the sixteenth century. The prisoners are led out of the city gates into the meadows beyond, where they are transferred to the secular authorities to be burnt (above right).

Right As one of the first inquisitors of Cartagena (Colombia), and later of Lima and Mexico, Juan de Mañozca presided over some of the most violent autos-da-fé in the history of the Inquisition in the Americas.

Below Interrogating a suspect. The Inquisition was an intensely hierarchical institution: note how the chairs of the inquisitors are higher than that of the subject.

The Court of the Inquisition by Francisco Goya. Painted following his career as a court artist,

Goya's dark portraits of the Inquisition are among the most famous visual representations.

Above Torture by the Inquisition. In contrast to this engraving, torturers were usually masked. Often water was poured down the throat of a victim strapped to a hard table or *potro.*

Opposite, top This engraving dates from the early nineteenth century when torture by the Inquisition was a thing of the past. However, such was the success of the propagandists against the Inquisition, and of the Inquisition itself in sewing the idea of its power, that the popular perception was that torture continued.

Opposite, bottom Victims were hoisted into the air using pulleys and let drop a little way during interrogation.

Cardinal Francisco Jiménez de Cisneros. As inquisitor-general of Spain in the early sixteenth century, Cisneros safeguarded the institution after its brutal excesses in Cordoba, under Inquisitor Lucero, had threatened its very survival.

A penitent wearing the *fuego revolto*. These were given to those who had been condemned for execution, but had confessed and accepted Christian communion. They were then garrotted rather than burnt.

Lisbon, c.1553. The Inquisition had been granted full powers in Portugal following papal bulls of 1536 and 1547. At autos-da-fé, stakes were erected along the waterfront (foreground, centre).

Scene of an auto-da-fé on the waterfront in Lisbon, with the royal palace in the background.

The Inquisition in New Spain (Mexico). The first trials led under inquisitorial authority outside Europe occurred in Mexico City in 1528, before spreading throughout Latin America, to Goa and to some Portuguese settlements in Africa, such as Cape Verde, Luanda (Angola) and São Tomé.

Above Standard of the Spanish Inquisition (*left*) and that of the Inquisition of Goa (*right*).

Right Portrait of Sir John Hawkins. Survivors from Hawkins' stricken ship, the *Jesus of Lubeck*, were later convicted as Lutheran heretics, becoming the first victims of the court of the Inquisition in Mexico.

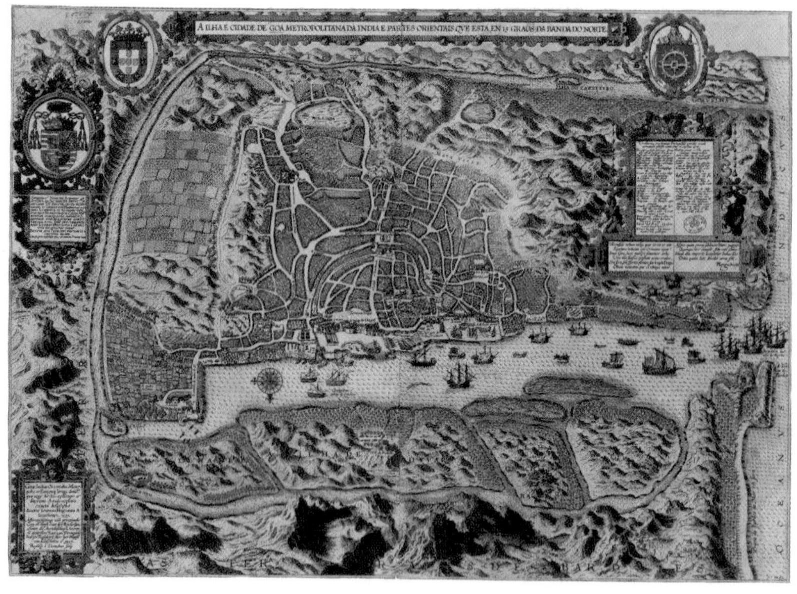

A sixteenth-century map of Goa. This colony became the bloodiest of all the Portuguese tribunals, concentrating most on 'crypto-Hindus' – secret Hindus who pretended to be Catholics.

Above, left and right Isabel de Carvajal being tortured prior to her death at the 1596 auto-da-fé in Mexico City.

Right Mariana de Carvajal was burnt at the stake during the same auto-da-fé in which her sister Isabel and brother Luis perished. They were the nieces and nephew of the Governor of Nuevo León, Luis de Carvajal y la Cueva.

Right (detail beneath) Depiction of the Grand Auto-da-Fé in Madrid 1680, one of the most ostentatious ever staged in Spain. By the latter seventeenth century, autos-da-fé had become vast elaborate affairs, but the costs involved in staging them meant that they became increasingly infrequent.

Below An artist's impression of an exorcism in Spain, a practice that had become commonplace by the seventeenth century.

An auto-da-fé in Lisbon in the eighteenth century. The Inquisition remained very powerful in Portugal in the first half of the century, with autos-da-fé continuing to 'relax' penitents to death in large numbers, generally for the crime of crypto-Judaism.

The destruction of the Inquisition in Barcelona on 10 March 1820. As the Inquisition had sanctioned violence for so long, the destruction of Inquisition offices and archives quickly became a popular activity.

Lisbon 1637

JUST THREE YEARS before the revolt of Portugal against the Spanish king Philip IV and the end of the joint monarchy tensions were reaching their peak in Iberia. In Peru the large colony of Portuguese merchants had been hit by a series of inquisitorial arrests (led, it will be no surprise, by Juan de Mañozca) which had seen the incarceration of eighty-three people and the questioning of 110 more. The belief spreading in Spanish society that the Portuguese were Jews led to these traders being accused of a crypto-Jewish plot.[24] Eleven of them would be killed in the great auto of 23 January 1639.

Events and feelings in the colonies and the homelands were, then, connected. But in many parts of Portugal denunciations to the Inquisition frequently reflected the more parochial, daily concerns of the citizenry. This was the case in Lisbon in April 1637, when information began to be received concerning a 'witch', Cecilia da Silva, who lived in the countryside outside the city. Silva, if witnesses were to be believed, was an extremely dangerous person whose heretical activities needed to be stopped at all costs.[25]

One witness described Silva's activities in some detail. She had portraits of St Erasmus, whom, the old woman Silva said, did whatever she asked. Silva could see devils painted alongside St Erasmus, and said that she knew how to perform spells so that these devils would do her bidding. Many people had come to see her because of this and given her money and offerings, and all this had made Silva a rich and doubtless envied member of the community.

The effects of Silva's notable powers were especially severe on a certain Antonio de Bairros, a trader who lived in the same area as she did. For many years Bairros had been having an affair with one Marta Gonçalves, who was a great friend of the witch. It was publicly rumoured that the affair had only lasted so long because of Silva's spells, and one day a servant of Bairros called Antonia had seen a slave belonging to Marta Gonçalves arriving with an offering for Silva and a message complaining that Bairros did not come to her house any more. Why bring an offering if not for some service in return? Why complain about Bairros? In a society where the slightest event could be seen to come within the purview of the Inquisition, this was inflammatory indeed.

One of the most diabolic aspects of Bairros's 'bewitchment' was that Marta Gonçalves was 'old and with facial deformities'; his wife in contrast was beautiful, young and gentle. Yet the spells of the witch Silva were so strong that Bairros had nothing to do with his household, which was the cause of great sadness to his wife. Bairros himself described the occult forces which drove him to humiliate his wife and himself in full view of the gossips: 'Many times some inner force has constrained him to go to the house of Marta Gonçalves whilst standing in the street or many times even when lying in bed . . . Often he sees himself in his house with his wife and children and then finds himself in the house of Marta Gonçalves without knowing how he got there, and many times he finds himself taken there as if with chains of iron'.

All this was said to be witchcraft; and yet one suspects that the accusers of Cecilia de Silva, marvelling at Bairros's infidelity with this 'ugly old woman' Gonçalves, were poorer students of human psychology than they were of the daily activities of one another. It may well have been precisely Gonçalves's apparent repulsiveness which was so attractive to Bairros, this respectable trader who had married a respectable wife. In Bairros the inner drives and contradictions which make all of us human needed an outlet, an outlet which could be found in this person who symbolized everything that he had outwardly rejected in himself and in his choice of spouse.

Cases such as this reveal that it was by no means just in the New World that superstition was rife; indeed, the archives of the Inquisition make it plain that Portugal and Spain were countries riddled with superstition at the time. Denunciations of witchcraft centred on women living alone, stealing cattle by night, their houses filled with clues of their participation in the occult such as strands of hair and loose teeth.[26] Diviners were accused of reading events in distant places by gathering all sorts of peculiar objects such as beans, a whelk, a rag and various coins. Two of the beans would be put in the mouth of the person seeking information, one to represent them and one their loved one. Ten beans were thrown onto the table, and read by seeing to which object they landed nearest. Sometimes these diviners would even pass on their occult knowledge to a friend, who would then give up the practice after they found, to their great surprise, that it was never accurate.[27]

This was a widely credulous society. Yet while people at large were often finding indications of pacts with the devil in the behaviour of their neighbours – observed in minute precision – the Inquisition itself was less credulous. As we saw in the Prologue, Portugal and Spain were among the few European countries that experienced no mass witch-hunts during these years, and indeed the Inquisition often sent people packing when they came to denounce the diabolic pacts of their neighbours.[28] By the early 18th century inquisitors in Portugal no longer believed that witches went to coven meetings and could use spells to curse others.[29]

Here is the curious paradox of an institution that was able to see that some of those claiming to fly by night to covens were mentally ill, and a population many of whom still believed that such events were part of daily life. Yet the explanation for this is quite simple: just as the witch-hunts in northern Europe expressed powerful social drives and contradictions which required a scapegoat, so in Iberia the Inquisition had already targeted its own scapegoats, in the shape of the *conversos* and the *moriscos*. Witches were no longer necessary; fantastical enemies were not required as others had already been invented.[30]

For the citizens of Portugal and Spain, however, things were different. Envy and jealousy, those quotidian emotions, could be exorcised daily in gossip and spying on neighbours, rivals and enemies. A moral purpose could be served by watching people who may have been pure of blood but were open to being contaminated by other types of heretical activity and by their own fantasies of demonic possession and magic.

There was of course no need to be a *converso* or a *morisco* in order to enter into a pact with the devil or to practise witchcraft. All Old Christians were equally susceptible to this sort of behaviour. Thus the sense in a large part of the general population that witches were ubiquitous and of interest to the Inquisition – even if it was misplaced – fostered an atmosphere in which the daily practices of all classes of people came under scrutiny. Just as under Inquisitor-General Valdés in the mid-16th century concentration on the

Lutheran threat had widened the possibilities of suspicion, so now interest in beliefs beyond Islam and Judaism meant that every member of society could be an object of vigilance.

As it happened, Valdés had also been a key figure in the expansion of inquisitorial vigilance to Old Christians, as a leader of the movement that became known as the Counter-Reformation. In the aftermath of the Carranza case which had convulsed the Spanish elite in the 1550s the Inquisition in Spain had moved on to examine the collective attitudes of the nation.[31] The Inquisition began to move out from urban centres, making regular visits to rural districts and, in the second half of the 16th century, prosecuting with increasing severity minor offences which were expressive of ignorance or anger rather than heresy – bigamy and blasphemy being particularly targeted.[32]

In order to achieve this reach, Valdés undertook a thoroughgoing reform of inquisitorial institutions. He reorganized inquisitorial finances by securing for the Inquisition the right to charge rents on *canonjías*, specific ecclesiastical posts. He greatly expanded the network of inquisitorial officials from the cities to small towns and villages throughout Spain. He revised the rules governing the administration of the Inquisition, and by the end of his life had secured the institutional pre-eminence of the Inquisition over all other civil and ecclesiastical courts in Spain.[33] Thus, like many of the most terrible persecutors who followed him in other places and at other times, Valdés was a meticulous administrator.[34]

The advance of the Inquisition was accompanied by a massive programme of religious indoctrination, following the impetus of the Council of Trent,[35] perhaps the most important council ever held by the Catholic Church. The aim was to achieve uniformity of behaviour in keeping with Catholic doctrine and morals through a concerted effort of indoctrination.[36] The irony was that most Old Christians were already good Catholics, and did not understand why the Inquisition should have anything to do with them.[37] Had they not supported the establishment of the Inquisition? They found it difficult to grasp how this institution of persecution could so suddenly turn on its supporters and be used to repress them.[38]

The way in which the atmosphere in Spain changed between the formation of the Inquisition and the reforms of Valdés is best exemplified by looking at blasphemy. In the instructions issued by Inquisitor-General Diego de Deza in Seville in 1500 it was specifically stated that words uttered 'with anger or ire' were not heretical but blasphemous, and should not come under the province of the Inquisition.[39] By the 1560s all that had changed, and the most innocuous remark thrown out in the heat of the moment could be enough for a denunciation to the Inquisition. Thus, in 1560 the trader Melchior de Berrio from Granada was sentenced to three years in the galleys for having offended the Holy Sacrament;[40] in 1562 the labourer Luis Godines from Cordoba was tried for saying that 'the tithe could go to the devil since the devil invented it.'[41] Now everyone, Old and New Christian alike, had to watch what they said, and to whom they said it.

To read through the archives of the Inquisitions of Portugal and Spain is to develop the general impression that blasphemy and swearing were as common then as they are now. Indeed, it does not seem as though the fact that the Inquisition dealt with these crimes had much effect in stemming them; anger is not something easy to repress, and the same clearly holds for the words that go with it.

Blasphemy tended to come into one of three categories. The first was general disparagement of the Church and its institutions. Luis Godines's dismissal of the tithe in Cordoba is one good example of this; another comes from Marco Antonio Font, a royal bailiff in Valencia in the early 17th century who was sent to arrest a man who claimed to be an official of the crusade. Font greeted him with the challenging (and blasphemous) remark, 'So you're from the crusade are you? I shit on the crusade, I'll wipe my arse with the papal bull and with the crusade'.[42]

The second type of blasphemy was when the offender expressed overt scepticism of God sometimes bordering on atheism. This was quite common, and people often blasphemed when they lost their faith in God.[43] At times the blasphemous expression was merely a version of common sense, as when the Old Christian labourer Afonso Annes declared near Porto in Portugal in 1569, 'God could not be in the sky and in the church at the same time'.[44]

Perhaps the most explosive type of blasphemy, however, was that which reflected what the Inquisition saw as sexual deviance. One of the most common types of blasphemy was to assert that the condition of a married person was better than that of a friar. Such a view was in direct opposition to that of St Thomas Aquinas, who had held that total chastity was superior to any other condition, as it was the best route to perfection and a relationship with God.[45] This philosophy was of course meat and drink to the (theoretically) celibate friars themselves, but could be expected to hold less sway among the general population. Typical of those who fell foul of this rule was Alonso García in Cordoba, who had declared that 'it was not a sin to sleep with a woman if you paid her'.[46] In Évora the way these blasphemies related to daily life was graphically revealed when Fernão Matheus was accused of saying that it was not a sin to sleep with two sisters; his sister-in-law Isabel Díaz was accused shortly afterwards of saying that it was not a sin to have sex with her brother-in-law.[47]

The punishments meted out for this sort of self-betrayal were more minor than those directed at *conversos* or *moriscos* but usually stretched to lashes and sometimes exile, the galleys and/or prison. For the Inquisition to secure a conviction people had to monitor their neighbours for any sign of nonconformity. Thus while in the colonies the Inquisition's presence in daily life was often seen in the denunciation of slaves renouncing God or practising some form of 'sorcery', in Iberia the state of mind which it fostered led to vigilance over the most mundane of conversations.

It is in this context that we can see why historians tend to think of the Inquisition as one of the first modern institutions. With its organization and ability to check on the lives of its citizens, it was a forerunner of the organizations which cast such a shadow over human beings in the 20th century. It is true that some historians today hold that this facet of the Inquisition has been exaggerated and that the Old Christians perceived it as a remote tribunal.[48] But the reach of the Inquisition was something which varied with the period in question. In the late 16th and early 17th centuries its reach within rural communities was immense, with an administrative presence even in small towns where there was no tribunal. Yet although this reach contracted, collective memory ensured that in its later years the scope of the Inquisition was imagined to be far greater than it actually was.

★

If you enter a restaurant in Spain today and carefully examine the menu, you may notice something specific to Spanish culture. Any soup or stew described as *'a la Española'* or *'Castellana'* is served with slices of ham or pieces of roast pork in it. A popular chain of restaurants in Madrid is called the *Museo del Jamón* (Museum of Ham), and once you have pushed your way past the dozens of legs of ham curing from the rafters this is as good a place as any to test out one of these dishes. One of the most ironically named dishes of all is *Judías con Jamón* – Jewesses with ham – or rather, as it is today, beans and ham.

Turn from the restaurants to the culinary emblem of Spain, the tapas bar. Here, you can sit on a stool beside the bar and the barman will hand you a plate of food to whet your appetite while you cradle a cold beer. Look at the food you have been given: pork scratchings, a piece of *chorizo*, some prawns, a collection of pickled shellfish. It is rude not to eat it, and so you comply, even though it may be stale or cold. You will probably not notice that these offerings – like many portions of tapas – are against both Islamic and Jewish dietary laws.

Turn back the clock over 300 years to the island of Majorca, the jewel of the Balearics. Here in the late 17th century a large community of *conversos* still lived in the capital of the island, Palma, occupying a ghetto known as the Sagell. One summer's day in 1673 a group of local bigwigs gathered in the garden of one of the richer *conversos*, Pedro de Onofre de Cortés. Also present were Gabriel Ruiz, a familiar of the Inquisition and Antonio de Puigdorfila, who was related to the bailiff of the Inquisition. Miguel Pont, a shoemaker, described what happened next.

> Among other things that [the visitors] had brought and set out to eat was a stew with blood sausage made of pork, and one of the brothers [of the *converso* Pedro de Onofre de Cortés] – he does not remember which – wanted to eat some of it, whereupon the other Cortés said to him: That is blood sausage, pork! And they ate none of the stew but rather some fish and fruit that they had. Then the aforementioned Antonio de Puigdorfila said to them, Why do you not eat this? And he insisted that the damned Jews eat. But they said that it would make them

> ill; and the rest of those present then laughed and said to one another: Look, the Jews have refused to eat the stew![49]

Here, then, was a social dynamic where the visitors generously brought food to a house where, if *conversos* did keep some aspects of the Jewish law, they would be unable to eat it. Such generosity was a challenge and a veiled threat. It spread through the culinary tradition as a means of testing people, keeping watch over their orthodoxy and gaining a hold over those thought to be suspicious. As both Islam and Judaism banned the consumption of pork, offering it to a *converso* or a *morisco* was the perfect way to humiliate someone while pretending to keep to the rules of Christian charity. The refusal of people to eat pork is constantly present in the cases of *conversos* and *moriscos* before the Inquisition, and testifies to how the ideology of the Inquisition percolated the most basic human activity of all, eating.

For *conversos* and *moriscos* the nature of culinary vigilance varied. For *conversos* the question of the consumption of pork was critical and, as the Italian traveller Leonardo Donato noted in 1573, 'they are observed in their works and their ways of life with such attention that, even if they prevaricate in the smallest Christian rite, they are seen as suspicious of heresy and punished'.[50] For *moriscos* an additionally dangerous period came during Ramadan, when the slightest hint that they were not eating during the day could lead to a denunciation, in another instance of the interplay of sham generosity with the ideology of the Inquisition. In 1578 a *morisco* in the district of Valencia was accused of refusing to eat or drink throughout the day during the fast of Ramadan when working with some Old Christians at a house, even though 'they invited him to eat and have snacks'.[51] The same year an Old Christian denounced four *moriscos* who had come and worked on his land during Ramadan in 1577 and had neither eaten nor drunk throughout the day.[52]

Evidently, in order for such accusations to be made, the suspects would have to be observed constantly, with the question always lurking as to whether or not they would eat or drink. One can imagine the pleasure and tension in the witnesses as they watched. One suspects that many would have taken more delight in proven sedition than in vindicating the suspect.

It is clear that such extreme vigilance began very early in the Inquisition's history. When the *conversa* Maria de Cazalla – later accused of being an *alumbrada* – was attending mass in the Castilian town of Guadalajara in 1525, Diego Carrillo observed that she lowered her eyes when the sacrament was raised and then turned them to look at the church door.[53] This sort of accusation was commonplace, and it is difficult not to feel simultaneous amusement and revulsion at the hypocrisy of people denouncing others for not observing the sacrament with sufficient attention, when for their own part they were clearly more interested in observing the behaviour of potential heretics than they were in offering their own reverence to the body of Christ.

Such questions concerning this sort of evidence do not seem to have occurred to the inquisitors, however, and church was one of the prime locations where the behaviour of *conversos* and *moriscos* was examined. In 1566 one *morisco* was reconciled in Granada 'since when the priest raised the Holy Sacrament he was seated with his head lowered and his hands covering his eyes so as not to see it'.[54] Thirteen years later the *morisco* Gómez Enreymada – banished from Granada after the failed uprising – was denounced by eight witnesses for behaving suspiciously when the sacrament was raised by the priest.[55] The intensity with which people were watched over is illustrated by the fact that three witnesses denounced the *morisco* Miguel Melich in Valencia for not having confessed for a whole year;[56] clearly, all of them had been watching him and keeping notes.

Perhaps the most extraordinary example of vigilance comes from a case of 1597 when the *morisco* Bartolomé Sánchez was arrested with his whole family. One of the witnesses, a neighbour, maintained that Sánchez washed himself even after defecating. One can only conclude that even this most private of bodily functions was considered fair game, something which perhaps should not surprise us in a society where the mere fact of washing was thought suspicious.

But if catching people out when shitting was legitimate, the problem was that this was merely society shitting on itself. Given the extraordinary diligence with which members of the community watched over the *conversos* and *moriscos* in their midst, it is difficult not to conclude that it was precisely this grounding in vigilance which enabled it to be transferred to members of the Old Christian community itself. Expertise in securing evidence for the persecution of others would be turned back on the dominant community. Thus again was the persecuting institution able to turn skills and practices developed in one context against the very people who had supported its creation in the first place.

The effect on society was stark. As the historian Juan de Mariana put it, the secret investigations of the Inquisition 'deprived people of the freedom to listen and talk among themselves'.[57] Since the slightest slip of the tongue could lead to a denunciation, humiliation and the loss of privileges, the society of vigilance became the society of suspicion, and of division.

LET US RETURN TO the gory days right at the start of the history of the Iberian Inquisitions – to Seville in 1484 and the first Instructions issued for the operation of the Inquisition by Inquisitor-General Tomás de Torquemada. The sixth chapter of the Instructions declared as follows:

> The said inquisitors should order that [heretics and apostates] cannot hold public offices, nor benefices, that they cannot be attorneys, nor landlords, nor druggists, nor spice merchants, nor doctors, nor surgeons, nor bloodletters, nor brokers. And that they cannot wear gold or silver or coral or pearls or any such thing, nor precious stones, nor wear any sort of silk or camlet . . . and that they cannot ride horses, or bear arms for the whole of their lives on penalty of being found guilty of relapsing [into their heresy].[58]

In 1488 in Valladolid Torquemada took things further and ordered that the children and grandchildren of heretics be banned from all official positions.[59] We have seen in this chapter how these prohibitions were enforced through the case of the granddaughter of a *relajado*, Antonia Machado, prosecuted in Mexico in 1604 for wearing silk clothes with a golden fringe.* Such prosecutions were not at all uncommon; in 1587 several descendants of people 'relaxed' or

* See page 213.

reconciled by the Inquisition were fined in Hellín in Murcia for wearing silk and carrying knives.[60]

Something of the anxiety of those touched by these prohibitions comes across from the case of Jerónima de Vargas, who in 1560 made a heartfelt plea to inquisitors to allow her to wear silk, taken as a sign of nobility and honour in Castilian society. Jerónima's parents had been reconciled in Cuenca eighteen years before, when she was two years old, and she feared that if her husband, a member of the petty nobility, discovered that she could not wear silk then he 'would not give her a good life or provide a marital life [sleep with her]'.[61]

It is worthwhile thinking again about what Torquemada's original Instructions of 1484 implied. For if people are to be prevented from wearing certain types of clothing and jewellery, from riding horses and bearing arms, and from entering certain professions, then it is obvious that they will have to be watched over. From the very start, then, the Inquisition set out rules which insinuated mutual vigilance into society. Thus while it was not the Inquisition which did all the watching, nor all the accusing, it was the rules of the Inquisition which created the atmosphere from which this followed.

Yet at the same time one should not fall into the trap of making the Inquisition the scapegoat for the failings of human beings. The admonition to be nosy was one which many people were only too happy to follow. Most of us, if we are honest, will admit to enjoying the discussion of mutual acquaintances. Gossip is communal, it is fun, and best of all it allows us to talk about the failings of others rather than think about our own. By giving such behaviour moral legitimacy, the Inquisition took a brilliant step towards ensuring its own popularity, allowing the desire to gossip to be concealed behind the desire to do good.

From the legitimation of gossip came, as we have seen, the spread of the Inquisition into all walks of public life. In Portugal teachers and midwives were required to be examined on their lives and customs before being given a licence.[62] In Sicily no foreign schoolteachers were appointed without inquisitorial permission, and autos spread from the capital, Palermo, to the cities of Catania and Messina on the east coast.[63] Yet this constant promotion of conformity would have the same effect on human society as a drought has on a river. People stagnated as innovation and creativity were leached out of society by the more immediate gratifications offered by gossip and revenge.

Chapter Ten

THE ADMINISTRATION OF FEAR

. . . instead of talking of 'the inquisitor of Peru' it was more accurate to talk of 'the Peru of the inquisitor' . . .

At this moment we seem to have reached to the heart of neighbourly odium. Questions mentionable and unmentionable circle the towns and their acid decay. How did the Inquisition penetrate the everyday? What made people submit to administration and its brittle soul? We have seen that there was a sense of complicity, of pleasure at the licence to spy. But to take advantage of this passivity there had to be an organization ready to take command.

The tale is a familiar one, though foreign in its antiquity. The minutiae of its procedures is, as we have seen, something which marks the Inquisition out as a modern persecuting institution, one of the first of its kind. With the administration of persecution went the possibility of stealing power, and from power came the corruption of what was supposed to be an institution of purity. The Inquisition, theoretically an instrument of the divine, was nothing if not human.

This corruption is no surprise. As the story has unravelled, it has been punctuated by bloodthirstiness and frequent instances of sexual predation by inquisitors. Often, indeed, the two have been connected. Lúcero in Cordoba, Mañozca in Lima and Mexico, Salazar in Murcia, these inquisitors arranged large-scale burnings even as they satisfied their baser desires, and they were by no means out of the ordinary.* According to the social bonds of the time, these

---

* See pages 1–5, 65–68 and 120–124.

overbearing men had something alluring about them – the power to punish, and the power to forgive.

As these examples show, corruption was as commonplace in the colonies as in Portugal and Spain. The same held elsewhere. In Cartagena, the hub of the slave trade to South America, abuses of power occurred on a daily basis as vast numbers of contraband African slaves arrived in America in appalling conditions. Perhaps, then, the Spanish settler Lorenzo Martínez de Castro should not have been surprised in 1643 to find himself a resident of the inquisitorial jail.

On the arrival of Martín Real, an inquisitorial visitor of inquiry from the *Suprema* in Spain, Martínez de Castro had written and described the activities of Inquisitor Juan Ortiz with his wife, Rufina de Roxas. Ortiz had recently begun the unusual practice of taking Rufina's confession in a session that lasted all night. As Martínez de Castro rhetorically put it, 'What business is so serious that a married woman has to have her confession taken all night, and what scribe could possibly exist who would write down her declaration? What divine law orders an inquisitor to commit public adultery, so that if I had killed my wife it would have been on his account?'[1] The sense of outrage and scandal is to be expected, but there is nothing in the complaint to indicate surprise; rather, merely the hope that the grievance would be listened to. It was, and over the next six months Real tried to get to the bottom of what had, or had not, gone on.

Martínez de Castro's wife, Rufina, was only seventeen-years-old in June 1643 when her problems began. Freshly arrived from Seville, one can surmise that she was still adjusting to life in the New World and to the urges of her body. Probably, she found her older husband boring, domineering or both. Such is the implication of the fact that in the first half of 1643 she took to giving him 'wild aubergines', which, her slave Thomassa had told her, would make him sleep so that she could go out by night and do as she pleased – and, perhaps more importantly, not do as he pleased.[2]

Rufina's problems began when she told Thomassa not to confess to a priest her part in this mild drugging of her husband because, she informed her, it was not a sin.[3] This order of Rufina's was overheard by a mulatto carpenter, Pedro Suárez. Here was a chance for some excitement. He determined to denounce her to the

Inquisition.[4] Suárez does not come across from the evidence as a particularly devout person; far more likely is that the motivation for his betrayal was his own thwarted desire for Rufina.

In any event, on the very same day that Suárez went to denounce her the messenger of the Inquisition in Cartagena came to Rufina's house and ordered all of her female slaves to come in for questioning. Rufina fell into a panic. She rushed to a priest for advice, and was told she should go to the Inquisition at once to make a full confession. The peculiar values of that distant time and place are revealed by the fact that, in the Inquisition's eyes, her sin was not the drugging of her husband, but the advice to her slave Thomassa not to confess her part in it.

On her way back from seeing the priest Rufina met a friend of hers, Inés. Inés clearly knew a thing or two about Inquisitor Juan Ortiz. She suggested that Rufina throw herself at his feet; it would help, she added, if she put on her jewels and finest clothes so that she looked as beautiful as she could. Rufina did as she was told and went to visit Ortiz that evening. The man who accompanied her and her female slave through the narrow streets that night, keeping them safe from physical threat, was none other than Pedro Suárez, her accuser.[5]

Rufina spent half an hour with Ortiz that evening, with her slave Ana just outside in the darkened corridor. She emerged announcing to Suárez that the inquisitor had declared that this was not a matter for the Inquisition but nevertheless went to see Ortiz the following evening, accompanied again by Suárez. Ortiz told her to come back by day two days later, dressed in black and carried through the city by her slaves to make an official confession.[6] This would just be a formality for her to go through so that any question of an offence against the faith was forgotten.

Ortiz, however, had clearly learnt how to snare women like Rufina. Once her guard was down, the shift from relief to fear was one which could provoke other extreme feelings. When she arrived on the appointed day at six in the morning with her slaves, Ortiz changed his approach. He tore into her angrily, and said that it was now clear that the Inquisition would have no option but to arrest her; she was to come two days later by night and see if there might be any remedy.[7]

The hapless Rufina did the inquisitor's bidding. Passing through Cartagena in the moonlight, she arrived on the evening in question again with Suárez and her slave Ana in tow. Ortiz asked her if she had come accompanied by a man. Yes, she had; her protector Suárez was waiting for her. She should not have brought him, said Ortiz. Such people, he continued – no doubt thinking of Suárez's own accusation of Rufina – were not to be trusted, and moreover he had invited her 'so that she should come to his bedroom, leading her to understand that he wanted her to stay the night with him'.[8]

Rufina made an excuse and left. She was summoned again two days later. This time, she confessed to the *Suprema* visitor Martín Real, she had worn a white shift and a skirt embroidered with green taffeta. She had arrived late at night and gone in through the side door of the inquisitor's lodgings, not by the front door as on previous occasions. This time she did spend the night.[9]

At first one is shocked by the abuse of power. But consider again how Rufina described the clothes she had worn on the night Ortiz seduced her. This is the description of someone who had taken great care with her appearance before setting out, and, moreover, who by going in via the side door had known what would await her. It is the statement of someone appalled by power, but yet finding this emotion sublimated into a feeling of intense attraction and the release of submission.

Here we touch on the emotional landscape of one of the more disturbing scientific experiments of the 20th century. In 1961 Stanley Milgram sought to test human response to people in authority. Participants were ordered to administer increasingly large electric shocks to an unseen person in a nearby room. There was in fact no person being tortured and the participants heard the shouts and cries of an actor, yet in spite of the screams two-thirds of the participants gave the largest shock of all, which could have been lethal.

Authority and power compel. Inquisitor Ortiz had played his hand with skill, showing Rufina his potential for compassion before making her fear his power. Such power perhaps accentuated her feelings of loneliness in this alien city so far from her home in Spain. Here, where the streets were filled with American Indians and African slaves, and where the sufferings of those unloaded from slave ships were constantly apparent, the consequences of disobedience and powerlessness were obvious. Authority became all too easy to obey.

The inquisitorial visitor Real, when he uncovered the truth of the matter, concluded that Rufina had sinned by sleeping with Ortiz; the inquisitor's failing, in contrast, had been in not punishing her for her crime against the faith. It may seem extraordinary that the Inquisition saw the liaison as Rufina's sin rather than the inquisitor's, but this was the (misogynistic) world view of that institution.

Men such as Ortiz are difficult to forgive. Inquisitors had to have legal training and were not usually friars but rather priests who had not taken holy orders.[10] Perhaps this makes such failings as these less hypocritical, but only marginally so. In the end what one finds is that power was concentrated to such an extent in the hands of these agents of God that many of them were unable to resist the opportunities that followed. Strengthening the powers of the Inquisition entailed strengthening the corruption of power; the inquisitors were in fact 'neither demons nor angels . . . just men, in all their glory and all their wretchedness'.[11]

THE POWER OF INQUISITORS does not just emerge in their sexual activities; it touched every aspect of their lives: their dress, their behaviour to their colleagues and their pride. To observe how power could corrupt an inquisitor's sense of what was and was not permitted, we shall examine the will of the inquisitor-general of Portugal, Dom Francisco de Castro. Castro was a key figure in the Inquisition's power struggle with John IV, the first king of Portugal after the split with Spain in 1640. In his efforts to make the Portuguese state solvent, John IV passed a law in 1649 barring the confiscation of goods by the Inquisition from *converso* merchants. Unhappy at this threat to its revenues, the Inquisition then engaged in a protracted power struggle with him, bolstered by the papacy, who did not recognize John and allowed see after see to fall vacant as bishops died.

Following the death of the first Portuguese inquisitor-general, John III's brother Cardinal Henry, these individuals had generally had a chequered reputation. In 1621 a letter had been written urgently to King Philip IV* saying that the Portuguese Inquisition was on the verge of ruin because of the corruption of Inquisitor-General Fernando Martines Mascarenhas. A council needed to be formed to resolve the problems, and its members should be neither related to the inquisitor-general nor in his debt.[12] Clearly, there was a feeling that Martines Mascarenhas was not entirely above worldly affairs.

Similarly, the wardrobe of the venerable inquisitor Francisco de Castro as revealed in his will illustrates a different sort of corruption, but one which was no less endemic. It gives some idea of the lifestyle which this individual followed in his battle with heresy. In his wardrobe were pieces of camlet, dressing gowns, capes, jerkins, knickerbockers, black silk socks, a sunhat made of damask and bonnets, all stored in leather trunks, damask bags and large chests. In fact, let us not make the mistake of thinking that the inquisitor-general had just this one damask hat. No! He had two flat hats with green ties to wear at court and another for when he was travelling plus two hats made of palm leaves, adorned with taffeta and embellished with black and green ribbons.

This was not an individual forced to go short of the necessities of life. Even the spittoon and the travelling urinal which he took with him on journeys to catch his holy spittle and urine were made of silver. He had no shortage of mirrors with which to admire himself. He had a golden dinner service, large tablecloths for when he was having banquets and smaller ones for more personal use. In the midst of such opulence Inquisitor-General Francisco de Castro managed to enshrine the necessary social hierarchies; while he and his colleagues ate from golden plates, his servants ate off dishes made from tin.[13]

All this was in keeping with the pride and ostentation to which inquisitors were given. The Inquisition was a body driven by status, as its rules of operation make clear. At autos inquisitors sat on chairs and other officials sat on benches. In court the prosecutor was given a chair, but it was smaller than the inquisitors' chairs; in Galicia, one prosecutor responded by ordering that his own subordinates take off their bonnets when talking to him.[14] All power flowed via the

* Of Spain, and Philip III of Portugal.

hierarchy to the inquisitors, who only deferred to the authority of the scriptures; everyone else deferred to them.

Does one suppose that all inquisitors began life as hypocrites who would be prepared to say one thing and do another? This would be too simplistic; the most famous inquisitors are those that did appalling things,[15] while the many who were 'just doing their job' and progressing inexorably up the career ladder tend to be passed over.[16] Perhaps, indeed, the view that inquisitors either followed the Mengele or the Eichmann school of persecution is also too easy an answer. Human beings, as the archives of the Inquisition show, have countless ways of working out their inner torment.

What we do see, though, when looking at the lives of inquisitors and of inquisitorial operatives in general, is the endless abuse of power. Inquisitors like Juan Ortiz in Cartagena, with his predatory conquest of the young bride Rufina de Roxas, were anything but atypical. Indeed one of the best arguments against those historians who downplay the impact of the Inquisition is the very impunity with which inquisitorial staff abused their power. Had the Inquisition not been feared and its power disproportionate, some of the terrible things that officials felt able to do would surely not have been tolerated.

Santiago de Compostela 1609

IN GALICIA, spiritual heartland of Spain, destination of the great pilgrimages from France and across Spain, all was not well between the two inquisitors. As a network of Judaizing *conversos* was uncovered around Santiago, Inquisitors Muñoz de la Cuesta and Ochoa began to write letters complaining about one another. In July 1607 Muñoz de la Cuesta had accused Ochoa of insisting on doing things only the way he wanted and of stringing out trials of impoverished prisoners unnecessarily, creating a financial burden for the tribunal. Then, in 1609, when the number of prisoners taken in Galicia was such that the *Suprema* ordered additional buildings to be constructed to house the prison, Muñoz de la Cuesta accused Ochoa of taking over some of these buildings in order to expand his own apartments. The *Suprema* censured Muñoz de la Cuesta for the disagreements between the two men, so, feeling that he was in danger of being sacked, Muñoz de la Cuesta arranged for an anonymous letter to be sent to the *Suprema* alleging all sorts of irregularities on the part of Ochoa.[17]

Tired of the constant sniping between the two inquisitors, the *Suprema* arranged for a visitor to come and examine the affairs of the tribunal. They appointed the inquisitor of Zaragoza, Delgadillo de la Canal, who rapidly formulated over sixty charges against *both* inquisitors, including the fact that each of them had embezzled confiscated goods into the hands of their friends.[18] However, it was their open sexual peccadilloes which were perhaps most astonishing for men who were supposed to uphold the sanctity of the divine law; it is worth recalling again that inquisitors were supposed to prosecute, among other blasphemies, the statement, 'Simple fornication is not a sin'.*

Among the charges laid at the door of Muñoz de la Cuesta was that he went to orchards on the fringes of the city and seduced young women there. He had brought a girl called María to Santiago, even though she was only fifteen or sixteen years old, and showered her with gifts. He accompanied married women to the theatre and invited them on a daily basis to his rooms in the tribunal offices; it was public knowledge that he slept with them, and that he had even attempted to seduce nuns through third parties.[19] Although he was suspended from his post in 1612 none of these manifest failings prevented him from being appointed inquisitor of Barcelona in 1615[20] – something which says a lot about the competition.

Ochoa was little better. He had bombarded a married woman, Quitería Rodríguez, with presents until he had persuaded her to move to Santiago and live with him openly in sin. She had been with him for several years, and all the inquisitorial officials were forced to call her *señora* – my lady. When he had eventually been forced to separate from her, he had gone around the tribunal crying and sobbing, calling out, 'Oh, my beloved Quitería!' Eventually he had hit upon the ruse of inviting her back with her cuckolded husband Juan Piñeiro, whom he had appointed to a post in the

---

* See page 121.

bureaucracy. Ochoa had then taken to presiding over inquisitorial hearings with Quitería beside him, while she had been known to protest at the unreasonable volume of paperwork and at the thoughtless and selfish cries of the prisoners in their jail cells.[21] Clearly, Ochoa had decided that it was better to be a hypocrite than to induce the sin of bigamy by marrying Quitería; otherwise he might have ended up having to prosecute his beloved or, worse still, see her prosecuted by his arch-rival Muñoz de la Cuesta.

This remarkable case reveals the chasm between inquisitorial theory and practice. Although in theological theory simple fornication was most definitely a sin, these inquisitors saw nothing wrong with enjoying it in practice. In fact, they were all for it. Moreover, cases such as these are much more common than one might think. In Barcelona in 1592 Inquisitor Alonso Blanco was accused of slipping out in the middle of the night to visit the local brothels.[22] And sixty-six years before, when the city of Granada was trying to persuade Charles V against instituting a tribunal of the Inquisition there in 1526, its councillors wrote:

> When the [inquisitorial] judges are bad, as can occur since they are human beings and not saintly like the Holy Office [*sic*], when they arrest virgins and respectable young married women, or when they order them to come secretly before them as the Holy Office requires, they have been known to do with them as they will, which the women only slightly protest against because of the great fear which they have [of them] . . . and meanwhile the scribes and officials of the Holy Office, being single men, as they are in some places, do the same thing with daughters and wives and female relatives of prisoners, and this is easy for them, as the favour will be granted in return for knowing something about the case.[23]

It is worth stopping to think about what this actually meant. An institution established with the aim of purifying religious practice and combating its corruption was responsible for forcing married and single women to prostitute themselves for the sake of the men they loved or for fear of the consequences if they did not. Such events were not universal. They may not even have occurred in the majority of tribunals. But they clearly were not rarities either. It is difficult not to conclude that if there was a corrupting agent in the Iberian world at this time it was actually the Inquisition.

For inquisitors power was everywhere, and they took advantage. Some kicked prisoners in the face if they did not get the right answer or simply to intimidate.[24] The way some of them saw their charges is revealed by Miguel de Carpio, inquisitor of Seville between 1556 and 1578, who saw his mission as to 'burn and embrace people' – as if these two actions were in some way related – and wanted to 'relax' some prisoners rather than reconcile them simply because they were poor – luckily for them this was not always carried out, since other inquisitors were more moderate, and all such decisions were taken by vote.[25]

When one looks at the frankly astonishing evidence of abuse of power and of inquisitors' capacity to say one thing and do another, the gulf between theory and practice becomes ever more disturbing. In theory, therefore, the Inquisition came down hard on officials accepting gifts, and the very first rules of the institution from 1484 made it clear that this was not acceptable;[26] fourteen years later, in the instructions written in Ávila in 1498, inquisitors were told not to impose high fines simply in order to get paid, and were ordered to live 'honestly in their dress and adornments of their person as in every other respect' – a veiled allusion to sexual misconduct.[27] Yet these orders were contemporaneous to numerous cases of corruption and bribery.[28]

Thus the theory and rule of the Inquisition were never the whole story, and to look at its history by reading its decrees is to miss the point. Like all institutions, the Inquisition was loathe to relinquish power once it had got hold of it. Thus it might pretend dismay at the cases of bribery and corruption, but these were themselves testament to the power of the institution, something of which it was all in favour. Power was too addictive to be sacrificed on the altar of morality. Rather than coming down hard on its own malefactors, the Inquisition often moved them on to another place, as they did with Muñoz de la Cuesta. There was no sense of shame; but it was a little inconvenient that morality was in fact the justifying principle of everything which the institution did.

*

Concentration of power was not, of course, the product simply of the personalities of the inquisitors. It required a detailed administrative machinery which channelled authority into the institution and to its functionaries. It also required the agreement of the state in this process since, as we have seen, the Inquisitions of Portugal and Spain were products of local conditions rather than of papal imposition.

The Inquisition's development of its administrative machinery was slow. In Spain the first tribunal was instituted in 1480 (Seville) and the last not until 1659 in Madrid. In Portugal and Goa, in contrast, the four tribunals were all founded within twenty-five years of each other in the mid-16th century. In Spain the *Suprema* had six members – five ecclesiastical councillors and one prosecutor – and the king was allowed to nominate two lay members from the Council of Castile; in Portugal the inquisitor-general was allowed to nominate members of the General Council of the Inquisition directly, which could lead to the sort of allegations of corruption that we saw in the case of Fernando Martines Mascarenhas.[29]*

The bureaucratic differences between the two Inquisitions were matched by some differences in targets. As we have seen, the Portuguese Inquisition never dealt with *moriscos* or large numbers of Lutherans, unlike in Spain. With the *moriscos*, this was because Portugal had been reconquered from the Muslims much earlier and had assimilated them by the time of the Inquisition. As for Lutherans, at the height of the panic in Spain in the late 1550s the Portuguese Inquisition had only just got off the ground and was still happy to concentrate on the threat of the *conversos*.

Nonetheless, the period of the joint monarchy (1580–1640) led to a growing fusion of bureaucratic styles. As the inquisitor-general of Portugal, Francisco de Castro – he of the damask hat – put it in 1632, 'The mode of procedure conforms to law and is, according to the information that we have, substantially the same as that which is used by the Inquisitions of Castile'.[30] This meant that many of the reforms which the Inquisition had undergone in Spain in the 16th century, when the Portuguese Inquisition had still been experiencing its growing pains, became characteristic of both institutions.

---

* See page 236.

In Spain, as with the expansion of the institution to prosecute Old Christians for blasphemy, bigamy and Lutheranism, bureaucratic growth coincided with the watch of Inquisitor-General Fernando de Valdés, the arch-enemy of Archbishop Carranza of Toledo.* Valdés reorganized the administration of the Inquisition in line with the needs of the Counter-Reformation. He put the Inquisition's finances on a surer footing by securing annual rents from the churches (*canonjías*).[31]† He also standardized inquisitorial procedures with general instructions issued in 1561, regularized visits to rural areas so that remote spots were covered more frequently, and established the Inquisition in areas where it had not previously had a presence.[32]

However, perhaps the most important bureaucratic reform instituted by Valdés was his reorganization of the familiars of the Inquisition in a decree of 1553 known as the Concordia. Familiars were spies of the Inquisition, expected to report anything suspicious; they were often asked to help with the arrest of suspects, and were given drawings of fugitives to help track them down.[33] Until the time of Valdés they had been sparse in Spain, but under him the Inquisition appointed familiars according to the size of each settlement. Granada, Seville and Toledo had fifty familiars each, Cordoba, Cuenca and Valldolid forty, Murcia thirty, Calahorra and Llerena twenty-five, towns of up to 3,000 residents (*vecinos*) ten, towns of up to 1,000 residents six, towns of up to 500 residents four, and towns of fewer than 500 residents two if needed.[34]

This rationalized network of spies facilitated the movement of the Inquisition into daily life[35] and fostered the growth of the power of individual inquisitors and other functionaries. At their peak there were over 20,000 familiars in Spain.[36] Henceforth, until the institution declined from the mid-17th century onward, even small towns could not be sure of being free of spies who would report misdemeanours to the authorities. By 1600 even the isolated province of Guatemala in Central America had between sixty and one hundred, and there was no colonial town that was without its familiar.[37] In Portugal, meanwhile, although there had been only eighteen familiars before the union with Spain in 1580, by 1640

---

* See pages 129–142.

† See page 222.

another 1,600 were in place.[38] From now on it would not just be inquisitors who routinely abused their powers; their sidekicks, the familiars, would also become a burden on the people in the towns and villages of Portugal, Spain and the colonies.

Lisbon 1627–8

THE PORTUGUESE CAPITAL suffered during the sixty years of the joint monarchy. The ships still came and went from the dockside at the Tejo. They sailed out to sea past the royal palace and the beautiful tower at Belén, shadowed by the green hills of Sintra. The dock still groaned with goods unloaded from Brazil and India, with porters hauling them up the narrow streets and passageways, towards the marketplaces and the homes of the nobility. Nevertheless, the decline was real. The greater emphasis placed by the (Spanish) monarchs on the Spanish empire meant that Portuguese colonial outposts began to suffer. Spain was not a country without enemies, and Portugal's association with its neighbour made its imperial settlements into targets for the Dutch, who were still fighting the 80-year conflict with Spain which would eventually lead to their full independence in 1648.

The problem for Portugal was that whereas the wealth of the Spanish empire in America came from great mining centres in the interior of Mexico and Peru, the Portuguese empire was based around coastal ports and was therefore much easier to target. Between 1603 and 1641 the Dutch attacked Goa (1603 and 1610), the Spice Islands (1605), Gorée (Senegal: 1619 and 1627), Mozambique (1607 and 1608), Malacca (1616, 1629 and 1641), Macao (1622 and 1626) and Mina (modern Ghana: 1637).[39] Resentment of the Spanish empire in Portugal was therefore intense, as was the sense of decline which would accelerate during Portugal's war for independence from Spain (1640–68). In these circumstances the presence of a group of people – familiars – who did little and expected others to shoulder their share of the social burden added to the problems.

A classic instance of what went on was the case of Amador Fernandes, a familiar of the Holy Office in the 1620s. Fernandes must have been a threatening presence in the streets of Lisbon. He was about thirty-five years old and strongly built, his chin shaded by a black beard; whenever he opened his mouth people could count the gaps in his teeth, picked off by disease like trees by a hurricane.[40] Fernandes earned his living by selling books but it appears that much of his time was spent on other, less reputable activities.

Fernandes had been made a familiar in 1625. In 1627, the year before accusations began to be received about him by the inquisitors of Lisbon, he used his privileges in an unusual way. Donning his familiar's habit and going out into the crowded streets of the city, he waylaid a man leading two mules and requisitioned them – this alone reveals the impunity with which familiars could act when on official business. The mules, he informed their owner, were needed for inquisitorial purposes. Fernandes proceeded to use them to go to a bullfight that afternoon.[41]

This sort of thing was routine behaviour for Fernandes. When he caught the *reconciliado* Manoell Pinto not wearing his penitential *sanbenito*, he turned a blind eye when a bribe was offered; Pinto knew of two other *reconciliados* who had achieved the same result. One familiar, Antonio Antunes, recounted how Fernandes went around buying the deeds of debt of people he disliked, just so that he could go and threaten them with the Inquisition if they did not pay up.[42] In March 1628 he lied to a group of *conversos* that he had been ordered to arrest one of their friends, just in order to frighten them.[43]

Fernandes was clearly someone who enjoyed his ability to instil fear. It must also be recognized that he was thought of as a poor example; three of his accusers before the Inquisition in Lisbon were themselves familiars scandalized by his behaviour. The picture which they painted of him does not inspire confidence in his ability to discharge his inquisitorial duties with probity. One of these familiars, Antonio Teixeira, described him as 'the worst man in the country'.[44] Another, Manoel Pires, was Fernandes's brother-in-law; Pires had few illusions about a man he described as 'one of the worst men in the world for swearing and committing egregious actions [*mal obrar*]'.[45]

The fact that other familiars denounced Fernandes shows that there were some checks and balance to the system, yet his reputation as a person of bad character also forces us to ask why on earth the Inquisition appointed him in the first place. Practices and rules varied a little between districts,[46] but often the reality was that the appointment of familiars was left to the whims of inquisitors and was therefore open to widespread abuse. As one inquisitor put it in 1596, 'he suspects that in the same way as he has received presents because this is said to be a normal way of doing things, so do other officials, and that he has received presents in connection with some applications to become a familiar'.[47] In such circumstances it is not surprising that hypocrisy and abuse of power were often synonymous with the activities of familiars.

What did this mean for daily life in the world of these inquisitorial functionaries? The way in which Amador Fernandes seized property and issued threats reveals a system where power depended on the whim of those who had it. One could not be secure in one's possessions or in the chastity of women since inquisitors or familiars might seek to steal these away. This was a world of arbitrariness, a world in which it was not possible to feel safe.

In the Portugal of Amador Fernandes – as in the cases we saw above of the behaviour of inquisitors in Spain – the gap between theory and practice was once again all too obvious. Thus in 1739 a rulebook composed for familiars in Portugal reveals both how they were supposed to behave and how they actually behaved. Familiars were supposed to be people 'who behaved well, people of confidence and recognized abilities'.[48] The fact that often they were not is revealed by the next requirement, that 'they should have property from which they can live well' – presumably so that they did not extort bribes from others. Familiars were not to 'aggrieve or annoy anybody on the pretext of the privileges which they enjoy' (so we can assume they did this frequently); they were to 'speak about the *conversos* cautiously, so that it is not obvious that they hate them' (obviously they did hate them, and frequently went around whipping up hatred against them); and they were not to ask for loans from *conversos* or accept gifts from people who had dealings with the Inquisition (clearly it was common practice to solicit bribes in return for silence or information).

Although the number of familiars declined from the mid-17th century onward,[49] particularly in Spain where the Inquisition required a greater degree of wealth before making an appointment, their hypocrisies and bad character were a constant from beginning to end. They often did not bother to wear even a figleaf of piety. In 1566 the familiar Juan de Gonbao of the kingdom of Valencia was punished for the very (un)Christian declaration: 'I renounce God and will take a devil for my master if the devil has not taken the soul of my mother to hell'.[50]

This lack of a moral compass poisoned the activities of the familiars. Two years later, in a decree of Zaragoza, the familiars of Aragon were universally acknowledged to be so corrupt that they all had to be sacked and sixty new ones created in their place. The sorts of things that had gone on before are revealed in the articles of the decree, which among other things stipulated that familiars who were tradesmen or merchants should be prosecuted by secular judges for committing fraud in weights and measures and provisions, and that familiars should not arrest anyone without having an inquisitorial warrant to do so.[51]

Evidently, for some, to be a familiar was hardly a religious choice. It was rather to have the freedom to do as one wished in the knowledge that penances, if imposed, would come from the Inquisition itself, which had a vested interest in ensuring that punishments were minor. The power of familiars is illustrated best by the fact that the Inquisition had to prosecute people who pretended to be familiars in order to do as they pleased. False familiars sometimes robbed rich labourers, going into their houses and taking what they wanted at will.[52] Other impersonators of familiars arrested *converso* women and then tried to have sex with them.[53]

How dreadful familiars must have been if people would stand mutely by and watch themselves be robbed by them or by people pretending to be them. There was no shame or pretence of shame. Power *was* (im)morality, as the familiar Francisco Ramírez of the region of Albacete realized. Ramírez, the familiar, who as a young man had been wont to take the clothes off the image of Jesus in the local church, don them and then roam the streets of the town by night pretending to be a ghost; who thus disguised would go to a house to carry on an affair with its owner; who had made another friend pregnant and persuaded her to have an abortion. Once this devout individual was made a familiar, he changed little. He began threatening all those against whom he had taken a dislike. The lives of others were for him playthings. He took against one local deacon, and chased him through his home town of Yeste, waving a pistol in the air.[54]

THE LINK BETWEEN familiars and the inquisitors themselves was the offical known as the commissary. These were paid officials resident in the larger towns who managed the affairs of the local familiars and received depositions. Often, however, commissaries were little better than familiars.

In 1592 a memorial was written by the clergy of Peru denouncing the behaviour of the commissaries throughout the country, and also in Potosí.* The commissaries, the clergy said, were violent, dishonest and argumentative. In Cochabamba (modern Bolivia), the commissary Martín Barco de Centinera revenged himself through the Inquisition on all his personal foes. He usurped royal authority, drank himself silly and boasted publicly of his affairs with married women. The inquisitors of Peru denied none of this, but merely said that getting good officers was difficult. This was the best they could do.[55]

What does this imply about how the Inquisition saw the powers which it had? This observation reveals that abuse of power was seen almost as inevitable, and as a minor failing compared to the prospect of the absence of this power altogether. Power would inevitably be abused, but at least in such cases it would be inquisitorial functionaries and not others who were abusing it.

The impunity with which inquisitorial officials operated is revealed by such cases. There were frequent disputes between them and royal officials, who protested that they did as they pleased. When a servant of an inquisitor had a fight with a prostitute in a brothel in Barcelona in 1565 the officials who arrested him were themselves thrown into the inquisitorial jail for three months.[56] As we have seen, the Council of Granada accused minor functionaries of the Inquisition of bribery and sexual exploitation.[57†] There were

* Then in Peru, now in Bolivia, and capital of the world's silver trade in the colonial period.

† See page 239.

of course some kinder officials, but they were not always encouraged; when Miguel de Xea, an assistant in the inquisitorial jail in Toledo in the early 1590s, took to letting some prisoners out into courtyards and allowing messages to reach them, he was denounced by nine people and himself tried by the tribunal.[58]

The Inquisition did attempt to arrest or at least censure those who misused their powers, but abuses continued inexorably. As far as the familiars of Portugal and Spain were concerned, their freedom of action and disdain for others stemmed directly from the privileges which the Inquisition itself had secured for them. In Portugal, from 1562 onwards familiars were 'exempt from paying extraordinary taxes, demands, loans and any other charges requested by the royal councils or the towns where they are resident . . . nor can their houses, storehouses or stables be requisitioned by the army . . . and likewise nor can their bread, wine, clothes, straw, barley, wood, chickens, eggs, horses, mules and pack-animals be so requisitioned'.[59]

These were exemptions and freedoms shared by no other members of society. Officials of the Inquisition were constantly claiming rights and privileges, such as freedom from taxation or free lodging when travelling. The exemption from having their homes or goods requisitioned by royal armies was also a fact of inquisitorial life in Spain, and the subject of widespread anger. The unpopularity of familiars in Iberian societies is shown nowhere more graphically than by the fact that, in Catalonia alone, there were hundreds of attacks on them over the history of the Inquisition.[60] Eventually, in 1634, with the Iberian empires approaching crisis point, Philip IV of Spain withdrew all exemptions, pleading necessities of state;[61] yet as we have seen in this chapter, often this did not prevent familiars from continuing to do as they wished.

The abuses of power committed by officials of the Inquisition from the loftiest inquisitor to the poorest jailer make plain the power of this institution in Iberian societies. The Italian traveller Leonardo Donato said in 1573 that the Inquisition was of 'such extreme and tremendous authority . . . that I really do not believe there to be a greater one in Spain'.[62] By the early 17th century people were requesting it to do things which had nothing to do with its role, such as punishing people exporting money from Spain.[63] They applied to it because it was the most powerful body in Spain, and because it had a power which people had come to know, and to fear.

AS THE INQUISITION moved through its more than three centuries of existence naturally its structures evolved. One should not pretend that its administrative reach was always universal and all-powerful and, as we have seen, the number of familiars declined rapidly in Spain in the 17th century. Yet we should also not doubt that the Inquisition touched most aspects of most people's lives for most of its life. By the 17th century it was seen by some as a state within a state in Portugal,[64] and it had what was unquestionably the largest and most powerful bureaucracy in the country.

The precision of inquisitorial administration at some points in its history is remarkable. In Spain in the late 16th century all descendants of Jews and Muslims had to register with the Inquisition.[65] Such precision continued long into the 18th century. In 1723 the small provincial town of Aguilar de la Frontera near Cordoba provided a list of all the *sanbenitos* hung in its churches. There were a total of 132, including those of twelve people who had been 'relaxed' and 111 penitents between 1594 and 1723.[66] The list reveals both the reach of the Inquisition in provincial Spain, and also how this reach was constantly in the minds of the people through the *sanbenitos* hung in the churches.

What did the presence of these *sanbenitos* imply? It meant that each Sunday, as the parishioners attended mass, they were reminded of the reality of heresy, and of the fact that it could well be in their midst. Even as the host was elevated, the sermon preached and prayers offered, the threat of impurity was in the minds of the faithful. Thus did fear coexist with prayer even at the most exalted moments of religious devotion.

The practice of hanging *sanbenitos* in churches with the names of penitents continued throughout the life of the Inquisition in Spain. Documents exist showing that measures were periodically put in place to restore the *sanbenitos*,[67] some of which, by the end of the Inquisition's history, were nearly 300 years old. Only between 1788 and 1798 did a commission begin to examine the origin of the practice and whether or not it ought to be continued.[68]

Another indication of the bureaucratic fastidiousness of the

Inquisition can be seen in the inventories which it compiled of the goods of its prisoners. As soon as a person was arrested, a notary would enter their home and produce a list of their possessions. These inventories are extraordinarily detailed. Every last handkerchief or sheet was noted down. Thus, when Francisco Piñero was arrested by the Inquisition in Cartagena in 1636, his inventory included the following items:[69]

- One mattress
- Four cedar chairs with broken seats
- Two handkerchiefs
- Cloths from Rouen
- Napkins
- Pillows
- A black silk jacket
- An old parasol

One imagines that the officials did not make use of the broken-seated cedar chairs or the old parasol. They proceeded cautiously with every aspect of their investigation. Having examined the contents of Piñero's wardrobe, they decided that one rotten hat and some old black stockings that were also mouldy should be thrown out; these were, it was felt, unlikely to add much to the Inquisition's finances.

This emphasis on the minutiae of daily life is what makes Inquisition archives such a fascinating store of material. Yet this fastidious bureaucracy is also testament to the mentality that we saw in Chapter Three in the torture chamber in the sense that what was written down was somehow legitimated. Once a theft had been noted, it had been legalized, and thus record-keeping could be used for ill as well as good.[70]

Precise administration and abuse of power were two sides of the same coin: the enormous power of the Inquisition in Iberian societies. It was because the Inquisition wielded so much power that its employees were often able to act disgracefully and get away with it, and it was because the Inquisition was so powerful that it was able to create such a thorough and meticulous bureaucracy.

Thus the world learnt that an excess of power and an excess of administration often go together. The ability to determine on paper the probity of individuals and to decide what should happen in places which the scribes would never see made the exercise of administrative power a remote activity. The powerful could be shielded from the consequences of their actions.

The culmination and catharsis of such power came, collectively, in the autos. By the middle of the 17th century, as we saw in the Prologue, these were lavish and pompous affairs. Something of the ceremony and importance of these events is revealed by the fact that in the auto of Cordoba of 1627 the second largest expense after building the stage was in paying for the candle wax.[71] Of all the details one can find, this is perhaps the most expressive of the extraordinary theatricality of those public shows.

Yet the very cost of these autos at a time when the Spanish economy was in decline made them increasingly infrequent. The 17th century also saw the rise of the so-called *autos particulares*, more local affairs which did not require so much of an outlay.[72] After all, the costs of staging an auto had risen by over 4,700 per cent between 1554 and 1632 in comparison with inflation of only a little over 100 per cent.[73] Such vast extravagance is testament to the insatiable expansion of the Inquisition, but it was clearly unsustainable and only presaged a long decline.

IT IS HARDLY ORIGINAL to assert that great empires have always eventually fallen into decline. Power is heady and all-consuming, but eventually it fails. Thus we study with fascination the ruins of civilizations such as those that once dominated Easter Island, the Maya, Tiahuanaco in Bolivia and Great Zimbabwe. The dissipation of power appears to be something inherent to it, but it is perhaps not something that the powerful can bear to accept on a conscious level.

The story of the Inquisition is not alien to this dynamic. Spain was the most powerful country in the world in the 16th century and it was at this time that its persecuting institution, the Inquisition, reached its zenith. Yet the Inquisition's projection of power and its incessant seeking after enemies created the conditions for a decline from which the imperial power itself never recovered.

Administration was not irrelevant to this process. As we have seen in the last three chapters, the inquisitorial infrastructure was increasingly applied to tasks which from an objective position seem pointless. Such tasks occupied vast amounts of time and energy which could have been put towards more productive work. The very diversification and spread of the inquisitorial machine was a symbol of the institution's power but also a condition of the stagnation which developed as Spain stuttered towards the end of the 17th century and the crisis of the War of the Spanish Succession (1701–14).

In thinking of this process of power's self-destructiveness, it is worth thinking back to the process of the creation of the *morisco* enemy and their expulsion. We saw there that this was the choice of a society which could have assimilated the converts but chose to marginalize and humiliate this ambiguous group, in so doing vaunting its power. But it was in fact precisely this expulsion of the *moriscos* which precipitated the most serious decline in Spain.

In 1525, following the forced conversions of Aragon's Moors after the *germanía* revolt,* the prospect of unconverted Muslims leaving the country terrified the nobility. They wrote a long letter to Charles V, maintaining that the prosperity of the whole kingdom depended on the Moors, and that Aragon would be ruined if they left. It was the Moors who did all the harvesting, performed all the crafts, and whose rents sustained the churches, the monasteries and the nobility.[74] The nobles remained supporters of the *moriscos* throughout the 16th century, sponsoring their petitions to be freed from inquisitorial jails[75] precisely because the profitability of their agricultural estates depended on them. *Moriscos* provided the backbone of the agricultural economy in Aragon and Valencia and it was sheer folly to expel them, but, as we have seen, this is precisely what the country did, in accordance with an ideology of demonization in which the Inquisition had been pivotal.

The effects were stark. In June 1610, once the expulsion of the *moriscos* had been decreed, the viceroy of Aragon described how the nobility had lost 80 per cent of their income virtually overnight and were in danger of being bankrupted by their creditors.[76] Entire towns were deserted. In Asco, Catalonia, the town was emptied, the houses crumbled, the vines, olive groves and plantations of mulberry

---

* See pages 124–125.

trees went to seed.[77] With the loss of the majority of Aragon and Valencia's labourers came hyperinflation as the *moriscos* sold off their goods for a fraction of their true worth.[78] The situation there became so bad that people who turned to agriculture were exempted from military service.[79]

Such measures achieved little, however. By 1638 the total number of settlements in the kingdom of Valencia had fallen from 755 to 550, a decline of almost one third, with 205 former *morisco* villages simply abandoned.[80] Four per cent of the entire population of Spain had left,[81] and with it much of Spain's agricultural expertise. This picture was mirrored in Castile, where the population fell by almost 15 per cent between 1591 and 1631.[82] Populations continued to decline throughout the 17th century, and only in 1787 did the kingdom of Castile recover the population level of 1591.[83]

The results of this decline – precipitated in part by the expulsion of the *moriscos* – were dire. In 1620 William Lithgow described Spain as 'neither well inhabited nor populous: Yea, so desartuous that in the very heart of *Spaine*, I have gone eighteene leagues (two dayes journey) unseeing house or village . . . and commonly eight leagues without any house'.*[84] Depopulation accompanied decline, and Lithgow, who had travelled widely in Asia and Africa, felt that 'the most penurious Peasants in the world be here, whose Quotidian moanes, might draw teares from stones. Their Villages . . . wanting Gardens, Hedges, Closses, Barnes . . .'[85]

The comprehensive bureaucracy of the Inquisition thus presided over a comprehensive decline, and when one thinks of the stagnation fostered by the institution, the seas separating intention and reality become oceans. The Inquisition was supposed, after all, to safeguard society, but with it had come decline. It was supposed to purify the faith, but how were people supposed to believe in the faith when its guardians behaved so shamelessly? Far from safeguarding the faith, the Inquisition often only fostered cynicism. Just as it had invented enemies rather than destroying them, so it corrupted society rather than purifying it.

The gulf between intentions and results may seem extraordinary to some, yet it supports the view of some psychoanalysts that 'the

* A league is equivalent to approximately three miles.

fact that someone sincerely believes in a statement is not enough to determine his sincerity'.[86] For example, just as a person or institution may claim to be motivated by religious ends when the goals are purely political, so political aims can be cited when the goals of some dramatic and violent action are purely religious. To judge the Inquisition by its actions and effects and not by its stated intentions and beliefs, the institution was not a champion of purity or the security of society; in the end, it fostered corruption and decline.

Lima 1587

HERE IS THE TALE of the 16th-century inquisitor of Peru, Antonio Gutíerrez de Ulloa. The qualities of this man were eloquently expressed by the viceroy of Peru, Fernando de Torres y Portugal, who declared that 'instead of talking of "the inquisitor of Peru" it was more accurate to talk of "the Peru of the inquisitor"'.[87] Precisely what the viceroy meant was revealed in an inquisitorial visit of inquiry made by Juan Ruiz de Prado in the late 1580s.

It emerged that Gutíerrez de Ulloa, like so many inquisitors before and after him, had a strange attitude to his position. The affairs with married women – Catalina Morejón, Catalina Alconchel and the wife of the farrier Sancho Casco – come as no surprise. Gutíerrez de Ulloa however went further even than the (admittedly strong) competition. He began an affair with the young noblewoman María Delgado Tello when she was only eleven years old, and fathered a child with her who he packed off to live near the silver mines in Potosí.[88] Gutíerrez de Ulloa, indeed, soon became the terror of the young women of Lima, entering their rooms by night dressed as a young suitor, in silk stockings and a short cape. He made his housekeeper pregnant. His lovers had public arguments one of which Gutíerrez defused by letting the one he was seeing out by a secret door while the one he was not seeing shouted from the street. He accompanied some of his flames to their properties outside Lima and abandoned his post for weeks. And when he met a love rival near the house of a woman whom he was going to sleep with he stabbed him and left him for dead.

By the time Ruiz de Prado arrived, Gutíerrez de Ulloa had been an inquisitor in Peru for almost twenty years. The visitor formulated over 200 accusations against him. One would expect that in a case of such severity Gutíerrez de Ulloa would have been stripped of his post and punished, but instead he managed to drag it out for so long that Ruiz de Prado's finances ebbed away and he had to leave before he could arrest him. What, then, was Gutíerrez de Ulloa's punishment? He was made an inquisitorial visitor himself, of the province of Charcas (the north of modern Argentina), and left in December 1594 for Buenos Aires.

How can one measure the effects of centuries of abuse of power and bureaucratic stagnation? The decline of Iberia and the comparative poverty of its ex-colonies compared with North America are possible yardsticks, but there are others. In the early 1990s, when I was an employee of the Municipality of Santiago, Chile and provided with lodging as part of my contract, I was offered an iron for my laundry. The iron, however, took several months to get hold of; the problem, my contact informed me, was that the mayor of Santiago had to sign the contract for the release of the iron, and he was usually either busy or absent.

Many people will have similar stories of bureaucratic inertia from around the world. It may be an oversimplification to suggest that such practices are a direct legacy of the administrative bonanza which accompanied the Holy Office, but it is not perhaps inaccurate to suggest that an attitude was cultivated of respect towards administration and of the importance of administration in society, and that this attitude has endured.

What was created most of all was a state of mind. As one scholar so eloquently put it, 'What difference is there between the inquisitorial *sanbenito* and the yellow star imposed upon the Jews in the thirties and forties in several European countries . . . or the brands applied to slaves in so many countries of the Americas in the course of the nineteenth century? . . . Evidently, the inquisitorial mind is still alive'.[89]

Chapter Eleven

THE THREAT OF KNOWLEDGE

Thus silence has been imposed on the learned;
and as for those who ran to the call of science, as you say,
great terror has been inspired in them.

By the middle of the 17th century the Iberian peninsula was moving onward only in desolation. Decline hung in the emptying fields and the atrophying cities. Where had it all gone wrong? With the secession of the Dutch United Provinces from Spain in 1568? At the death of the heirless Portuguese King Sebastian in a pointless war in Morocco in 1578? During the failed Armada launched from both countries in 1588? With the temporary loss of parts of Brazil to the Dutch from the 1620s to the 1650s? The list lengthened into the second half of the 17th century with no respite.

Eventually, Spain had to acknowledge its limitations. After twenty-eight years of conflict Portugal achieved separation from Spain in 1668 but lasting damage had been done to both countries and their empires. Although Portugal had managed to recover Angola (1648), São Tomé (1649) and Pernambuco in Brazil (1654) from the Dutch, its empire in the *Estado da Índia* was irreparably damaged. Bombay (*Bom Baia*) was transferred to English control in 1661 as part of the dowry of Catherine of Bragança with her marriage to Charles II, and the chain of ports from Mombasa to Mozambique Island in east Africa would come under severe attack from the empire of Oman from 1650 onward. By 1700 Portuguese power in east Africa north of Mozambique was finished.[1]

For Spain, meanwhile, control of Portugal and its colonies had gone, and in 1648 the independence of the United Provinces was acknowledged. The Spanish population was falling and the state effectively bankrupt. Spain's American colonies were declining in importance with the rise of North America. The last Spanish king of the 17th century, Charles II, was both physically and mentally disabled, drooled frequently, and proved to be impotent; his death led to the disastrous War of the Spanish Succession.

What we are looking at here is the decline of imperial powers which had once stretched around the globe. In these circumstances, the inquisitorial bureaucracy which we have observed, bedevilled by minutiae which by any objective standards are meaningless, seems incomprehensible. Yet the emphasis on the steady accumulation of pieces of paper betrays a mentality unable to deal with the reality before it: the reality was of an empire and society in precipitous decline: unable to face it, the inquisitorial mentality took refuge in useless documents designed to safeguard the honour and nobility of the nation.

In such circumstances opinions which diverged from the chosen picture of reality were unwelcome. The truth perhaps hurts most – and provokes most anger in – those who are increasingly distant from it. Thus in Spain in particular the broad current of European thought groping towards the Enlightenment in the latter 17th century was unpalatable and had to be prevented from polluting the nation. This movement of scientific inquiry, raised on the shoulders of Bacon, Descartes, Locke and Spinoza, was a direct challenge to the inquisitorial world view. The Inquisition could sense from afar that here was an ideology which could deal it a mortal blow in a way that the *conversos* and the *moriscos* never had.

The Inquisition was right to be suspicious, for some of the more important roots of this ideology did indeed penetrate back to the very people whom the inquisitors had pursued remorselessly for so long, the *conversos*. The development of the scientific world view was in fact deeply connected with the waves of persecution which the Inquisition had first unleashed in Spain at the end of the 15th century, 200 years before this era of decline.

⋆

Zaragoza 1485 to Bordeaux 1592

ON THE LAST DAY of February in 1533 a son was born to Pierre Eyquem and Antoinette Lopez in south-west France. Eyquem was a prominent local dignitary who would later be mayor of Bordeaux and a councillor at Court in Périgeux. The name Lopez was, however, less obviously French. This is not the first time that we have met it in our story, however, for Antoinette Lopez's family had migrated across the border to France during the first onslaught of the Spanish Inquisition, with the persecutions that afflicted Zaragoza in 1486 after the assassination of Inquisitor Pedro de Arbues.* Midnight assassinations, autos burning in the enclosed streets of the city, an atmosphere of paranoia and vengeance; here lay some of the more unexpected origins of the modern scientific world view.

Antoinette Lopez's father had been called Pierre López de Villanueva. When the autos tore into the *converso* community of Zaragoza in the late 15th century many including Pierre fled to France, but not all members of the family were as fortunate. His father, Micer Pablo López de Villanueva, and his father's father, Juan Fernando López de Villanueva, were both burnt in the autos in Zaragoza which followed the sensational assassination of Arbúes.[2] It is worth pausing for a moment to imagine the mindset which the refugees must have taken with them. These were the grandchildren and great-grandchildren of people who had, often voluntarily, left the Jewish faith for Christianity.† They had then been rejected by their new religious community, and persecuted for their origins. It would be surprising if some of these people had not begun to doubt the validity of all religions. Certainly, it was precisely such scepticism which was implanted in the family of the López de Villanueva.

The son born to Pierre Eyquem and Antoinette Lopez in February 1533 became known to the world as Michel de Montaigne. Montaigne, in the view of some philosophers today, was *the* central figure in the evolution of modern sceptical philosophy, a forerunner

---

* See page 22.

† For a discussion of these conversions in the 14th and 15th centuries, see page 18.

to Descartes and Hume and the rise of the scientific world view.[3] In the 16th century he was the most eloquent champion of a brand of thinking known as Pyrrhonian scepticism, which held that there was never enough evidence to determine whether knowledge was possible, hence all judgment should be suspended[4] – a sort of agnosticism as to whether anything could ever be known.[5]

These ideas were reformulated by Montaigne and advanced in his famous *Essays*, still read today for their scope, wit and literary style. Many of the views put forward in the *Essays* were testament to Montaigne's belief in the validity of individual ideas and opinions. In his essay on the education of children, he noted that he was putting forward 'my humours and opinions: I give them because they are what I believe, not because they are what everyone should believe'.[6] His understanding of the gulfs that separate different views of the world and how each can appear valid to those that hold them was summarized in his statement in his famous essay on cannibals that 'people call barbarous that which is foreign to them'.[7]

It is the relevance of insights such as these even today, over 400 years after their formulation, which reveals Montaigne's innovativeness to his contemporaries. It is worth reflecting on the contrast between his belief in the essential independence of thought and expression and the ideology of the institution which had persecuted some of his ancestors in Zaragoza. As far as the Inquisition was concerned, it was precisely independence of thought and belief that was most dangerous and in need of punishment; should it therefore surprise us if one of the descendants of its victims championed the very ideas which the Inquisition found most dangerous?

This does not mean that Montaigne saw his *Essays* as deliberate challenges to the Inquisition or the ideology that lay behind it. One must be clear from the outset that Montaigne was not brought up as a crypto-Jew. While his mother's father came from Zaragoza, his mother's mother Honorette Dupuy was from an old Gascon Catholic family,[8] and Antoinette was brought up as a Protestant.[9] Montaigne himself was raised, like his father, to be a Catholic, but quickly became fascinated by both Reformation and Counter-Reformation thought. One must acknowledge this Christian background, but one must also recognize that Montaigne's *converso* background places some of his ideas in an intriguing perspective.

One idea to emerge from Montaigne was his emphasis on the distance between intention and action. Like a 16th-century Freud, Montaigne was aware that the two were quite different things. As he put it at one point, 'deeds must go with words . . . the real mirror of our ideas are the courses of our lives'.[10] One might say, for example, all kinds of beautiful things about loving one's neighbour and charity, and the need to sow peace and harmony in troubled parts of the world, but if one spent one's life waging war against people and sowing enmities among them it was difficult to argue that love and charity were one's deepest intentions; or as Montaigne noted in his essay on freedom of conscience, 'it is very common to see very good intentions, if they are conducted without moderation, drive men to produce very vicious results'.[11]

One sees here Montaigne's despair at the role of passion in the lives of human beings and his emphasis on moderation. His most influential essay on scepticism is called the *Apology of Raimond Sebond*, and in it Montaigne stresses that religion should not be guided by passion but by faith. There is, he wrote, 'nowhere such excellent an hostility as a Christian hostility. Our zeal wreaks marvels, when it bolsters our tendency towards hatred, cruelty, ambition, avarice, detraction, rebellion . . . Our religion is supposed to be made to extirpate vices; but it conceals, nourishes and incites them.'[12] Again, the tension between intention and action is evident, as is Montaigne's conviction that true religion should not be guided by passion, which only leads people astray.

In the *Apology of Raimond Sebond* Montaigne attacks the idea of Christian universality, both by pointing to the irrational passions which so often underlie religion, and by arguing for relativism. 'We receive our religion in our own way and through our own hands, and no differently from the way in which other religions are received . . . [in other circumstances] another religion, other witnesses, similar promises and threats could in the same way imprint in us a contrary belief . . . we are Christians in the same way that we are Périgordins or Germans.'[13] He argues that, rather than using our inherently flawed reasoning to reach God, simple faith is the way forward for a 'good man [*homme de bien*]',[14] lest there be an attempt to subject the divine power to the legal interpretations of men.[15] This philosophy is called fideism.

The key to the argument is Montaigne's scepticism.[16] Such scepticism was in fact what saved Montaigne's reputation in the eyes of religious orthodoxy, for it was used by the Counter-Reformation – following the argument advanced by Montaigne – to argue that faith alone was the route to salvation. The possibility of absolute scepticism was used by Catholic theologians to engage Calvinists in particular in debates which ended up leading them towards a total scepticism which made their own viewpoint meaningless – and left faith in dogma as a rational position.[17]

At the same time, however, this development of an agnosticism of knowledge was the beginning of a long road. It would be taken up enthusiastically by philosophers and champions of science such as Francis Bacon and Galileo* to push Europe towards the scientific outlook which, in the 18th-century Enlightenment, would come to challenge decisively the theological view of the world held by institutions like the Inquisition. Montaigne's version of Pyrrhonian scepticism was one of the most important sources of a movement which would eventually lead all branches of knowledge into a sceptical crisis from which the modern scientific outlook would emerge.[18] In the 18th century, as we shall see, it was this outlook which would become the principal bugbear of the Inquisition as it decayed towards extinction.

It is worth pausing for a moment to recall the way in which both *conversos* and *moriscos* were hardened into heresy by the persecution directed at them. These were cases, as we have seen, of the Inquisition at some level creating the heresy which it proceeded to persecute and which it saw as its greatest threat. In the case of the Enlightenment a comparable process was at work, as we see in the case of Montaigne. The circumstances created by the Inquisition gave rise to the forces which rebelled against it through a new ideology: the scientific world view.

For while Montaigne was no crypto-Jew, he was aware of his background. He wrote a long exposition of the history of the Jews of Spain in an essay dealing ostensibly with the attachment which some people have towards dying, with his excursus on the history of the Jews and *conversos* being much the longest example in this

---

* Later of course himself tried by the Roman Inquisition for his ideas.

essay.[19] The first publisher of his *Essays*, Simon Millanges, was the son of a *converso*, and the book was printed on 1 March 1580, the date of the Jewish festival of Purim that year. Purim was the most symbolic festival for those *conversos* who were crypto-Jews for it deals with keeping to the Jewish faith in times of oppression.* Montaigne declared in his introduction that the 'date [of publication] was intentionally chosen, to permit companions to understand its hidden message'.[20] Here is undeniable evidence of *converso* influence in Montaigne's thought in spite of the fact that only one of his grandparents had indeed been *converso*.

This statement implies that Montaigne's real beliefs were hidden behind outward opinions and suggests contentions such as that in the *Apology of Raimond Sebond*, 'The pest of mankind is the opinion of knowledge. This is why ignorance is so enjoined to us by our religion as a vital element in our belief',[21] while supposedly supporting his fideism, were intended as irony. For *conversos* and descendants of *conversos* such as Montaigne the use of 'dual language and equivocation' had become an accepted means of concealing subversive opinions behind those that were outwardly acceptable.[22] This was something which Montaigne, a voracious reader, would have known all too well, hiding the dynamite which was his scepticism behind the façade of his greater devotion to faith which he pretended to derive from it.[23] This was a tactic which would be employed in an analogous context by Charles Darwin in his 1859 publication of *Origin of Species*.

When one considers this, the continual exhortations in Montaigne's *Essays* towards relativism and against the role of the passions in religion, and his emphasis on the importance of measuring people by actions and not words, it is difficult not to conclude that the history of his maternal ancestors in Zaragoza must have had at least some impact on the evolution of his philosophy.[24] By its very persecution, the Inquisition fostered an atmosphere in which those it persecuted came to question all received truths. In such an atmosphere a new ideology would develop, one which was sceptical of all claims to divine right and justice, and which would herald the

---

* This is because the heroine of the festival of Purim, Esther, was herself a sort of crypto-Jew.

modern age – the very modern age which would ultimately bring the Inquisition down.

IT IS INSTRUCTIVE to read accounts of how the attentions of the Inquisition affected the attitudes of *conversos* and *moriscos* towards religion. In both cases, while no doubt some had their faith in their ancestral Islamic or Jewish creed strengthened, as they fled to North Africa (if *morisco*) or the Ottoman empire (if *converso*), those who remained in Portugal and Spain were forced into a double life which often turned them towards a sceptical outlook.

Living as a *morisco* often required a sort of ambiguous, double existence. The reality for some was summed up by an Old Christian in the town of Daimiel in Castile in the 1530s, who said to the *morisco* Lope Cambil, 'When you were Muslims, you always told the truth, but now you never do'.[25] Meanwhile, as we saw from the *morisco* uprising in Andalusia 1568–70, some of what *moriscos* did was hardly consonant with Islamic practice.*

Scepticism was, however, more apparent among *conversos*. A typical *converso* view which was frequently denounced to the inquisitors was that 'there was nothing more to existence than being born and dying'.[26] The social position of these converts encouraged scepticism. As the bishop of Porto Alegre (Brazil) put it in the 16th century, these people, 'pretending to be Christians, are neither Jews nor Christians'.[27] The lack of full instruction in either religion could often lead towards atheism.[28]

An ambiguous religious outlook was often married to geographical instability. Many *conversos* travelled constantly around both Europe and the colonies in Africa, America and Asia, as we have seen with the Carvajal family. These wanderings gave them a position between different worlds and, together with their religious ambiguity, created an environment in which they often found it impossible to adopt any one particular mindset, or religion, as entirely their own.[29]

Such feelings are easy to understand today in our equally fragmentary lives. Where one can freely enter so many different contexts and worlds, morality comes more and more to seem like a

---

* See page 173.

child of custom. Not for nothing did a traveller exclaim in the early 17th century, 'For who would have thought, that I who had seene so many sexs [*sic*: sects] and varieties of Religion, dispersed over the face of the earth, could have stucke fast to any Religion at all'.[30] Thus, with their perennial travelling and the perennial insecurity that was their lot, did the *conversos* become prototypes for the modern sceptic.[31] The *conversos* were permanent travellers because the persecutions of the Inquisition made them feel unsafe in any part of the Iberian world, Europe or the colonies. Scepticism was therefore not just a result of the memory of persecution, but also originated from the social condition which had become the lot of the *conversos*. In this situation, Michel de Montaigne was not to be the only *converso* descendant to develop a sceptical philosophy which would directly challenge the ideology of the Inquisition.

Montaigne studied for seven years at the Collège de Guyenne in Bordeaux. It had perhaps been here that *converso* intellectual influence had been brought most strongly to bear, for this important educational establishment had been founded in 1533 by the Portuguese *converso* André de Gouveia, who brought many other *conversos* to the faculty. In 1547 Gouveia was replaced by another *converso*, Jean Gelida, the tutor of Montaigne and, twenty years later, of another *converso* student who was to be almost as important in the development of scepticism.[32] This was the Portuguese doctor Francisco Sanches, whose book *That Nothing Is Known** would dovetail with Montaigne's views and lead directly to the ideas of Descartes and Spinoza.

Sanches was born in northern Portugal in 1551. Along with many Portuguese *conversos* of the time, his family moved to Bordeaux in 1562 as the attacks of the Inquisition on Portuguese *converso* families became ever stronger. Like his father Sanches trained as a doctor and spent most of his life in Toulouse. Here he held the university chairs of medicine and philosophy and lived as a practising and devout Christian – so much so that his two sons became priests.[33]

In his book – published in Lyon in 1581 – Sanches proclaimed time and again his complete scepticism. The first line of his book

* *Quod Nihil Scitur* in the original Latin.

declares, 'I do not *know* even this one thing, namely that I know nothing',[34] an assertion repeated in various guises throughout the book. From this starting point Sanches proceeded to demolish the Aristotelian theories of logic and science that had come to dominate scholastic circles, arguing that it was impossible to have certain or perfect knowledge of the rational world. This led Sanches to a very early form of empiricism in which he argued that direct study and verification of physical phenomena were the only paths to knowledge of the natural world.[35] As he wrote, challengingly, in his introduction, 'Let them be deceived who wish to be deceived; it is not for them I write, so they need not read my works . . . I would address myself to those who, "not bound by the oath of fidelity to any master's words", assess the facts for themselves, under the guidance of sense-perception and reason'.[36]

Montaigne and Sanches were between them, as one leading scholar has put it, 'responsible for a re-examination of old claims to knowledge by thinkers in the seventeenth century'.[37] They were the two philosophers to make 'a major contribution to the diffusion of sceptical ideas [in the sixteenth century]'.[38] Moreover, Sanches's reading of Aristotle was heavily indebted to the humanist Joan-Lluis Vives, and in particular to Vives's book *De Disciplinis*.[39] Vives had been born in Valencia in 1493 and studied in Italy before settling in Bruges until his death in 1540. He was a friend of Erasmus and Thomas More and a prominent figure in the humanist movement sweeping Europe;[40] perhaps it will come as no surprise to learn that, like Montaigne and Sanches, Vives was a *converso*.

Joan-Lluis Vives had direct personal experience of the Inquisition and its methods. His great-grandfather Pau Vives had been condemned in one of the very first autos of the new Inquisition, in Valencia in 1482.[41] Then in 1500 the Inquisition had uncovered a secret synagogue in the house of his grandfather Miguel where his father Lluis had been implicated in heretical ceremonies. This time the family members were reconciled, but in 1522 the Inquisition struck again, arresting his father Lluis and four other relatives. His father was burnt at an auto in 1524, together with his uncle Joan Maçana and effigies of his mother Blanquina March (who had died in 1508), and of his great-aunt.[42]

Some have argued that the *converso* background of Vives is

testament precisely to the lack of a specifically *converso* ideology influencing intellectual ideas in the 16th century.[43] Vives, certainly, was no crypto-Jew, yet as we have seen, he influenced Sanches in his powerful development of a sceptical philosophy to match the scepticism of which individual *conversos* were often accused. And, like Montaigne and Sanches, Vives held that absolute truth could not be known by the human mind, believing that the sceptic's aim should be to see whether or not trustworthy – if not entirely accurate – knowledge could be obtained.[44] At one point he wrote, 'We are ignorant of the beginning, development and causes of every single thing'.[45]

Where the impact of the Inquisition on Vives's philosophy can best be traced, however, is that like Montaigne and Sanches he was a devoted champion of the priority of reason.[46] While, unlike Montaigne and Sanches, he favoured reaching probable forms of truth rather than abandoning the conceit of knowledge altogether, like them he feared the triumph of passion over reason. If reason was abandoned, he wrote, the danger was that 'we will fall into absurd fictions and end up pursuing fickle dreams instead of wise doctrines'.[47] The type of fickle dreams he had in mind was revealed in a letter which he wrote to his friend Erasmus in January 1524 in which he described his hope that the popularity of Erasmus in Spain might lead the Spaniards 'to soften and to dismantle certain barbarous conceptions of life, conceptions with which these penetrating but uneducated and inhumane spirits are imbued'.[48] It is worth bearing in mind that it was in January 1524 that Vives's father Lluis was incarcerated in the inquisitorial jail prior to being burnt to death; the 'barbarous conceptions of life' which he feared need no further explanation.

Here a pattern begins to emerge, surely, in the origins of the sceptical philosophy that came to dominate the Western tradition during the Enlightenment. Persecution, it turns out, could not only lead to a general current of scepticism among *conversos* in their travels around the world; it could also lead the intellectuals among them to formulate ideas which assisted in the overthrow of all received certainties. These figures preached scepticism and the need to obtain knowledge by observation of the natural world – what became known as scientific experiment. It was the very experience of persecution which led to these intellectuals developing a concrete ideology which, between the 16th and the 18th centuries, helped along with many others to shatter the certainties upon which the ideology of the Inquisition was based.

The influence of this first generation of *converso* sceptics was far-reaching. Sanches's *That Nothing Is Known* was reprinted in Frankfurt in 1618[49] and may have been read by René Descartes – in Frankfurt in 1619 – as he worked his way towards writing his famous work on scepticism, *Discourse on Method*.[50] Descartes was in turn studied by Baruch Spinoza, a Jew from Amsterdam whose family had previously been *conversos* and had moved to Holland to be able to live as Jews.[51] Spinoza rejected Judaism and developed a form of scientific empiricism and a metaphysical system which was essentially Godless and prefigured some of the Enlightenment ideas which so bedevilled the Inquisition in the 18th century. Spinoza's ideas sprang from the strong current of *converso* scepticism, and there were many ways in which Spinoza reformulated both *converso* literary styles and ideas.[52]

It would be a mistake to take these ideas too far. No one can say that all or even most of the credit or blame for the rise of sceptical philosophy should be laid at the door of the *conversos*. But the fact that perhaps the three most important sceptics of the 16th century – Montaigne, Sanches and Vives – were all from families with experience of the Inquisition, and that the champion of a Godless world view where knowledge was obtained by scientific experiment in the 17th century – Spinoza – also came from this background is suggestive.

As we saw in the last chapter, the corruption of the Inquisition at home led to decay in the very things it wished to preserve. Abroad, its history of persecution led to the development of philosophies which would further undermine it. Every extreme action, perhaps, provokes an extreme reaction. And thus like every authoritarian institution or government did the Inquisition possess the seeds of the tendencies which would destroy it.

IN 1499 A PLAY was written which, together with Cervantes's *Don Quixote*, has widely been hailed as one of the masterpieces of Spanish literature. The play is called *La Celestina*, and deals with the doomed love of a young rake called Calisto. Calisto loves a noble lady called Melibea, but loves her in despair as he is not of her station. However, Calisto's servant Sempronio introduces him to a local procuress called Celestina, who specializes in the arcane (but important) art of restoring maidenheads to 'virgins'. Celestina lures Melibea towards Calisto, but the young gallant dies falling off a ladder while leaving Melibea's house in the dark, and his bereft lover responds by killing herself. Replace the impossibility of bridging snobbery with the impossibility of reconciling feuding noble houses, and here is much of the plot of *Romeo and Juliet* a century before Shakespeare.

In *La Celestina* the storyline combines beautiful disquisitions on many fine human emotions with some extremely powerful writing. A feature of the text, however, is the existence of phrases which could also convey an inquisitorial meaning. In the opening scene Calisto declares to Sempronio that 'the flame which kills one soul is bigger than that which burnt a hundred thousand bodies'.[53] This flame, for Calisto, is his love for Melibea, but when he is challenged by Sempronio as persevering with something bad, Calisto responds, 'You know little about steadfastness', to which Sempronio answers, 'Perseverance in sin is not constancy, but is called stubbornness and pertinacity in my country'.[54] When considering an inquisitorial subtext here, one must bear in mind that heretics condemned to burn were called *pertinaz* in the language of the Inquisition.

Another servant, Parmeno, tells Calisto that 'you lost the name of a free man when you allowed your will to become captive'[55] (as the *conversos* had become captives to inquisitorial jurisdiction when they had converted to Christianity). When Celestina describes the suffering of Parmeno's mother, who has been processed in an auto for witchcraft, she relates how 'with false witnesses and severe tortures they made her confess what she had never done'[56] and how she had been told by a priest that 'the Holy Scripture held that the fortunate were those who suffered persecution in the name of justice, and that they would inherit the kingdom of Heaven'.[57]

Such clear instances of an inquisitorial subtext do not occur on every page of *La Celestina*, but they are undoubtedly present, although they should not be used as the only prism through which to interpret the play.[58] But they are an important element of its context, and it will by now come as no surprise to learn that the author of *La Celestina*, Fernando de Rojas, was born in Castile in around 1476 to a *converso* family. When he was ten years old, in 1486, his future father-in-law was reconciled by the Inquisition, while his father-in-law's parents were exhumed and their bodily remains burnt.[59] Having written the play as a young man, Rojas became an upstanding figure in society, a barrister, and even acted in some inquisitorial trials, but when one reads some of the passages of *La Celestina* there can be little doubt that Rojas's *converso* background was one of the emotional sources for the play.

There were large numbers of *conversos* among the most important writers of golden age Spain. The very first picaresque novel, *Lazarillo de Tormes*, written in 1554 by an anonymous author and depicting Spanish society from the perspective of an individual at its bottom, is known to have been written by a *converso*,[60] as was the great poetry of Luis de Góngora.[61] Even Cervantes had some *converso* ancestry, and some historians have gone as far as to suggest from the sort of food that he ate that Don Quixote himself was supposed to be a *converso*.

Just as there is no coincidence in the fact that some of the most important early sceptics were *conversos*, so there is no coincidence about the prevalence of *conversos* among the most important Spanish dramatists, poets and novelists of the 16th century. The dissonance which existed between the *converso* individual and his ambiguous place in society created an alienation which was the starting point for the literature of the golden age, and indeed for the alienation at the heart of all modern literature.[62]

There were, it is true, other reasons for the predominance of *conversos* in writing and philosophy. Their Jewish ancestors had come to Christian Spain in the first place from the far more cultivated Muslim kingdom of Al-Andalus; there they had inherited a tradition of scholarship and literature unavailable to the militaristic Christians, for whom excessive intellectual activity would have obstructed the reconquest.[63] This inevitably meant that a disproportionate number of thinkers and writers were *conversos*, but it also meant that thinking and writing came to be associated with heresy.

The impact of this began to be felt in the 16th century, when the *converso* class as a whole gained a reputation for being clever (*agudos*). When the *converso* bishop of Granada and confessor of

Queen Isabella, Fernando de Talavera, tried to convert the Jews, one chronicler wrote, he found that 'as [the Jews] are naturally clever and can quote the Holy Scripture so readily, they often argued against what was preached to them'[64] whereas most people apparently simply accepted it. In another case a teacher at the University of Salamanca in 1572 was held to descend from *conversos* simply because '[his father and uncles] were all very clever'.[65]

The association of intelligence and independence of thinking with *conversos* and thus with heresy began with the persecution of the followers of Erasmus in the 1530s, when, as we saw in Chapter 5, large numbers of intellectuals were arrested for deviance from the orthodoxy. Rodrigo de Manrique, the son of Inquisitor-General Alonso Manrique, who was sidelined in those years, described the situation eloquently in a letter to Joan-Lluis Vives of 9 December 1533 after the arrest of the well-regarded humanist Juan de Vergara:

> When I consider the distinction of his spirit, his superior erudition and (what I value most) his irreproachable conduct, I feel great sadness that some great wrong may be done to this excellent man. Thinking of the intervention of those who have laid impudent calumnies at his door, I tremble at the thought that he has fallen into the hands of men lacking in dignity and culture who hate men of value, and who think they are doing a good and pious work in making wise men disappear for the sake of just one word, or because of a joke. What you say is right: our country is a land of envy and arrogance; you could add: of barbarity. Because it is well understood there that one cannot possess a certain degree of culture without being full of heresy, error and *converso* stains. Thus silence has been imposed on the learned; and as for those who ran to the call of science, as you say, great terror has been inspired in them.[66]

Historians who favour the general role of the Inquisition in the formation of Spanish society have often tried to exonerate it from this charge of being 'anti-knowledge',[67] yet in the protracted 18th-century debates on the issue the defenders of the Inquisition cited works of theological science rather than natural science in their arguments. The general attitude of the inquisitorial hierarchy towards individual talent and scientific advances can be seen in several cases: that of Manuel de Tovar Olvera, a Spaniard accused in Mexico around 1660 of having a pact with the devil because he was able to control a herd of mares which usually kept ten or eleven men busy;[68] or the extraordinary case in the early 18th century when the Inquisition in Lima proceeded against a pilot simply because he had guided a ship from Callao (the port for Lima) to Valparaíso in Chile in less than half the previous record time.[69]

It is cases like this that confirm the validity of the view of the great historian H.C. Lea on the Inquisition: 'The real importance of the Inquisition is not so much in the awful solemnities of the autos-da-fé, or in the cases of a few celebrated victims, as in the silent influence exercised by its incessant and secret labours among the mass of the people and the limitations which it placed on the Spanish intellect'.[70] The pursuit by the Inquisition of Erasmian intellectuals stifled the development of ideas, and the lack of informed debate about the great scientific issues of the day became a factor in the decadence which engulfed the world south of the Pyrenees in the 17th century.[71]

The effects were stark. By the early 17th century no Spanish press used Greek characters – an extraordinary fact considering that just one century before the Universities of Alcalá and Salamanca had been centres of Hellenism.[72] Such was the fear of science that in 1640 all the works of Copernicus were placed on its index of prohibited books by the Inquisition.[73] The great works of literature acquired by Philip II and placed in the library of his funereal palace at the Escorial went unread, and were in fact left uncatalogued until the beginning of the 19th century, when the work was undertaken by a Frenchman.[74]

Henceforth, erudition and reading were to be undertaken with caution. A new opponent was secured for the Inquisition which, in the 18th century in particular, became the major preoccupation of the institution: the book. As one inquisitor put it in the late 16th century: 'the truth is that the [doctrine of the heretics] is nowhere so much communicated and distributed as through the medium of books, which, as mute teachers, talk continuously; they teach all the time, and in all places . . . the typical adversary and enemy of the Catholic faith has always relied on this efficient and pernicious medium'.[75]

In such an atmosphere books were as worthy of condemnation as people and were burnt before the people together with heretics at autos.[76] In 1579 the inquisitor-general of Portugal ordered that they should be incinerated until not even the ashes remained.[77] But of course writers and thinkers were not above satirizing such events. Cervantes included a scene mocking the burning of books at an auto in *Don Quixote*, where the books of chivalry which the poor deluded knight had amassed were, as Cervantes put it, 'relaxed' by the secular arm of his housekeeper – thrown onto a bonfire in the courtyard to keep Don Quixote from reading any more of them.

The burning of the books in *Don Quixote* was a forerunner of other such literary scenes of which the most famous today is perhaps the scene in Umberto Eco's novel *The Name of the Rose* where the blind friar of a Benedictine monastery, Jorge, burns down a secret stash of priceless books rather than seeing their heresies spread. Ideas are dangerous. Like viruses they can be contagious. They must be stamped out. A future vision of the same concern was brilliantly imagined by Ray Bradbury in his novel *Fahrenheit 451*, memorably adapted for the cinema by the French director François Truffaut. In Bradbury's vision books are too dangerous for the population and are held to breed elitism and divergence from the accepted norms of society; 451 degrees Fahrenheit is the temperature at which the paper used to bind books catches fire, and firemen no longer put out house fires but burn books. Thus is a security cordon erected against ideas which might, it is feared, destroy the state, a security cordon that was first erected by the Inquisition.

It is not an insignificant comment on the human condition that, no sooner had the printing press been developed in the late 15th century, than people tried to censor what could be printed. It turns out that there is always a side of humanity – the side in authority – which fears the products of human creativity and tries to suppress them.

In Spain the potential of books to threaten the national identity became apparent during the early conflicts with the Muslims in Granada. Cisneros's ceremonial burning of thousands of Islamic books in Granada in 1501 was followed by an edict issued on 12 October of the same year ordering the burning of all Islamic books 'so that there should be no memory of them and no one should have the occasion to err in their faith again'.[78] The potential danger of books clearly penetrated the royal consciousness for the following year, on 8 July 1502, the *Reyes Católicos* passed a law that no printer or bookseller could publish without their royal permission.[79]

It did not take long for the Inquisition to become involved in censorship. In 1505 Inquisitor-General Diego de Deza attempted to prohibit a book by the grammatical scholar Antonio de Nebrija on the Bible[80] even though the book had not yet been completed.[81] Deza fell from grace after the Lucero affair, and his successor Cardinal Cisneros allowed the book to be published. Nonetheless, a precedent had been set.

By the 1520s the inquisitorial machine was beginning to investigate books as they entered Spain, and when in 1523 one French ship was found to have a small crate of Lutheran books, sixteen places were visited over the region of Guipúzcoa (the Basque country) to ensure that they had not become dispersed.[82] By the 1530s bookshops were being visited all over Aragon, and the association of the Inquisition with censorship had become irreversible.[83]

The instructions set out for visiting bookshops in the search for banned books were precise. First, the inquisitorial functionary was to order the shop to close and ask the owner for a list of all the books that he had – which the owner was obliged to keep. Then the functionary had to ask if there were any books which needed to be added to the list. Then the functionary was to check the list and see if any were from the latest catalogue of banned books. Finally the functionary had to check all the books on the shelves and cross them off against the owner's list. Ideally, the rules of operation suggested, visits should be made early in the morning so as not to damage trade.[84]

Booksellers are not today thought of as great adventurers, but in this era in Iberia this is what they were. One does not imagine such shops, filled with ponderous books accumulating dust, as owned by risk-takers, yet this was the reality. One can imagine the booksellers being torn between the demands of the Inquisition and the fact that banned books gave them the greatest profits. Thus while the bureaucracy clamped down on seditious ideas in another way it encouraged them.

The hazards which daily afflicted booksellers were many; books were frequently impounded, threatening them with bankruptcy. In the late 16th century Vicencio Millis, a bookseller from the market town of Medina del Campo, appealed to the inquisitorial authorities. His father Jacob had sent him thirty-three bundles of books from Lyon in France which had been impounded at the port in Bilbao to be inspected. This process was taking so long that Millis wrote to ask that the inspection occur in Medina del Campo instead, so that at least he could sell the ones which were passed fit for the general public.[85]

It is true that, from their own perspective, the Inquisition had much to dislike about some of these books. Heretics were also adopting wily ruses to get their seditious – and salacious – material into Spain, including in 1604 offering inquisitorial functionaries afternoon tea when they went to inspect their ships in port for banned books.[86] Sometimes they printed heretical books with the names of printers based in Catholic cities and sent them to their allies in Spain to smuggle in through Seville concealed within orthodox and decent books which aroused no suspicion.[87]

The reality was that a country with such a lengthy coastline could never be proof against this invasion of foreign books and ideas. One man was found with 250 prohibited works in his library in 1651.[88] Books could be smuggled over the passes of the Pyrenees, or concealed in clothes, trunks and hidden compartments in ships. They could be rowed ashore by starlight outside the major ports and then never seen again. There was a constant demand for them since as the cliché so accurately puts it, nothing excites so much as prohibition.

But while censorship could not prevent ideas from entering Spain, it could limit them to a very small section of society and act as a declaration of intent in which learning and innovative scientific thought were frowned upon; and this, was indeed precisely the effect of the first indexes of censorship.

Like a stubborn backache which refuses to disappear whatever position one adopts, we find ourselves back with an old foe, Inquisitor-General of Spain Fernando de Valdés. This is, we should recall, the same Valdés who destroyed his rival Archbishop Carranza of Toledo, expanded the scope of the Inquisition from *conversos* and *moriscos* to the Old Christian population, and reorganized the administrative structure of the Inquisition so that familiars were found in every small town across Spain. With his unequalled genius for administering persecution and repression, it was Valdés who presided over the creation of the first genuinely wide-ranging Spanish index of censorship in 1559 – at the height of his campaign to snare Archbishop Carranza.

Given all the cases we have seen of family members and friends denouncing one another, it should not surprise us that again personal enmity should have had such a decisive influence on the subsequent cultural history of Spain. The 1559 index was developed precisely as a means of discrediting Carranza's *Catechism*, one of the main thrusts of the investigation against him.*

In February 1559 under Valdés's leadership the *Suprema* ordered that all works in Spain dealing with the Bible which had been published in vernacular languages outside the country should be seized, adding in a letter to the Inquisition in Seville that commentaries on Carranza's *Catechism* should be confiscated, and that 'in order for it not to appear that only this book is being examined [i.e., it was precisely only this book which *was* of interest], it would be good to publish edicts ordering the seizure of all books written in the vernacular dealing with Christian doctrine'.[89] Matters moved swiftly, and by 20 March the *Suprema* was already talking of a 'catalogue of books' to be printed 'as soon as possible'. Eventually, publication came in August 1559, the very same month that Carranza was arrested.

It is true that there were precedents for this move by Valdés. Prior to this first index, lists of suspect books had been published by the Inquisition in 1540 and 1545[90] and prohibitions of Lutheran books stretched back to 1521.[91] The first full index had been published in 1551, but there was nothing distinctively Spanish about it, as it reproduced a list published in Louvain (in modern Belgium – then under the control of Charles V) in 1550.[92]

What was different about Valdés's 1559 index was that, in the midst of the persecution of the Lutheran threat in Valladolid and

---

* See page 130.

Seville and the pursuit of Carranza, with threats supposedly looming on all fronts, the opportunity was taken to ban not only religious books but works of all genres. The novels of Bocaccio appeared on the list, together with the picaresque novel *Lazarillo de Tormes* and other works by some of the most important writers of the early 16th century.[93] For the first time, censorship was expanding from the religious sphere.

It would however be a mistake to pretend that Valdés and Spain were acting in isolation. The first papal index of banned books had been issued by Pope Paul IV in 1557, as a result of discussions at the Council of Trent[94] and Portuguese indexes had been issued in 1547 and 1551.[95] Valdés also operated with complete royal approval, since in 1554 the Council of Castile had been made the sole authority to issue licences to print books,[96] and in 1558 Philip II had published a law prohibiting all booksellers from selling or possessing any book banned by the Inquisition on pain of death, and banning the possession of books written in the vernacular and published outside Spain without royal licence.[97] Knowledge had become a commodity to be monitored.

Valdés, as might be expected, did not rest with the establishment of the index. Censorship itself was centralized; the *Suprema* ordered at the height of the Carranza case that nothing could be censored without its approval.[98] From 1558 onward printers were supposed to be visited once every four months, and sometimes the production of suspect works was suspended.[99] A royal decree of 1558 imposed for the first time systematic control on the import of books, and a further thirty-three royal letters were written on the subject through to 1612.[100] Increasing numbers of *calificadores* were appointed, religious people in each district of the Inquisition who were sent books to read and approve or censor for orthodox eyes.[101] If the physical purity of the nation was increasingly bound up with ideas of blood, its mental purity was associated with preventing corruption by 'impure' ideas.

Just as the association of knowledge with heresy discouraged people from taking to learning, so this 'trial of the book' also had enormous effects on society. By the 1560s, just a few suspect lines were enough for a book to be banned; a work by Carranza's lawyer Dr Navarro was denounced in 1572 simply for having a few words in favour of the archbishop.[102] The number of books prohibited swelled like a cancer, from 699 under Valdés in 1559 to 2,315 under Inquisitor-General Quiroga in the index published in 1583. In this *Great Index of Prohibitions** books by Abelard, Dante, Machiavelli, More, Rabelais and Vives were banned, together with everything ever translated from Erasmus into Spanish and twenty-two of his works in Latin, and classical authors including Herodotus, Tacitus, Plato, Pliny and Ovid. Prohibition was extended to images, coins, portraits, medals, songs and statues.[103]

The poor inquisitorial staff! How was it possible to contend with a world in which so much heretical material was to hand? One went into a neighbour's house and saw a blasphemous image on a medal. One tried to ignore it, and began to study a book for some peace of mind only to be outraged by a statement betraying a lack of orthodoxy. Closing one's eyes to the sins of the world, one heard blasphemies in the siren-like voices of a choir. The four *calificadores* of Cordoba wrote to the *Suprema* in 1584 that there were so many books on the list that they would never finish their task of censorship if they were not provided with reinforcements.[104]

This was a society in which to be orthodox was to be perennially hot under the collar. The potential for outrage grew all the time, with the gargantuan appetite of the publishing industry. In 1559 the index of prohibited books was fifty-nine octavo pages[†] in length; the indexes of 1707 and 1747 would be over 1,000 pages in folio.[‡105] It was increasingly possible to feel scandalized and affronted, as the vituperative letters of the *calificadores* made clear: such-and-such a passage was *escandaloso* (underlined – scandalous), *malsonante* (underlined – sounded bad), *perjudicial a la fe* (underlined – prejudicial to the faith).

The willingness to be offended and to react with violence is a typical expression of a victim mentality. The Inquisition had created a world view that felt under siege and therefore felt justified in its

---

* *Gran Índice Prohibitorio.*

† An octavo page is 20 centimetres high.

‡ A folio page is 30 centimetres high.

persecutions. But the siege was laid more by internal repressions than by the deeds of enemies.

What occurred in Spain did not occur in inquisitorial isolation. In Portugal censorship commenced in an organized fashion as soon as the Inquisition was launched there in 1536. By 1539 books had to be approved by the Inquisition to be published, and in 1540 Cardinal Henry delegated censorship to three Dominican friars.[106] It was not only published books that were censored; works were subject to preventive censorship – submitted for approval before publication and amended accordingly.[107]

By the last quarter of the 16th century censorship in Portugal was well established. Every book had to be approved by the General Council of the Inquisition, local religious figures where the book was published, and by the palace authorities (*Desembargo do Paço*).[108] By 1581 lascivious books and comedies and plays in which religious people were portrayed were banned.[109] Among the books confiscated in a sudden visit to bookshops in 1606 were *La Celestina* and *Don Quixote*.[110]

In the New World all works of the imagination and profane books and theatre were banned throughout the colonial period.[111] Ports were checked everywhere, with regular inspections of ships even in remote districts such as Guatemala.[112] With such a vast remit censorship was in many ways harsher than in Spain.[113] As soon as ships docked in Mexico near Veracruz, inquisitorial commissaries inspected the luggage of all passengers and sailors for books, making an inventory and sending it to the customs house for clearance.[114] Foreign printers were prosecuted, and the majority of correspondence between the tribunal in Mexico City and regional commissaries related to the book trade.[115] In 1690 the number of inquisitorial visits to English ships to search for banned books was such that the English ambassador in Mexico City complained to the Inquisition.[116]

It is of course a mistake to pretend that censorship was exclusively an Iberian phenomenon. Louis XV of France (1715–74) threatened authors and printers of seditious books with death[117] while 294 books were prohibited in Britain between 1524 and 1683.[118] Yet when one compares this number to the 2,315 banned in the 1583 Spanish index alone, it becomes apparent that censorship in Iberia was of a different order to that elsewhere. It may not always have been effective, and banned books did seep in little by little, but the ideology behind it created an atmosphere in which many types of learning became suspect. Perhaps even more damaging than official censorship was the self-censorship which such a climate fostered, as people feared being cast adrift if they strayed from the prevailing ideology. Thus from small beginnings and individual bans did an entire world of ideas fall into inertia. A permanent sense of insecurity among intellectuals was created which meant that there was a fear of new ideas and discoveries.[119] Intellectual activity was turned into the mere repetition of pre-established schemas, and Iberian intellectual life fossilized,[120] becoming a mirror of the economic and political paralysis which took over from the 17th century onward.

This curious and sad history is difficult to imagine among the archives of Portugal and Spain, with their venerable tomes and lovingly preserved documents. Yet occasionally, if one looks hard enough, the legacy is there. In Lisbon one venue for my research was the archive of the palace of Ajuda, set on a high promontory above the estuary of the Tejo and the tower at Belén. The dirty cobbles of the streets below were more reminiscent of working-class districts in Montevideo or Santiago de Chile than a European city, and the palace itself was an anomaly; for above the workaday difficulties and sacrifices of one of the poorer cities of Europe were pendulous halls of marble, with shelves reaching like Towers of Babel into the architraves, stacked with books almost as high and as thick as a person.

In the palace of Ajuda one can sit surrounded by copies of Mercator, ancient globes, dust and silence. Here, at least, books are valued and preserved. But in the excessive respect accorded to them is a hint of the polarities of previous centuries, where elites had had access to forbidden knowledge while the rest of the population was deliberately denied it.

*

Cartagena de las Indias 1634

SOMETHING OF THE UNUSUAL moral compass which the Inquisition developed under the twin impulses of expansion and fear of knowledge coalesced in a remarkable case in Cartagena, Colombia in 1634. The ship *Nuestra Señora de Monserrate* arrived in port from Cacheu in Guinea-Bissau, captained by one Diogo Barassa, with over 300 contraband slaves hidden under the poop deck, who had lived in appalling conditions throughout the forty days of the voyage from Africa.[121]

Arriving on 30 July, the ship was visited by the inquisitorial secretary, who was concerned to see if any banned books were on board. The conditions on such ships were described in graphic detail during a subsequent visit the same year to a different ship, this time from Angola. On that occasion the secretary wrote,

> There were a large number of male and female blacks hidden behind some grass mats which covered them. They were so crammed in and piled on top of one another that it was only with extreme difficulty that I managed to pass the entrance and go into the space beneath the poop deck, and even then it was impossible for me to get more than halfway in since the blacks were so closely knit. The heat was so immense that I could not bear it and so I turned back and made two sailors from the ship go forward with lit candles between the blacks. There seemed to be more than 400 of them hidden there.[122]

On the *Nuestra Señora de Montserrate* from Cacheu the inquisitorial secretary proceeded to make a thorough examination. However, he found no books prohibited by the Inquisition and so was content to finish the visit without taking any action.[123] Prohibited books might have been anathema to the Inquisition, but the appalling conditions of the contraband slaves did not on this occasion even rate a mention by the inquisitorial flunkey. Theologically, the inaction of the official was justified, since the papacy had granted some moral legitimacy to the slave trade as a mode of saving souls. Perhaps, indeed, the more souls squeezed into those putrid sanctuaries of rotting wood rolling across the ocean, the better. But this surely reveals to us only that no dogma is godlike enough to warrant our unflinching approval.

It was of course a different vein of this very same dogma which led to the attempt to bar certain types of literary production from Iberian society. As we saw above, by 1583 many great authors had been banned, including Dante, Erasmus, Thomas More and Ovid. Although inquisitors were more interested in theology than works of literature[124] the greats continued to be excluded. In the late 16th and early 17th centuries there were repeated complaints about the impossibility of getting hold of Machiavelli in Spain,[125] and in 1659–60 a protracted debate began in Zaragoza and Madrid regarding Bartolomé de las Casas.

Las Casas' *Brief History of the Destruction of the Indies* is today recognized as one of the classic historical texts dealing with the Spanish discovery of America, but things were seen very differently in the 17th century. In 1659 the first person to propose censoring this work, the Jesuit Francisco Minguijon, did so saying that these 'injurious tales to the Spanish nation should be seized . . . even if they are true'.[126] The following year five Franciscan friars agreed, saying that the book was 'for the most part a defamatory libel against the Spaniards, injurious, pernicious, and denigratory, and an excuse for foreign nations to hate and abominate the Spaniards, which is enough to make it scandalous'.[127] As another *calificador* put it, as 'the excesses have been remedied . . . it should be prohibited and it falls within law 16 of the expurgatory index of 1640 which deals with words and clauses which detract from the reputation of neighbours'.[128]

In such an ideology truth no longer mattered; the appearance of truth was everything. Literature, though it remained the province of culture, was produced in the awareness that it did not escape the eyes of the censors. *La Celestina* – banned much earlier in Portugal – was expurgated many times before being banned in Spain in 1793, three years after the prohibition of all Montaigne's essays.[129] The entire works of Rabelais were banned in Spain in 1667, including the book for which he is now best remembered, *Gargantua and Pantagruel*.[130]

As the Enlightenment – and the Inquisition's reaction against it – proceeded in the 18th century, so did the number of banned books. Authors banned included Condorcet, Hume, Locke, Montesquieu, Pope, Rousseau, Swift and Voltaire; Laurence Sterne was banned in 1801 and Gibbon's *Decline and Fall of the Roman Empire* – surely too close to the bone – followed in 1806.[131] In the bookshop of Estanislao de Lugo, raided in 1817, books seized included works by Berkeley (*Dialogues Concerning Natural Religion*, now seen as a key work of philosophy), Erasmus, Gibbon, Locke, Milton (*Paradise Lost*), Montesquieu, Rabelais, Rousseau and Voltaire.[132]

By any modern standard, these authors rank among the towering figures of Western literature and philosophy; the Inquisition wanted nothing to do with them.

As we have seen in the last few chapters, it was the social effects of the Inquisition which became most pronounced in the 17th century. As the global influence of the Spanish and Portuguese empires diminished, so did the physical reach of the Inquisition and its capacity to inflict its violence. This reminds us that the Inquisition was essentially a political institution, and that, as we have also seen, Catholic theology and papal authority merely served the authorities as an excuse and a justification.

In Portugal in the later 17th century, for instance, the papacy was once again a restraining influence. When, in July 1672, some of Lisbon's wealthiest *conversos* were arrested, the papacy eventually issued an ultimatum to the regent Dom Pedro demanding an inquiry into the trials and threatening suspension of the Inquisition.[133] Around this time an anonymous account was circulating in Rome of the terrible practices of the Portuguese Inquisition. Little had changed since the early days of the institution: there was still routine torture; lawyers were not allowed to see the evidence against defendants; the most genuine Catholics were most likely to be condemned. When the executioner at an auto in Coimbra was forced by the struggles of his victim to slacken the rope a little, the dying man cried out, 'Jesus!'[134]

In Spain, meanwhile, the emphasis on pomp and ceremony at autos meant that these were rarer, but they tended to be violent affairs when they did occur. A legacy of the union with Portugal was the association of all Portuguese with crypto-Judaism,* with the result that numerous Portuguese victims were convicted of this

---

* See page 202.

crime through to the 18th century. In Majorca a terrible series of trials unfolded against the *converso* community of Palma which resulted in the reconciliation of 250 *conversos* at five autos in 1679 and the 'relaxation' of thirty-seven of these for relapsing in an auto of 1691.[135] In Madrid, meanwhile, one of the greatest autos in the history of the Inquisition occurred in 1680, when twenty-three people were 'relaxed' on a stage 58 metres long and 30 metres side dominating the Plaza Mayor in the centre of the city.[136]

This auto occurred almost exactly two centuries after the first auto in Seville in 1481 and showed that even though people were no longer burnt and garrotted every year, the Inquisition could still descend with fury on communities when it wished to. It is difficult today beneath the brightly painted balconies of the Plaza Mayor to imagine such a terrible scene, but memories of horror and brutality fade quickly; it is only in their social legacies that something of the cultural memory of fear can be discerned.

What comes across most of all, perhaps, is the joylessness of it all. Pleasure was anathema to the censors. Some paintings and playing cards were banned from the mid-17th century onward for their offence to dogmatic morality.[137] By the end of the 18th century complaints were being received about the words of hymns sung in church.[138] Some of the works of Goya were banned.[139] It was possible to object to any aspect of cultural endeavour: literature and philosophy, song and craft, painting and theatre. The ideology behind this process drove the decline of the Iberian powers in two key ways: first by helping to foster an ideology – scepticism – which would deal a mortal blow to the Inquisition during the Enlightenment, and second by helping to ensure the intellectual stagnation of the culture from which the Inquisition had grown, rendering it incapable of dealing with this threat when it emerged in the 18th century.

Other societies in other times and places have exhibited some of these tendencies. But the Inquisition was the first to leave detailed records of its road to self-inflicted ruin. In its painstakingly recorded loss was indeed a tragedy, for here lay all the debris of that emotion which can drive some human beings to destroy the very things that sustain them.

Chapter Twelve

THE NEUROTIC SOCIETY

. . . they feel fits of madness and they go to look for them and their spiritual guides kiss them and . . . put their hands on their breasts and over their hearts, telling them that these contacts are not sinful, that they do them to make them happy . . .

THE MONASTERY OF BORJAS was in the district of the tribunal of Zaragoza, venue of the assassination of Inquisitor Arbues and home to the forebears of Montaigne. It was here that a bizarre case began in 1705, at the height of the War of the Spanish Succession. The case centred on a nun in the local convent, Sister Theresa Longas. Longas had entered the convent as a teenager. At once she had provoked comment, dressing herself with flamboyance and refusing to offer charity to those nuns who were sick.[1] Such questionable behaviour, however, was merely the prelude to an extraordinary career in the convent which led to Longas being accused of literally hundreds of charges before the inquisitors of Zaragoza.

The charges were summarized: '[Longas is] a famous liar, a hypocrite, scandalous, impertinent, impious, abusive of the Holy Sacrament of the Eucharist and of the exorcisms of the Church, irreverent, suspected of having an illicit relationship with her spiritual director . . . a boastful faker of prophecies, revelations, apparitions, communications from the saints and of miracles'.[2] With such a charge sheet it was clear that all was not peace and light within the sacred walls of the Borjas convent.

The case had developed gradually. At the age of nineteen Longas had taken a new spiritual director in the convent, a Franciscan friar called Manuel de Val. Tongues started to wag immediately, since Val was also young, only twenty-seven years old. There was good reason for the gossip since Longas 'took to communicating with so much frequency and excess in the confessional that she was there every day for an hour and a half or two hours in the morning, and after lunch he [Val] would return to the confessional where he remained with [Longas] until dusk, and on some days he would return again at night'.[3] Quite when Longas had the opportunity to commit the number of sins implied by such protracted confessions was not clear, since she appeared to spend every waking hour with Val; perhaps the sins were committed in the confessional itself. On one occasion Val only left the convent at three in the morning after having 'administered communion' to his 'daughter of confession'.

Soon enough Longas and Val were fast friends. Many nuns in the convent were scandalized by the 'pleasure which they could see in the feelings of both of them' whenever they looked at one another.[4] One can imagine the glowing smiles and the mutual enjoyment of the tension and envy which their pleasure provoked. On one occasion the two of them helped tend a nun who was sick. Their solicitude was not, however, all that it appeared. They took advantage of the situation to go at night to a nearby room to discuss spiritual matters. It was unclear what spiritual matters were being discussed as the nuns heard volleys of laughter echoing from the room.[5]

Longas and Val took to eating from the same plate and drinking water from the same glass.[6] Val began to remark on the extraordinary spiritual prowess of Longas, who, he claimed, had visions, and of whom he said that all her works were prodigious and touched by divinity.[7] Longas developed a following of adepts in the convent, people who perhaps admired her bravado. Naturally, this made her foes all the more vituperative. Matters came to a head nine years after the beginning of her relationship with Val, when Longas made an audacious bid to become the convent's abbess.

Longas retired to her cell. No, she said, she would shun the world. She did not require material sustenance. No, she would only take bread and water from Friday through to Sunday, and she would survive off chard and beans for the rest of the week. Yes, she was disciplining herself, lashing herself repeatedly in the confines of the cell so that its walls were smeared with blood.[8] Such an extraordinary show of discipline and devotion was undermined in the eyes of some by the fact that Longas's room sometimes smelt of bacon and chocolate but the devoted nun took things further. She fasted for forty days without food and drink; breadcrumbs and pots for making hot chocolate were, however, sometimes found by the door of her cell.[9] Nevertheless, the performance had its desired effect, and Longas was elected abbess.

Once she had become first among equals, the problems in the convent really started. Longas made use of her position to torment her adversaries. Spurred on by her confessor Val, she claimed to have visions of nuns from the convent who had died, saying of one dead nun that she had had horrible visions of her in hell. This dead nun was blamed for noises that were heard by some – Longas and her followers – in the convent; Longas's adversaries claimed they could hear nothing. Tensions peaked as some of the nuns started to have fits whenever the noises occurred.

In an attempt to face down the ghostly noises Longas and Val took a group of nuns to the choir stalls of the convent chapel. As soon as they entered Longas leapt back and screamed, 'Don't you hear it? Don't you hear it?' Val joined in, saying in a frightened voice, 'What's that?' cowering and indicating that he could hear the same noises as the abbess. Not all of the nuns were convinced, and one of them replied to his question, 'Father, it's the air going up the chimney'. Longas shooed the other nuns away and was seen in prolonged conversation with Val; at one point his voice rose and he asked her, 'Condemned for ever?' The answer, of course, was yes.[10]

Many now claimed that they could hear the noises. Longas and Val exorcized the poor nuns, who were increasingly desperate. The cell of the dead nun so disliked by Longas and said to be responsible for all the noises burst into flames at three o'clock one morning; the night before, Longas had been seen alone carrying a bucket of hot coals. Indeed, she and Val were clearly not as distraught as the rest of the community, since Val was seen one evening with a white flower in his hand, with Longas at his feet, both of them laughing about something or other.[11]

In all, Longas was charged with 377 offences. Her defence was piecemeal and she was found guilty. The Inquisition ordered her to abjure her errors and spend six years in seclusion in her cell. She was to emerge only to hear communal mass among the very nuns whose behaviour she had precipitated with her own cravings for power and attention.

The scenes from the convent reveal how after over two centuries of hard work excising heresy from the heart of Iberia, the Inquisition had built an increasingly neurotic society. Today, it is difficult to use the term 'neurotic' without thinking of Freud. Freud saw neurosis as a state which followed the repression of some of a person's instincts. This repression was, however, ultimately unsuccessful, and the instincts were able to achieve their goals, drawing on creations of the person's fantasies to do so. But in achieving these goals, reality was distorted, and the fantasies emerged as a substitute.* This is a fairly precise description of the goings-on at the Borjas convent, and indeed of much of Portugal and Spain during these centuries.[12]

This sort of behaviour was not confined to the repressed atmosphere of the convents. It was just as apparent among the holy women known as *beatas*, found in the towns and villages of Iberia. *Beatas* were secular women living in the community, held to have special powers to mediate with the divine.[13] Unlike married women and nuns they did not accept the authority of any particular man, and this gave them an unusual position of freedom and power in a deeply misogynistic society.[14] The Church hierarchy was unhappy with this situation and increasingly forced *beatas* to follow the rule of one or other of the spiritual orders. The Inquisition also began to discredit *beatas* through repression and misrepresentation.[15] The stage was set for a series of extraordinary denunciations.

One condition of being a *beata* was that she had to make a private vow of chastity. This led to some calling them 'brides of

---

* In recent years the ideas of Freud have come under sustained attack from numerous quarters. Freud is accused of suppressing actual cases of sexual abuse (Masson 1990), of scientific laxity in the development of psychoanalytic theory (Eysenck: 1985 and Crews: 1993), of willfully mythologizing his own role in the development of psychoanalytic ideas (Eysenck: 1985) and of the fact that the psychoanalytic process itself fails to demonstrate any measurable success in its treatment of patients (Stannard: 1980). Thus in spite of the unquestioned influence Freud's ideas have had, the critical strength of psychoanalysis has been shaken. I use some Freudian terminology in this book because of my own argument that, although Freud's use of certain concepts is questionable, this does not mean that the concepts themselves are invalid. The concept of neurosis clearly does describe some phenomena which do occur. See Green (2007: Appendix A) for a fuller discussion.

Christ'.[16] These women dressed in simple habits and shunned material considerations; they were living exemplars of the purity of the Virgin herself. Yet chastity and purity were not qualities for which all *beatas* were known.

Cordoba 1718 to Villar 1801

On 24 April 1718 a *beata* was reconciled by the Inquisition of Cordoba. She had perverted the beliefs of four Franciscan friars, one of whom asked to be garrotted rather than suffer the indignity of wearing a *sanbenito*. The poor friar's sense of humiliation was understandable. The *beata* had 'through the cunning of the devil' enticed an image of the baby Jesus to speak to the friars and give them precise and unusual instructions as to the best means of securing their salvation.

What the image of the baby Jesus had told the four men was that no soul existed below the hips and that their salvation required them to have sexual intercourse with the *beata*. It was only after this intercourse that they would become sanctified. However, in order to ensure the efficacy of their salvation they needed to strip naked and lubricate themselves with certain oils, with the friar and the *beata* rubbing the oil into one another from top to bottom. Once they had done this there was no need for them to receive communion or confess provided that they follow certain precise preparations before saying mass. These preparations required them to kiss the *beata*'s breasts and then to look at the host, where they would see that she was herself visible in the sacrament with her breasts prominently displayed.

There were numerous other remarkable teachings and prophecies of this unusual leader of friars. The *beata* informed them that she was to have four children, one by each of them, and that these offspring would go to the four corners of the world preaching the *beata*'s remarkable divine law. And when any of them had toothache, there was a sure-fire way of alleviating the pain – sticking her tongue into the mouth of the patient.[17] The four friars had accepted her teaching unquestioningly, and no doubt with a feeling of release that all their emotions and urges could at last find a holy outlet.

EIGHTY-THREE YEARS LATER, in Villar, a case was brought against the *beata* Isabel María Herraínz, who over three years had developed a large following in the town. Most of her male followers, it may come as little surprise to discover, were themselves in religious orders. The remarkable powers of Herraínz were confirmed by her servant Manuela Perea, who said that she herself had seen the baby Jesus at the breast of her mistress on numerous occasions. A group of her female followers known as the *endiabladas* – the bedevilled – took to barking, roaring and dancing in front of the church, screaming at those not in their group until the *beata* ordered them to be quiet.

One of Herraínz's followers, Atanasio Martínez, revealed the sort of goings-on commonplace in her circle. Martínez had got to know Herraínz in Cuenca, where he used to take his hat off whenever he passed her home and received 'an interior light from the mystery hidden within [her house]'. One day, when praying in Cuenca, he realized that God inhabited the *beata* and, following 'an inner impulse, he embraced her, and kissed her on the face and on the breasts which were decently covered with a cloth'. Soon Martínez came to call the *beata Señor* – the Lord – and took to expressing his love of God by kissing her face and putting his tongue in the mouth of the Lord and kissing her naked nipples with his eyes closed, 'knowing it to be an infallible truth that these acts were executed by the Lord himself in union with himself [Martínez] without any influence from carnal desires'. Curiously, once these demonstrations of Martínez's sincere love for the Lord were over, he found that his feelings of anxiety ebbed away, and the *beata* Herraínz would say to him, 'Your grace may leave having received all of the sacraments'.

When the behaviour of Herraínz became widely known, Martínez was arrested by the Inquisition. Put in jail, he would go mad whenever Herraínz's name was mentioned. After his intimate relationships with 'the Lord' he believed that he had Jesus in his chest. On one occasion he put his finger in his mouth, licked it, and spat at the doctors who were examining him so that they would receive the kingdom of Jesus Christ.

Herraínz had been feted by many priests – all aged between thirty and fifty years old – who had experienced the same sort of intimacy with the Lord as Martínez. Four of them would surround her bed during private meetings. But there was nothing untoward here since, as the servant Manuela Perea told the inquisitors, when one of them got into bed with her the bedroom was filled with light and angels encircled the bed.

The *beata* summoned another priest to her room and stripped naked. Hugging the priest to her breasts, the *beata* shouted, 'I feel it here, I have it here, I see it here, this is where God has placed his love for the highest ends of his providence. Come here, your grace, ask of it what you will, adore it, your grace, kiss it, do not be afraid, this is what God desires, this is his wish, this is what pleases him'. The priest did as he was ordered, kissing and adoring the Lord where he had been told to, and even touching it with his hand, although, as he stressed to the Inquisition, 'without feeling even remotely any effects of sensuality . . . but rather love for God, respect for the Lord and devotion to the Holy Virgin'.[18]

Such extraordinary cases were all too common in 18th-century Spain. *Beatas* were often accused of faking miracles. Some pretended to levitate; others would suddenly announce to companions that the Virgin was in front of them or that Jesus had given them a crown, and then would slap themselves and say that the devil had taken it from them.[19] In many cases such fantasies were clearly designed simply to obtain an easier life but from today's standpoint it seems that there must often have been an intense conjunction of desire and repression.

Why did people sincerely believe in the divinity of these *beatas*? The answer must be that they dealt with some deep needs, with some of the distortions of reality that repression had forced people to accommodate. On a physical level they clearly provided an outlet for the increasingly repressed sexuality of Iberia under the sway of the Inquisition. On the psychological level, however, these cases were symptomatic of the effects of the cult of the Virgin.

It is worth bearing in mind that one of the most common blasphemies prosecuted by the Inquisition related to doubting the truth of the virgin birth. While some refused to believe that a virgin could give birth, others could use the sexual activities of *beatas* to show that supposedly pure women were like everyone else. The sexual impurity of some *beatas* fulfilled a psychological need for a supposedly pure woman who was in fact not pure and not a virgin; on an unconscious level, *beatas* represented society's deep resentment of the uses made of the story of the Virgin, and its collective belief in its impossibility.

MANY PEOPLE LIKE a miracle. In Mexico the most important religious shrine today is that of the Virgin of Guadalupe, now on the northern fringes of Mexico City. The shrine commemorates miraculous visions of the Virgin said to have been had by an indigenous labourer, Juan Diego, in 1531 just ten years after the conquest of Mexico. In July 2002 Pope John Paul II came to Mexico City to canonize Juan Diego. Millions of people thronged the Reforma boulevard in the city to witness the passage of the pope as he made his way to the shrine of Guadalupe to canonize an individual who some historians now doubt ever existed. Many of the people who came were from Mexico's indigenous communities and one of them said on TV, 'This canonization is for all of us'.

Perhaps similar feelings were prominent in the minds of those who adored *beatas*. How much better, after all, to adore holiness in the flesh than to think back to increasingly distant stories of the doings of Jesus and Mary in a far country that no one had ever visited. Yet when this credulity was stretched to allow all sorts of forbidden fruits, the real motivations behind such innocent desires were revealed.

Here it is worth recalling the religious atmosphere of the 1520s and the first persecutions of Old Christians by the Inquisition in Spain. One of the groups that came under close scrutiny was the *alumbrados* or illuminists, and one of the more unusual doctrines of a member of this group, Antonio Medrano, was that 'devotees could embrace one another naked as well as clothed'* – not something found in many religious works, either then or now, but an

---

* See page 117.

idea testament to the sort of feelings being worked through as the Inquisition advanced through society.

As the 16th century unwound, *beatas* and *alumbrados* became increasingly associated in the minds of inquisitors, and each carried connotations of illicit sex. In early cases of persecution of *alumbrados* in the region of Toledo sexual activity had been a minor part of the accusations, but it was to become a much stronger element as time wore on. The next group of *alumbrados* was uncovered in the dusty region of Extremadura in the 1570s. They were revealed by an itinerant monk from the region, Alonso de la Fuente, who realized that curious modes of religiosity were at work when he came across a niece of his near Badajoz who 'showed great signs of holiness . . . being yellow, dirty, thin, going about groaning, sweating and downcast'.[20]

The woman was a *beata*, and confessed to de la Fuente that her master had told her to confess in such a way that 'she felt a huge weight of bad thoughts, revolting considerations, carnal feelings, faithless ideas, heresies, blasphemies against God and the saints and against the purity of the mother of God . . . that she felt dead, consumed, mad and without reason or the body of a woman; and that she bore it all with patience, since her spiritual advisor told her that all this was a sign of perfection and of being on the right path'.[21] If being a tortured, wretched misery was indeed seen as perfection, one wonders what hell would have looked like to these spiritual guides.

De la Fuente, for one, knew at once that 'all the teachers of this wickedness were ministers of the AntiChrist'.[22] In the town where his niece lived the leader of the local *alumbradas* was one Marí Sánchez, who, said de la Fuente, 'was celebrated as a very holy and wise women . . . and she had reached such a state of perfection that she was given communion every day as a spiritual necessity, because she was so hungry for the Sacrament that if she was not given it on any day she fell ill in bed and gave out a thousand groans and suffered cruel torments and behaved like a woman who had been bitten with rabies'.[23] In today's language one might say that if she didn't receive communion this *beata* had a neurotic fit.

The leaders of this group were Hernando Alvarez and Cristóbal

Chamizo, who were both punished in an auto in Llerena in 1579.[24] These father-confessors had exceptionally efficacious methods of inducing neurotic symptoms in their 'daughters of confession'. They would declare that only they were to confess the women. They would instruct their charges to fast and discipline themselves with lashes at least once every five days. They would tell them to pray rigorously and contemplate the meaning of the passion of Christ. After some time undergoing this austere, self-mutilating programme, the priests would ask the women if they felt anything.[25]

An anonymous report for the Inquisition described what happened next:

> Those who perform this prayer with feeling experience hot flushes, ardour, and pain in specific parts of the body, in the heart, in the chest, in the back, in the left arm and in ulcerous places; they faint, suffer from seizures, palpitations, tiredness, rabidness, anxieties, and other strange things. Then their confessors tell them that these come from God and the Holy Spirit. Some of these *beatas*, when they perform these prayers, see visions, hear noises and voices, suffer great fears and frights, and they cannot look at images or go to church . . . and it seems to them that the Christ who they are contemplating appears as a man and they suddenly feel great carnal temptations, and it really seems to them that they touch him sexually until he is polluted [ejaculates]. This is then the excuse for their guides to teach them to look on them as men as well, and they fall in with them putting mouth against mouth and limbs against limbs and the guides say pretty and loving words to them, such as 'Flesh of my flesh, bones of my bones' . . .[26]

Chamizo was found guilty of deflowering numerous *beatas*. The symptoms provoked by his mode of confessing went beyond the purview of inquisitorial explanation:

> As soon as these women confess with their guides, they feel a strange affection for them, and they become lost in great temptations of the flesh. Soon they feel fits of madness and they go to look for them and their spiritual guides kiss them

> and embrace them and put their hands on their breasts and over their hearts, telling them that these contacts are not sinful, that they do them to make them happy, to console them and to help them to get rid of these feelings . . . and some of them go further with these contacts, putting their tongues in their mouths and touching them in their private parts and throwing themselves naked onto the bed with them.[27]

Such strong currents of repressed energy were unleashed by these methods of prayer and contemplation that some women were able to melt wax with their bare hands when they were in the midst of this inflamed passion, known to them as 'devotion'.[28] In the 1620s an even more widespread outbreak of *alumbradismo* would be experienced in Seville, led by a *beata* called Catalina de Jesús and her sidekick, the priest Juan de Villalpando. Once again a confessor would take advantage of his position to touch up his 'daughters of confession', and there were so many people in this group that over 500 people gave evidence against Villalpando.[29]

Both Extremadura and Seville, where these *alumbrados* were found, were places from which large numbers of men had left to go to the New World,[30] places of longing, desires and sadness. But most of all they were places where these phenomena had to co-exist with sexual repression, watched over by the same ideology as accompanied the rise of the Inquisition. These conditions fostered the development of neurotic symptoms in those for whom repression was most severe. This usually meant women unable to marry for lack of men. The social forces unleashed with the expansion to America had thus also triggered the mass exploitation of women by men, an exploitation that took place on a hitherto unimaginable scale.

THE ROLE OF the Inquisition in propagating repression was a complex one. By the time of the discovery of the disturbed behaviour of the *alumbrados* of Extremadura in the 1570s the Council of Trent had placed the sexual behaviour of Catholics within the scope of inquisitorial inquiry. It was the Council of Trent which made monogamous marriage the sole legally and morally acceptable form of social behaviour, and it was the Inquisition which was charged with overseeing the daily repression of 'sexual deviance' – sex outside marriage.[31] Bulls of 1559 and 1561 required the Church to examine the behaviour of priests in the confessional, and soon increasing attention was being given to sodomy and bigamy. What the French philosopher Michel Foucault called the 'cycle of the forbidden' had begun.[32]

Sodomy – homosexual sex – was tried by both the Inquisitions of the Crowns of Aragon and Portugal, though not by the Inquisition of the Crown of Castile. The first trials for sodomy in Aragon had been as early as 1531, in Barcelona,[33] while in Portugal sodomy came under the Inquisition's jurisdiction in 1555,[34] and was the second most common crime tried by the Inquisition there after crypto-Judaism.[35] The right of Portuguese inquisitors to inquire into sodomy spread to Goa in 1567.[36] Women and men were covered by the inquisitorial definition of sodomy, as lesbianism was included, though the number of trials for this was very small; there were several cases of women denounced for lesbianism in Brazil in the 1590s[37] but it was decided in 1646 that women should only be prosecuted for their part in anal sex.[38]

Many cases of sodomy which came before inquisitors were testament to the harsh, isolated nature of existence in the 16th, 17th and 18th centuries. Migration to and from ports and between areas of seasonal work meant that Iberia was a place full of inns where strangers would bed down in the same room as one another before continuing on their journeys.[39] These people may have been shepherds tending flocks, servants of powerful figures or muleteers and carters transporting goods from one end of the country to the other. They had to supply their own food and entertainment. Inns would have been filled with pulsing energies, tiredness and physical frustrations exacerbated by temptation. Beds were often shared with strangers as the key was thought to be to maintain bodily warmth with four in a bed not uncommon. This meant that those so inclined deliberately frequented inns looking for willing partners.[40]

Besides the chance homosexual encounters of the road, there were ugly stories of abuse. Francisco da Cruz worked in the convent of St Catherine in Évora and was accused by several young men of touching their private parts when sharing the same bed,[41] while a friar from the Dominican monastery of the same city was notorious in the early 17th century for trying to rape young men in the district. One of his targets, Manoel Pires, was only able to escape by punching the fat, tall man and knocking him to the ground.[42]

While today we may draw a distinction between such predatory and abusive attempts at a homosexual encounter and consensual sex, the Inquisition did not. Since the Middle Ages sodomy had been associated with heresy.[43] The act of sodomy was seen as a violation of the natural order and something increasingly significant when the state's presence was encroaching on many aspects of life, and when it desired to impose the notion of a natural order and hierarchy.[44] Thus all acts of sodomy, whether violent or not, needed to be prosecuted.

In pursuing homosexuals, the Inquisition was far from alone in Europe. More people were executed for sodomy in Calvinist Holland between 1730 and 1732 than in the entire history of the Portuguese Inquisition.[45] Thus the repression of homosexuality by the Inquisition was not in any way unique; nevertheless, it was testament to the atmosphere of sexual repression which was also expressed through the pursuit of bigamists.

Bigamy is not seen as a major problem today, but in the 16th and 17th centuries it was rife. This was for two main reasons: first, that legitimate sexual relationships could only take place within marriage, and second, that this was a world where people were criss-crossing the oceans in an attempt to make their fortunes, and slaves could be uprooted from one place and deposited in another.

Thus many bigamists punished by the Inquisition in the Americas were slaves who had been taken away from their wives or husbands and had decided to marry again.[46] Sometimes people had more prosaic reasons for committing bigamy; this was the case with a man accused in Lisbon in 1666 of having married a rich widow so that he could get hold of enough money to keep his first wife and their children.[47]

What the Inquisition's dealings with bigamy reveal most of all is a form of institutional blindness reminiscent of the official searching a ship for banned books and ignoring the slaves stacked up like matchsticks in the hold. For when one reads some of the cases prosecuted by the Inquisition in this area it is clear both that they were expressive of lives of sadness, fear and danger, and also that the Inquisition had little empathy for the people caught up in the midst of these emotions.

Recife (Brazil) 1663

ANTONIO MARQUES DA SYLVA came before the inquisitorial representatives to accuse his wife, Maria Figeuira de Abreu, of bigamy. Sylva was a desperate man with a desperate story; the Inquisition was his last hope. He had married his wife sixteen years before in the city of Bahia, and after living with her for three years and having children, he had sailed for Portugal on business. It was a decision which was to have disastrous repercussions for the rest of his life.[48]

En route to Portugal, Sylva's ship had been seized by English pirates and he had been taken to Harwich in England. He was imprisoned for eleven months before being allowed to go to Portugal. After a few years there saving money, he had left as a passenger on a ship travelling to the island of Madeira to pick up wine. From Madeira Sylva had planned to go on to Brazil, but his ship had again been captured by pirates and this time he had been abandoned in the Azores.

Sylva was clearly out of favour with the heavens. He had been forced to return again to Portugal, where for some time he was unable to get the money together to return to his wife. At last, in August 1661, eleven years after he had left Brazil, he set sail in an English ship for Rio de Janeiro. He arrived safely, but Rio was almost 1,000 miles from his familial home. Setting sail from Rio for Bahia, the ship he was travelling in sank off the coast of Espirito Santo and Sylva swam ashore without anything in the world except the clothes on his back.

After such an extraordinary series of adventures the prospect of home must have seemed a sweet dream indeed. Yet perhaps Sylva had also learnt to adopt a little fatalism; in Espirito Santo he learnt that his wife had married again and that if he appeared she and her husband would kill him. However, Sylva felt that he probably had little choice but to continue. He had no money, no possessions and no contacts anywhere but in his old home. Arriving in Bahia, he fell ill and spent three months in hospital. He did not try to find his wife; he kept his head down even after leaving hospital and going on to Recife, until one night his wife, having heard that he had reappeared, sent for him and took him to her house.

For two months Sylva and his wife lived together. He pretended that he was her brother-in-law, as anything else would have aroused suspicion. Maria told him not to worry and that she would give him the money to return to Portugal, but one night she and her second husband Francisco Alvares Roxo tried to move him out of the city to the house of Roxo's aunt. Realizing that this was the prelude to killing him, Sylva escaped and told inquisitors his story; the inquisitors arrested Sylva's wife, and the case began to unravel.

Stories like Sylva's reveal the root cause of much of the bigamy of the time: the unpredictability and danger of life in the age of the discoveries. Sylva's wife Maria was clearly afraid of the consequences of the Inquisition's discovery of her sin and by no means the only bigamist to contemplate the murder of an inconvenient extra husband or wife.[49] At times, exiled men married again in their place of exile, to the deep sadness of their first wives, who would come crying to the door to hear news of the people that they had loved, and lost.[50]

The penalties for those found guilty of bigamy were harsh. As late as 1774, in Portugal they included whipping and between five and seven years in the galleys for men, and six and eight years in exile in Angola or Brazil for women.[51] Meanwhile, in both Aragon and Portugal sodomy could lead to being 'relaxed' to the secular arm. Just as sex outside marriage was perceived as sinful, multiple marriages or, in the Inquisition's enigmatic phrase, 'pollution outside the natural vessel [non-vaginal sex]' could not be tolerated in a society governed by moral values.

Once again, we find ourselves in the gulf between the intentions and the effects of the Inquisition. With these notions of sexual conformity, the Inquisition claimed to desire a morally pure society and yet, as we have seen with the *beatas* and *alumbrados*, the society of which it was the moral guardian encouraged sexual neuroses which led to results which were anything but pure. There was an outward concern for morality, but no thought to what this might do to people's inner emotions. A fastidious concern with the details of a case history blinded investigators to the emotional and moral significance of their subject.

The level of repression aimed at ordinary sexual activity emerges casually from details. Take the Frenchman Charles Dellon in Goa in the late 17th century: with ships constantly coming into port bringing men looking for sex and a little release, Dellon was told by a Portuguese to cover up the crucifix above his bed if he brought home a woman to sleep with.[52] Natural impulses had been made taboo and the enforcer of this code was the Inquisition. In such circumstances outbreaks of mass insanity such as those which periodically centred on *beatas* were almost inevitable. Such neurotic acts of sexual fulfilment were a vital defence mechanism, and one of the only ways of exorcising the demons festering within.

Mexico 1691–1717

At last, by 1717 the conflicts that had raged in Europe over the succession to the Spanish throne were over. The Bourbon Philip V had been acknowledged as king although not without some bitterness even within Spain, where many people feared the consequences of a French dynasty for Spanish society. Was France not the gateway to northern Europe and all manner of heresies? In the 18th century the French would embrace free thinking, and France would become one of the economic power houses of the Atlantic world and alien to the enclosed intellectual and cultural worlds of Iberia. Was this not, indeed, the beginning of the end for the neurotic society?

In the colonies the end of the War of the Spanish Succession ought to have brought a measure of peace. Privateers such as William Dampier and Alexander Selkirk – model for Defoe's *Robinson Crusoe* – were no longer able to attack Spanish provinces as enemy territory.[53] Great settlements such as Mexico City, with their aristocrats, their riches hauled from the mines and the whitewashed walls of their houses, ought to have been secure. Yet in spite of the lancing of external boils, the inner demons which increasingly afflicted the societies of the Iberian world were not so easy to deal with.

Thus in the convent of Jesus María in Mexico City, strange events began to beset Sister Margarita de San José in 1717. Sister Margarita found herself constantly beset by temptations to commit all sorts of sacrilegious acts. She wanted to remove her rosary. She longed to scourge crucifixes. She was suddenly overcome by the desire to extract the host from her mouth, stab it through the middle and then fry it in oil. Possessed by fury and a sort of inflamed rage, she would run out of sung mass during the creed. Sometimes she would even lose her temper with the priests officiating at holy ceremonies, and launch vleys of vituperative insults at them.[54]

To Sister Margarita and those who brought her case to the attention of the inquisitors, it was clear that she was possessed by the devil. Indeed, Sister Margarita confessed as much. The devil tempted her continuously to offend God, and had led her to write a contract of slavery to him. She had done this, borne away by rapture; the contract had been signed by Margarita, in her own hand, as 'the slave of Satan'. Now she found that whenever she tried to contemplate the divine mysteries and the works of Jesus Christ she was incapable of thought. And when she was advised to frequent the company of nuns of unimpeachable sanctity, she burst into maniacal floods of laughter.

As the historian Fernando Cervantes recognized, this is a clear example of someone suffering from neurotic delusion. The furious subconscious hatred of her religion which coursed in her breast was attributed by her to the devil, and then everything was permitted. As Freud himself noted, 'neuroses of . . . early times emerge in demonological trappings'.[55]

It is easy to imagine what had led Sister Margarita to this state: forced by her parents into the convent, perhaps, forced to repress her desires, surrounded by symbols and teachings which told her that her desires were sinful and yet unable to resist the feeling that they held a truth which was equally as valid as the ideology which had corralled her into the ritual cycle of prayer, fasting and lamentation. How wretched this poor woman must have been; how blessed by her surrender to the promptings of the devil, which at least allowed her feelings some form of expression.

This account is not pure hypothesis. In Iberian societies of the time girls chosen by their parents to be nuns were dressed in nuns' clothing when small.[56] Those passed over by men were asked if they were not soon planning to enter a convent for a life of contemplation.[57] In such circumstances it should not be a surprise that repression so often led to neurosis.

The way in which extreme religious orthodoxy – such as that encouraged by the Inquisition in Iberian societies – led directly to neuroses had already been revealed in a town to the north of Mexico City. In 1691 the case had come before the Inquisition of the demoniacs of Querétaro. These demoniacs had been uncovered by a group of austere Franciscan missionaries after the friars had embarked on an unusual form of preaching in the town.[58]

The Franciscans of the Propaganda Fide movement had arrived in Querétaro in 1683 where they had set up a demanding routine of prayer and contemplation which involved mass sleep-deprivation. As soon as the hours of the choir finished at two thirty in the morning they would busy themselves by walking through the town with crosses, ropes and crowns of thorns. They forced their lay followers to slap their faces, drag them with ropes and trample on them. Soon their preaching had achieved a 'universal reformation of customs': games, feasts and parties stopped, as did dances and comedies. Some women gave up their dresses for coarse Franciscan habits and took to leaving the family home without a word and attending three-hour-long sermons, where they proceeded to cry almost continually – not, one suspects, with happiness.

By December 1691 the asceticism of the missionaries was beginning to have startling effects. After each evening's preaching a new demoniac emerged from the Franciscan mission. One woman, Francisca Mejía, was possessed by the devil, who spoke through her mouth, left bite-marks on her body and ripped her Franciscan habit to pieces. She herself was completely dumb and would only open her mouth if saintly relics were applied to it; whenever this occurred she suffered violent convulsions and tormenting pains elsewhere in her body. When the devil spoke through her he said that he had been placed in her by a group of four witches; on being exorcised, Francisca expelled four avocado stones, about half a pound of pebbles from a river which looked like small nuts, a small toad and a snake which slunk out of her ear.

Another of those possessed was Juana de los Reyes. The strangest objects emerged from her body, especially from her private parts; these included an iron spindle, a bag containing twenty pins, and also a bundle of black wool from her lungs. By 1 January 1692, 400 devils were said to inhabit Juana's body, although 200 were good enough to announce that they would be leaving immediately. She swelled and turned blue, and the Franciscans said the last rites; the next morning, miraculously, she gave birth to a baby, although as her Franciscan spiritual guide the friar Pablo de Sarmiento explained, devils were well able to obtain human semen and transfer it.

The reality of such cases of exorcism, of confessions turning into sexual games, of inflamed manifestations of feeling, is the mass repression, coercion and abuse of women by men. The only cases where gender roles were reversed centred on *beatas*, and the Inquisition did its utmost to clamp down on these people.

The spectacle of a gang of repressed men preying on a group of repressed women, sexually exploiting them and catalyzing the expression of their neuroses is not an edifying one. Nevertheless, this was precisely what happened in Querétaro. Some members of other religious orders recognized the nature of the phenomenon. One Carmelite wrote that 'the number of the possessed [has] grown so large that it [surpasses] all possible credulity' and that women roamed the streets of the town with mad, vacant expressions on their face. As we have seen, the Inquisition was less credulous than many members of the society as far as witchcraft and devil possession was concerned, and the case was rejected out of hand by the inquisitors of Mexico City.

Events like the exorcism of Juana de los Reyes in Querétaro remain a reality in the modern world. Exorcisms are far from uncommon, and we should not pretend that they themselves are proof of neuroses. There are many who devoutly believe that they deal with some kind of demonic possession. And yet, where religious manifestations clearly overlie repressed sexual urges expressed by uncontrollable bursts of energy and extraordinary acts of sexual catharsis, most reasonable people would agree that some form of neurosis is at work.

Particular to the world presided over by the Inquisition was that exorcism was often related to sexual exploitation of the possessed woman – almost always it was a woman who was exorcized. Reading through the records, it becomes clear that while this was a mental form of possession, it was increasingly exorcized by a possession that was entirely physical.

This was something which had indeed long been obvious in Mexico. Over one hundred years before the events in Querétaro, the Dominican Francisco de la Cruz was arrested in Mexico City in January 1572. He was said to have had disturbing visions. After several sessions of interrogation Cruz confessed that he had had an affair with a certain Leonor de Valenzuela, and that in December 1570 he had discovered that she was pregnant.[59] Cruz had returned to his monastery in a state of deep agitation at the news and had begun to pray. Soon, he had been introduced to one Catalina Carmeño, whose daughter María Pizarro claimed to have visions. María Pizarro carried on absurd conversations with angels and saints, and on being introduced to Cruz informed him through an angel that his child with Leonor de Valenzuela, to be called Miguelico, would be a saint.

With his conscience thus salved, Cruz went to tell Valenzuela that a saintly child was to be born and that he would be abandoned at her door. Not surprisingly, given his relief, Cruz was highly taken with Pizarro's angel. The angel had even told him that he would not commit any further mortal sins (father any further children). Yet Cruz found temptation a difficult cross to bear. Valenzuela was one of five sisters, and finding himself with her and some of her siblings he kissed them repeatedly and almost, as he put it, fell into lasciviousness. Going to ask forgiveness from the angel (Pizarro), he was told by the voice of God (Pizarro) that the angel was very cross and, as Pizarro put it, was quite right to be so.[60]

Perhaps it is not too cynical to suggest that it was Pizarro herself who was cross at Cruz, and secretly longed for him. Certainly, her impressive visions of angels now began to attract the attention of other members of Mexico's religious communities. She described how the angel appeared to her in the shape of a beardless man, with long hair falling below his ears. She described how she spoke to the saints, and they told her to do good works, but then she confessed that she did in fact have a pact with the devil.[61]

Such possession clearly needed exorcism. Two friars began to sleep in her room to protect her from the devil. The Jesuit Luis López tried to exorcize her, but the devil immediately possessed her and she had visions of terrible black slaves and felt as if her tongue was being tied down with iron bolts. The devil made insatiable demands for jewels and velvet and taffeta and pearls and necklaces, which she conveyed to her exorcists López and the Dominican Alonso Gasco.[62] The devil also had sexual intercourse with her several times, appearing in the shape of a gentleman and promising to marry her.

Whatever the truth of her relationship with the devil, she certainly had sex with her exorcist López. After several nights sleeping in the same room as her, kissing and embracing her in an attempt to exorcize the devil, López had extinguished the light and forced her to share his bed, where he had taken her virginity and caused her to bleed copiously.[63] Thereafter, Pizarro noted a curious correlation. Whenever her exorcist Luis López slept with her, so did the devil. Then, another of the friars exorcizing her, Jerónimo Ruiz de Portillo, adopted the same technique as López, and slept with her several times.[64]

The Inquisition held that this was all evidence of a pact with the devil, and María was reconciled in a sentence of 1 June 1573; by now seriously ill and increasingly insane, she died that December, aged just twenty-three. Yet the real cause of her illness was at hand, as one intelligent friar, Pedro de Toro, realized. He noted that 'the origin of the illness with demons that overcame doña Maria . . . was that her mother wanted to enter her into a convent to be a nun, partly because she thought that she would never be able to run a house and serve a husband and partly because this was a way of getting her to forego her inheritance of a sum that had been left to her by her aunt'.[65]

All the origins of neurosis were there: the need to seek attention, the despair of facing a lifetime of repression. The exorcists satisfied María's inner need for sexual expression as they did their own, but her neurosis led inexorably to her death. One thinks of the good sense shown by the friar who understood the causes of her illness, and realizes that religion did not in itself lead to darkness and excess; people's personalities allowed them to use religion in this way.

Exorcisms became common in Iberian societies from around the middle of the 16th century. While in the first half of the 16th century, those claiming visions were suspected of seeking material gain or some sort of fame, such common-sense scepticism evaporated thereafter.[66] This change coincided precisely with the rise of the Inquisition as guardian of the moral condition of Spain; from repression came fantasy and a sexual style of exorcism.

By the 1620s and 1630s public exorcisms in churches were ordinary occurrences. Possession became an almost daily phenomenon and many of those requiring exorcism were none other than the *beatas*.[67] The sort of exorcism which went on is revealed by a case from Alicante of the 1630s, where the *beata* Francisca Ruiz was exorcised by her spiritual guide, the canon of Alicante cathedral Lorenzo Escorcia. A witness who visited the house described what went on during the exorcisms:

> [She] found Francisca Ruiz on the floor with her mouth open and Lorenzo Escorcia hitting her and saying: 'You are present, obey me, get out of there'. And Francisca Ruiz was still stretched out and unable to speak . . . and the said Lorenzo Escorcia put his arm under the skirts of the *beata*, putting in his hand and reaching so that the arm was covered beyond the elbow, between her shirt and her flesh, and [the witness] did not see what he did, although it seemed to her that he must have reached her natural vessel [vagina] . . . and then the canon took a slipper from his sister Lelia, and beat her repeatedly on her buttocks, above her dress, and then beat her on her whole body saying 'Obey me, come out of there'. But nothing [else] happened.[68]

Ruiz was not the only person to be exorcised by the sadist Escorcia. In the Augustinian convent of Alicante three nuns said to be possessed suffered his exorcisms; one of their colleagues noted how the devils only seemed to come to the convent when Escorcia himself arrived.[69] Far from exorcizing devils, the exorcist, through his excitation of neurotic delusions, merely turned them from a fantasy into a reality. But then this should not surprise us, for this was merely another instance of the way in which, throughout its history, the Inquisition had invented enemies and heretics just in order to exorcize them.

PERHAPS IT IS UNFAIR to blame the Inquisition for the sorts of neurotic symptom observed in this chapter. One can prove anything by pointing to extreme examples and every society has its neurotics; it is only necessary to watch one of today's reality TV shows to confirm the truth of that. Perhaps, even, in treating the symptoms of the neurosis, the terrible fits, convulsions and delusions, did not the exorcists actually deal with their root cause – sexual repression – using their own form of sexual predation? Were not the priests who led the *alumbrados* in Extremadura in the 1570s right when they said, 'these [sexual] contacts are not sinful, that they do them to make them happy, to console them and to help them to get rid of these feelings . . .'?[70] And of course one ought to bear in mind that the Inquisition did not sanction any of these goings-on.

Instead of concentrating on extreme symptoms, we should try to picture life in the villages, towns and cities of the 17th century. As Spain fell into the chaos of the War of the Spanish Succession in 1701, Portugal was on the verge of an economic boom that would follow the discovery of gold in the Minas Gerais of Brazil. Lisbon was full of English merchants, who described life in the Portuguese capital with a mixture of admiration and bafflement.

The houses of the city were plastered on the outside and the doors and windows made of a coarse marble; inside, the floors were of brick or tile, and each window had a balcony. The roads were paved as far as three leagues outside the city, and every league or so there would be a cistern with good water for pack animals.[71] This physical reality was, however, pervaded by an atmosphere of religious zeal. One merchant wrote in 1701: 'The religious persons of all sorts are commonly reckoned one-third, and some say three-fifths of the whole. The clergy are thought to be posest [sic, possessed] of one-third of the land . . . If one strikes a priest one is liable to have ones hand cut off.'[72] There were, he said, at least 6,000 mendicant friars in Lisbon, and they refused to eat mere scraps but wandered the streets begging in a loud singing tone, going from house to house with a linen bag thrown over their shoulders.[73] Mass was said in the churches every day from six in the morning until noon – the priests had to have something to do – and people would commonly say their prayers in the middle of a conversation.[74] At dusk bells rang from the churches; people were expected to stop what they were doing in the street to say the Ave Maria, and even street performers and carriages stopped in the street for this purpose.[75] But at least there was now an agreement between Portugal and England not to try English Protestants under the Inquisition.

Clearly, this was a society in which almost every action was determined by religion. The same was true in Spain, where by the 18th century great care was taken to stop even a crumb from the host becoming stuck in the communicant's teeth; sick people were given a glass of water after taking communion and asked, 'Has the Majesty gone down?'[76] When the bells were rung in the evening, as in Portugal, actors and spectators at theatrical performances fell to the ground crying, 'God! God!' and parties were abruptly brought to a halt in people's homes.[77] If a priest passed bearing the eucharist, he would be in a chair carried by porters, and everyone had to stop and fall to their knees, beating their breast until he had passed; if anyone did not, there was the danger that the priest would call them a heretic.[78]

These do not come across as societies where joy and spontaneity were prized or even possible but rather as places where everything was subordinated to the proclaimed requirements of religious orthodoxy. The Inquisition, as the champion of this orthodoxy, had been the main enforcer of this code and, as we have seen in this chapter, its move into moral censure in the late 16th century coincided with the emergence of the first symptoms of more widespread neurosis across society. Thus, while the Inquisition was not in itself the direct instigator of the sexual frolics of *beatas* and *alumbradas* and indeed prosecuted them, it was the moral force behind the social atmosphere which created them.

All this was a far cry from the situation in Portugal and Spain before the Inquisition. The Silesian noble Nicolaus von Popplau, visiting Lisbon in 1485, described how the Portuguese were 'ardent in love', how the women dressed so that you could see half of their bosoms and how they were 'mad with sensuality, like the men, ready for anything'.[79] The Italian traveller Federico Badoardo described in 1557, just as the Inquisition was beginning to censure moral behaviour, how the Spaniards 'eat and drink with excess, and this combined with the heat of the climate means that they give themselves enthusiastically to the pleasures of love, and that the women are open to all types of vice'.[80]

It would appear then that there had been not a little sexual freedom in the late Middle Ages.[81] Brothels had been widespread, opening up rapidly during the colonization of the Canaries in the early 16th century, for instance.[82] At the start of the 16th century nudity was not taboo, and people were happy to dress and wash themselves in front of others.[83] But all brothels would be closed by royal decree in Spain in 1623[84] and, as we have seen, by the beginning of the 18th century a different scale of values had come to dominate life in Portugal and Spain.

How then are we to explain these extraordinarily repressed societies? Where misplaced sexual energy melted candles. Where the level of delusion was such that women could believe themselves to have a pact with the devil, since the devil always appeared in the same form, as a student who wanted to have sex.[85] Where priests and *beatas* believed that their sexual longings were divine blessings. Where violence, sadism and masochism were integral to the exorcism of the possessed. The measure of emotional violence and self-mutilation is difficult to take, but when we consider that a typical act of penitence in the late 17th century was to place a hand in the flame of a candle, keep it there for as long as possible, and reflect that the fires of hell were eternal,[86] it becomes apparent that a level of repression existed which could only lead to the terrible expressions we have seen in this chapter.

In the Freudian interpretation of society repression is an essential part of the contract by which human beings enter civilization; we have to repress certain of our desires in order to interact with others and share communal goals. Where people are well adjusted, these repressed desires are expressed in Freudian slips, in dreams or literature, but where people develop fixations neuroses can develop. In such cases the repressed desires still exist, but repression forces the rejected aspects of the libido to express themselves in a roundabout, distorted manner.

Perhaps it will help to think back to the level of violence which accompanied the emergence of the new Inquisition in the late 15th century. As we have seen, that violence was eventually replaced by a more systematic, if less combustible, attitude to persecution. But repressive violence did not cease; in need of another outlet, it would appear, from the neuroses that we have observed, to have been redirected back at its original source, at the societies of Portugal and Spain.

This is a classic example of what Freud called the 'return of the repressed': the return of repressed desires. This in itself helps to remind us that violence, once unleashed, is difficult to reign back in. It festers. It is transferred – from *conversos* to Lutherans to *moriscos* and then back to the Old Christians. This violence may emerge in imperial expansion, but eventually it will return home to roost.

So, once the Inquisition had been established and persecution institutionalized, the groundwork for the neurotic society was done. The exorcisms and their accompanying laughable delusions were merely reminders of the dangers which must always follow from persecuting an enemy when our biggest enemies are always, if we dare to be honest with ourselves, to be found within us. Violence and repression can perhaps only pursue their circular paths back to those from whom they originated.

FOR SEVERAL YEARS I trawled the archives of the Inquisition in Portugal and Spain. In both Lisbon and Madrid the national archives are located in neo-fascist buildings constructed under the Iberian dictators of the 20th century, Franco and Salazar. Each time one of the thick, yellowing bundles of paper was brought to my desk and I unbound the cloth ties around it and began to read, a little of the parchment would disintegrate. When I had finished and returned the documents, motes of dust would sit where I had been reading, reminding me of the fragility and impermanence of life, and of moral standards.

Like almost everyone I had heard of the Inquisition. But when I began to make those lonely trips to the archives I had no idea of the enormities I would discover. The world felt darkest during the tales of terrible woe, of sadism and the loss of self. For how could such systematic abuse be measured in systems, analyses, science? It went beyond words. At times I was saddened not so much by the stories I read as by the remorseless compulsion with which I returned to read, which often felt like a reflection of the remorselessness with which the inquisitors themselves had conducted their investigations. But then I would come across a story of resistance and the sadness of those heavy, dusty reading rooms would lift.

At times, too, the decline that accompanied the woe would console. By the first decade of the 18th century the Inquisition's social architecture of moral and cultural inertia was reaping its reward. Yet its leaders still carried on as if little had changed. Once Philip V had been confirmed as the new king of Spain and the war of succession had ended, condemnations increased again; there were fifty-four autos during his reign (1700–46), and seventy-nine people were 'relaxed' in person and another sixty-three in effigy.[87] In Cuenca five Judaizers were 'relaxed' in person in 1721; three more in person in Valladolid in 1722, and twelve more in Granada in 1723.[88] In Portugal, where there was no great war to interrupt the inquisitorial process, the violence did not abate. Eight people were 'relaxed' in Lisbon in 1732 and another seven in 1735.[89] Twelve more followed in 1737, including one from Brazil, and another eleven in 1739 (with another Brazilian case).[90] And seventeen people were 'relaxed' between 1744 and 1746 in Lisbon alone.[91] The vast majority of these cases in both countries related to crypto-Judaism – the 'Portuguese heresy'.

In Spain the reforming government led by the Bourbons did attempt to curtail inquisitorial power. In 1713 Philip V's minister Melchor de Macanaz proposed withdrawing subsidies from the Inquisition; the Inquisition responded by launching an investigation into Macanaz, who fled the country.[92]

This partial revival of the Inquisition in the early 18th century in Spain is again testament to the fact that the institution waxed and waned with royal power, and was thus fundamentally propelled by secular and not religious goals. It had declined in the second half of the 17th century with the drooling King Charles II, and now had a last spurt of vigour under the impetus of a new royal dynasty. Yet although the Inquisition looked to have recovered its dynamism, the neurotic societies which it had helped to create were about to get their own back. For in the first half of the 18th century the 'crime' which increased most in the Inquisition's eyes was that of solicitation by priests in the confessional, something which itself was testament to the type of society which had evolved under its watch.

Valencia 1784–1805

AS THE 18TH CENTURY drew to a close an extraordinary case began in Valencia which epitomized some of the currents running through society on the Iberian peninsula. It all related to the unusual disciplinary methods which the Franciscan friar Miguel de Palomeres used on his 'daughters of confession'. Palomeres first came to the attention of the authorities in 1784 after being denounced by one Ramona Rica, a twenty-nine year old from the city who wanted to become a nun. The story which emerged reads like a handbook of sado-masochism.

The problem with Rica's desire to enter a convent was that she was unable to read, and one day, after seven months of tuition, Palomeres became angry because she had not learnt her day's study portion. Thereupon he:

> ordered her to lift up her skirt from the behind as he wanted to whip her, to which [Rica] resisted . . . but sensing that after receiving the punishment she would give more attention to her study, she decided to obey him, and did so a few days later, after which [Rica] fell ill with a minor indisposition and asked [Palomeres] to come and confess her. [Palomeres] complied coming to confess her in her bed, which he did before leaving the room at once without saying a word. After three or four minutes he came back in and gave her a study portion, at which point [Rica] told him that she would pay more attention

> if he punished her as he had done before; at which he gave her the punishment, ordering her to take off her clothes and to lie on her stomach, at which he whipped her, and then fondled the parts which he had whipped.[93]

Soon, Rica recovered. After a time she went to see Palomeres and said that she was worried that Palomeres did not administer this discipline with noble aims, and that he enjoyed touching her flesh. This led to a merry dance of further sado-masochistic activity, as over the coming weeks Palomeres whipped her often, sometimes with Rica on the floor, at other times with her on the edge of the bed; however, no longer did these acts of discipline follow Palomeres' ritual confessing of his charge.[94]

Palomeres was called before the Inquisition to defend himself in 1784, but he argued successfully that Ramona Rica was a stubborn student who was pertinacious in her false beliefs and therefore required rigorous disciplining. Yet four years later he was accused again, this time by Gertrudis Tatay, another would-be nun who had gone to him for instruction. Again, at times he had whipped her buttocks, and at others he had looked her over in the flesh as he had administered his punishments: 'and many times without it being a day of confession he made her go to his house to receive tuition, and sometimes he disciplined her with an iron whip and at others he pardoned her'.[95]

Once again the attention of the Inquisition had been drawn to the activities of Palomeres, but the prosecutor did not proceed. Then in 1805 two more women, Pasquala Monfort and Josefa Marti, denounced Palomeres. Marti described how she had frequented Palomeres' house over a period of two months of confession during which he had forced her to kneel with her buttocks in the air, hitting her so hard with his iron whip that twice he broke it and the blood often reached the floor. One day he forgot his whip and used a hair shirt to tear the skin of her buttocks to shreds before fondling the results of his butchery. Marti became convinced that Palomeres 'was not guiding her soul well' and ceased to go for confession, but she continued to go to be disciplined for a further two years.[96]

People like Palomeres were known to the Inquisition as 'flagellants'.* Whereas in the 16th and 17th centuries cases of soliciting priests were commonplace and cases of flagellants isolated, in the 18th century flagellants became increasingly common.[97] This tells us that by the 18th century repression had worked its way right through society and was decisively affecting people's emotional behaviour. When one thinks of Marti returning for her whipping for two whole years and of Rica saying that 'she suspected Palomeres did not have noble intentions in whipping her, and that he enjoyed touching her flesh [i.e., she realised that her own intentions were not pure and that she enjoyed him touching her flesh]', one has a glimpse of the mutual repression and coercion expressed in these acts of pseudo-religion, of domination, submission and inner despair. It was no accident that the women who responded to Palomeres wanted to be nuns; consciously, they desired their own repression, but unconsciously the repression wreaked wounding effects upon them.

The relationship between confessors and their 'daughters' had definite sexual connotations.[98] The archives of the Portuguese and Spanish Inquisitions contain innumerable cases of priests who took advantage of the undercurrent of passion to solicit the women whom they confessed. During the inquisitorial visit to the islands of the Azores in 1618 numerous priests were denounced for soliciting in the confessional[99] and in Lima in 1595 sixteen priests were tried for soliciting, including one, Melchor Maldonado, who was accused by sixty-seven women;[100] one priest in Lima was denounced by ninety victims.[101]

It would be wrong to be too judgemental of these priests. If you put sexually repressed men in an enclosed place with sexually repressed women, this sort of thing is likely to occur. The level of the problem is revealed by a handbook called *Antidote to Soliciting Priests*, published in Spain in 1778 (and recommended by one correspondent to the Inquisition for censorship, since it could fall into the wrong hands).[102] This and the way solicitation mutated into flagellation in the 18th century reveal the extent of the symptoms of the neurotic society by this time.

---

* Although there is little evidence that many of them whipped themselves – as is the implication of the English term.

In pondering the emotions and desires which must have coursed around those confessionals during those centuries when the Inquisition was the moral enforcer of Iberian society, the priest Francisco Martínez comes to mind, accused in Zaragoza in 1683 of saying to a married woman, 'The black eyes of your grace have stolen my heart'.[103] Battered by his desires and the conflicting need to repress them, Martínez found his way to a certain poetry.

Yet not everyone was capable of cleansing their inner demons. The nature of inquisitorial repression ensured that neurosis deepened the malaise of the societies which it was supposed to guard. Repression had at first been projected outwards at the perceived enemy, but it had returned unerringly to haunt Iberia on the threshold of the industrial age.

Chapter Thirteen

PARANOIA

. . . the number of men enlisted in this Congregation is truly appalling, since according to their books and public pronouncements it reaches four million . . .

In Portugal the discovery of gold in the Minas Gerais of Brazil led to Lisbon becoming one of the busiest ports in Europe in the 18th century. The king who benefited from most of the profits, John V, squandered them on the construction of a baroque palace at the small town of Mafra, to the north-west of Lisbon. Over the border in Spain the accession of the Bourbon dynasty with Philip V meant that the squabbles that had characterized the late 17th century were over, and Spain was connected to the wealthier kingdom of France to the north. In Iberia a period of consolidation had set in.

However, the influx of a new Francophile aristocracy brought its own problems to Spain. France was to be at the heart of the Enlightenment in the 18th century, and it was precisely the ideals of the Enlightenment which were seen by the Inquisition as the great enemy during the last century of its existence. The crypto-Jews from Portugal in the first years of Philip V's reign were, increasingly, replaced by new targets, enlightened thinkers known as Jansenists, and Freemasons.

The way in which any group could be perceived as a threat is revealed in a case against the German bullfighter Antonio Berkmeier towards the end of the 18th century. Berkmeier was thrown into the jail of the Inquisition and accused of 'trying to found a society to reform the world and with the purpose of realizing the goals of the Old Testament, claiming that not all of its prophecies have yet come to pass'.[1] In order to further the aims of this seditious society,

Berkmeier was said to fake visions and apparitions of God and Jesus Christ, which enabled him to 'seduce' various people to join his society.

Berkmeier's first accuser was one Juan Joseph Heideck, a compatriot of his, who saw the danger of the group in part in its internationalism. 'The said society', he reported, 'is composed not only of musicians and Swiss soldiers, but also of other Germans, Frenchmen and Spaniards'. The society aimed to subvert not only religion but also the state and the government, and each day new members were joining. Another witness described how Berkmeier and his acolytes gathered by a fountain with a group of Germans to discuss their new religion; something of the danger of the group was shown by the fact that Berkmeier, in the words of his accuser, 'has a book, and perhaps also some papers'.

Berkmeier was a freethinker typical of those the Inquisition saw as most threatening. He had written a book called *El Tonto Sobrenatural – The Supernatural Fool* – which suggests not so much a hankering after the Old Testament as scepticism of everything supernatural. Summoned at the end of August 1798 to answer the charges, he wrote long and detailed answers to the questions put before him. Something of the inequities of inquisitorial justice is revealed by the Inquisition's choice of an interpreter for Berkmeier, none other than Juan Joseph Heideck, the man who had accused him, and by the fact that Berkmeier languished in jail for four years before his responses to their questions were condemned as heretical.

It is clear that the most important thing was seen to be to crush Berkmeier's group immediately; once the agitator was incarcerated, the orthodoxy of his views could be examined at the inquisitors' leisure. This attitude towards societies and gatherings of people stemmed directly from the fear which the Inquisition had developed of Freemasonry in the 1730s. Freemasonry had been condemned by Pope Clement XII in April 1738 in his bull *In Eminenti*; the bull had been confirmed by Cardinal Firrao, secretary of the Vatican state, on 14 June 1739, in a document in which the mere suspicion of Freemasonry was stated to be a capital offence.[2]

The rise of Freemasonry in Europe had begun in the early 18th century, and had been marked by the publication of the *Constitution of Masonic Orders*, published in 1723. The Masonic orders reinvented the initiation rites of the Masons of the Middle Ages, including keeping the secrets of the lodge. It was this secrecy which seemed so suspicious to their enemies, although the secrecy largely appears to have related to the interpretation of certain ritual ceremonies and to have had little to do with religion or politics.[3]

Nonetheless, authorities such as the papacy moved swiftly to condemn the movement. Following the papal prohibition of 1738, the major impact of Cardinal Firrao's activities was in Portugal, where he wrote to Inquisitor-General Cardinal da Cunha ordering him to pursue the Masons. Da Cunha prohibited Freemasonry in an edict of 28 September 1738, and five major trials followed in 1743.[4] One victim, the Swiss Protestant John Coustos, described his experiences with a certain amount of artistic licence.[5] He recounted how the cells were so dark that it was impossible to read. Prisoners were not allowed to groan, sigh, pray loudly or sing psalms, and were beaten if they did. When he was tortured, the door of the torture chamber was covered with mattresses so that his cries would not reach the rest of the prison, while the cords were tightened so much in the *potro* that they cut through to his bone. The torture only lasted for fifteen minutes, but it reduced him to such a state that for three months afterwards he could not bring his hand to his mouth. When he was eventually sentenced to four years in the galleys, where he was chained to another prisoner by the feet and had to perform menial tasks, he wrote how the relief of being away from the fear of the Inquisition was such that the galleys seemed comparatively pleasant.[6]

With the Inquisition, little seems to have changed. This held for both the system of inquisitorial practice and the grounds for arrest in the first place. For something of the darkness in which this question was mired had been revealed in Cardinal Firrao's original instructions to Inquisitor-General Da Cunha regarding the Freemasons, in which he had urged him to 'find out fully the nature and recondite purpose of this company or institution of [the Masons], so that the papacy can be informed with precision'.[7]

Inquisitor da Cunha had followed Firrao's instructions. He had summoned people who had attended Masonic dinners before him to find out what their nefarious purposes might be (even though those purposes had already been condemned) only to be told that 'in the said places nothing whatsoever was discussed against the

Catholic religion, and that their purpose was simply to eat well and entertain themselves with a little music, each of them contributing a few escudos towards the cost, with some money also to be given to the poor'.[8] Moreover, Da Cunha went on in a letter to Firrao, as soon as they heard of the Papacy's condemnation of Freemasonry, 'they entirely abandoned these conventicles'.[9] After the thorough interrogation of nine members of these lodges, even the examining inquisitor declared that 'the said meetings and society are in no way opposed to the faith or to good customs'.[10] Yet none of this prevented the banning of Freemasonry and the arrest and torture of Coustos and other Masons in 1743. In other words, the papacy and the Inquisition had prohibited something and set about punishing it without even knowing what it was, and had then continued the persecution despite discovering nothing heretical. This was to take that inquisitorial speciality, the invention of heresy, to new heights.

On 18 May 1751 Pope Benedict XIV confirmed the bull of prohibition of the Masons issued by his predecessor Clement XII. An anonymous memoir described the reasons behind this move: 'Although up till now it has not been possible to find out with any degree of certainty the mysterious secrets of this sect, these can only be abominable to God and the authorities, swearing as they do a profession of complete freedom, and admitting people of every class and religion into their society'.[11]

Such equalities of class and religion were deeply heretical and, coincidentally, challenged the status quo as well. Benedict XIV was convinced of the vast army of heretics to be found within the 'mysterious sects' of the Freemasons. He had written a letter pointing out that there were 90,000 members of Masonic lodges in Naples 'so it is said'.[12] The master of the Neapolitan lodges wrote to him politely to point out that there were four lodges in Naples with a combined membership of around 200.[13]

In Spain King Ferdinand VI, who had succeeded Philip V in 1746, issued an edict against the Masons on 2 July 1751 at the urging of his confessor, the Jesuit Francisco Rávago. Rávago had written a long memorial in which the threat to the Spanish nation indeed appeared stark. After all, as Rávago had pointed out, 'the number of men enlisted in this Congregation is truly appalling, since according to their books and public pronouncements it reaches four million'.[14] Rávago, however, was sceptical of such outlandish claims, and was happy to limit membership to an eighth of this, around half a million. Nevertheless these 500,000 Masons were, said Rávago, a terrible threat to the monarchy. For one thing, most of them were soldiers. Moreover, their leader was 'a bellicose king of whom it is not impertinent to say that he would aspire to a universal conquest and monarchy if he had the means for it'.[15] And this threat was not merely hypothetical, since if these half a million people were joined in an army they would be able to conquer the whole world, and it was not inconceivable that they would be put up to this by the king of Prussia. Therefore one was obliged to wonder or suspect if the Freemasons did not desire the conquest of all Europe; and since in a matter of such gravity mere suspicion was enough, even without evidence or certainty measures needed to be taken at once.[16]

One can only wonder at the sheer insanity of Rávago. Yet such insanity had long been brewing. The charges echoed those levelled at the *moriscos*, similarly accused of planning to invade Spain with the help of large numbers of foreign allies, put up to it by the duke of Berne and various French/Turkish/Portuguese supporters.* They, too, had had a 'desire' for 'universal conquest'. It does not take the most unreconstructed Freudian to imagine that the desire for worldwide domination was in fact the saintly Rávago's.

Ferdinand VI nevertheless heeded his confessor's advice. With the edict published and hordes of Freemasons supposedly spreading the length and breadth of Spain, strings of vague denunciations followed. One friar, Torrubia, published a book in 1752, the year following the edict, saying that Freemasons were homosexuals who deserved to be burnt. Torrubia admitted that he did not actually know the precise characteristics of Freemasons, but this did not appear to matter. After all, as he pointed out,

> The blacks are certainly black, even though we do not know the origin of their Aethiopic tincture. Cockerels sing at a certain time in the day even though we do not know what makes them do it. No one so far has denied their black colour to the

* See page 182.

> blacks or their songs to the cockerels, just because they are ignorant of where these attributes come from . . . so Freemasons can hide from us what they know and what they have sworn not to say, but not what we see. We already know their colour and song. And we know that they are wicked.[17]

In the light of such inexorable logic, the die was cast. The following year a series of letters reached the Inquisition of Cordoba, claiming that there were 6,000 Masons at court, although some said there were 12,000. The members of the sect met twice a week in the house of one Zenón de Somodevilla, in front of a picture 'of an especially lascivious woman with a naked man who is committing the base act of fornicating [with] her'.[18] This Zenón de Somodevilla was grand master of a sect of 14,000 families, all of whom were paid salaries. He must, however, have been a devastatingly inept scion of darkness, since even with such a following he never did quite manage to bring about his wicked revolution.

In the face of such terrible threats and tremendous armies of Masons one would expect there to have been thousands of inquisitorial trials, yet in the entire archive of the Spanish Inquisition just two cases exist: one from 1751, when Ignacio Le Roy denounced himself as a Mason, and another in which a Frenchman called Tournon confessed to being a Mason and was expelled from Spain.[19] There were a few more cases in Mexico, where 200 lashes were given to the Venetian painter Felipe Fabris for Freemasonry in 1789, and further isolated cases followed there in 1793 and 1795.[20] Yet this is a low count for a situation in which half a million soldiers were said to be clamouring for the destruction of the monarchy.

The threat to the nation had been invented. Freemasonry had been denounced as a crime, even though the Inquisition did not know how to define it and it would not in all probability exist in Spain until the Napoleonic Wars.[21] Moreover, those who did join Masonic lodges may also often have been motivated by interest in something forbidden; as the master of the Neapolitan lodges wrote to Benedict XIV 'my curiosity was piqued to get to know personally something that was attacked so vituperatively by some, and praised to the hilt so much by others'.[22]

*

THE FREEMASONRY FANTASY which developed in 18th-century Iberia was but one of many. There had been the *converso* plot to deliver Castile into the hands of the Mosaic law at the end of the 15th century; the Lutheran plot which led to the great conflagrations of Valladolid and Seville in 1559; the extraordinarily complex plots of the *moriscos* in the late 16th century to hand Spain over to the Muslims, Protestants and *conversos*;[23] and the great plot of the Portuguese *conversos* in Lima in the 1630s – all meticulously documented, and thoroughly foiled by the Inquisition. There was the inquisitorial document in Portugal which referred to 200,000 *converso* families existing in Portugal in 1624 when there were no more than 6,000 'full-blooded' *conversos* left in the country.[24] Then there was the threat posed by heretical books, when the existence of a few copies of Calvin and Bibles in the vernacular prompted claims that 30,000 books by Calvin were circulating, together with 6,000 such copies of the Bible in vernacular.[25] There was, it is true, some threat to Catholic ideology in Spain from the printing press, but the number of forbidden books was magnified beyond all proportions.

In order to assess the substance of these fears, one must ask: was there ever a plot of the nature which the Inquisition claimed to have uncovered? The answer lies in the facts. The *moriscos* never did ally themselves with the Calvinists and the *conversos*, or with the Turks or Huguenots, to destroy Spain. The *conversos* never did overwhelm Portugal with their birthrate. No hordes of Freemasons allied themselves with the king of Prussia to destroy the Bourbon monarchy. Some enlightened members of the aristocracy did possess banned books in the 17th and 18th centuries, but only a few – there were never thousands of 'licences for heresy' in circulation threatening to destroy the nation.

Not once did any of the complex plots which the Inquisition claimed to have uncovered come to fruition. Not once were any of them close to success. One must, therefore, conclude that the plots were often invented and that where there were plots, the hostility of the enemy groups stemmed mainly from their persecution. The church had often compartmentalized people's fears so as to deal with them more thoroughly, and it was this tradition which the Inquisition put into practice in Iberia as it purported to deal with first one threat, and then another.[26] Yet in spite of the threats to their existence, the

Church and the monarchies of Portugal and Spain stubbornly lived on, even as the society around them decayed. It was easiest to blame this decay on internal and external threats, and on the constancy of their attacks, yet the biggest damage was done precisely by the unceasing pursuit of the largely invented enemies.

In studying one particular aspect of the Inquisition, one can get sucked in by the paranoia, to sympathize with the 'threat' posed by the *moriscos*, or by the Lutherans sweeping Spain (but curiously not Portugal), or by the *conversos*. Inquisitorial functionaries wrote persuasively of the problems which they faced and of the dangers which everywhere were to hand. But when one considers the common factors at work in each case, it becomes clear that what we are dealing with *is* paranoia, a constant search for threats in order to crush them. It is only by considering the whole that the individual threads within the Inquisition become clear.[27]

There is one final case which should be described, to remind us just how the paranoid society developed under the Inquisition. This is one of the most extraordinary cases in the records, that of the 'witches' of Urdax and Zugarramurdi in the Basque country in the early 17th century. This was the last occasion when people were burnt for sorcery under the Inquisition in Spain but it also shows just how near paranoia was to the surface of everyday life in Iberia.

Zugarramurdi 1608–10

IN THE HILLS OF the Basque region just south of the border with France, inner conflicts were reaching a crisis in the early 17th century. Mutual enmities were many, but while the regions of Aragon and Valencia were purging their distress through the expulsion of the *moriscos*, no such outlet was available in the Basque country. Thus it was that the enemy – who was ubiquitous and ready to pounce – manifested itself through the discovery of witch covens. These covens had made terrible inroads into the communities of these isolated regions, as an officer of the inquisitor described in some detail.

The inquisitorial official told how when a person decided to become a witch, they were visited two or three hours before midnight on the chosen night by a member of the coven, who 'anoints them with some stinking dark green water on their hands, temples, breast, genitals and on the soles of their feet, and then takes them flying through the air, leaving by the door or through the window which are opened for them by the devil'.[28] At the coven meeting the devil would appear in a chair made of gold or dark wood which looked like a great throne. He had an ugly, sad face, appearing 'like a black man with a crown of little horns and three big ones, so that as if like a ram he had two of them at the sides and one on the forehead, and with these horns he illuminates all those who are at the coven with a light that is brighter than the moon'.[29]

It was hardly surprising that most people who met the devil were frightened. When the devil spoke he sounded like a braying mule. He always seemed annoyed, his expression was always melancholic, and he always spoke in a sad voice; this, combined with his 'round, large, open, shining and terrible' eyes, his goat's beard and his goat-like torso, was enough to cow most people.[30] They adored him, kissing his left hand, his mouth, his chest and his genitals, and then lifting his tail and kissing his ugly, dirty, stinking behind. The devil then made a mark on the novice with his fingernail, drawing blood, and gave them a toad as a guardian angel. The novitiate was taken to dance around a fire with the other witches, where they entertained themselves in sinful excess, to the sound of flutes and tambourines, until dawn.[31]

This sort of account is familiar today, in particular in the light of *The Crucible*, Arthur Miller's portrait of witch-hunts in Salem, Massachusetts. Miller's classic play, written in part as a commentary on McCarthyite America in the 1950s, has become part of the cultural furniture for those who wish to examine the psychology of paranoia and persecution. *The Crucible* was a reminder of the power of the past to speak to the present, and of how the particular can be universal; its imaginative portrait of a witch-hunt could be substituted for the persecution of supposed communists in America, or for events in Urdax and Zugarramurdi more than three centuries before.

The goings-on in the Basque region first came to the attention of inquisitors when María de Ximildegui, a twenty-year-old woman, returned to Zugarramurdi from south-west France; here she claimed to have attended covens numerous times. Arriving back at her home village, Ximildegui claimed that another woman, María de Yurreteguía, was a member of the local coven in Zugarramurdi. Confronted by this accusation, Yurreteguía denied it repeatedly, but her accuser spoke so persuasively that the villagers began to believe her. Eventually, Yurreteguía fainted, and when she came round she confessed that it was all true.[32]

Having confessed, Yurreteguía found herself pursued by witches. The devil called for her personally, and the witches disguised themselves as:

> dogs, cats, pigs and goats, and put the queen of the coven Graciana de Barrenechea in the figure of a mare, and then went to the house of María de Yurreteguía, which belonged to her father-in-law . . . and entered the house by the doors and through the windows which were opened for them by the devil: and there they found that María de Yurreteguía was in the kitchen surrounded by many people who had gathered with her that night to keep her company and protect her from what had happened on the previous nights, and because she had told them that that night there would be a coven meeting and that the witches would come to abuse her. And the devil and Miguel de Goyburu, king of the coven, and other witches, hid themselves behind a seat, and raised their heads to locate her and see what she was doing, making signs to show that she should go with them. And her aunt and teacher, María de Chipía, and one of her sisters, positioned themselves high up on the chimney, making signs to ask if she wanted to go with them, and she defended herself, shouting and indicating where the witches were; but those who were with her could not see them, because the devil had bewitched them and thrown shadows over them so that only María de Yurreteguía should see them, and she shouted out: 'Leave me alone, traitors, do not pursue me, I have already had enough of following the devil!'[33]

The next day the astonished residents of Zugarramurdi found that the devil and his acolytes had been so furious that they had torn up fruit trees and vegetables and destroyed the water mill by splitting the wheel and leaving the millstone on the roof.[34]

There is an evident connection between these extraordinary fantasies and the repressed energies and neurotic symptoms that we saw in the last chapter, but what emerges in Zugarramurdi is how the neurosis quickly fed into paranoia. The neurotic delusions of Ximildegui and Yurreteguía rapidly spread along with their fears. Shortly before New Year 1609 a dozen or so neighbours broke into the houses of those they suspected of being witches to look for the demonic toads they thought were protecting them. None were found, but those under suspicion were dragged to the priest to be tortured if they did not confess. By January many had admitted the 'truth', and a commissary of the Inquisition was sent for to compile a report.[35]

It soon became apparent that the case was a farce. Yurreteguía told her aunt María Chipía that she had confessed falsely to save herself and advised her to do the same. Six of those who had confessed went to the Inquisition's headquarters in Logroño to say that they had declared falsely under threat of torture. But the fears, once unleashed, were not so easy to put away. An inquisitorial visitor who arrived in Urdax in August 1609 was informed that the friar Pedro de Arburu was a witch even though he was found sleeping in bed at the time of the coven meetings. Was it not obvious that this was a counterfeit body, placed there by the devil to give him a false alibi?[36]

Paranoia spread. In the neighbouring region of Navarre the priest Lorenzo de Hualle gave sermons in the village of Vera in which he described how over three-quarters of the residents of the village were witches, and that this was a fact which he would repeat a thousand times. He confined a large number of children and adults in his rectory for over forty days, during which time no one could leave unless they confessed to diabolical activities. This led to Hualle's triumphant exposure of the sect in Vera, although as he wrote to the inquisitorial envoy from Logroño, 'The men and women under suspicion . . . declare without flinching that there are no witches but that I fabricate them in my house; that everything I say in church is a lie and a fable and I am not to be believed; that I get people to affirm things that do not exist at all by means of promises and threats'.[37]

Just as in Miller's Salem, the witches of the Basque country had been invented. Neighbour had denounced neighbour and nieces had denounced aunts. Just as the Inquisition had created an atmosphere in which no one could be free of suspicion of heresy, so everyone was thought capable of being a witch. At the auto in Logroño in November 1610, six witches were 'relaxed', and a further five burnt in effigy; already, in inquisitorial jails thirteen had died in epidemics.[38]

The *Suprema*, it is true, commissioned an inquiry led by the most sceptical of its inquisitors in the Logroño tribunal, Salazar, hoping to dampen down the paranoia. Salazar concluded that almost three-quarters of the confessions were false. Over 1,000 of the cases he examined were of children under twelve, and many of them could not even say how they had managed to go to the coven meetings. There was, in fact, no evidence for the existence of the witches at all.

Salazar pointed out that it might be best to cease the hunt altogether. After all, in neighbouring south-west France, where there had recently been a similar outbreak of witches, they had all disappeared of their own accord after the bishop of Bayonne had prohibited further mention of them in conversation or in writing.[39] Thus did the threat to the social fabric depend so deeply on the paranoia which had invented it in the first place.

By 1750 in Spain there was widely said to be a three-pronged attack by the forces of evil on the forces of good. Two of the prongs consisted of Freemasons and philosophers.[40] One of these foes had, as we have seen, largely been invented and the other was to lay the foundations for the world as we know it today; this says much for the condition of the inquisitorial mind in the 18th century. The third prong was the Jansenists, by the early 18th century the main intellectual preoccupation of the Inquisition.[41] However, as with the Freemasons, precisely what Jansenism consisted of was open to question. Once again it turned out to be highly useful to invent a label with which to create an enemy.

Originally, the matter had been straightforward. Jansenists were followers of Jansenius, whose book *Augustinus* was published in 1640 and immediately condemned as heretical by the papacy.[42] Yet by the

18th century the movement had become more amorphous, and contained both those who desired a spiritual renewal in opposition to the currents of the Enlightenment, and those who supported a new humanistic rationalism rather as Erasmus had done in the 16th century.[43]

The spiritual element in 18th-century Jansenism was in many ways a revival of the movements to interiorize piety which had always been such anathema to the Inquisition.[44] The Spanish Jansenists wanted to rescue Spain from her increasing intellectual isolation from the rest of Europe, but also stressed their national heritage. Often, they drew on works by some of the early intellectual enemies of the Inquisition, *conversos* such as Sanches and Vives, as well as on better-known thinkers such as Descartes.[45] They also looked to the theological writings of other *conversos*, people such as Luis de León and Juan de Ávila.[46]

When one takes a step back to think about the implications of the intellectual foundations of 18th century Jansenism, it becomes clear that the Inquisition was correct – up to a point – in its identification of a threat. Members of this movement sought intellectual renewal through the writings of many thinkers whose ideas the Inquisition had condemned two centuries before, and from philosophers whose ideas were similarly suspect. Yet the fact that so many of these ideas had come from *conversos* serves to show yet again that the Inquisition had merely helped to establish the ideological currents which then came to pose such a challenge.

What many Jansenists in Spain really stood for in the 18th century was an attempt to blend spiritual renewal with the principles of the Enlightenment.[47] This meant that Jansenists often opposed the jurisdiction of the papacy.[48] They tended to argue for the expansion of royal power over the Inquisition, something that became known as regalism.[49] This gave them a political outlook which was enough, together with their sympathy for some Enlightenment ideas, for them to become associated with the forces which were then chipping away at the edifice of inquisitorial ideology.

The irony was that the Jansenist movement itself had been in part created by the Inquisition, since it was inquisitors, led by Jesuits, who in the first half of the 18th century had defined its enemies as 'Jansenist'. One Jansenist wrote in 1803 that the Jesuits 'have always deliberately ensured that the idea of Jansenism is horrific and yet obscure and confused, so that it can be applied to all those who . . . support the reform or abolition of their company'.[50]

The connection to the Jesuits had come because in the first half of the 18th century the Inquisition in both Portugal and Spain was increasingly dominated by the Society of Jesus.[51] The Jesuits saw Jansenism as a specifically anti-Jesuit doctrine associated with France and Voltaire.[52] When two Jesuit friars were asked to compile the Spanish index of censorship in 1747 one of them simply copied an edict of 1722 called the Jansenist Library, and thereby included all the books which he reviled.[53] Some friars in other orders were furious, and one declared that the so-called Jansenist books in the index were no such thing[54] – which shows just how vague the concept was, and how easy to appropriate for ideological ends.

The protests against the index of 1747, and at the role of the Jesuits, had serious consequences in Spain, with some contemporaries going so far as to say that doubt had been cast on the index's legitimacy.[55] In Portugal the Jesuits and the Inquisition were soon to suffer an even more damaging setback. Far more serious than the phantom enemy of the Jansenists was a real foe, the one man who did more than anything to put an end to the Inquisition's stranglehold on society there: Sebastião José Carvalho e Melo, the chief minister of Portugal better known to posterity as the marquis of Pombal.

A GOOD if doubtless apocryphal story is told of Pombal. In 1773 he was said to have been irked by a proposal of King José I. José, like many before and after him, had suggested that all those with Jewish ancestry should wear a yellow hat. A few days later Pombal came to court with three such hats tucked nonchalantly under his arm. José was understandably bewildered. He asked what they were for, and Pombal answered that he merely wished to obey the king's orders. 'But', José is said to have asked, 'why do you have three hats?' 'I have one for myself', replied Pombal, 'one for the inquisitor-general, and one in case Your Majesty wishes to cover himself'.[56]

Pombal was a child of the Enlightenment. He wanted nothing to do with José's proposal to revisit old forms of discrimination, and proceeded to follow up his humiliation of the king by proposing the abolition of the legal distinctions between Old Christians and *conversos*. As Pombal held absolute power in Portugal, he was successful, and so managed to blow away the raison d'être of the Portuguese Inquisition.

Pombal's rise to such power over the crown was directly related to another moment that had changed the history of his country, the terrible earthquake that destroyed Lisbon in 1755. The first tremor had struck the city just after 9.30 a.m. on 1 November 1755, All Saints' Day. The tremor had lasted for two minutes, and been followed by seven minutes of violent shaking. The quake had been accompanied by terrible groaning noises, as if the very rocks on which the world was built were entering their death agony.[57] Great cracks opened up in the city streets, and subterranean fires could be seen below.[58]

This first tremor destroyed the palace of the Inquisition in the Rossio and the king's palace on the waterfront. One mansion lost 200 paintings including a Reubens and a Titian, a library of 18,000 books and 1,000 manuscripts. In the royal palace 70,000 books were lost. Thirty-five of Lisbon's forty parish churches collapsed, many onto praying parishioners. The dust thrown into the atmosphere by the destruction made the sky go black,[59] and the devastation was completed by a second tremor, at around 11 a.m., which led to a tidal surge in the Tejo after which only 3,000 of the city's 20,000 houses were habitable.[60] The wave destroyed ships and flooded the streets. Fires broke out, fanned by a north wind, and people fled the city in panic, believing that the world was about to end.[61]

Beautiful Lisbon, guarded by the Castle of St George and appearing to visitors as if in an amphitheatre,[62] graced with big skies stretching out into the Atlantic, was utterly destroyed. The streets were reduced to piles of ash and broken stones and the charred remains of walls.[63] The cities of the Algarve suffered similar devastation.[64] The force of the earthquake can be measured by the experience of the terrified residents of Mafra, who saw the vast palace of John V raise and lower itself, move from side to side, creaking and groaning with the earth and threatening to lay bare the vanity of all monuments to human ambition.

With Lisbon brought to its knees, Pombal was given full control by José I; he was the only minister who seemed equipped to deal with the situation. Pombal acted swiftly, executing looters and disposing of the many dead by taking them out to sea, attaching weights to their bodies and casting them into the deep. Then the rebuilding began, and the structure of the modern city of Lisbon was created; the pleasant wide streets which stretch down from the Rossio to the Tejo were all built in this period. But the Inquisition was not to experience such a renaissance.

Feelings ran high in Lisbon after the earthquake. This was a city, and a country, which had spent over two centuries in the grip of the scapegoating Inquisition. Many people, moreover, can only have seen the events as divine punishment for wrongs committed. A new scapegoat was needed, and Pombal, whose power was growing all the time – he would be made count of Oeiras in 1759[65] – settled on a group which he saw as inimical to the Enlightenment values which he wished the new Portugal to adopt: the Jesuits.

As in Spain, the Jesuits in Portugal had an important role in the Inquisition in the 18th century. But this did not stop rumours circulating about them soon after the earthquake. Pombal himself wrote a series of anonymous pamphlets accusing the Jesuits of all sorts of crimes including running the communities which they controlled in Paraguay with slave labour.[66] The Jesuits were said to encourage disobedience to the pope, to support treason and regicide, and to have created their kingdom in Paraguay with the sole purpose of enriching themselves.[67]

The pamphlets began to work. On 21 September 1757 all Jesuits were expelled from the royal palace. More denunciations followed, as people sensed that a new scapegoat was in the making. Four months later, in January 1758, the canons of Lisbon wrote that the Jesuits favoured lying about the past, libelling the government or a person in order to weaken them, and wishing the death of a neighbour if it was in their own interests – all charges which surely reveal prevailing attitudes towards the Jesuits.[68]

Pombal moved inexorably towards his target. In the summer of 1758 an alleged plot was uncovered against José I led by the noble house of Távora, in which some Jesuit priests were said to be involved. Several were arrested on charges of treason, and on 3 September 1759 the Society of Jesus was expelled from Portugal. Still festering in the dungeons of the Inquisition was one of the 'plotters', Gabriel Malagrida, and on 21 September 1761 he was burnt to death in front of the crowds on the waterfront in Lisbon, the last person to be burnt by the Inquisition in Portugal. The Jesuit Malagrida represented everything that the enlightened Pombal detested. After the 1755 earthquake he had preached to the people that the disaster was punishment for Portugal's sins. He was also said to encourage people to see him as a saint, and to foster credulity among the masses. He was the perfect scapegoat for an enlightened despot such as Pombal.[69]

The treatment of the Jesuits created an international scandal and led to the exclusion of Portuguese envoys from the Vatican for nine years. Yet this in itself was an opportunity for Pombal to encroach further on Church power in his attempt to build a modern state. Even though he was now in his sixties, he was a man of indefatigable energy, and moved on to the biggest target of all, the Inquisition.

As a believer in free trade and Enlightenment ideas, Pombal was not a man with any love for the Inquisition. He saw it as backward and as constraining economic growth through its persecution of the commercial class of *conversos*,[70] and he delighted in removing its powers. Pombal made censorship a state function in 1768, taking it out of the hands of the Inquisition.[71] In 1769 he made the Inquisition subordinate to royal commands and ordered that all confiscated property be passed to the state.[72] The 1773 decree abolishing legal prejudice against *conversos* followed,* and in this document Pombal could not help noting that such prejudice was contrary to the spirit and canons of the universal Church,[73] thereby undermining the entire rationale from which the Portuguese Inquisition had proceeded and showing once again how some of its principles were contrary to true Catholic theology.

Pombal followed these decisive moves with a decree abolishing the Inquisition of Goa in 1774 – although it was subsequently re-established for a time.[74] While in Portugal persecution of *conversos* had continued to predominate, in Goa from 1650 onward the main attention of the Inquisition had moved to prosecuting the crime of Hindu 'gentility' – people practising Hinduism while being baptized Christians.[75] As late as 1768 people were burnt for this crime in an

* See page 328.

auto in Goa,[76] and Pombal evidently felt that such barbarism did not fit with the modern state which he wished to construct.

Such sweeping reforms must have bewildered the people of Portugal. In 1750 the Inquisition had been a rock of society, its position unimpeachable; by 1774, although Pombal had not abolished it, he had made it subordinate to the crown and paved the way for its complete removal. Moreover, the persecuting institution had in a sense turned in on itself, burning in its very last auto a member of the Jesuit religious order which had offered so much support to it over its history.

Yet this should not be surprising. The Inquisition had after all always been an institution for channelling the scapegoating desires of the most powerful sectors of society and for fostering paranoia. The ruling classes always chose the scapegoats, consciously or unconsciously, and after the earthquake of 1755 it was Pombal who was impregnable, not the Inquisition; Pombal's choice of scapegoat for the earthquake was what mattered, and he fastened on the Jesuits.

In this key moment in the history of the Inquisition, then, the persecution which it had always directed outward turned in.[77] The paranoia which it fostered meant that threats to society were always credible; this time, however, the threat was its ally the Jesuits. Thus the culture of paranoia swung back on the Inquisition like a boomerang. Weakened, stagnant and at bay, the Inquisition would be unable to resist the violence of its own power.

Seville 1767–77

UNDER ATTACK IN PORTUGAL, in Spain the Inquisition remained utterly committed to fighting the Enlightenment. Thus while France basked in the intellectual renewal of Diderot, Montesquieu and Voltaire, in Spain proponents of the ideas of these thinkers were attacked. A show trial was needed and the Inquisition fastened on the government orderly of Seville and quartermaster-general of Andalusia, Pablo de Olavide.

Olavide was the sort of internationalist the Inquisition loathed. He had been born in Lima in 1725 and only come to settle in Spain at the age of twenty-seven. In his mid-thirties he had travelled widely in France and Italy, and on returning to Spain in 1764 had opened a Parisian-style salon which was precisely the sort of vehicle for new ideas which the Inquisition could not abide.[78] Two years later, in 1766, depositions against Olavide began to be received.

The first accuser was Carlos Redonc, a servant of the marquis of Cogulludo, who described Olavide's palace, Valdeaveiro, as containing hundreds of 'extremely scandalous paintings' which could 'provoke sensuality'.[79] Another witness, Francisco Porvelo, expanded on the 'provocative' paintings, saying that they had 'women, who by all appearances were young, with uncovered legs and breasts, having dealings with hermits'.[80] Meanwhile scandal was exacerbated by the fact that Olavide had chosen for his bedroom a former oratory where mass had been celebrated.[81] All this, and the large number of books that Olavide possessed[82] – a suspicious fact in itself – were enough for him to develop a reputation as an enemy of religion.

This reputation was clearly widespread. On hearing the news of Olavide's appointment as orderly in Seville, the count of Santa Gadea declared, 'This Olavide observes the same religion as the mule who draws my carriage'.[83] Nonetheless, Olavide settled into the grand surroundings of Seville's royal alcázar,[84] with its beautiful gardens, ornate patios and fine Islamic architecture stretching back to the period of the *convivencia*. Here, in his apartments overlooking the spires of Seville's enormous cathedral, Olavide merrily proceeded to scandalize his peers.

By 1768, just a year after his appointment to Seville, new accusations were being lodged with the tribunal of the Inquisition. Olavide only served meat on Fridays in his lodgings, in contravention of the custom of avoiding it on that day. His rooms were again filled with 'provocative' paintings of scantily clad women. He was said to own a portrait of the great enemy of the Inquisition, Voltaire, and some even said that he had met this figurehead of the Enlightenment. He had told a young woman that if she ever considered becoming a nun, she should reject the idea as if it had come to her from the devil. And, to cap all these slights to religious orthodoxy and devotion, he listened to mass while resting on a walking stick and did not even raise himself at the elevation of the host.[85]

What all these denunciations of Olavide really revealed were the growing divisions within Spanish society. This was no longer a society of one faith, attitude and purpose. The arrival of the Bourbons in the 18th century had led to the creation of an influential minority of intellectuals touched by the French Enlightenment.[86] Olavide was representative of this class: he openly mocked the Spanish mode of prayer and said that enlightened nations were right to laugh at it; he called preachers fanatics and confessors fatuous, and was widely known as 'the great Voltaire'.[87] The Inquisition decided to make an example of him.

The depositions against Olavide accumulated throughout the 1770s like kindling for a fire. The extraordinary detail of the case which was eventually mounted reveals the extent to which the bureaucracy of the institution was stifling it. There were eleven files in the trial, each meticulously handwritten and containing an average of around 500 pages; over 140 witnesses were called to prosecute a man who was, in the final analysis, a blasphemer. At last, in October 1775, the *Suprema* wrote to the king outlining the crimes of which it wished to accuse Olavide.[88]

Not only was Olavide a blasphemer and a doubter in miracles, affirmed the Inquisition, he had declared that if the authors of the Gospels had never written them the world would be a better place. He was 'contaminated by the errors of Voltaire, Rousseau and others who have constituted the greatest infamy of our century'. Worse still, he had introduced public dances and masked parties to the towns of the brown hills of the Sierra Morena, north of Seville. His mockery of the Catholic hierarchy was epitomized by his sudden question to a priest in the town of Nueva Carolina: 'What does your grace think of fornication?'[89] The scandalized priest did not deign to record his reply.

The arrest warrant for Don Pablo de Olavide was finally issued on 14 November 1776.[90] He was taken to the inquisitorial jail in Madrid and his goods sequestered: his white silk socks, golden tobacco box, his purse filled with gold coins. Olavide was eventually reconciled in a humiliating auto in 1777, before spending three years performing penances in various monasteries. In 1780 he managed to flee to France, where he would spend most of the rest of his life in exile.

The Inquisition had channelled its fight against Enlightenment ideas into this one battle, having, in the words of one historian, 'chosen Olavide'.[91] This meant that many people in Spain saw him as the repository of all evil. One witness described how Olavide was commonly reputed at court to be a 'heretic or a Jew'.[92] A song was heard that epitomized the scapegoating process and the shifting but constant threat which Spanish society believed itself to have been under for the last 300 years:

> Olavide is a Lutheran,
> A Freemason, an Atheist;
> He's a Gentile, a Calvinist,
> He's Jewish, and he's Aryan.[93]

Of course Olavide's ideas were threatening to the Inquisition, yet the way in which the threat was inflated, as shown in this song, to encompass all known ills is revealing of the paranoia which the Inquisition had created.

Everyone experiences moments of paranoia in their lives. We develop unfounded fears that people do not like us. We worry about things we have said long after those we have said them to have forgotten them. We see threats where there are none. But then, when we recover our sense of proportion, we recognize the paranoia for what it was, and our own part in it.

Historically, there has often been a connection between authoritarianism and paranoia. The violent dictator of the west African nation of Guinea in the 1960s and 1970s, Sékou Touré, was convinced there was a permanent plot against his regime. In Chile, meanwhile, some in the police believed that while under Pinochet the main threat had been posed by communists, in the 1990s the danger came from drug traffickers. The demise of Pinochet (and the communists) did not, sadly, mean that the threat to society had gone.

ON 18 MAY 1776 Ignacio Ximénez, the notary of the Inquisition of Cordoba, received a letter from the priest of Nueva Carolina, the town in which Pablo de Olavide had scandalized the local priest. The letter denounced Olavide for sowing dangerous ideas among the farmers of Nueva Carolina from a book which he had brought from France: 'It was proposed', the priest wrote, 'to teach in the Agricultural and Industrial Society some chapters from the Dictionary relating to industry, factories, and trade'. The priest was outraged, since, as he pointed out 'I knew that according to the French prohibitions there were dangerous chapters in this work . . . and it was my obligation to oppose such a reading'.[94]

Fear of enlightened ideas was such in inquisitorial circles that books advancing new scientific and technical ideas were often suppressed. When in 1748 the mathematician Juan Jorge wrote a book defending the idea that the sun was at the centre of the solar system, Inquisitor Pérez Prado sought to ban it on the basis of the trial in Rome the previous century of Galileo.[95] Meanwhile, in tandem with this fear of science, the inquisitorial censors, the *calificadores*, wrote disapprovingly of countries where there was 'freedom of conscience'[96] as if such freedom was intolerable. Phrases in books were denounced as being, as one friar, Andrés de la Asunción, put it in 1783, 'accomplices in tolerance'.[97]

Asunción was symbolic of the anger felt by many of his class in the late 18th century. He censored thoroughly a book called *The Clamour of Truth*, published in Madrid in 1776. In this book Asunción objected particularly to the injunction, 'Tolerate your brothers whatever their religion, in the same way that God tolerates them'. This meant that a true Catholic had to 'dissimulate, silence themselves, suffer their mockery of the monastic life, of the clergy, of the Inquisition . . . you have to eat with them, live with them, talk with them'.[98] Asunción's hackles were also raised by, 'Patience and meekness . . . are the strongest of weapons . . . and their use can never be excessive'. Was this not to desire 'the extinction of anger in dealing with the impious, that is the strangling of a holy anger which satisfies a holy vengeance on he who offends the creator'? Asunción was clearly a member of that class that felt permanently hot under the collar.

This anger sprang from the feeling that Spain was a society under siege. The intellectual weapons of its enlightened enemies in France were becoming sharper and sharper, and censorship became the main preoccupation of the Inquisition in the second half of the 18th century. Between 1746 and 1755 Voltaire, Montesquieu and Rousseau all wrote key works, and the Inquisition responded by banning their entire oeuvres in 1756.[99] Thirty-six edicts banning books were promulgated between 1747 and 1787, to be posted on the doors of churches and convents, with sixty books banned in the edict of 1750 alone.[100]

By 1797 it was clear to supporters of the Enlightenment in Spain such as Gaspar de Jovellanos – by then minister of justice – that the Inquisition derived most of the power it still had from its role in the censorship of books.[101] The *calificadores* of books were usually of very mediocre intellectual calibre. Many of them could not read any language but Spanish, even though most of the works they censored were written in French; in Logroño French books had to be sent to Madrid as no one there could understand them.[102]

The increasingly hysterical banning of works central to the modernizing world beyond the Pyrenees sank Spain into an ideological pit of its own making. The enlightened classes from which people such as Jovellanos sprang had no difficulty in getting hold of the books[103] as the censors became increasingly incapable of holding back the tide,[104] but the edicts polarized society and meant that most people remained ignorant of new ideas. Spain was dividing into two camps: a bourgeois liberal faction and a conservative non-bourgeois wing,[105] a division that would take centuries to heal.

The new divisions were encapsulated in the trial of two brothers, Bernardo and Thomas Iriarte, whose cases began in Madrid in 1778. The Iriartes were successful figures in Madrileño society in the 18th century, with Thomas a novelist and Bernardo having served as a diplomat in London before joining the Ministry of State on his return.[106] The brothers ran a sort of salon in Madrid where religious ideas were discussed, causing scandal to the more orthodox who came across them. One of these, Joseph Antonio de Roxas from Chile, noted how he had heard them say to one another that the ignorance of Spain derived only from the Inquisition.[107]

This was a perennial refrain among the enlightened classes in Spain in the 18th century. There were many who supported the Inquisition, as Jovellanos himself admitted, but influential figures in the arts and politics saw it as responsible for the growing material and intellectual backwardness of Spain in comparison with the rest of Europe. That such people scorned the pro-inquisitorial masses of Spain and its priests emerges from the accusations made against the

Iriartes by none other than their brother, the friar Juan Iriarte, a Dominican in the Canaries.

Juan found the mockery of his brothers too much to bear. They enjoyed nothing more than laughing at his religious beliefs and his claim that he was able to perform exorcisms. They also inveighed against the truth of the gospels and the pointlessness of saying mass.[108] The ideological divisions which were beginning to surface in Spanish society are revealed no better than in Juan Iriarte's statement that he often 'provoked discussions on religion to see if his suspicions [of the faithlessness of his brothers] were well-founded'.[109]

There is no doubt that the Iriarte brothers delighted in provoking the faithful. One November in the early 1770s Bernardo, talking with the friar Felix de la Guardia in the library of the El Escorial palace built by Philip II, asked la Guardia if he spoke French; on hearing that he did he shared with him a book which he was reading on the subject of onanism or masturbation – an activity which it is fair to assume not all friars abstained from. La Guardia was understandably offended, and said that such books ought to be burnt. Not at all, joked Iriarte; the book taught nothing bad, only about a sin of nature, that of voluntary ejaculation – and it was for this precise reason after all that he had had thirty-six noble ladies put to the sword, rather than be tempted by this vice any more himself.[110]

Bernardo Iriarte's behaviour was indeed intolerable, but the weight of his scorn and of the anger of his accusers reveals a society where neither side had any time for the other. For those interested in new ideas, the stagnant intellectual environment of the time must itself have been intolerable. One of Bernardo Iriarte's accusers was the librarian of El Escorial, the friar Juan Núñez. El Escorial was the most important library in Spain, but Núñez described a conversation he had had with Iriarte in which he had declared that he was a great supporter of the Inquisition's prohibition of books. 'I wish they would prohibit more', the great librarian had said to Iriarte.[111]

This fear of new ideas was, at bottom, a sort of self-realization. The Inquisition knew that the Enlightenment heralded its destruction, and, like all institutions, it would do everything it could to stave off its demise. Yet this process in itself required a certain amount of self-knowledge to develop.

Thus, as we have seen, secrecy was one of the institutional characteristics of the Inquisition, but in 1751 the Inquisition's supporter, Francisco Rávago, railed against 'the horrible oath that the Masons swear to keep secrets'.[112] Or, as Rávago's Jesuit colleague Luengo put it in 1786, 'the quality of these [Masons] can only be perverse . . . it is enough to see their desire to hide everything . . . if everything is innocent, good and irreproachable, and offends no one, neither the State nor religion, what does it matter if everything is known?'[113] What was true of the Masons also held for the Inquisition.

Such unconscious self-knowledge had also dawned in Portugal, where in the last code of practice of the Inquisition, written in 1774, the inquisitors wrote, 'Madness . . . [can exist] in the fixation in the imagination of the madman on a certain point of view to which he is an irrevocable adherent, so much so that he only shows his insanity when the said point is mentioned, while speaking otherwise in an ordinary and correct manner'.[114] What was the essence of the Inquisition, if not the irrational pursuit of often invented heresies in people who otherwise spoke reasonably about many things? This disquisition on insanity and the denunciations of secrecy reveal a slow, unconscious dawning of self-knowledge. But it was too late. The Inquisition could not be saved from the collapse which had been provoked largely by its own view of the world.

Chapter Fourteen

THE FAILURE OF FEAR AND THE FEAR OF FAILURE

. . . opposed to the sovereignty and independence of the nation and to the civil freedom of Spaniards . . .

IN 1789 REVOLUTION swept across France. Over the next twenty-five years Iberia would be overrun by the forces which were unleashed. The Portuguese royal family was forced to flee to Brazil in November 1807 as a result of the Napoleonic invasions; the following year the Spanish monarchy was replaced by a puppet king; and the first liberal constitution in Spanish history was proclaimed at the southern port of Cádiz in 1812. The entire imperial edifice disintegrated in a puff of Napoleonic smoke, its American colonies breaking away in independence movements led by Simón Bolívar, Bernardo O'Higgins and José de San Martín.

It was not just political change which turned Portugal and Spain upside down. The new freedoms swept away centuries of ideological and sexual repression. The Inquisition, recognizing itself in mortal peril, lashed out like a wounded beast at the liberties fanning out from France across Europe. On 13 December 1789 the Spanish Inquisition declared war on all books and ideas originating in France, noting how the leaders of the Revolution championed everything which it opposed:

> Under the specious guise of defenders of freedom, they really work against it by destroying the social and political order, and thereby the hierarchy of the Christian religion . . . in this way they pretend to found this chimerical freedom on the ruins of

> religion, a freedom which they erroneously suppose to have been given to all men by nature, and which, they say with temerity, has made all individuals equal and dependent on one another.[1]

Thus we can summarize the enemies and friends of the Inquisition in 1789: its enemies were freedom, equality and interdependence; its friends were the status quo and the hierarchy. The institution proceeded earnestly with its attempts at censorship. The banning of books and the searching of libraries became its main function. Its secret archives swelled with vast numbers of case files, as more and more books were published promoting what it saw as outrageous ideas.

The sheer range of books banned in those years is testament both to the boom in publishing and the incapacity of the Inquisition to do anything to stem the tide. A two-page pamphlet entitled 'A Burlesque Sermon to Laugh and Pass the Time' was censored in 1802 for its quips such as 'Firewater has more virtue than holy water' and its description of the carriage driver who 'thinks himself in eternal damnation whenever he is not at his drinking station'.[2] Lascivious books recounting 'profane loves' were banned in their entirety.[3] The *Barber of Seville* was prohibited for its mockery of the joyless life of upstanding moral virtue.[4] Works lampooning and demonizing the Inquisition proliferated, and were denounced as 'impious, full of temerity, seditious, and injurious'.[5] But these works were increasingly popular.

Libertinage and mockery of the Inquisition, and of everything it held dear, became unstoppable. Fans imported from France were censured in 1803, as by opening and closing them a Capuchin friar and a woman could be seen in 'indecent postures'; the fans were sold around the Plaza Mayor and the Puerta del Sol in Madrid, and there was 'barely a woman who did not have one, since they are the height of fashion'.[6] And when a friar protested some years later at the sale of some china ornaments depicting indecent figures, the vendor refused to give them up to him, and her son added, 'Perhaps the good father would like to entertain himself with them in his room'.[7]

Nothing was sacred any longer. In 1799 a play was put on about

Christ's Passion during Lent in Barcelona. The Inquisition was appalled at the idea of a mortal man playing Christ and succeeded in having the play prohibited, but the very fact that it had been staged in the first place reveals the atmosphere of the times, and the growing divisions between supporters and opponents of the inquisitorial world view.[8] These divisions increasingly reflected tensions within Spanish society. They pitted rural against urban, liberal against conservative. The Inquisition, through such doctrines as *limpieza de sangre* and its steadfast refusal to accommodate any new ideas, was as responsible for the divisions as anyone.

In an article by Nicolás Morvilliers published in 1782 in Paris he described Spain as 'today a nation in paralysis'.[9] The cause, in Morvilliers' eyes, was the fear of knowledge and science as expressed through inquisitorial censorship of books.

'The proud and noble Spaniard is ashamed of educating himself, travelling, of having anything to do with other peoples', Morvilliers wrote.[10] 'The Spaniard has scientific ability', he added, 'and there are many books for him to read, and yet this is probably the most ignorant nation in Europe . . . every foreign work is impounded, tried and judged . . . a book printed in Spain goes through six acts of censorship before seeing the light of day'.[11] The result, in Morvilliers' view, was the stagnation of the natural sciences in Spain at a time when they were all the rage in the rest of Europe. 'What is owed to Spain? . . . Art, science and commerce have been extinguished . . . In Spain there are no mathematicians, physicists, astronomers or naturalists'.[12]

The article caused a furore in Spain, with numerous people launching vituperative attacks on it pointing to the health of the sciences there. Yet, on closer examination these 'sciences' were all taken in the humanistic sense, and referred to subjects such as grammar, jurisprudence and theology. No one could come up with examples of luminaries in natural science from Spain.

The divisions between the Enlightenment and ultramontane supporters of absolute papal authority and the Inquisition became more stark, as supporters of the Enlightenment defended Morvilliers. One of them, Cañuelo, described the condition of Spain in drastic terms: 'Our poverty and ignorance have never been greater', he wrote. 'But we console ourselves', he went on with bitter irony, 'with the thought that our wealth is still not so great that we have actually got enough to be able to eat and to clothe ourselves . . . We need chickpeas, beans . . . we need meat; half of Spain is short of bacon; we have to import all the fish we eat except that which is freshly caught; we are in greatest need of eggs, which are brought from Berne to be sold in the Plaza in Madrid'.[13] Everything from thread to make clothes to furniture and children's toys was imported, and had to be paid for in silver and gold, he said. 'But let us console ourselves and rely on our apologists. They will make us believe that we are the richest and most powerful nation in the Universe, and even that we have reached the greatest peaks of worldly happiness . . . and thus will they keep us in ignorance'.[14]

By the late 18th century ignorance was indeed characteristic of most parts of Spain outside the cities. Typical was Villacañas in the district of Toledo, where in the 1770s Andrés de las Blancas claimed to have the ability to save young men from military service. This was because, he told his neighbours, he had made a pact with the devil to give away his son Lorenzo. Lorenzo would disappear one dusk, ostensibly to go and see his diabolic master in Toledo, and return at midnight with powders and other ingredients whose stench was so revolting that they made people's throats gag. For a fee of between sixty and one hundred *reales*, Las Blancas would supply this magical concoction to his clients, making the father and the son take it while fasting. Then the hapless dupes would put their hands into a jar and recite the following rhyme:

A demon am I,
I am the devil's mate,
My hand goes down to test
The currents of my fate.
My payment is rewarded,
Should freedom be my guide;
I take the devil's name
and put my hand inside.[15]

Such goings-on were not uncommon; it was still widely thought that the right spell could make the face of a malevolent witch appear in a barrel of water.[16] When the lame beggar Ignacio Rodríguez offered to sell charms to women which would seduce the men of their choice into a sexual relationship, he managed to convince many of them that these amazing charms would only work if the women first had a sexual relationship with him; once this had been consummated, all they had to do was mix the charms with their pubic hair and their desires would be realized.[17]

Some defenders of the society of which the Inquisition was the moral guardian have asserted that Spain was the 'least superstitious society in the world' in this period.[18] In the light of such stories as these, however, and of the goings-on we saw involving *beatas* and exorcisms in Chapter Twelve, this seems a curious judgement to make. Much of the population undoubtedly remained extremely gullible and superstitious; but these qualities were in opposition to the movement favouring the Enlightenment in intellectual circles.

It was, however, such circles, with their greater access to the levers of power and the ideas sweeping across the rest of Europe, who had the momentum. Thus it was that as the 18th century ended and Napoleon's forces began to sweep across Europe, the episodes of resistance which had sporadically punctuated the history of the Inquisition finally moved into the ascendancy.

In order to secure and maintain its place at the heart of society, a persecuting institution must have popular support. As Hugh Trevor-Roper put it, 'without the tribunes of the people, social persecution cannot be organized'.[19] Once the social tensions have been defused, however, the masses slink back into their respectable lives and any blame falls on the institutions which received their silent sanction. Thus does society scapegoat scapegoating institutions for its own crimes.

The Inquisition always was a popular movement in Portugal and Spain.[20] As soon as it was established, had people not rushed to denounce *conversos*?[21] Was the Inquisition perhaps a product of the popular mentality, rather than its cause?[22] In fact it was both; the Inquisition could not have arisen without popular support, but it then used the powers vested in it to shape the ideas of the people.

Was there any way the rise of the Inquisition could have been stopped? There were of course the local factors at the beginning: the tensions between Old Christians and *conversos*, the civil war in Castile, growing urbanization. There was much specific to Portugal and Spain, in particular the cultural mixture which was then unique in Europe. The Inquisition was, in the end, an ideological prop for developing a 'pure' nation and culture from 'impurities' – the ideological counterpart to the violence of the defeat of the Moors and the expulsion of the Jews.

Violence, of course, was nothing new in the world. What was new, and reached beyond the boundaries of Iberia, was the institutionalization of violence. The power of the Inquisition was a symbol of the growing force of the state, a force which went with modernization. It was the beginning of totalitarianism. And yet in the worlds of the Inquisition the popular support for aggression, expansion and persecution was always in tension with a resistance.

We have seen signs of this resistance at various points throughout our story: the *converso* plot to kill inquisitor Arbues in Zaragoza; the constant Aragonese complaints directed at the tribunal until the mid-16th century; the repeated attacks on officers of the Inquisition by *moriscos*. These were not merely isolated cases: at the zenith of protests against Inquisitor Lucero in Cordoba in September 1506 a mob stormed the Alcázar and freed all the prisoners;[23] there were two popular uprisings against the Inquisition in Spain in 1591;[24] and a mob stoned an inquisitor in Rio de Janeiro in 1646.[25]

These pressures for and against persecution mirror the struggles in the minds of countless individuals, in all of us perhaps, between the impulse for love and the impulse for destruction. This was at the heart of the psychological drama of the Inquisition and it is not a little consolation to see that throughout its history there were people capable of allowing their good impulses to triumph. For as well as all the tales of horror and cruelty, the archives of the Inquisition are occasionally touched by softer emotions. Incarcerated in the inquisitorial jail in Malaga in 1620, William Lithgow found his spirits raised by some of the staff. One of the Moorish slaves in the inquisitorial jail hid a handful of raisins and figs in his shirtsleeves once a fortnight, beginning the night after Lithgow had been tortured; the slave was crippled in all his limbs, and had to drop the fruit out of his sleeves onto the floor, where Lithgow would lick them up one by one. Then when Lithgow fell ill an African slave tended him for four weeks, bringing food daily and secreting a bottle of wine in her pocket for him. Lithgow was so touched that he composed a poem for her, which ended, 'For she a savage bred, yet shews more love / And humane pitty, than desert could moove'.[26]

Perhaps Lithgow sensed that the Inquisition was indeed a desert of emotion – a place for mutilation and self-mutilation, and for repression. Yet away from this desert there were always members of society willing to risk their lives or reputations to protect the persecuted. In Portugal some Old Christians opened inquisitorial letters and showed them as a warning to *conversos*.[27] Many Old Christians hid *conversos* who were hoping to escape.[28] And we have already seen how at the time of the forced conversions of Jews in 1497 some Christians hid Jewish children rather than have them seized from their parents by the authorities.* Yet perhaps the most moving way of all in which Old Christians stood together with *conversos* and showed that there must always be brave individuals who stand up to persecution was when some of them adopted the Jewish religion themselves, and died in the autos as a result.[29]

Seville 1720

ON 25 JULY 1720 a thirty-six-year-old friar, Joseph Díaz Pimienta (also known as Abraham Díaz Pimienta), was garrotted before being burnt at an auto in Seville, convicted of the crime of crypto-Judaism. Pimienta had led an extraordinary life of adventure, double-dealing, weakness of mind and, in the end, great courage. What had appalled the inquisitors most about this friar was that he was an Old Christian, and he was made to suffer the ultimate penalty for his acceptance of Judaism.[30]

Pimienta had spent most of his adult life in the Caribbean. He had studied grammar and morals – this last apparently without much success – in Puebla de los Ángeles, the second city of Mexico, which lies deep in its fertile valley between the ancient temples of Cholula and the city of Tlaxcala. From Puebla he had gone to Cuba, where he entered a monastery in 1706 at the age of twenty-two. Something of Pimienta's tempestuous character is revealed by the

---

* See page 52.

fact that he at once had violent disagreements with some of his fellow friars, and escaped the monastery two months later, spending ten months living with his parents before returning to the monastic life.

One can discern that all was not well with Pimienta in the Cuban monastery. After a further eighteen months he asked to be able to complete his studies elsewhere, but was refused. Chafing at the restrictions of the monastic life, Pimienta fled again. First he went to Caracas. From Caracas he made his way up the Caribbean coast, through the jungles of Darien and past the former Mayan heartlands of the Yucatán, until he reached Veracruz, the Caribbean port that served Mexico City. This was where the Carvajals had arrived in the New World 150 years before, the port where Luis de Carvajal, the governor of Nuevo León, had helped to overcome the pirate John Hawkins; it was still attractive to chancers and people wishing to reinvent themselves.

From Veracruz Pimienta climbed into the highlands around Puebla, where he forged his baptismal papers in order to obtain written permission to be a priest. Yet his life of constant travelling in the fetid lowlands of the coast, in the highlands, from one outpost of colonial barbarity to another, had not calmed his spirit. He returned from Puebla to Veracruz, and after four months went back to Havana. He was stripped of his priestly titles in Cuba by the bishop, who had learnt of his forged papers. He returned to the monastery, twice, and escaped, twice – each time he was put in the stocks on his reappearance. He was pardoned and decided to try to return to Mexico. He was short of money, so he decided to steal some mules of his mother's. He was spotted by one of her servants, and fired on him, injuring the man. He knew that the authorities were after him, so he took ship with some English pirates who dumped him on an isolated headland on the Cuban coast. At this point Pimienta made for Trinidad, where he decided to re-enter the priesthood.

What is one to make of this envoy of the divine? As a priest in Trinidad, he began an affair with a married woman whose husband threatened to kill him. He took to going about with pistols, and shot one mulatto after an argument. Then, with his options rapidly narrowing, he sailed from Trinidad to the nearby island of Curaçao, just north of the Caribbean coast of South America. This was controlled by the Dutch and home to a large Jewish population descended from the Jews of Portugal and Spain. Pimienta had decided to become a Jew; such a choice was understandable in this deeply religious person, especially as he had heard that people were given money to convert, sometimes as much as 300 pesetas.

In Curaçāo, however, things did not go as planned. Pimienta cooked up a story of coming from a good Jewish family and being forced to convert to Christianity by the Inquisition. He was aiming to take the money and run. The Jews, however, insisted on instructing him in their faith first, and took him to live in a village where he was taught important prayers and rituals. He was eventually accepted into the faith and given some money, but Pimienta, who appears to have found it impossible to stick at anything for more than a few months, found the ritual demands of Judaism increasingly onerous. Moving to Jamaica, he tried to throw a copy of the New Testament onto a fire but seemed to see blood coming from it, which he took as a sign to leave Judaism.

Pimienta had clearly become a man tortured by unresolved desires. Twice he went to the synagogue in Jamaica but he recited Catholic prayers during the service. Then he heard that the Inquisition was after him again, so he escaped from the island with fifteen Indians and a Jew; something of the inner conflicts now devouring him emerges in his attempt to exorcise his frustration by flogging the Jew, forcing him to eat ham and making him recite the names of the Holy Trinity. But Pimienta was then himself turned on by the Indians with him and left for dead after a fight. He dragged himself through the jungles of the South American coast until he reached a camp, where he was seized, put in chains and taken to the nearest Spanish settlement at the Río de la Hacha. From there he was taken before the court of the Inquisition in Cartagena, where he was reconciled and deported to spend the rest of his days in Spain.

Penniless, Pimienta sought help from the crypto-Jews of Cádiz. He wrote to the commissary of the Inquisition there that he was a Jew and would always remain one – in order, he told the commissary later, to deceive the crypto-Jews and reveal their heresy. The Inquisition arrested him. He declared that ever since his reconciliation in Cartagena he had been a good Christian. Then he changed his mind and said that he had really been a Jew ever since his time in Curação. He said that he had kept the Jewish sabbath in prison, and refrained from eating ham and any meat not killed according to Jewish law.

For two months in the inquisitorial jail of Seville efforts were made to save Pimienta. But perhaps all he really longed for was release from his endless sufferings. He stubbornly maintained his Judaism. On 22 July he was told that he would be killed in the auto three days later, and at length, in his journey through the crowds of the streets of Seville, he repented and begged for Christian mercy. This confused and saddened Old Christian, spent by his life of adventure and confusion in America and Europe, was given the clemency of being strangled by the executioner, before his lifeless corpse was burnt and its ashes billowed up into the unyielding skies above.

HOW COULD AN Old Christian adopt Judaism? Spanish Christians were imbued from a young age with an ideology that demonized the Jewish and Muslim faiths and made them aware that accepting the tenets of these religions could lead to their deaths. Yet Pimienta was not alone, and throughout the history of the Inquisition there were cases of Old Christians who did the same.

Moreover, it was not just that a few Old Christians became heretics. Aspects of both Jewish and Muslim culture filtered into Iberian society and were widely adopted by the Old Christian population. Many of these practices lasted down to the 20th century. In the 1970s the Spanish researcher José Jiménez Lozano investigated the cultural practices of people living in the rural heartlands of Castile, and found that many of the older people recalled customs which, unbeknown to them, came straight from Judaism. All fat was removed from meat when it was slaughtered, and blood spilt on the ground was covered up. Cold meals were called *adafinas*, the name given by Jews in Spain to their sabbath meals, which were cooked on Friday and eaten cold on Saturday. The bodies of the dead were washed, and women underwent forty days of quarantine with no sexual contact after giving birth. Most extraordinary of all, in the town of Palencia he found that bread without yeast was made during Easter, a legacy of the Jewish practice of eating unleavened bread during Passover, which occurs at the same time of year.[31] His respondents all thought of themselves as devout Christians, yet, as Jiménez Lozano wrote, had they been observed by the Inquisition, they would without question have been arrested for heresy.

These were not just isolated rural practices. The custom of cooking food in oil rather than lard, now seen as typically Iberian, is in origin a Jewish one, denounced by the 15th-century supporter of the Inquisition Andrés Bernaldez.[32] And large numbers of people observed elements of Judaism in the 20th century in Portugal and Brazil – as many as 20,000 in Portugal, according to one researcher, even though not many of these can have been of 'pure' *converso* stock.[33] Thus in spite of the best efforts of the Inquisition to excise heresy, the reverse had happened: traits of the hated heresy had spread through Iberian society, touching not only people of Islamic and Jewish descent, but the whole culture.

This evidence is all the more extraordinary when we consider that, as we saw right at the start of our story, *conversos* in 15th-century Spain were not in the main active crypto-Jews and had moved away from the faith of their ancestors. Thus it was not a question of the Inquisition persecuting heretics and not even a question of the Inquisition encouraging its first targets, the *conversos*, to become heretical; the reality was that even some people who had little or no Jewish ancestry were pushed towards heresy by the atmosphere created by the Inquisition.

In considering why this might be so, one is reminded of some of the people we have come across in this story: the Old Christian ladies who flocked to Erasmus's ideas precisely because he was so attacked in some circles, or the head of the Masonic lodges in Naples who became a Mason for the same reason. Persecution and demonization can make a group more attractive. The desire to break taboos and prohibitions runs very deep in human beings, after all, as Eve showed in the Garden of Eden. Moreover, the customs of the *conversos* were constantly read out to the population during the inquisitorial edicts of grace which warned people what heretical customs they needed to guard against.

It was in fact the acts of demonization and persecution which ensured that the threats to society persisted. On some unconscious level, therefore, imperial, expansionist Iberia desired the persistence of these ideas, as enemy threats against which it could define itself. This self-definition through hatred of the enemy was powerful, but it also fostered paranoia, delusion and ultimately the collapse of the very imperial edifice which the Inquisition sought so hard to sustain.

THE LAST CENTURY OF the Inquisition in Spain saw several attempts at reform. Philip V's minister Melchor de Macanaz had produced a programme in 1713 calling for secularization of the state, and seeking to reform the Inquisition as part of this. In Macanaz's vision the *Suprema* would be served by a royal secretary, turning it effectively into just another ministry, while censorship would have come under royal and not inquisitorial aegis, with *calificadores* being appointed by the crown and not the Inquisition. However, as we have seen, such ideas did not endear Macanaz to the Inquisition, which began a case against him and drove him to flee to France.*[34]

Nevertheless, in tune with events in Portugal under the marquis of Pombal, in the reign of Charles III (1759–88) the state in Spain progressively encroached on the territory of the Inquisition. In 1768 attempts were made to rein in the Inquisition's powers of censorship, and a decree of 1770 restricted it solely to matters of faith, and excluded crimes such as bigamy. The 1790s saw various proposals for reform, one of them led by the first great historian of the Inquisition, Juan-Antonio Llorente, who was also the Tribunal's secretary. But for one reason or another these later reform programmes all failed, and the Inquisition staggered towards its end.[35]

By 1800 what energy the Spanish Inquisition had left was directed at coming books from France. But the inquisitors themselves were increasingly influenced by French ideas, and some of them were accused of the very crimes of Jansenism and excessive tolerance of which they accused others.[36] A case in point was the last ever inquisitor-general of Spain, Ramón José de Arce. Arce was said to be polite, enlightened and to have had an affair with the marquessa of Mejorada. When Napoleon's army occupied Madrid

* See page 310.

on 22 March 1808 Arce resigned the following day and emigrated – to France.[37]

It was the coming of Napoleon which really spelt the end for the Inquisition. Napoleon had first invaded Portugal after disputes with the Portuguese king John VI over the French blockade of English ports. After forcing the Portuguese royal family to flee, the French proceeded to occupy northern Spanish cities. The Spanish king Charles IV was deposed by an aristocratic faction and his son, Ferdinand VII, replaced him; Napoleon removed them both to south-western France 'for their safety' and installed his brother Joseph on the Spanish throne.

On 4 December 1808 this government issued a decree abolishing the Inquisition in Spain. Within ten days eight members of the *Suprema* had been arrested, the offices of the Inquisition in Madrid sacked and large amounts of money confiscated. Napoleon's forces occupied much of Spain and suppressed the tribunals. In Rome Pope Pius VII had been imprisoned by French troops, which meant that the very idea of the Inquisition had to face difficult questions regarding its spiritual legitimacy.[38]

With the Spanish empire in chaos, a Cortes was convened in the southern port city of Cádiz, which was not in Napoleon's hands. Guerrilla fighting raged across Spain, and it was clear that whatever the outcome of the war between the French, Spanish guerrillas, the Portuguese and British troops fighting in Iberia under the future duke of Wellington, Spain would never be the same again. The Cortes was convened on 24 September 1810, and comprised liberals, royalists and a significant proportion of clergy – almost a third. Just two days after its inauguration one of the leaders of the liberal faction, Agustín de Argüelles, raised the issue of freedom of the press.

The debate lasted several weeks. Argüelles argued that freedom of the press was the source of Britain's prosperity, but one of the ecclesiastical deputies, Canon José Isidro de Morales, replied that it was 'completely irreconcilable with the canons and discipline of the Church and with the very dogma of the Catholic creed'.[39] One of the other things that was irreconcilable, it can be seen, was the gulf between the two parties at the Parliament.

Eventually, on 18 October 1810, the decree permitting freedom of the press was passed. At once a barrage of pamphlets, magazines, newspapers and books commenced attacking the Inquisition. The liberal press was swisher, better written and had a wider public than its conservative rivals. It swiftly took the high ground in the ideological battle. Although after six months some pamphlets in support of the Inquisition began to appear, it was already too late. A port full of ships and sailors from the northern European countries where Enlightenment ideas were in vogue,[40] Cádiz was one of the most liberal cities in Spain.

The Inquisition rapidly became a symbol for everything seen as wrong with the old order. There was, moreover, a sense that the Inquisition had never been weaker. One of its opponents at the Cortes of Cádiz described it as a 'colossus . . . with a brilliant golden head, the chest and the arms made of silver, the stomach and the muscles of copper, the legs of iron; but half of its feet are built from mud, and so it is very easy to knock it over'.[41]

The momentum would be impossible to check. In 1812 a commission was appointed to examine whether the Inquisition should be re-established in Spain in the event of the defeat of the French, and whether it was compatible with the liberal constitution which the Cortes had issued on 12 March 1812. The commission noted the many problems: the pope was imprisoned and the inquisitor-general had resigned, so the question of what authority the Inquisition would report to was a difficult one to resolve. Moreover, it was suggested that the Inquisition was 'opposed to the sovereignty and independence of the nation and to the civil freedom of Spaniards, which this Parliament has desired to ensure and consolidate'. The commission proposed instead a system working through the bishops to inquire into heresy: the stage was set for abolition.

It is worth looking at some of the tactics used by the liberals against the tired old colossus that for so long had exerted its influence over Spain. The Inquisition was given a character by the pamphleteers which it had not really had for over sixty years, with torture and executions described as if they were still ongoing. Polemicists described the Inquisition as responsible for the decadence of Spain, the disappearance of practical sciences, agriculture, industry and business. Interestingly, these same accusations had been levelled at the Jesuits earlier in the 18th century, and had been responsible for the order's expulsion from Portugal in 1759 and Spain in 1767.[42]

Where the accusations remain the same and it is only the identity of the accused group which changes, it is reasonable to suspect that the group is being made to take the blame for something whose causes are different. How many enemies had Spain had to live with! *Conversos*, Lutherans, *moriscos*; Freemasons, Jansenists, the Enlightenment; sodomites, bigamists and blasphemers; and now, Jesuits, and the Inquisition. In each case the charges of threatening the strength and identity of the Spanish nation were made. But in each case, there was a more complex dynamic at work, one which required a scapegoat to be found.

Once again, the dynamic met with success in Spain. The campaign was so convincing that when crowds burst into offices of the Inquisition in the organization's death throes they expected to find instruments of torture set out for the maiming of its victims. This was even though nobody alive could recall ever having witnessed a public auto and very few of the crowd had ever known anyone who had been arrested by the Inquisition.[43] Repression had returned to its source: the scapegoat for all of the ills of Spain had become none other than the original scapegoating institution.

THE POLEMICS WHICH swung into action during the dying days of the Inquisition and old regime were the first full public debate on the past in Spain. The divide which we have seen growing between conservatives and liberals crystallized around the different perspectives on the Inquisition and what these said about the history of Spain.

In the late 19th century, one of the champions of the conservative view of Spanish history which again had come to predominate in intellectual and political circles, was Marcelino Menéndez y Pelayo, a man whose excesses of intellectual precocity were matched only by his excessive verbal diarrhoea. At the age of twenty-seven he published an eight-volume history of non-orthodox thought and thinkers in Spain, including much material on the Inquisition, which remains read today. Menéndez y Pelayo was a staunch defender of the role of the Inquisition in the formation of Spanish society. He held that 'intolerance is an innate law of the healthy human understanding':[44] the active intelligence reached the truth and then sought to impose it on others, being intolerant to their ideas.

As I visited the archives in Portugal and Spain, the initial affront which such an idea might have created began to be replaced by different emotions. For what were these mounds of yellowing papers but an attempt to impose a vision of the world? Here these papers lay, patiently awaiting their distillation and dismemberment by each passing generation of historical researchers, confined in their protective boxes, wrapped tightly by cloth ribbons. They were journeys into the past and into the psychology of the past which had made the present, but they were also journeys which at some level made the pain and discord of the present easier to bear by displacing it onto the traumas of those who no longer suffered.

It became difficult to dismiss entirely the insight of Menéndez y Pelayo into the intolerance of the human mind. Blame was increasingly easy to place on those one held responsible for various evils: one could blame the inquisitors for their venality and surrender to power, the torturers for their sadism, imperial warmongers for their wars from which liberal intellectuals had often benefited indirectly. Thus the liberal view also required its enemies, who, as with the enemies of the Inquisition, renewed themselves with the changing of the intellectual seasons and the passing of time.

Was the inquisitorial state of mind then in some way an inevitable precursor to the modern human condition? There is no doubt that it has had plenty of successors, by analogy at least. There was the Stasi network of informants known as the *Inoffizielle Mitarbeiter*, which spread across East Germany during the cold war like inquisitorial familiars, monitoring the politically incorrect; and the executioners of Mao Zedong, who severed the larynxes of their victims so that they could not protest just as the victims of autos had been gagged, and who charged the families of the dead for the bullets used to kill them just as victims of the Inquisition had had to pay the people who flogged them.[45]

It had been discovered that administration was a vital tool which could be used to project failings onto others. Human psychology was, then, at the heart of the story of the Inquisition. But if the historical literature spoke with precision of inquisitorial structures, of the statistics of autos, of the detail of the inquisitorial trial process and of its activities all over the Iberian worlds, it very rarely entered into the psychology behind what had gone on in an effort to understand what had actually motivated the persecution.[46]

This always seemed a mistake. And yet in the climate in which the research was conducted, one could see how such an omission could come about: the volume of information about the atrocities and the creeping advance of the persecuting culture, the accumulating 'evidence' of the threat, all inevitably pushing consumers of this information into relating to it on its own terms, so that it became difficult to perceive it from any external perspective and gain a psychological understanding of what was really going on.

In the decades that followed the demise of the Inquisition the task of understanding the psychological dynamics involved was increasingly passed to novelists. Classic examples are Dostoyevsky, with his devastating vignette 'The Grand Inquisitor' in *The Brothers Karamazov*, and Kafka's portrait of a bureaucratized inquisitorial pursuit in the story of Joseph K., recounted in *The Trial*. Who can forget K's quest for a meaningless piece of paper, of whose name he is always in ignorance, and his sudden execution after a meeting in the cathedral?

Another writer who used this theme was Elias Canetti. Like myself, Canetti was a descendant of the Iberian Jews who had been among the initial targets of the Inquisition. This made objectivity difficult and yet it also perhaps allowed a level of empathy which, one hopes, rather than trampling upon the emotions produced by the Inquisition, released them. One of Canetti's most famous works is his novel *Der Blendung*, published in Austria in 1935 and translated into English under the author's supervision as *Auto-da-Fé*. In this book Canetti – who won the Nobel Prize in 1981 – portrays the psychological breakdown of a scholar, Peter Kien, living in a central Europe increasingly dominated by authoritarianism in the years leading up to the Second World War. Hoodwinked out of his apartment by his housekeeper Thérèse and the fascist caretaker Benedikt Pfaff, Kien descends into an underworld from which he cannot re-emerge.

Canetti's book reprises the satire of the inquisitorial Auto which had first been composed by Cervantes over three centuries before.

In Canetti's disturbing vision the background to Kien's madness and collapse is the growing aggression, violence and scapegoating of a society on the brink of genocidal war. This world is unable to take responsibility for its own enormities. Obsessed by his own vision of the truth in his books, surrounded by a culture of incipient persecution, beaten, intense, mad, Kien is no longer able to live with what he has created in the microcosm of his ordered flat. In this space of such learning and culture, its creator, Kien, decides to burn down the flat, burn down the books, and destroy himself in the process.

The debate on the commission's proposals for the future of the Spanish Inquisition was inaugurated in Cádiz on 4 January 1813. Agustín de Argüelles, one of the members of the commission, came to the defence of its findings, reiterating the difficulties involved in re-establishing an Inquisition when there was no inquisitor-general, and adding that the institution had not promoted the purity of religion, but rather helped in eroding it by 'encouraging accusations . . . and relying on the probity of the judges, who are as full of wretchedness as any men'.[47] He went on to accuse the Inquisition of having dried up the sources of the Enlightenment and chased out of Spain all men of genius and enlightened ideas.

Argüelles was supported by the count of Toreno, who again stressed the absence of an inquisitor-general and the Inquisition's opposition to the Enlightenment, and added, 'The Inquisition has always gone about watching over and investigating the conduct of wise men and the intelligentsia . . . I cannot think of any enlightened person I have known who has not been under threat from the Inquisition'.[48] There were, though, many who spoke out in favour of the Inquisition. Some deputies noted that the nation was not comprised just of the enlightened or those who liked novelty, but of ordinary folk, and that these people desired the Inquisition to remain. Others stated that the Cortes should have nothing to do with belief, and should limit its remit simply to defending the faith, which as far as they were concerned meant maintaining the Inquisition.

The critics of the Inquisition in the Cortes proceeded to pull off a trick. On 16 January, as many of its supporters attended the funeral of the bishop of Segovia, the liberals rushed through a law declaring that 'the Catholic and apostolic religion will be protected by laws which conform to the Constitution'.[49] The Inquisition was doomed; on 22 February 1813 the decree of abolition was approved. Prohibited books went on sale at once, their sales boosted by being advertised as 'works prohibited by the Inquisition'. In the masked parades during Lent people dressed as bishops with burning axes went from plaza to plaza reading out the decree of abolition. In Cádiz, centre of bourgeois and internationalist Spain, celebration was in the air.

These events were mirrored in Portugal and the New World. In Mexico the leader of the independence movement, Miguel Hidalgo y Costilla, a liberal priest from the region of Querétaro, was charged in December 1810 by the Inquisition with 'rebellion and heresy'. Hidalgo was said by numerous witnesses to have doubted the coming of the Messiah, to have said that the Bible had only taken its complete form in the third century AD, and that St Teresa of Ávila had been deluded because of her self-flagellation and repeated fasting.[50] It was said that in his house a 'large group of common people gather perpetually to eat, drink, dance and chase women'.[51] Priests were said to dance with vials of holy oil around their necks, and the church ornaments and vestments were used in masked balls. On Christmas Eve the host had been hidden on the altar; the officiating priest suspected it had been stolen and had to hunt for it, just so that the congregants could find something to laugh at.[52]

Hidalgo maintained that he would never have been accused of heresy but for his support of the independence movement. However, the vigour with which the Inquisition pursued him may have been due to the fact that he spread stories among his followers about it. To the horror of Inquisition officials, he claimed that 'the inquisitors were men of flesh and blood; that they could make mistakes; and that their Edicts were driven by passions'.[53] Many priests agreed with Hidalgo, and one of them, the friar José Bernardo Villaseñor, announced that the edict issued against the 'heretic Hidalgo' was 'fit for using to wipe your bottom'.[54] Hidalgo and his followers then marched on Mexico City but in early 1811 retreated north, where they were defeated in March. Hidalgo was given a summary trial by the Inquisition before being shot.

Hidalgo, however had not died for nothing. Mexican independence soon followed, and by June 1813 the decree of abolition from Cádiz was public knowledge and the tribunal in Mexico ground to a halt. The same occurred in Lima, while in Chile the municipal council of Santiago had removed the ecclesiastical rent from the cathedral *canonjía* dedicated to the Inquisition almost two years earlier, in September 1811. Cartagena in Colombia had seen violent demonstrations demanding the abolition of the Inquisition the same year.[55]

In Portugal, meanwhile, events were no less dramatic. The Inquisition had been declared abolished by liberals following the flight of the Portuguese royal family from Napoleon's troops in 1807; the offices of the Inquisition were sacked, and the inquisitor-general fled to south-western France.[56] A definitive edict suppressing the tribunal in Goa was published on 16 June 1812.[57] The viceroy wrote suggesting that all the trial documents be burned and they have never been found. The Inquisition was finally abolished officially in Portugal on 31 March 1821 by the constitutional government[58] after the upheavals of the Peninsula War had come to an end.

By this time the decree of abolition passed by the Cádiz Cortes in 1813 had finally come into effect in Spain. After the ejection of French troops in 1813 King Ferdinand VII had returned to Spain and reinstalled the Inquisition, briefly. But a revolution had occurred in January 1820, again centring on Cádiz, and Ferdinand had only managed to retain his throne by promising to respect the constitution passed during the earlier Cádiz Cortes. Ferdinand proceeded to release prisoners from the inquisitorial jails and to pass a decree suppressing the Inquisition on 9 March 1820,[59] a decree ultimately converted into a law of abolition in 1834.

As soon as Ferdinand VII's decision to abide by the constitution of Cádiz was published on 8 March 1820 people took matters into their own hands. In Madrid a crowd of several hundred went to the jail of the Inquisition, where they freed seven detainees, all of them political prisoners. Those freed refused to be carried aloft in triumph to their homes; a tailor offered himself for the role instead, even though he had never had anything to do with the Inquisition. Then the crowd made a bonfire of all the furniture and paperwork that they had taken from the palace.[60]

The scapegoating of the scapegoater could not be checked;

repressed feelings and anger returned with an awesome inevitability. The jails of the Inquisition were stormed in Seville and Valencia on 10 March. In Palma, Mallorca the inquisitorial palace was destroyed.[61] In Barcelona the mob arrived at 1 p.m. on 10 March outside the palace of the captain-general, demanding the declaration of the constitution. He agreed, and they made for the inquisitorial palace with the aim of putting an end to the Inquisition for good. They forced the gates of the prison, as in Madrid, and freed the prisoners. More bonfires were lit, plumes of smoke rising into the sky as the trial records and archives of the Catalonian tribunal darkened the skies overhead.[62]

Poor Iberia! Portugal and Spain, once the seats of the greatest empires in the world, had been reduced to ruin. Divisions ruled. The Inquisition had tried to produce a united ideology, had persecuted threats when and where it had found them, but had only managed to preside over imperial decline. It could not be said that the persecution of the enemy had contributed to prosperity or the enhancement of people's lives. Repression had followed, and frustration. From frustration came anger, and then mutual rancour.

The stage was set for increasing bitterness. In time the divisions would slide into the terrible conflict of the Spanish Civil War and the mutual antagonism of conservatives and liberals which foreshadowed Portugal under Salazar. The enemy never vanished. The Inquisition had helped in its pursuit, yet the split which had in consequence been opened up would become wider than an ocean. Thus in Portugal and Spain had paranoia bled prosperity into decay. It was the imperial society's intolerance and pursuit of phantom threats which had ground its own empire into the melancholy runnels of oblivion.

Notes

For a list of abbreviations used in these notes see page 412.

Prologue

1 Bethencourt (1994: 79) describes the arms of the Inquisition in the Spanish dominions. My account of this autos-da-fé is taken from Liebman's (1974) translation of Bocanegra's eyewitness description of the event.
2 Liebman (1974) 38.
3 Ibid. 41–5 for the description of the stage, which was 44 *varas* long and 28 *varas* wide, a *vara* being equivalent to 85 centimetres.
4 Ibid. 50–4.
5 Ibid. 54.
6 Ibid. 57.
7 Wiznitzer (1971b) 144–5; Wachtel (2001a) 116–20. During Sobremonte's trial, his son recited a Jewish prayer that Sobremonte had taught him, and it emerged that he was seen as a rabbi in Mexico and had celebrated his marriage to Marí Gomez according to Jewish law. Sobremonte had been reconciled by the Mexican Inquisition in 1625; his second offence permitted the sentence of relaxation – death – to be pronounced. His trial is published in BAGN (1935–7) Vols 6–8.
8 Liebman (1974) 62–3.
9 Ibid. 65.
10 Ibid. 63.
11 Ibid. 64.
12 Ibid. 39.
13 Ibid. 24.
14 Ibid. 24–5.
15 AGI, Santa Fe 228, Expediente 63.
16 AGI, Santa Fe 228, Expediente 81A, nos 6–7, 9.
17 Ibid. nos 12, 18; Mañozca threatened these poor folk with the galleys and loss of office if they did not back down.
18 Ibid. no. 19.
19 Ibid. no. 30.
20 Ibid. no. 33.
21 The appointment was made in 1623 – see Lea (1908) 476.
22 AGI, Quito, Expediente 20A, no. 5.
23 Ibid.
24 Ibid. no. 8.
25 Toribio Medina (1887) Vol. 1, 191.

26 Liebman (1970) 57. See Wachtel (2001a: 134–9) for an analysis of how there was an elision between the idea of some Jewish rituals and making love in the language of the Mexican crypto-Jews.
27 Pérez Canto (1984) 1134.
28 Liebman (1970) 64: '*Quem canta, seu mal espanta;/Quem chora, seu mal aumenta:/ Eu canto para espalhar/a paixão que me attormenta*'. The translation is my own.
29 Palmer (1976) 63.
30 Chinchilla Aguilar (1952) 227.
31 PV, 272.
32 Toribio de Medina (1890) Vol. 1, 283.
33 Hakluyt (1600) 727.
34 AHN, Inquisición, Libro 1028, 160r–164r. During his trial Drake always protested that he had realized, on arriving at Asunción (and falling into the hands of the Spanish), that he wanted to be a Catholic. The documents do not relate what happened after his release from the monastery, though the likelihood is that he remained in Peru as the Inquisition in America often placed bans on travel for former *reconciliados* from Protestant countries who might be tempted to repeat their former errors.
35 Blázquez Miguel (1986b) 83.
36 Ibid.
37 Blázquez Miguel (1990) 28.
38 Blázquez Miguel (1986b) 64.
39 Blázquez Miguel (1990) 29–30.
40 Contreras and Henningsen (1986) 113–114; Bethencourt (1994) 365.
41 García Cárcel and Moreno Martínez (2000) 87.
42 Bethencourt (1994) 365.
43 Marques (1972) 292, 399, 402.
44 Mario Cohen (2000) 56.
45 Paiva (1997) 189.
46 Kinder (1997) 61–6.
47 Ruiz de Pablos (ed.) (1997).
48 An excellent statement of this view is Pinta Llorente (1953–8) Vol. 2, 61.
49 Trevor-Roper (1984) 113; Paiva (1997) 347–9.
50 Rawlings (2006) 2.
51 Sierra Corella (1947) 17.
52 See Tomás y Valiente's (1990) introduction to the second edition of his book on torture, originally published in 1973 during the Francoist era.
53 This is how to interpret Pinta Llorente's blaming of the decline of Spain in the 18th century on university lecturers (1961: 123–4) or his statement that 'today we know absolutely the paternal and merciful spirit which almost always accompanied the actions and procedures of the Spanish Inquisition. He who puts the honour and glory of God, and the maintenance of a moral order, above all else . . . has to admit the excellence of this national institution' (81).

54 This is a curious gap in the historiography of the Inquisition. While amongst Portuguese and Spanish authors it is understandable that there should be a focus on their own national histories, authors in English have concentrated on Spain: Lea (1906–7) devoted a chapter of his work on Spain to Portugal, as if it was some kind of Spanish province, while both Kamen (1965, 1997) and Monter (1990) looked only at Spain. The best comparative work of the Spanish, Portuguese and Roman tribunals is Bethencourt (1994).

55 Thus the protocol of the auto in Mexico described in this chapter can be compared to that of the auto in Évora in 1623 (Mendonça and Moreira (1980: 135–40)); they can be seen to be very similar, although the standards of the Inquisition in Spain and Portugal were different (Ibid. 134).

56 Almeida (1968) Vol. 2, 401.

57 These points of similarity are drawn out by Vainfas (1989) 190.

58 Lea (1963) 128.

59 Kagan and Dyer (2004) 11.

60 These acts as breaks with the past are cited by Bethencourt (1994) 22.

61 Lea (1906), Vol. 1, 163.

62 Almeida (1968) Vol. 2, 387–9, 403, 414.

63 Llorca (1949) 61, 68; García Cárcel and Moreno Martínez (2000) 33–4. Persecution under the the later Italian Inquisition was also far less exacting than in Portugal and Spain. Only 2–3 per cent of prisoners were tortured in Venice in the 16th century, far less than was the case at that time under Portuguese or Spanish tribunals. Fewer people were executed under the Inquisition in Italy in the 16th century than during the conflicts between Catholics and Protestants in England between the reigns of Henry VIII and Mary Tudor (Grendler (1977) 52–8).

64 García Mercadal (ed.) (1999) Vol. 2, 354, 371.

65 AHN, Inquisición, Libro 937, folio 14r.

66 This view is in opposition to that of some scholars such as Dedieu (1989: 57) and Domínguez Ortiz (1993: 26) who stress that the tribunal was ecclesiastical. While of course the interests of most of its officers were overwhelmingly theological in direction, there can be no doubt that in the wider political context the separation of the Iberian tribunals from Rome made them into fundamentally political institutions.

67 F. Ruiz (1987) 40–1.

68 AHN, Inquisición, Legajo 2022, Expediente 24, folio 4r: '*no es sino mierda y mas mierda*'.

69 This is in spite of the destruction across Spain of large numbers of documents during the Napoleonic Wars and the ensuing liberal revolution, which meant that the archives of the tribunals of Cordoba, Granada and Seville were almost completely destroyed (García Fuentes (1981) xi).

70 Lithgow (1640) 479–80.

71 García Mercadal (ed.) (1999) Vol. 1, 582.

72 García-Arenal (1978) 42–3.

73 AHN, Inquisición, Libro 938, folio 168r: the case of Pedro Mufferi of Chelva, near Valencia, dating from 1602.
74 Benassar (1987) 178.
75 Ibid.
76 Ibid.
77 Contreras and Henningsen (1986) 120; for a fuller discussion of the imposition of the reign of fear see Contreras (1987) 53–4.
78 Benassar (1987) 183.
79 As we shall see, it is not for nothing that some historians see in the Inquisition the basic elements of modern totalitarian regimes. See Lewin (1967) 9; Gilman (1972) 168.
80 Bradley (1931) 319–22.

One – The End of Tolerance

1 Thus in 1484 the *Reyes Católicos* had had to order the elite of Ciudad Real not to shelter 'heretics' to protect them from the Inquisition, which had been installed there in 1483; Beinart (1974–85) Vol. 4, 295–6.
2 Pinta Llorente (1961) 56.
3 There is considerable academic argument as to the nature of these conversions. The traditional view of this wave of conversion was that it largely followed the violent pogroms against the Jews which broke out in Seville in June 1391 and spread rapidly across the country to places such as Cordoba, Toledo, Cuenca, Majorca, Valencia and Barcelona (Baer (1966) Vol. 1, 96–110). Though some recent historiography supports this view (Netanyahu (1995a) 148–51), Norman Roth has argued persuasively that there was much royal defence of the Jews (see also Suárez Fernández (1980) 215) and that those who were forcibly converted to Christianity could have returned to Judaism had they wished to (2002: 33–45); instead, he sees the voluntary conversions among the elites as precipitating a spiritual crisis in Spanish Jewry which led to waves of voluntary conversions, fuelled by the firebrand preaching of St Vincent Ferrer. Certainly, the fact that some *Jews* themselves participated in the pogroms suggests that the traditional view is in need of a little revision (Blázquez Miguel (1989) 127–8).
4 García-Arenal (1996) 165.
5 Monter (1990) 6.
6 Pinta Llorente (1961) 60–1; such actions make Menéndez y Pelayo 's claim (1945: Vol. 3, 433) that the resistance in Aragón was 'light' (*leve*) difficult to comprehend.
7 Monter (1990) 7–9.
8 Ibid. 9.
9 There were more Moors in Aragon than anywhere else in Spain other than Granada; in the countryside they outnumbered the Christians (García

Mercadal (1999) Vol. 1, 301) and it was their skills in ploughing, cultivating and irrigating which supported the lifestyle of the nobility. A local saying went, '*Quien no tiene moros, no tiene oro*' – Whoever has no Moors has no gold (Ibid. Vol. 1, 388).

10 I have drawn this general account of Zaragoza from the Venetian ambassador Navajero's account of 1525 – García Mercadal (1999) Vol. 2, 16.

11 Trasmiera (1664) 4–5.

12 Ibid. 52–3.

13 Zurita (1610) Book 20, 341.

14 Ibid. 342.

15 Ibid.

16 Sabatini (1928) 217.

17 Llorente (1841) 144.

18 Zurita (1610), Book 20, 342.

19 Trasmiera (1664) 73–4.

20 Ibid. 82–3.

21 Sabatini (1928) 221; Llorente (1841) 158–9.

22 Sabatini (1928) 222–3.

23 Jama (2001) 35–47.

24 It is of the first importance that the initial anger of the *conversos* was matched by that of *caballeros* and *gente principal*: Zurita (1610) Book 20, 341.

25 Amador de los Ríos (1960) 29, 69.

26 Green (2006) 30–1; Fonseca (1995) 15 (following Barradas de Carvalho). The shift in importance from a geography of human places to one of physical spaces accompanied the modernization of consciousness and the growth of an abstract, scientific world view.

27 Bernis (1978) Vol. 1, 16–17.

28 Ibid. Vol. 1, 20–3.

29 Ibid. Vol. 2, 20 – the view of Alonso de Palencia, Henry IV's chronicler.

30 Ibid. Vol. 2, 21.

31 Ibid.

32 Castro (1954) 126.

33 Ibid. 121; moreover Islamic influence also extended to the Jewish community, in the architecture of its great synagogue known as *El Tránsito* in Toledo, for instance, and in its literature and theology (Ibid. 446; Roth (1994) 170–82).

34 Castro (1972), xxix.

35 Fletcher (1992) 143.

36 Roth (2002) 66.

37 Roth (1994) 133.

38 Nirenberg (1998) 138–9.

39 Fletcher (1992) 138.

40 The Christians in Spain could not have accomplished the reconquest if they had dedicated themselves to intellectual ideas (Castro (1972) lii).

41 Escandell Bonet (1984a) 270.

42 The evidence of the Florentine ambassador Francesco Guicciardini – García Mercadal (ed.) (1999) Vol. 1, 578.
43 Bernáldez (1962) 15–16.
44 Ibid. 18.
45 Ibid. 15.
46 Valera (1927) 5.
47 Douglas (1984) 4, 38. I am indebted to my doctoral supervisor, Paulo Farias, for bringing this insight to bear on the position of the *conversos*.
48 Pérez de Guzmán (1965) 43.
49 Sicroff (1985) 52–3.
50 Benito Ruano (1961) 186.
51 Ibid. 188.
52 Ibid. 187–8.
53 Pérez de Guzmán (1965) 39.
54 Ibid. 45–6.
55 Ibid. 46.
56 The importance of the weakness of John II in this matter is noted by Sicroff (1985) 56.
57 Benito Ruano (1961) 206.
58 Ibid. 193: *'facen otros géneros de olocaustos e sacrificios judaizando'*.
59 Ibid. 193, 194–5.
60 Netanyahu (1995) 357–9.
61 Ladero Quesada's analysis from Badajoz, Toledo and Andalusia shows that, in the last third of the 15th century, only 10–15 per cent of *conversos* were involved in commerce, and that the vast majority (between 50 and 77.5 per cent) were artisans (1992: 42–4)); in Osma's bishopric at the end of the 15th century only 3.1 per cent of *conversos* were active in commerce (Valdeón Buruque (1995) 56).
62 Valdeón Buruque (1995) 71–81.
63 Fromm (1951: 69) is particularly good at showing how the inconsistencies in an argument may reveal the underlying feeling which propels it.
64 In the early 15th century, less than 20 years after the events of 1391, the Jews of Évora in Portugal complained that the Jewish quarter in the town was not big enough, which meant that the cost of owning houses was prohibitively expensive and many Jews were emigrating to Castile (Almeida (1967: Vol. 2, 389); in 1467, riots and forced conversions of Jews in Tlemcen, North Africa, caused a rabbi, Yeshu'ah ha-Levi, to migrate to Toledo: as ha-Levi put it, he 'came to the land of Castilla to keep [his] life from danger for a while' (Hirschberg (1974) 388–9). The dichotomy between the violence directed at *conversos* and the absence of any similar behaviour towards Jews is noted in Sicroff (1985: 85).
65 Suárez Fernández (ed.) (1964) 21; Roth (2002) 50–1, 82–5.
66 The idea that resentment of the *conversos* derived from hostility towards urban centres is explored more fully in Green (2007: Appendix B); see also Ladero Quesada (1999) 314.

67 Beinart (1974–85), Vol. 4 (1985) 8–11.
68 Ibid. (1985) 26.
69 Beinart (1981) 67.
70 Bernáldez (1962) 96–8.
71 This is the unanswerable argument of Netanyahu (1966).
72 Roth (2002) xix.
73 Baer (1966) Vol. 2, 272.
74 The evidence of Pulgar on Toledo, cited in Benito Ruano (2001) 31.
75 Beinart (1971a), 435.
76 Kamen (1997) 40.
77 Sabatini (1928) 124–5; see also Kamen's (1997) discussion of the evidence from Ciudad Real.
78 Kamen (1997) 60.
79 Gitlitz (1996: 18–19): 'In many ways it [the Inquisition] helped to create the very culture it was dedicated to eradicate'; see also Novinsky (1972: 37); Azevedo (1974: 108).
80 Mariana (1751) Vol. 8, 186.
81 Ibid. Vol. 8, 185.
82 Bernáldez (1962) 76.
83 García Mercadal (ed.) (1999) Vol. 1, 380–1.
84 Bernis (1978) Vol. 1, 39.
85 This was the report of Nicolau von Popplau *c.* 1485 (García Mercadal (ed.) (1999: vol. 1 298). On the extraordinary influence of *conversos* at the court of Isabella see also Amador de los Ríos (1960) 683–4.
86 Collantes de Terán (1977) 74–8.
87 Ladero Quesada (1976) 49.
88 Pulgar (1943) Vol. 1, 310.
89 Llorente (1841) 112–13.
90 Beinart (1981) 10–20. A recent account of Espina's *Fortalitium Fidei* is Vidal Doval (2005); little is known of Espina's origins, although he appears to have written largely for a court audience and to have been attempting to propitiate a faction at court. Once thought to have been a *converso* himself, this is now seen as unlikely; see Netanyahu (1997).
91 Barrios (1991) 19; the foundational bull only makes mention of the *converso* heresy (Llorca (1949: 49–50), which makes García Cárcel and Moreno Martínez's (2000: 43) claim that the 'Inquisition was not only created to resolve the *converso* problem' extraordinary.
92 The suggestion of Llorente (1841: 111).
93 León Tello (1979) Vol. 1, 531–2. Even those who came forward during the period of grace had to give part of their goods to help in the war against Granada; see Jiménez Monteserín (ed.) (1980) 90.
94 Gil (2000–1) Vol. 1, 35; note also Edwards (1999: 55–6), who suggests that the role of the civil war in the establishment of the Inquisition was that the factions in Andalusia became allied to factions in the civil war between Isabella and her rival claimant to the throne Juana la Beltraneja, who was

supported by Portugal. Edwards suggests that by linking opposition to her claim to Judaizing *conversos* and establishing an Inquisition, Isabella legitimized her position as monarch.

95 Kamen (1997) 7. This pattern is in keeping with Adorno et al. (1950) and Ackerman and Jahoda's (1950) findings on the way in which anti-Semitism – and indeed all acts of demonization of others – can be a defensive psychological strategy for the warding off of mental illness; in the case of Castile the 'illness' can be interpreted as the civil wars and the demonization as the invention of the *converso* Judaizers.

96 Barrios (1991) 20.

97 Gil (2000–1) Vol. 1, 93–110.

98 Domínguez Ortiz (1971) 34.

99 Gil (2000–1) Vol. 1, 123–38.

100 Pulgar (1943) 337.

101 Blázquez Miguel (1989) 90–1, 134.

102 Barrios (1991) 20; Bernáldez (1962) 100.

103 Barrios (1991) 20.

104 Ibid.

105 Bernáldez (1962) 99.

106 Llorente (1841) 121

107 Kamen (1997: 47) and Netanyahu (1995a) suggest that the death of Susán on the scaffold is a myth, since he is said to have died before 1479. However, it was documented by Bernáldez, who is usually a reliable chronicler for names and dates; this inclines me to believe that the story is true.

108 Sabatini (1928) 127.

109 Bernaldez (1962) 101.

110 Gil (2000–1) Vol. 1, 155.

111 Collantes de Terán (1977) 109–13.

112 Ibid. 103.

113 Bernáldez (1962) 101.

114 Ibid. 99.

115 Martínez Millán (1984) 12; this was a part of the modernization of administrative structures completed by the *Reyes Católicos* (Escandell Bonet (1980a: 275); Benítez Sánchez-Blanco (1983: 65); Ruiz (1987: 42)).

116 Beinart (1974–85) Vol. 1, xvi–xvii.

117 Ibid. 2–25.

118 Ibid. 41–69.

119 Ibid. 275.

120 Ibid. 302.

121 Ibid. 92–130.

122 Ibid. 17–18.

123 Ibid. 391–2.

124 Ibid. 254.

125 Blázquez Miguel (1990) 28.

126 Another defendant, Maria González la Panpana, the wife of Juan Panpan,

said that she had refused to Judaize with her husband and had not gone with him when he had left the city ten years before so as not to follow his doctrinal errors. Again, her account was largely confirmed by priests, but even though she had confessed to what had only been minor wrongdoings during the period of grace, she too was burnt. Ibid.; Beinart (1974) Vol. 1, 71–89.

127 Ibid. 36.

128 Llorca (1949) 68–9.

129 León Tello (1979) Vol. 1, 512–14.

130 Bethencourt (1994) 45.

131 Domínguez Ortiz (1993) 37.

132 Pulgar (1943) Vol. 1, 336; this makes Kamen's (1997: 60) estimate of 2,000 deaths up to 1530 look like an underestimate.

133 Bernaldez (1962) 102.

134 López (1613) 365, 369.

135 Ibid. 369.

136 Jiménez Monteserín (1980) 111 – the situation throughout Spain in 1488 according to instructions drawn up in Valladolid.

137 Blázquez Miguel (1990) 29; Monter's figure of 80 deaths by 1530 for Zaragoza is probably an underestimate (1990: 18).

138 BL, Egerton 1832, folios 37v–38v.

139 Monter (1990) 17.

140 La Mantia (1977) 42–3.

141 Ibid. 38.

142 Monter (1990) 18; La Mantia (1977) 44, 53.

143 Llorente (1841) 140.

144 The classic modern statement of this view is López Martínez (1954); it is no coincidence that this is one of the most egregious works of anti-Semitism in the history of writings on the Jews of Spain.

145 The key work arguing for the racialization of the movement of which the Inquisition was a spearhead is Netanyahu (1995a).

146 Unlike other European countries the vernacular had been the language of governance in Spain since the 13th century (Castro (1954) 357). Anderson (1991: 12–18) has persuasively argued that the use of the vernacular was an important element in the rise of European nationalism, and the fact that this occurred much earlier in Spain than elsewhere in Europe would explain why the institutionalization of persecution also occurred earlier. This use of the vernacular was itself the legacy of the *convivencia* and the role of Jews in transmitting Arab culture to the Christian powers of the north (Castro (1954: 451–8). For a more general discussion of this process see Green (2007) Appendix B.

Two – Spreading the Fires

1 Caro Baroja (1978) Vol. 1, 145.
2 CRP, 967–8.
3 Ibid. 972–7.
4 Ibid. 972, 978–9.
5 IAN/TT, Inquisição de Évora, Proceso 8779, folios 1r–3r; 6r for his age.
6 Ibid. 6r—v.
7 Ibid. 3r, 8r.
8 Ibid. 66v; the trial of Jorge exists in the IAN/TT but access is denied owing to the bad condition of the document. The skeleton outline of Jorge's case in the index in IAN/TT confirms that the arrest of Jorge was also on 10 January 1545.
9 Ibid. 67r.
10 Roth (1959) 54.
11 Tavares (1982) Vol. 1, 425; Herculano (1854) Vol. 1, 108.
12 IAN/TT, Inquisição de Évora, Proceso 8779, 66v; confirmed in Toro (1982) 278–9.
13 Thus Gaspar de Carvajal died in Benavente (Ibid. 279), as did Álvaro and Jorge's father Antonio (ibid.); subsequent members of the family lived in Salamanca and Medina del Campo (ibid.).
14 Godinho (1969) 425.
15 Boxer (1948) 1.
16 Godinho (1969) 829.
17 Herculano (1854) Vol. 1, 184 – complaints from the Cortes of Torres Novas, 1525: King Manoel I had died in 1521.
18 Marques (1972) Vol. 1, 80.
19 IAN/TT, Inquisição de Évora, Proceso 8779, 17r–v.
20 Góis (1949) Vol. 1, 11–12.
21 Ibid. Vol. 2, 223–6.
22 Costa Lobo (1979) 130.
23 The evidence of Nicolaus von Popplau (*c.* 1485) – García Mercadal (ed.) (1999) Vol. 1, 289, 295.
24 Lobo (1979) 117.
25 Douglas (1984) 38.
26 Révah (1971) 483.
27 Góis (1949) Vol. 1, 42.
28 Osorio (1944) Vol. 1, 81.
29 Tavim (1997) 83–84.
30 Osorio (1944) Vol. 1, 81.
31 Ibid.
32 Lobo (1979) 34.
33 This is all taken from Góis (1949) Vol. 1, 254–7; see also Bernáldez (1962) 505.

34 Azevedo (1922) 59.
35 IAN/TT, Inquisição de Évora, Proceso 8779, folios 23r–v.
36 Ibid. 27v–28r.
37 Ibid. 134r–137v.
38 Azevedo (1922) 61–3.
39 AG, Vol. 1, 116; Nunes's account of his experiences among the *conversos* of Lisbon is published in AG, Vol. 1, 103–18.
40 Ibid. 107–15.
41 Ibid. 343–4.
42 Tavares (1987) 113.
43 Monteiro (1750) Vol. 2, 424.
44 Saraiva (1985) 41.
45 Herculano (1854) Vol.1, 262–4.
46 Ibid. Vol. 2, 1–90; Almeida (1968) Vol. 2, 387–401; Tavares (2004) 146.
47 The foregoing two paragraphs are taken from Góis (1949) Vol. 2, 112.
48 Mendonça and Moreira (1980) 121.
49 Almeida (1967) Vol. 2, 404–6; Azevedo Mea (1997) 61–5.
50 Azevedo (1922) 95.
51 Almeida (1967) Vol. 2, 414–415.
52 Remedios (1928) Vol. 2, 50.
53 Roth (1959) 73.
54 IAN/TT, Inquisição de Évora, Proceso 8779, folio 158r.
55 Toro (1982) 279; Espejo and Paz (1908) 41.
56 Toro (1944) Vol. 1, 40.
57 Baião (1921) 21.
58 The evidence of a Polish ambassador dated 1524; García Mercadal (1999) (ed.), 770.
59 *Documentos de la Época de los Reyes Católicos*, 338–9.
60 Contreras (1987) 48.
61 Barrios (1991) 31.
62 Ibid. 31–2.
63 García Fuentes (1981), xxii.

Three – Tortured Justice

1 Llorente (1841) 229.
2 Barrios (1991) 58.
3 Gracia Boix (ed) (1982) 96–101; for a more general confirmation of this see Anonymous (ed.) (1964) 153–4.
4 Barrios (1991) 57.
5 Herculano (1854) Vol. 1, 230; cited in Lipiner (1977) 171.
6 Meseguer Fernández (1980) 379–89; Fernández García (1995) 480.
7 Gracia Boix (1982) 30–1.
8 This slave almost certainly hailed from the Gold Coast.

9 Gracia Boix (1982) 31–77.
10 Ibid. 100–1.
11 Ibid. 101.
12 See for example Ackroyd (1998: 387) on the initial death sentence handed down to Thomas More in 1535.
13 Vainfas (1989) 191–2; Blázquez Miguel (1990) 79; Ceballos Gómez (1994) 121; Rawlings (2006) 2.
14 AHN, Inquisición, Libro 938, folios 37v–39v.
15 Ibid. Libro 938 folios 9v–22r.
16 Ibid. Legajo 2105, Expediente 26.
17 Carrasco (1983) 181.
18 Ibid. 182 n.38.
19 Ibid. 184.
20 Mott (1988) 79–81 comprehensively overturns Vainfas's (1989: 247) view that torture was not used in Portugal against crimes such as sodomy. Vainfas is one of those who holds that inquisitorial torture was not as bad as is sometimes thought.
21 Pulgar (1943) Vol. 1, 440.
22 Caro Baroja (1968) 38.
23 Jiménez Monteserín (ed.) (1980) 98 n. 15.
24 Barrios (1991) 36.
25 Monterroso y Alvarado (1571) folio 52r.
26 Vassberg (1996) 81.
27 Tomás y Valiente (1980) 53; (1994) 91.
28 Barrios (1991) 36.
29 See Lea (1906–7), Vol. 3, 1–30 on the general use of torture; many of the Latin American trials reveal this fact, for example AHN, Inquisición, Legajo 1620, Expediente 15.
30 Jiménez Monteserín (ed.) (1980) 426–7.
31 Toro (1944) Vol.1, 281, 285.
32 Fernández-Armesto (1982) 182–3.
33 Rumeu de Armas (1956) 141–2.
34 Wolf (ed. and trans.) (1926); Millares Torres (1981).
35 Alberti and Chapman (eds) (1912) 88: '*ser lutherano [el testigo] entiende es no oyr misa y hurtar*'.
36 Ibid. 120: '*la yglesia de ynglaterra no es yglesia sino sinagoga del demonio*'.
37 Ibid. 84.
38 Ibid. 84–5.
39 Ibid. 87.
40 Ibid. 84–101.
41 Something that is particularly apparent in the cases of *moriscos* in the late 16th and early 17th centuries. See for example AHN, Libro 936, folios 182r–184r, on Valencia in 1578–9.
42 Rêgo (ed.) (1971) 90.
43 IAN/TT, Inquisição de Lisboa, Livro 223, folios 99r–v.

44 Ibid. folio 99v.
45 AHN, Inquisición, Libro 1020, folio 514r.
46 Ibid. Legajo 1647, Expediente 13, folios 134r–v.
47 IAN/TT, Inquisição d'Évora, Livro 91, folios 197r–199r.
48 Eymeric (1972) 15.
49 Ibid. 23–4.
50 Ibid. 25.
51 Ibid. 63.
52 Sabatini (1928) 140–2; see also IT.
53 AHN, Inquisición, Legajo 1620, Expediente 11, folios 54r–56v, 72r, 74r.
54 Ibid. Legajo 1620, Expediente 18, folios 33r–33v.
55 Ibid. Legajo 1620, Expediente 15, folios 105r–v.
56 Pinta Llorente (1961) 72.
57 Mariana (1751) Vol. 8, 506.
58 Ibid. Vol. 8, 507.
59 AHN, Inquisición, Legajo 2022, Expediente 2, folio 3r.
60 See also Dedieu (1989) 142–3.
61 Mariana (1751) Vol. 8, 506–7.
62 AHN, Inquisición, Legajo 1647, Expediente 11, no. 4.
63 Thus Fernando de Rojas, the *converso* author of *La Celestina*, had acted as a lawyer in inquisitorial cases. See also Kamen (1997) 194.
64 Gracia Boix (1982) 201–2; the *instrucciones* of Torquemada (1484) make it clear that this payment depends on their financial capacity (IT: folios 6r–v).
65 Kamen (1997) 201–2.
66 Rêgo (1983) 117–118; Rêgo (1971) 126–7; the Portuguese case dealt more generally with 'deaths' in jail, but in the text stressed that in many cases this was death by suicide.
67 Cited in Souza (1987) 327; such evidence does not entirely bear out Lea's assertion (1906–7: Vol. 2, 509) that inquisitorial jails were better than their civil counterparts.
68 IAN/TT, Inquisição de Lisboa, Livro 218, folios 27r–28r.
69 Jiménez Rueda (ed.) (1945) 317.
70 Fonseca (1612) 126.
71 Dellon (1698) 5.
72 Ferrer Benimeli (1976–7) Vol. 3, 80, 429–32.
73 Eymeric (1972) 18.
74 AHN, Inquisición, Legajo 1620, Expediente 15.
75 Thus 22.9 per cent of those accused of Judaizing and and 12.8 per cent of those accused of Lutheranism between 1621 and 1700 in Toledo were tortured (Dedieu (1989: 79)).
76 González Obregón (ed.) (1935) 171–9.
77 Böhm (1984) 291.
78 González Obregón (ed.) (1935) 299–307.

Four – Escape

1 Ships left Lisbon for Cape Verde in February, according to the anonymous pilot (Anonymous (1551/2?).
2 Toro (1932) 280–1. The same can be gleaned from the account of his life given to the inquisitors in Mexico in 1589.
3 MMA, II, 441.
4 The view of the sailors who informed Valentim Fernandes *c.* 1506 – see Mauny et al. (eds.) (1951) 110.
5 Carletti (1965) 67.
6 Anonymous (1551/2?) 89. Most of the ships came from Seville or from the newly discovered lands in America, and the first consignment of slaves to go directly from Africa to the New World had left from this harbour in around 1514; the first legal consignment was taken by Lorenzo de Garrevod in 1517 (Correia Lopes (1944: 4)); however, slaves had in fact been leaving routinely from at least 1514 as part of contraband (Hall (1992) Vol. 2, 428).
7 Toro (1932) 280. The family also had connections in Benavente – it was here that Luis's sister Francisca would marry and raise her family.
8 IAN/TT, Inquisição de Évora, Proceso 8779, folio 66v.
9 Toro (1932) 281.
10 Saunders (1982) 55.
11 Ibid. 17.
12 Vogt (1973) 1.
13 The account of Hieronymus Münzer (1494) – García Mercadal (ed.) (1999) Vol. 1, 354.
14 Vogt (1973) 10.
15 Ibid.
16 Ibid. 12.
17 Saunders (1982) 76.
18 Ibid. 75–7.
19 Ibid. 52.
20 Toro (1932) 280–1; evidence of Luis de Carvajal's work in Cape Verde is also found in HGCV: II, 522.
21 Hall (1992) Vol. 1, 143–6.
22 Vogt (1973) 10.
23 Baião (1921) 202.
24 A vast literature exists mooting the possibility that Columbus himself was a *converso*. Supporters of the theory argue that Columbus used Hebrew letters as a monogram at the top of private correspondence; moreover, Columbus's contacts in Palos near Seville included several *converso* families, members of which were subsequently tried by the Inquisition. See David (1933) 66; Gil (2000: Vol. 1, 181); Gil cites the Pintos of Palos as contacts of Columbus, and that on departing Seville in 1492 he left his son Diego in the hands of

Juan Rodríguez Cabezudo, later reconciled by the Inquisition; Cohen (2000: 39–40) summarizes the arguments for the *converso* theory.

25 Wittmayer Baron (1969) Vol. 13, 134.

26 Liebman (1970) 47.

27 Liebman (1971) 475; (1970) 48.

28 Baião (1945) 17–23.

29 Fernández del Castillo (1982) 584.

30 Böhm (1963) 13.

31 Salvador (1978) 126–7. This was largely because of the absence of any other literate Portuguese. There are some excellent instances in this reference – for example, the notary of the council in São Paulo for years was Fructuoso da Costa, who had been exiled to Brazil because of his faith.

32 The Aboabs had been among the most important Sephardic families, with one – Isaac – a *gaon* or supreme guardian of the Law just prior to the expulsion from Spain in 1492 (Azevedo (1922: 20)).

33 Salvador (1969) 15; Samuel (2004) 69–79.

34 Salvador (1978) 130–4.

35 Todorov (1982) 146.

36 This is an echo of Davis's (1994: 16) point that the Jewish (as opposed to *converso*) communities of the Caribbean found the threshold of their emancipation in a region of slave labour. For a fuller discussion of this process of transference see Green (2007: Part I, Chapter 5).

37 The major works on the early modern history of Cape Verde are the HGCV, Correia e Silva (1995), Green (2007) and Hall (1992).

38 Anonymous (1551/2?) 85.

39 Ventura (1999) 121–33.

40 Carletti (1965) 7.

41 Saunders (1982) 14.

42 Carletti (1965) 7: 'Their Portuguese men love these black women more than their own Portuguese women, holding it as a certain and proved fact that to have commerce with them is much less harmful and also a much greater pleasure, they being said to have fresher and healthier natures.'

43 Ibid.

44 Ibid. 8.

45 AGI, Escribanía 119A, 15r–17r – a letter from Cape Verde of 12 May 1574 detailing this process for one of Duarte de Leão's later factors.

46 Carletti (1965) 14–15.

47 IAN/TT, Inquisição de Lisboa, Maço 25, no. 233.

48 One such was Antonio Duarte; Duarte lived in Buguendo with Jorge. Ibid. folios 24v, 38v.

49 Baleno (1991) 169.

50 Ibid.

51 Teixeira da Mota (1978) 8.

52 Révah (1971) 504.

53 IAN/TT, Inquisição de Lisboa, Livro 840, Folio 8r.
54 Silva (2004) 164.
55 These are the figures of 1582 from Francisco de Andrade, MMA, Vol. 3, 100.
56 IAN/TT, Inquisição de Lisboa, Livro 214, folio 13r.
57 ASV, Secretaria di Stato di Portogallo, 174v–175r.
58 Toro (1932) 21.
59 Jiménez Rueda (1946) 5–7.
60 Toro (1932) 108.
61 Jiménez Rueda (1946) 9.
62 Russell-Wood (1978) 33–4.
63 Havik (2004a) 104.
64 IAN/TT, Inquisição de Lisboa, Maço 25, no. 233, folio 4r.
65 Ibid. 4v.
66 IAN/TT, Inquisição de Évora. Livro 91, folio 41r.
67 Sweet (2003) 53–4; Mott (1988) 32.
68 Sweet (2003) 70–5.
69 Ibid. 73.
70 Fernández (2003) 82; this is borne out by the punishments meted out to both active and passive partners throughout the institution's history, but see Mott (1988: 111) who says that the active partner was condemned and Sweet (2003: 73) who holds that passive partners are assumed to be the criminal agent.
71 AHN, Inquisición, Libro 936, folio 114r.
72 Baião (1945) Vol. 2, 489.
73 Cited in Caro Baroja (1968) 34–5.
74 IAN/TT, Inquisição de Lisboa, Maço 25, no. 233, folio 4v.
75 Ibid. 24r–v.
76 Ibid. 42r.
77 Ibid. 42v–43r.
78 Ibid. 38v.
79 Ibid. 2r.
80 HGCV: II, 522.
81 Toro (1932) 281.
82 Camões (1973) 5.
83 Conway (ed.) (1927) 7–8.
84 Léry (1975) 19.
85 Ibid. 32–3.
86 Delumeau (1978) 39.
87 Green (2007), Part I, Chapter 4.
88 Toro (1944) Vol. 1, 26.
89 ENE, Vol. 10, 286.
90 Cohen (1995) 442–3.
91 Osorio Osorio (1980) 55.
92 AHN, Inquisición, Legajo 265, Inquisición de Toledo, Expediente 2.

93 AGI, Contratación 5539, Libro 5, 218v; the proof of *limpieza* of Luis Fernández Suárez from 12 April 1634, a nephew of the *converso* Antonio Núñez Gramaxo, one of the leading traders of Cartagena.
94 Lea (1906–7) Vol. 2, 308.
95 BA, Códice 49-X-2, folios 243r–245r; AGI, Justicia 518, no.1, Autos Fiscales; BA, Códice 49-X-2, folio 244r; AGI, Escribanía 119A, '*Los herederos de Duarte de León y Antonio Goncalez de Guzman con el fiscal de su Magd sobre pieças de esclavos*'.
96 Toro (1932) 281.
97 Ibid. 281.
98 Hakluyt (1600) 549.
99 Ibid. 18.
100 Ibid. 541.
101 Conway (1927) 10.
102 Ibid.
103 Thomas (1997) 157.
104 Hakluyt (1600) 558; Hawkins (1569) 3v–3r.
105 Jiménez Rueda (ed.) (1945) 414, 417.
106 Hawkins (1569) 5v–6v.
107 Hawkins (1569) 11v–15r; Hakluyt (1600) 560–2.
108 Hawkins (1569) 15v; Hakluyt (1600) 562–3
109 Jiménez Rueda (ed.) (1945) 419–20; Toro (1944) Vol. 1, 33.
110 Toro (1944) Vol. 1, 35.
111 Toro (1932) 47–9.

Five – The Enemy Within

1 Huerga (1978–88) Vol. 1, 367.
2 Ruiz de Pablos (ed.) (1997) 302. This account came from the escaped Lutheran from Seville known as González Montes. Though its veracity has repeatedly been questioned by historians, the editor of this recent published version takes issue with the critics to argue that although there are exaggerations in the account, much of it is undoubtedly true (Ibid. 88–103).
3 García Mercadal (1999) (ed.) Vol. 1, 316–17.
4 Ibid. Vol. 1, 320–1.
5 AHN, Inquisición, Legajo 1198, Expediente 32; the evidence for the case against Costa consists of an unnumbered copy of the original file appended to an inquiry concerning *limpieza de sangre* dated 1713. The remainder of the information concerning the case in this chapter is derived from this file.
6 See Vassberg (1996: 19) for some extraordinary examples of this.
7 Novalín (1968–71) Vol. 2, 188–9.
8 It should be noted that this case of Costa adds to the knowledge of trials and *relajamientos* of Lutherans in these very early years. The notion that there was a slow drip of persecution directed at Lutherans prior to the great trials

of Valladolid and Seville should therefore perhaps be somewhat revised (Tellechea Idigoras (1977: 26–8)).

9 Contreras (1987) 48.

10 Meseguer Fernández (1984) 350–6; Arzona (1980).

11 One of the best discussions of Cisneros's career and influence remains Bataillon (1937) 1–64.

12 Barrios Aguilera (2002) 78.

13 See for example Lea (2001) 109.

14 Bataillon (1937) 63–4.

15 During the *comunero* revolts of the Castilian cities 1520–1, for instance, a strong anti-inquisitorial flavour could be found; Contreras (1987) 48.

16 Hamilton (1992) 28–36; derived from the Edict of Grace issued in Toledo on 23 September 1525 and published by Márquez (1972) 272–82. This is a summary of the many charges laid at the door of the *alumbrados*.

17 Nieto (1970) 60 n.42.

18 Ibid.; Hamilton (1992) 26.

19 Ibid.; Márquez (1972) 62.

20 Hamilton (1992) 51–3.

21 Ibid. 56–61.

22 Ortega-Costa (1978) 31: '*que estando ella en el acto carnal con su marido estava más allegada a Dios que si estuviese en la más alta oraçión del mundo*'.

23 Llorca (1980) 273–4; Medrano was clearly sexually obsessed by Hernández, since among his personal beliefs were that a belt which she had given him was as holy as if a bishop had sent it, that she was the beneficiary of infinite grace, and that – fortuitously – it was 'impossible' for her to commit a carnal sin (ibid. 274).

24 Ibid. 69–77; Nieto (1970) 80–3.

25 Márquez (1972) 67.

26 Selke (1980) 622–3; Márquez (1972) 62.

27 Hamilton (1992) 53, 70–1.

28 Ibid. 63, 71–5.

29 Ibid. 2.

30 Menéndez y Pelayo (1945) Vol. 4, 98.

31 Hamilton (1992) 77–9.

32 Escandell Bonet (1984c) 436–7.

33 Bataillon (1937) 167.

34 Ibid. 254.

35 Ibid. 467.

36 Avilés Fernández (1984) 467ff.

37 Kinder (1997) 63.

38 Bataillon (1937) 473–526.

39 Kinder (1997) 63–8.

40 Alcalá Galve (1984) 793.

41 On inquisitorial interest in Teresa of Ávila see Llamas Martínez (1972); on her *converso* background see Caro Baroja (1970: 33–5) and Révah (1959: 38).

The original inquisitorial trial of Luis de León is published in CDIHE, Vols 10 and 11 (1–358), where his *converso* lineage is cited Vol. 10: 146–63; Sicroff (1985: 16–19) saw the Jewish ancestry of León as an important factor in the trial, though this is put into question by Marquez (1980: 101–13). While León clearly was a good Christian, his interest in the Old Testament and in Hebraic studies does point to a certain attachment to the faith of his ancestors.

42 Márquez (1972) 68; Selke (1980) 626.

43 This and all the accusations against Dr Sánchez are in AHN, Inquisición, Legajo 2023, Expediente 23.

44 Ibid. Expediente 10; Novalín (1968–71) Vol. 1, 226.

45 AHN, Inquisición, Legajo 2023, Expediente 22.

46 For this and all the list of accusations made against Salazar noted here ibid. Expediente 25.

47 Ibid. Expediente 9.

48 This detail and the rest of the material in this paragraph comes from AHN, Inquisición, Legajo 2012, Expediente 6.

49 Blázquez Miguel (1985) 25 n.8.

50 This detail and the rest of the material in the next two paragraphs comes from AHN, Inquisición, Legajo 2023, Expediente 29.

51 AHN, Inquisición, Legajo 2022, Expediente 1.

52 Ibid. Legajo 2022, Expediente 2.

53 Novalín (1968–71) Vol. 1, 235–6; once again, this shows the difficulty of arriving at concrete figures, as Monter (1990: 43) puts the number burnt between 1558–1568 at 100. Both accounts, however, cast doubt on Kamen's (1997: 97) assertion that this was 'a local phenomenon of passing importance'.

54 Lea (2001) 135–6.

55 Fonseca (1612) 11.

56 García-Arenal (1996) 107.

57 BL, Egerton MS 1832, folio 21r.

58 García-Arenal (1996) 107–8.

59 Lea (2001) 136–49; Domínguez Ortiz and Vincent (1978) 24.

60 BL, Egerton MS 1832, folio 21r.

61 Domínguez Ortiz and Vincent (1978) 26.

62 García Mercadal (ed.) (1999) Vol. 2, 60.

63 Ibid.

64 Lea (2001) 167 n.23.

65 Benítez Sánchez-Blanco (1983) 128, 139.

66 Novalín (1968–71) Vol. 1, 217–218.

67 Domínguez Ortiz and Vincent (1978) 28–9.

68 Fernández Alvarez (ed.) (1971–83) Vol. 4, 75.

69 García Mercadal (ed.) (1999) Vol. 2, 223, 280.

70 CDIHE, Vol. 5, 397–8.

71 Ibid. 425.

72 Salazar de Miranda (1788) 27–9; Menéndez y Pelayo (1945) Vol. 5, 19–20.
73 Ibid. 5, 20.
74 CDIHE, Vol. 5, 398.
75 Salazar de Miranda (1788) 30.
76 Ibid. 192–6.
77 Novalín (1968–71) Vol. 1, 9–11.
78 Ibid. 17–166.
79 Ibid. 64–66.
80 Ibid. 226.
81 Ibid. 170.
82 Tellechea Idigoras (1977) 119–20.
83 Ibid. 125; DH Vol. 1, 118 – the evidence of Bartolomé de las Casas, the famous bishop of Chiapas (Mexico) and champion of the Amerindians, who was a friend of Carranza.
84 Tellechea Idigoras (1968) Vol. 1, 83–4; (1977) 31.
85 DH, Vol. 1, 163.
86 Ibid. 85, 110, 175; cited in Tellechea Idigoras (1968) Vol. 2, 101.
87 DH, Vol. 1, 163.
88 Ibid. 162–3.
89 Tellechea Idigoras (1977) 123.
90 DH, Vol. 1, 123.
91 Tellechea Idigoras (1977) 35.
92 Ibid. 115.
93 Tellechea Idigoras (1968) Vol. 1, 177.
94 Tellechea Idigoras (1977) 31.
95 Menéndez y Pelayo (1945) Vol. 5, 40.
96 Tellechea Idigoras (1977) 31.
97 Tellechea Idigoras (1969) Vol. 2, 122 n.73.
98 Ibid. Vol. 1, 192–7.
99 Tellechea Idigoras (1978) 122.
100 On the letters to Philip II, see Novalín (1968–71) Vol. 2, 225, 227; letters of 16 May 1559 which provide ample proof of this. On the public rumours, CDIHE, Vol. 5, 407.
101 DH, Vol. 1, 212.
102 Tellechea Idigoras (1978) 35.
103 CDIHE, Vol. 5, 404.
104 DH, Vol. 1, 301–2.
105 Menéndez y Pelayo (1945) Vol. 5, 47.
106 CDIHE, Vol. 5, 465.
107 Ibid. 411, 468.
108 Ibid. 408, 468.
109 All this paragraph ibid. 411–12.
110 Ibid. 469–71.
111 Novalín (1968–71) Vol. 2, 216–21.
112 Kamen (1997) 98.

113 Menéndez y Pelayo (1945) Vol. 4, 446 n.2, 467.
114 Ibid. 441–3.
115 Ibid. 452.
116 Tellechea Idigoras (1969) Vol. 1, 129–33.
117 Tellechea Idigoras (1977) 53–62, 106–9; Menéndez y Pelayo (1945) Vol. 4, 478. This may be taken as perhaps an apocryphal story, since other accounts claim that Seso was gagged during the auto.
118 Monter (1990) 41–2; Novalín (1968–71), Vol. 2: 216–21 has the request for the dispensation.
119 BL, Egerton MS 2058, folios 7v–10v.
120 Novalín (1968–71) Vol. 2, 239, 248.
121 BL, Egerton MS 2058, folios 23r, 10v.
122 AHN, Inquisición, Legajo 2075, Expediente 1.
123 Ibid. Expediente 2.
124 Ibid. Expediente 3.
125 Ibid. Expediente 4.
126 Ibid. Expediente 6.
127 Contreras (1987) 55.
128 Ibid.; Bataillon (1937) 753–5.
129 Huerga (1978–88) Vol. 4, 10.
130 See for example Menéndez y Pelayo (1945) Vol. 4, 183–205; Dias (1975).
131 Tellechea Idigoras (1977) 61–90.
132 Tellechea Idigoras (1968) Vol. 1, 200–3.
133 Salazar de Miranda (1788) 155.
134 CDIHE, Vol. 5, 414.
135 Ibid. Vol. 5, 414–16.
136 Llorente (1841) 334–40.
137 CDIHE, Vol. 5, 456–7.
138 Contreras (1987) 56.
139 Sarrión Mora (2003) 56; a good summary of Cano's views on suspicious doctrines is in Alcalá Galve (1984: 813).
140 García Mercadal (ed.) (1999) Vol. 2, 312; Israel (1998b) 100, 144–6; Caro Baroja (1978) Vol. 1, 360.

Six – Terror Envelops the World

1 Chinchilla Aguilar (1952) 26–37.
2 Ibid. 37–8 for all the cases cited in this sentence.
3 Conway (ed.) (1927) 12.
4 Ibid.
5 Conway (ed.) (1927) 19–20.
6 Ibid. Appendix III.
7 Hakluyt (ed.) (1600) 569.
8 Ibid. 569–70. It is difficult to be sure as to the precise numbers arrested;

Phillips claims that there were over sixty, but evidence from trial records suggests there were only thirty-six *sanbenitos* in these years (Toro (ed.) (1932) 48–9) and see also Conway (ed.) (1927: 156–66) and Jiménez Rueda (ed.) (1945: 505–6) who suggest that only twenty people were tried in the auto of 1574. It is possible that Phillips exaggerated the numbers to play on Protestant fears of the Inquisition in Britain, but seeing as his account was only narrated to an interlocutor (Hakluyt) and not published for commercial gain, this cannot be taken as certain.

9 Hakluyt (ed.) (1600) 570.

10 The evidence of Robert Thomson from the 1560s (Conway (ed.) (1927) 19–20) and Henry Hawks from 1572 (Hakluyt (ed.) (1600) 549–50).

11 Ibid. 572.

12 The evidence of Miles Phillips – Hakluyt (ed.) (1600) 569.

13 Jiménez Rueda (ed.) (1945) 368–9.

14 Ibid. 377–9, 412.

15 Ibid. 460–80, 500–1.

16 Ibid. 281, 280.

17 Ibid. 301–2 for this detail on his attempted escape to China.

18 Toro (1944) Vol. 1, 36.

19 Huerga (1984) 955.

20 Toro (1944) Vol. 1, 128–30

21 Palmer (1976) 50.

22 González Obregón (ed.) (1935) 42.

23 Toro (1944) Vol. 1, 42–3.

24 González Obregón (ed.) (1935) 217.

25 Toro (1944) Vol. 1, 72.

26 Ibid. Vol. 1, 74–9.

27 González Obregón (ed.) (1935) 47, 54.

28 Ibid. 47–51 and Toro (1932: 213–14, 237–240). They kept Succot, Yom Kippur and Passover, eating maize tortillas instead of the unleavened bread *matzot*.

29 Toro (1932) 239.

30 AHN, Inquisición, Libro 1028, folio 227v; the evidence of Francisco Diaz from Lima c. 1592.

31 González Obregón (ed.) (1935) 217–18.

32 Ibid. 269.

33 Shastry (1981) 122–30; Scammell (1981) 167.

34 Subrahmanyan (1993) 68.

35 Boyajian (1993) 4–5.

36 Ibid. 13, 63–64.

37 This whole description is taken from the account of Pyrard de Laval (1619) Vol. 2, 42–75; the importance of slaves in the economy of Portuguese India is discussed more fully in Scammell (1981: 171–2).

38 Ibid. 169–70.

39 Subrahmanyan (1993) 230.
40 Baião (1945) 25; Shastry (1981) 71–2.
41 Subrahmanyan (1993) 230–1.
42 Baião (1945) 26.
43 Boyajian (1993) 31.
44 Baião (1945) 26; Rêgo (ed.) (1983) 10; Tavares (2004) 117.
45 Baião (1945) 27–35.
46 Laval (1619) Vol. 2, 56.
47 Ibid. Vol. 2, 60.
48 Ibid. Vol. 2, 94.
49 I am indebted for this point to the external examiner of my doctoral dissertation, Professor Francisco Bethencourt.
50 Ibid. Vol. 2, 94–6: '*ils ne font que mourir aux riches, et aux pauvres ne donnent que quelque penitence*'.
51 Baião (1945) 265; IAN/TT, CGSO, Livro 96, No. 3, folio 2r.
52 Boyajian (1993) 31.
53 IAN/TT, CGSO, Livro 96, no. 25, folio 1r.
54 Ibid. no. 4, folio 1v.
55 IAN/TT, CGSO, Livro 100, folios 40v, 47r.
56 Baião (1945) 68, 290.
57 Ibid. 290.
58 Toribio Medina (1887) Vol. 1, 57.
59 Toribio Medina (1889) 65–90.
60 Toribio Medina (1887) Vol. 1, 253–97.
61 Domínguez Ortiz (1971) 135.
62 This number includes Brazil (where the figures have recently been published by the noted Brazilian scholar Anita Novinsky). I am indebted for this point to the external examiner of my doctoral dissertation, Professor Francisco Bethencourt.
63 AHN, Inquisición, Libro 1030, folio 254r; the case of Juan Crespo de Aguirre arrested in 1622.
64 AHN, Inquisición, Libro 1028, folio 1r–v; the case of Francisco Bello Raymundo arrested in 1587.
65 Ibid. folio 4r; Pero Gutíerrez de Logroño arrested for witchcraft in 1587.
66 Ibid. 208v; the case of Pero Luis Henriquez from 1592.
67 AHN, Inquisición, Legajo 1620, Expediente 12, folios 1r–16r.
68 Lea (1908) 338–42 provides a good summary of these attempts.
69 Several examples are cited in Boyajian (1993: 73, 80).
70 IAN/TT, Inquisição de Lisboa, Livro 223, folio 194r – dated 16 May 1606.
71 AHN, Inquisición, Legajo 1198, Expediente 18 – Alonso de la Cruz Crespillo's application to be a familiar in Arica (the far north of Chile) in 1629.
72 AHN, Inquisición, Libro 1030, folio 213v.
73 AHN, Inquisición, Libro 1020, folio 327r–329r.

74 Souza (1987) has a potent analysis of the association of Brazil with ideas of the devil.
75 González Obregón (ed.) (1935) 5.
76 Ibid. 8–9, 12.
77 Ibid. 17; Toro (1944) Vol. 1, 204–5, 225–32.
78 González Obregón (ed.) (1935) 17, 20–2.
79 Ibid. 7–8.
80 Ibid. 40–2.
81 Toro (1944) Vol. 1, 335–42.
82 Ibid. Vol. 1, 343–6.
83 Rocha Pitta (1880) 2.
84 Ibid.
85 Gandavo (1858) 4.
86 Ibid. 5, 36.
87 Léry (1975) 95.
88 Ibid. 97–109.
89 Baião (1921: 141) shows that by 1543 there were people in Brazil with children in the jails of the Inquisition in Portugal for Judaizing. See also Salvador (1969: 83–4).
90 AG, Vol. 9, 204–5.
91 Godinho (1969); Novinsky (1995) 515.
92 Pereira (1993) 116.
93 Martínez Millán (1984).
94 This summary is made by Gonsalves de Mello (1996: 6).
95 Ibid. 167–96.
96 IAN/TT, CGSO, Livro 92, folio 53r; IAN/TT, CGSO, Livro 12a, folio 54r; IAN/TT, CGSO, Livro 99, folios 32v–33r cited in Green (2007) Part II Chapter 3.
97 Novinsky (1971) 437 n.34.
98 Salvador (1978), xvii.
99 Novinsky (1972) 60–1.
100 Ibid. 111.
101 See for example Kohut (1971) 35.
102 Toro (1944) Vol. 2, 8.
103 Ibid. 20.
104 Ibid. 199.
105 This is, famously, the argument of K. Anthony Appiah.
106 González Obregón (ed.) (1935) 131–4.
107 Ibid. 136–60.
108 Ibid. 457.
109 Ibid.
110 Ibid. 229.

Seven – The Islamic Threat

1 García-Arenal (1996) 157–63.
2 Fonseca (1612) 89–93.
3 AHN, Inquisición, Legajo 549, Expediente 7, folio 46r.
4 García-Arenal (1996) 165.
5 BL, Egerton MS 1510, folios 6r–7v – dating from *c.* 1502.
6 García-Arenal (1996) 165.
7 AHN, Inquisición, Legajo 549, Expediente 1. Note that there are no folio numbers in this document; all the other details of Arcos's case which follow are extracted from it.
8 See for example AHN, Inquisición, Libro 936, folios 182–184, 269r–270r, for cases from Valencia in these years which bear this out.
9 BL, Egerton MS 1510, folio 71r.
10 Even in the early years when there were some efforts made towards Christian education, these were limited towards teaching the absolute basics of Catholic ritual (Benítez Sánchez-Blanco (1990: 70–1)).
11 Lea (2001) 207, 214, 225.
12 BL, Egerton MS 1510, folio 74r.
13 Ibid. 75r; those *moriscos* who had not been baptized were to be persuaded rather than forced to the font.
14 Ibid. 124v.
15 Ibid. 127r.
16 Barrios Aguilera (2002) 294.
17 An example is the case of Angela Caxinçera from Gandia (AHN, Inquisición, Libro 937, folio 327r).
18 BL, Egerton MS 1510, folio 153v.
19 Ibid. folio 154r.
20 Barrios Aguilera (2002) 294.
21 García Mercadal (ed.) (1999) Vol. 1 334.
22 Barrios Aguilera (2002) 283.
23 Ibid. 284.
24 Ibid. 285.
25 García Fuentes (1981) 29–30, 40, 48–54, 66.
26 Cardaillac and Dedieu (1990: 21–2).
27 García Fuentes (1981) 70–6.
28 Cardaillac and Dedieu (1990) 22.
29 García-Arenal (1996) 65.
30 Ibid. 66.
31 Cardaillac and Dedieu (1990) 23.
32 Epalza (1992) 79–82.
33 Ibid. 56–7.
34 AHN, Inquisición, Libro 938, folio 219r.
35 AHN, Inquisición, Legajo 2105, Expediente 27; a case from Toledo in 1591.

36 This is the thesis of García-Arenal (1978: 10).
37 Domínguez Ortiz and Vincent (1978) 31.
38 AHN, Inquisición, Libro 937, folio 18r.
39 Ibid. folio 18v.
40 Ibid. folio 19r.
41 Ibid. folio 19v.
42 Domínguez Ortiz and Vincent (1978) 99.
43 Lea (2001) 144.
44 Gracia Boix (ed.) (1982) 227–8.
45 Monter (1990) 190.
46 Gracia Boix (ed.) (1982: 207, 210–11) transcribes two cases from the Inquisition of Cordoba of this dating from 1578.
47 Ibid. 207.
48 Carrasco (1983) 175.
49 Ibid. 181.
50 García-Arenal (1978) 43.
51 AHN, Inquisición, Legajo 2022, Expediente 8, folio 9r.
52 Dedieu and Vincent (1990: 82) see this as the real origin of *morisco* fear.
53 Lea (2001) 177–8; see also García-Arenal (1978: 25) for further examples of whole families being persecuted from the region of Cuenca.
54 Valencia (1997) 77.
55 Fonseca (1612) 110.
56 AHN, Inquisición, Libro 936, folios 151r–v, a case of 1577 from Valencia; Vidal (1986: 20), a case of 1578 from Zaragoza.
57 AHN, Inquisición, Libro 936, folio 14r – this is the opinion of the inquisitors of Valencia of 1566 on the attitude of *moriscos* to their *sanbenitos*; Fonseca (1612) 125.
58 That fear and hatred were the prime emotions of the *moriscos* towards the Inquisition was noted by Cardaillac (1977: 117–18).
59 Ibid. 101.
60 Lea (2001) 240.
61 Ibid. 240–1.
62 Ibid. 264.
63 Cardaillac (1977) 14; Domínguez Ortiz and Vincent (1978) 130.
64 Cardaillac (1977) 18–19.
65 Valencia (1997) 73.
66 Cardaillac (1977: 20–1) is excellent on the development of this process.
67 IAN/TT, CGSO, Livro 100, folios 15r, 17r.
68 IAN/TT, Inquisição de Lisboa, Livro 211, folios 192r–193r.
69 AHN, Inquisición, Libro 936, folio 16v (1566); ibid. folio 50v (1570).
70 Ibid. folio 40v (1568).
71 For example AHN, Inquisición, Libro 937, folios 10v–11r – Miguel Gil in the region of Valencia in 1587; AHN, Inquisición, Libro 938, folio 165r – the case of Luis Mijo Mandoll from 1602 converting an Old Christian.
72 Valencia (1997) 78.

73 Epalza (1992) 39.
74 García-Arenal (1996) 268–71.
75 Such a statement clearly implies a racial view of identity which some may feel is anachronistic for 16th-century Spain. Yet as we shall see this period also saw the growth of a new doctrine of purity of blood which was developed substantially along racial lines, with the consequence that such racial attitudes could have influenced the perception of the *moriscos* and their integration into Spanish society.
76 Domínguez Ortiz and Vincent (1978) 20.
77 BL, Egerton MS 1832, folio 22v.
78 Caro Baroja (1976) 123.
79 Domínguez Ortiz and Vincent (1978) 58.
80 Carrasco (1983) 187.
81 The classic work demonstrating this process is Perceval (1997).
82 Cardaillac (1978) 94–5.
83 Carrasco (1983) 187; see also Dedieu (1983: 503) who notes that Old Christians would often denounce the *moriscos* of Daimiel en bloc.
84 AHN, Inquisición, Libro 937, folio 343r – from 1590.
85 Reglà (1974) 65.
86 That is to say, one is here in the classic Freudian territory of projection; for a full discussion on the validity of the use of this concept in historical texts, see Green (2007) Appendix A.
87 AHN, Inquisición, Libro 938, folios 69r, 69v (two cases); ibid. 221r (a case from 1604).
88 AHN, Inquisición, Legajo 2105, Expediente 32.
89 AHN, Inquisición, Libro 938, folio 165v.
90 Ibid. folio 404r ff. – the rest of the detail of this case comes from this source.
91 Fonseca (1612) 106.
92 Ibid. 113.
93 Ibid. 95.
94 See for example numerous cases from 1588 in Valencia at AHN, Inquisición, Libro 937, folios 70v, 71r, 76v, 88r.
95 Vidal (1986) 200.
96 García Fuentes (1981) 221, 223.
97 AHN, Inquisición, Legajo 1786, Expediente 11.
98 Vidal (1986) 62.
99 AHN, Inquisición, Libro 937, folio 360r.
100 Lea (2001) 242–3.
101 Ibid. 483–7.
102 Carrasco (1983) 172.
103 Fonseca (1612) 219.
104 Domínguez Ortiz and Vincent (1978) 17, 71–2.
105 Lea (2001) 347–59.
106 Ibid. 362.
107 Perceval (1997) 126, 173–8.

108 Reglà (1974) 57–8.
109 Ibid. 172.
110 Ibid.
111 Ibid. 186.
112 Epalza (1992) 129.
113 Ibid. 146–8, 218–19.
114 Barrios Aguilera (2002) 413.
115 Fonseca (1612) 255.
116 García-Arenal (1996) 235.
117 Ibid.
118 Cardaillac and Dedieu (1990) 19.
119 Epalza (1992) 48; Cardaillac and Dedieu (1990) 15–16.
120 This was acknowledged by Pedro de Valencia when he urged that the Inquisition must not be charged with getting *moriscos* to relinquish their dress and customs, as 'with its exacting procedure they become more obstinate and begin to plot so that they do not give one another away' (Valencia (1997: 131)).
121 Thus in Daimiel in the 1530s there was an extraordinary poverty of knowledge of Islamic ritual among the *morisco* community (Dedieu (1983: 498)); by the late 16th century, all this had changed.
122 Marques (1972) Vol. 1, 80.
123 This insight is derived from Douglas (1984). One should note that Douglas herself has since modified the use of the concept of anomaly within a general cognitive theory, in particular as she suggests that outsiders cannot perceive necessarily what is anomalous within a given culture (*Journal of Ritual Studies*, 2004). However, in this case the anomalous is perceived not outside a given culture, but within it.
124 Reglà (1974) 113.
125 See for example García-Arenal (1978) 141–4 for a fascinating case of this.
126 Perceval (1997) 116.
127 Ibid.

Eight – Purity at all Costs

1 AHN, Inquisición, Legajo 1198, Expediente 32; this document has no folio numbers. All the subsequent information on Costa in this section derives from this file.
2 Graizbord (2004) 34.
3 Ibid. 37.
4 García Mercadal (1999) Vol. 2, 757.
5 Gil (2000–1) Vol. 3, 37. See also Schorsch (2004) 201 and Fredrickson (2002) 40. Debates are active as to whether racism had been invented in classical antiquity – the thesis of Isaac (2004) – or was a modern invention of western Europe. One should remember that racism against Africans was

current in the medieval period in the Islamic world. The evidence suggests, however, that in Europe the matter was more complex, and that prejudice tended originally to be directed from the religious and not the racial perspective until the 16th century (see Green (2007) for a full discussion of this idea).

6 Netanyahu (1997) 6 n.30. One should also bear in mind that there was no such thing as a 'race' of the Jews, as is made clear both by Netanyahu's examples and by Patai and Patai (1989).

7 I am grateful to Professor Francisco Bethencourt for formulating the matter in this manner at the 2004 C.R. Boxer Centenary Conference at King's College, London.

8 For a fuller discussion of the events of Toledo and their implications, see Sicroff (1985: 54–85) and Netanyahu (1995a: 356–82).

9 Sicroff (1985) 84.

10 Ibid. 57–81; one of these, Alonso Díaz de Montalvo, was an ally and friend of King John II of Castile.

11 Netanyahu (1995a) 584.

12 Blazquez Miguel (1988), 139.

13 Sicroff (1985) 117.

14 Ibid. 105–12; the statute was ratified by the papacy in 1495.

15 Blázquez Miguel (1988) 139.

16 The classic account of the struggle to get the statute accepted in the see of Toledo is Sicroff (1985: 125–72). On the statute of 1555, see Yerushalmi (1981: 15).

17 Sicroff (1985) 131.

18 See above, n. 8.

19 The key work on the doctrine of biologism which spread through theorists of *limpieza* in the 16th century is Gracia Guillén (1987). On the link between ideas of biologism and classical formulations of racism see Isaac (2004). There is indeed a direct comparison here with the type of ideology that became associated with the Atlantic slave trade, where slaves were described and loaded just like any other material 'good' – (that is, dehumanized) – and where the legend of the Hamitic curse was said by some to justify their slavery, the Hamitic curse being the punishment which God had meted out to the descendants of Noah's son Ham.

20 Blázquez Miguel (1988), 139.

21 Sicroff (1985) 315.

22 Ibid. 330–4; see also Domínguez Ortiz (1993: 48) on the specifically Iberian nature of this idea.

23 Iberia was perhaps peculiarly suited to this development since, as Saraiva (1985: 25) noted, this was a society where the identification of closed groups or castes with specific occupations had persisted; this was therefore a society in which there was a latent notion of caste purity which was open to being converted into a racial doctrine.

24 Kamen (1965) 125; however, although in this early work Kamen emphasized

the role of the Inquisition in propagating *limpieza*, in his more recent work on the subject he plays down the connection (1997: 242–253), using the attempted reforms of 1623 to argue that the Inquisition championed the dilution of the principle.

25 Bethencourt (1994) 363.

26 Sicroff (1985) 326.

27 AHN, Inquisición, Legajo 2105, Expediente 23.

28 Ibid.

29 This is close to the argument of Dedieu (1989: 341–2) that while the Inquisition did not invent the myth of *limpieza*, it expanded it to take material and moral profit.

30 AHN, Inquisición, Legajo 2105, Expediente 23; the case of Hernando de Villareal from 1587, attempting to get one son into a monastery and another accepted as a public scribe.

31 Baião (1921), Documentary Appendix, 3.

32 Caro Baroja (1978) Vol. 2, 324.

33 Remedios (1895–1928) Vol. 2, 64.

34 Green (2004) 24. Quiroga's maternal great-grandfather had the surname De la Cárcel'; *conversos* often took surnames of urban phenomena – the surnames De Mercado and De la Rúa are famous examples, and so the chances are very high that this individual was a *converso*.

35 Lipiner (1977) 17.

36 Isaac (2004) doubts the modernity of racism; however the classic work arguing this case is Comas (1951), and see also Green (2007: Part 4, Chapter 4).

37 Douglas (1984); the work of Freud is obviously of significance here.

38 García-Arenal (1978) 50–1.

39 García Fuentes (1981) 217, 251, 308–9, 311.

40 García-Arenal (1978) 51.

41 AHN, Inquisición, Libro 938, folio 173r.

42 García-Arenal (1978) 51.

43 García Mercadal (ed.) (1999) Vol. 2, 693.

44 Sicroff (1985) 346–7.

45 Valencia (1997) 137.

46 This was following the death of Sebastian I on the battlefield in Morocco in 1578, and then of Sebastian's uncle the aged Cardinal Henry in 1580.

47 Liebman (1970) 183.

48 Saraiva (1985) 114–16; Lea (1906–7), Vol. 3, 276–7.

49 Salvador (1978) 126.

50 Carneiro (1983) 124.

51 Saraiva (1985) 128–9.

52 Lea (1906–7), Vol. 3, 276.

53 Oliveira (1887–1910) Vol. 1, 576.

54 Ibid. Vol. 1, 568–9; ibid. Vol. 2, 63.

55 IAN/TT, Inquisição de Évora, Livro 90, folio 173r–v.

56 Oliveira (1887–1910) Vol. 2, 94.
57 Lipiner (1977) 123.
58 There are countless examples of this in the archives – see for example IAN/TT, CGSO, Livro 434, folio 45v for someone who was one-eighth New Christian convicted of Judaizing; and ibid. folio 126v.
59 IAN/TT, CGSO, Livro 184, folio 13v.
60 Gonçalves Salvador (1976) 7.
61 BL, Egerton Ms. 1134, folios 153r–v.
62 Coelho (1987) Vol. 1, 343 and 420–1.
63 Lea (1906–7), Vol. 3, 273.
64 AHN, Inquisición, Legajo 1198, Expediente 10. Note that there are no folio numbers in this document.
65 AHN, Inquisición, Legajo 1198, Expediente 2.
66 Ibid. Expediente 22.
67 Ibid. Expediente 16.
68 Ibid. Expediente 18.
69 For example ibid. Expedientes 28 (from 1722) and 30 (from 1723); this would seem to suggest a modification is required of the view (Kamen (1997) 253) that there were mere echoes of the idea of purity of blood in Spain in the 18th century.
70 Domínguez Ortiz (1993) 167.
71 The founder of the theory that the Inquisition was motivated by economics is Llorente (1818). Some contemporary historians do still hold to this view, for example Carneiro (1983: 49), although in general there has been a recognition that the reality was much more complicated. See for example Blázquez Miguel (1988: 83–4), who shows the financial precariousness of the Inquisition even in the first years after its foundation in the 1480s, when the crown only in fact got 2 per cent of all the confiscations between 1488 and 1497. Alpert (2001: 23–4) shows that even the large sums confiscated in the early 16th century were not enough entirely to fund the tribunal's activities; the classic work demonstrating the poverty of the purely economic interpretation is Martínez Millán (1984).
72 This is close to García Cárcel's (1976: 141–74) examination of inquisitorial finances in Valencia; he stresses that what mattered financially for the institution of the Inquisition was that it should be solvent for the crown, and that this raison d'être was predicated on its position as a state institution, which fluctuated along with the state.
73 Sicroff (1985) 221.
74 Domínguez Ortiz (1993) 81: Pérez Villanueva (1984) 1038.
75 Pérez Villanueva (1984) 1040.
76 Ibid. 1041.
77 Ibid. 1039.
78 Ibid. 1041.
79 AHN, Inquisición, Legajo 1198, Expediente 26, folio 6v; all the rest of the details of Angulo's case are taken from this trial.

80 All the material on this case derives from AHN, Inquisición, Legajo 265, Expediente 5.
81 AHN, Inquisición, Legajo 2962.
82 Personal communication from Ian L. Rakoff, a pupil at South African schools in the 1950s.
83 Mann (2005) 340.
84 See, for instance, AHN, Inquisición, Legajo 265, Expediente 14 for a case from 1628–33 which occupied a large amount of time and energy, investigating numerous small towns near Palencia and Castrogeriz, before it was decided that the people in question were pure of blood.
85 AHN, Inquisición, Legajo 2962 contains a case of this.
86 Gil (2000–1) Vol. 3, 33.
87 Rêgo (1983) 77.
88 Indeed one can argue that in Iberia, where religion was tied into the obsession with social hygiene, a society was revealed where collective psychology was still at odds with itself, and struggling to come to terms with the modern world. Douglas (1984: 35) suggested that there is a 'specialization of ideas which separates our notions of dirt from religion'. The tying in of the religious idea through the Inquisition to the notion of cleanliness emphasized the fact that the Inquisition was an institution at fundamental odds with modernity, and therefore likely to fight against it at every opportunity.

Nine – Every Aspect of Life

1 This and all subsequent information on Galván derives from Toro (1944: Vol. 2, 20–1).
2 Lewin (1967) 171.
3 The best recent summary of the debate as to the numbers lost to disease after the conquest of America is Mann (2005).
4 IAN/TT, CGSO, Livro 100, folio 37r.
5 IAN/TT, Inquisição de Lisboa, Livro 205, folios 231r–v.
6 Thus the number of ships sailing annually between Portugal and Goa in what was called the *carreira da Índia* declined from seven on average between 1500–99 to two on average between 1650–1700 (Disney (1981) 152). There is an excellent summary of the Portuguese crisis in Asia between 1610 and 1665 in Subrahmanyan (1993: 144–80).
7 Pyrard de Laval (1619) Vol. 2, 94.
8 Souza (1987) 210–15.
9 Ibid. 217–18.
10 Ibid. 239.
11 Ibid.
12 Palmer (1976) 158.

13 PV, 311–12 – a case of a woman, Margarida Carneira, accused of doing this by a lover that she had spurned.
14 Vainfas (1989).
15 Sweet (2003).
16 AHN, Inquisición, Legajo 1602, Expediente 7.
17 Ibid. 34r–v.
18 Sweet (2003) 74–5.
19 Ibid. 69–70.
20 See for Cartagena Splendiani (1997) Vol. 2, 41; Sánchez B. (1996) 41, and Toribio Medina (1899) 103; also idem. (1887) Vol. 1, 258 for a case from Lima. For several cases from Mexico see Palmer (1976) 150.
21 Cervantes (1994) 79–80.
22 Ibid. 79.
23 Palmer (1976) 94.
24 The best recent analysis of these events is in Wachtel (2001a).
25 All this material on Silva comes from IAN/TT, Inquisição de Lisboa, Livro 221, folios 518r–v.
26 See for example IAN/TT, Inquisição de Lisboa, Livro 208, folios 494r–v for a case from 1622.
27 IAN/TT, Inquisição de Lisboa, Livro 240, folios 250r–251v.
28 Paiva (1997) 84–6. This attitude eventually filtered through to the Spanish colonies in the New World too, with the Inquisition in Cartagena often passing jurisdiction over witchcraft cases to the civil authorities after 1650 (Ceballos Gómez (1994) 95), and repeatedly ignoring cases of purported 'witchcraft' in Mexico from the late 17th century onwards (Cervantes (1994) 125–41).
29 Paiva (1997) 86.
30 This argument is brilliantly formulated in Trevor-Roper (1984) 113; see also Paiva (1997) 347–9.
31 Contreras (1987) 58.
32 Pérez Villanueva and Escandell Bonet (eds) (1984) 703–5.
33 Martínez Millán (1984) 32–3.
34 One is reminded of Moore's (1987) argument that the rise of persecuting societies in medieval Europe resulted from the spread of literacy and the rise of a literate class.
35 Griffiths (1997) 95. The Council of Trent (1545–63) is widely considered one of the most important in the history of the Catholic Church. It was initiated in order to consider Catholic responses to Protestantism. The most important theologians in Catholic Europe attended, and developed clear doctrines on a wide range of issues, ranging from the mass and biblical canon to the concept of salvation.
36 García Cárcel and Moreno Martínez (2000) 58.
37 Dedieu (1989) 12–13, 139, 152.
38 Clearly, this was before the development of the Freudian theory of the

'return of the repressed' – which could be suggested to be an unconscious factor in this change of tack in the institution of the Inquisition.

39 IT, folio 14r.
40 García Fuentes (1981) 17.
41 Gracia Boix (1982) 151.
42 AHN, Inquisición, Libro 938, folio 229v.
43 See for example the case of Pedro Cabrera from Murcia in 1579; AHN, Inquisición, Legajo 2022, Expediente 8, folio 2v.
44 IAN/TT, CGSO, Livro 433, folio 22r.
45 Sánchez Ortega (1992) 24.
46 Gracia Boix (1982) 152.
47 IAN/TT, Inquisição d'Évora, Livro 86, folios 52v–53r.
48 See for example Dedieu (1989: 281).
49 Selke (1986) 67–8.
50 García Mercadal (ed.) (1999) Vol. 2, 371.
51 AHN, Inquisición, Libro 936, folio 171v.
52 Ibid. folio 168r.
53 Ortega-Costa (ed.) (1978) 49.
54 García Fuentes (1981) 58.
55 AHN, Inquisición, Legajo 2022, Expediente 8, folio 7r.
56 AHN, Inquisición, Libro 938, folio 163r.
57 Mariana (1751) Vol. 8, 506.
58 IT, folio 4r; published in Jiménez Monteserín (ed.) (1980) 89–90.
59 IT, folio 11r.
60 AHN, Inquisición, Legajo 2022, Expediente 18.
61 AHN, Inquisición, Legajo 4442, Expediente 18.
62 Oliveira (1887–1910) Vol. 2, 69–78.
63 La Mantia (1977) 60, 130.

Ten – The Administration of Fear

1 AHN, Inquisición, Legajo 1601, Expediente 18, folio 1v.
2 Ibid. folios 19r–v.
3 Ibid. 19v.
4 Ibid. folio 4r.
5 Ibid. folio 5r.
6 Ibid. folios 5r–6r.
7 Ibid. folios 7r–v.
8 Ibid. folio 8r.
9 Ibid. folios 8v–9r, 13r.
10 Dedieu (1989) 161.
11 García Cárcel and Moreno Martínez (2000) 131.
12 BL, Egerton MS 1134, folio 170r.
13 Baião (1942) 57–70.

14 Contreras (1982) 320–1. The prosecutor was later reprimanded for this unsanctioned demand.
15 Caro Baroja (1968) 30–1.
16 For an excellent analysis of the Inquisition as a career path, see Bethencourt (1994: 119). For how this operated in Sicily, with being an inquisitor a stepping stone to being a bishop, see La Mantia (1977) 36.
17 Contreras (1982) 328–33.
18 Ibid. 333–37.
19 Ibid. 339.
20 Blázquez Miguel (1990) 90.
21 Contreras (1982) 340.
22 Blázquez Miguel (1990) 90.
23 Barrios (1991) 31–2.
24 A good example is Lithgow (1640) 480.
25 Márquez (1980) 129.
26 IT, folio 8r; published in Jiménez Monteserín (ed.) (1980: 83–105).
27 IT, folio 12v; published in Jiménez Monteserín (ed.) (1980: 116–21).
28 See for instance the case of Pedro de Guiral, inquisitor of Ávila and Cordoba, from 1499 (Gracia Boix (1982) 30–1). Lucero is another obvious example of this.
29 Bethencourt (1994) 65, 71.
30 Baião (1942) 17.
31 Ibid.; Novalín (1968–71) Vol. 1, 231.
32 Contreras and Henningsen (1986) 116.
33 Ruiz de Pablos (ed. and trans.) (1997) 209.
34 Jiménez Monteserín (ed.) (1980) 366–70; see also Contreras (1982) 73.
35 Ibid.
36 Blázquez Miguel (1990) 104.
37 Chinchilla Aguilar (1952) 120–1.
38 Bethencourt (1994) 51.
39 Russell-Wood (1998) 24–5.
40 IAN/TT, Inquisição de Lisboa, Livro 217, folios 170r–190v.
41 Ibid. folio 171r.
42 Ibid. folio 172v.
43 Ibid.
44 Ibid. folio 184v.
45 Ibid. folio 190v.
46 See for example Blázquez Miguel (1990: 105) on how in Catalonia alone familiars were barred from holding public office.
47 Contreras (1982) 87 n.46.
48 *Regimento dos Familiares do Santo Oficio* (1739). Note that this publication has no page numbers.
49 Contreras (1982) 130.
50 AHN, Inquisición, Libro 936, folio 32r.
51 BL, Egerton MS 1832, folios 105v–108v.

52 Contreras (1982) 51–2.
53 IAN/TT, CGSO, Livro 433, folio 196r. People frequently pretended to be familiars; in one case, Bartolomé Gómez de Quesada was punished in two autos in the same year for this offence and eventually sentenced to two years in the galleys (García Fuentes (1981: 20–35).
54 Blázquez Miguel (1985) 37.
55 Lea (1908) 335–7.
56 Blázquez Miguel (1990) 91.
57 Barrios (1991) 30–1.
58 AHN, Inquisición, Legajo 2105, Expediente 28.
59 TA, folio i.
60 Blázquez Miguel (1990) 122.
61 Lea (1906–7), Vol. 1, 381–98.
62 García Mercadal (ed.) (1999) Vol. 2, 358.
63 Fernández Vargas (1980) 931–2.
64 Marques (1972) Vol. 1, 288–92.
65 BL, Egerton MS 1832: Segovia, 1575.
66 BL, Add. MS 21447, folios 137r–143v.
67 See for example Toro (1932), doc. 3: *Diligencias Sobre los Sanbenitos antiguos y Renovación de ellos . . .*
68 Paz y Melia (1947) 452.
69 AHN, Inquisición, Legajo 4822, Expediente 3.
70 Moore's (1987) argument that the development of a literate class was a key aspect of the formation of a persecuting society is of relevance here.
71 Martínez Millán (1984) 287–91.
72 Dedieu (1989) 273–7.
73 Ibid. 275.
74 Lea (2001) 159.
75 See for example the case at AHN, Inquisición, Legajo 4529, Expediente 2, that of Martin Vendicho from 29 March 1588, a *morisco* from Zaragoza.
76 Reglà (1974) 186.
77 Biarnés i Biarnés (1981) 112, 146.
78 Reglà (1974) 61, 142.
79 Biarnés i Biarnés (1981) 150.
80 Reglà (1974) 138–9.
81 Domínguez Ortiz and Vincent (1978) 203.
82 Casey (1999) 21.
83 Ibid.
84 Lithgow (1640) 451.
85 Ibid. 453.
86 Fromm (1951) 67.
87 Escandell Bonet (1980) 450.
88 All the material taken here for the case of Gutierrez de Ulloa comes from Toribio Medina (1887) Vol. 1, 265–82.
89 Benassar (1987) 183.

Eleven – The Threat of Knowledge

1 Newitt (1995) 175–6.

2 Jama (2001) 35, 60–1. It had been Pierre (Pedro)'s great-grandfather, and Antoinette Lopez's great-great grandfather Meyer Paçagon who had been the first member of the family to convert from Judaism to Christianity in around 1412, at the time of the famous disputation between Christian and Jewish theologians at Tortosa (Ibid. 34–5).

3 Popkin (1960) 43, 55. There were of course numerous intervening steps, but nevertheless the ideas of Montaigne were pivotal in this process.

4 Ibid. ix.

5 Fernández Santamaría (1990) 17. Pyrrhonian scepticism derived from the writings of the Greek philosopher Pyrrhon of Elis (*c.* 360–270 BCE), who held that reason alone could not give knowledge of the universe, and that as the senses could only give knowledge of how things appeared – rather than how they actually were in reality – all human knowledge was opinion.

6 Montaigne (1998) 66.

7 Ibid. 19: '*Chacun appelle barbarie ce qui n'est pas de son usage*'; see also his statement in the *Apologie de Raimond Sebond* that '*tout ce qui nous semble estrange, nous le condamnons*' ('we condemn everything that seems strange to us'): Rat (ed.) (1941) Vol. 2, 151.

8 Jama (2001) 60.

9 Popkin (1960) 44.

10 Montaigne (1998) 93.

11 Ibid. 221.

12 Rat (ed.) (1941) Vol. 2, 122.

13 Ibid. 123.

14 Ibid. 176.

15 Ibid. 223.

16 Ibid. 268.

17 Popkin (1960) 69–82.

18 Ibid. 86–112.

19 Rat (ed.) (1941) 47–68: '*Que le Goust des Biens et des Maux Depend en Bonne Partie de l'Opinion que Nous en Avons*' (tr.: 'That taste in Good and Evil Depends Substantially on our Opinion') – the relevant passage is pp. 50–2.

20 Jama (2001) 23–24: '*une date, intentionellement choisie, qui permettait justement aux compagnons d'entendre son message dissimulé*' (tr.: 'a date, chosen intentionally, which allowed only friends to understand its hidden message').

21 Rat (ed.) (1941) Vol. 2, 176.

22 Yovel (1989), x.

23 Jama (2001: 182–8) also believes that there are clear traces of Jewish theological leanings in the *Essays* when it comes to his views of God. See also López Fanego (1983: 371) on how wily authors inserted professions of

their devout faith and submission to ecclesiastical dogma inside works which as a whole are critical of that dogma.

24 This is indeed a view shared by many Montaigne specialists (see for example Malvezin (1875: 106–22, 128)) and specialists on the Iberian realities (Castro (1972: 15), Faur (1992: 105–6)).

25 Dedieu (1983) 498.

26 See for example Baião (1921) 122 – a case from 1541 from Lisbon. However it should be noted that this itself was an age-old rural saying in Iberia. I am grateful for this point to Professor Francisco Bethencourt.

27 Salvador (1969), xx.

28 Blázquez Miguel (1988) 50.

29 For an example of how this worked in practice, it is interesting to read Wachtel's (2001a: 85–89) analysis of the library of Manuel Bautista Pérez, an exceptionally well-travelled crypto-Jew from Lima in the 1630s who had spent time in both Guiné and South America; the library is suggestive of someone of a sceptical bent.

30 Lithgow (1640) 486.

31 The view of *conversos* as prototypes of modern individuals is not a new one, and has been propounded in Novinsky (1972: 162), Rivkin (1995: 408), Wachtel (2001a: 13), to name but three authors. This idea is examined in more detail in Green (2007).

32 Faur (1992) 108–9.

33 Sanches (1988) 4–19.

34 Ibid. 172.

35 Faur (1992) 96.

36 Sanches (1988) 168.

37 Ibid. 81; the words of Elaine Limbrick.

38 Ibid. 79; the words of Elaine Limbrick.

39 Ibid. 28–36.

40 There is a good summary of Vives's life in González González (1998: 25–6).

41 Garcia (1987) 91.

42 Ibid. 187; the trials of Vives's mother Blanquina March are published in Pinta Llorente and Palacioty Palacio (1964). In 1491 she had confessed of her sins within the period of grace and been reconciled, but, after her death in 1508, she was eventually condemned posthumously in 1529.

43 Kamen (1997) 130; Révah (1959) 38.

44 Fernández Santamaría (1990) 72, 104.

45 Ibid. 72.

46 Ibid. 123.

47 Ibid. 71.

48 Bataillon (1937) 166–7.

49 Gouhier (1958) 116 n.59.

50 Sanches (1988) 83–4.

51 Klever (1996) 20.

52 Yovel (1989), x, 28–36.

53 Rojas (1985) 22.
54 Ibid. 23.
55 Ibid. 59.
56 Ibid. 130.
57 Ibid. 129.
58 This was the mistake in Gilman's classic account of the play and the author's *converso* origins (1972). The idea that the *converso* interpretation should merely be one interpretation of *La Celestina* is advanced in Yovel (1989: 97).
59 Long and involved academic debates have occurred as to the origins of Rojas. Salvador Miguel (2001) disputes Rojas's *converso* origin, following Marquez (1980: 47–8), who argues that the statement in his defence by Rojas's father-in-law Álvaro de Montalbán that Rojas was a *converso* in an inquisitorial trial of 1525/6 was merely a rumour attributed to Rojas by the prosecutor of the Inquisition. Nevertheless, as Yovel (1989: 94 n.29) points out, the prosecutor could merely have been repeating a known fact, and there is no evidence that this was simply a 'rumour'. The clear *converso* themes throughout the play support the idea that Rojas was, indeed, a *converso*, as his father-in-law declared. Others have argued that *La Celestina* was a composite work of different authors, but this has been disputed recently by some specialists (Aguirre Bellver (1994)).
60 Faur (1992) 62–9.
61 Ibid. 57.
62 Castro (1972) 15.
63 Ibid. lii.
64 Ibid. 153.
65 Ibid. '*segun eran de agudos*'.
66 Bataillon (1937) 529; cited also in Kamen (1965) 75.
67 See the classic works of Menéndez y Pelayo, and more recently Kamen (1997); see also García Camarero and García Camarero (eds) (1970) for a summary of 18th-century views on the matter.
68 Cervantes (1994) 91.
69 Lewin (1967) 14–15.
70 Lea (1906–7), Vol. 1, v.
71 Saínz Rodríguez (1962) 85.
72 Castro (1972) 36.
73 García Cárcel and Moreno Martínez (2000) 325.
74 Castro (1972) 37.
75 Alcalá Galve (1984) 812.
76 See for example Novalín (1968–71) Vol. 1, 265.
77 Baião (1921) 36–7.
78 Barrios Aguilera (2002) 81.
79 Rumeu de Armas (1940) 15.
80 BL, Additional MS 10248, folios 107v–108r.
81 Bataillon (1937) 31–5 has a good elucidation of this case.
82 Bethencourt (1994) 174.

83 Ibid.
84 AHN, Inquisición, Legajo 4470, Expediente 6.
85 AHN, Inquisición, Legajo 4442, Expedientes 33 and 34.
86 AHN, Inquisición, Legajo 2963.
87 AHN, Inquisición, Legajo 4470, Expediente 12.
88 Kamen (1997) 119.
89 Novalín (1968–71) Vol. 1, 274.
90 Pinto Crespo (1983) 67.
91 Bethencourt (1994) 173.
92 Márquez (1980) 144–5.
93 Ibid. 146–8.
94 Sierra Corella (1947) 47.
95 Bethencourt (1994) 173.
96 Ibid. 87.
97 The text of this fundamental decree is published in Rumeu de Armas (1940: 17 n.1).
98 Pinto Crespo (1983) 39.
99 Ibid. 91–2.
100 Ibid. 99.
101 Ibid. 42.
102 Pinto Crespo (1983) 33.
103 García Cárcel and Moreno Martínez (2000) 321–3.
104 Gracia Boix (ed.) (1982) 218.
105 Márquez (1980) 150.
106 Révah (1960) 21–2.
107 Ibid. 21–4, 29.
108 Ibid. 27.
109 Ibid. 67–8.
110 Bethencourt (1994) 177.
111 Cohen (1995) 446; idem. (2000) 74; Chinchilla Aguilar (1952) 187: the *cédula* banning the circulation of profane books of 29 September 1543 is published in Sierra Corella (1947: 196–7).
112 Chinchilla Aguilar (1952) 189–90.
113 Jiménez Rueda (1946) 237.
114 Greenleaf (1969) 183.
115 Ibid. 184–5.
116 AHN, Inquisición, Libro 285, folio 200r.
117 Defourneaux (1963) 15.
118 Alcalá Galve (1983) 784 n.11.
119 Pinto Crespo (1983) 63–6.
120 Ibid. and idem. (1987) 185.
121 AHN, Inquisición, Legajo 4816, Expediente 22, folios 4v–9r; for a more detailed examination of this ship and of Diogo Barassa in general, see Green (2007) Part III: Chapter 3.

122 AHN, Legajo 4816, Expediente 22, folio 45v; I have modernized some of the punctuation in my translation of this passage.
123 Ibid. folio 11v.
124 Defourneaux (1963) 24–5.
125 AHN, Inquisición, Legajo 4436, Expediente 4.
126 AHN, Inquisición, Legajo 4480, Expediente 21, folio 2r.
127 Ibid. folio 4r.
128 Ibid.
129 Defourneaux (1963) 24–5: the expurgated editions had begun in Seville in 1539.
130 Ibid. 25.
131 Ibid.
132 AHN, Inquisición, Legajo 4469, Expediente 31.
133 Baião (1972) 222–69; Subrahmanyan (1993) 186. This was after lobbying from the famous preacher Antonio Vieira (himself arrested by the Inquisition in 1665) and *conversos* in Rome.
134 ACE, 36, 51, 62–3.
135 Selke (1986) 9, 189.
136 Jiménez Monteserín (ed.) (1980) 656, 688.
137 Paz y Melia (ed.) (1947) 135–7.
138 AHN, Inquisición, Legajo 4465, Expediente 30.
139 Paz y Melia (ed.) (1947), no. 392. These paintings are not named in the source: one was a sleeping Venus with a gold mark, a second of a sleeping nude, and a third of a poor woman lying on a bed.

Twelve – The Neurotic Society

1 AHN, Inquisición, Legajo 1808, Expediente 11, folio 13r.
2 Ibid.
3 Ibid. folio 14r.
4 Ibid. folio 16v.
5 Ibid.
6 Ibid. 17r, 18r.
7 Ibid. 19v–21v.
8 Ibid. 14v.
9 Ibid. 15r.
10 Ibid. folios 24r–29r.
11 Ibid. folios 30v–32v.
12 Freud (1961a).
13 Sarrión Mora (2003) 45.
14 Perry (1987) 152–4.
15 Ibid. 158.
16 Ibid. 151.

17 This remarkable story is published in Gracia Boix (ed.) (1982: 281–3).
18 This remarkable story is summarized in Sánchez Ortega (1992: 69–78).
19 See for example the case of Eugenia de las Heras, arrested by the Inquisition of Madrid for faking visions in 1802 – AHN, Inquisición, Legajo 3730, Expediente 21.
20 Huerga (1978–88) Vol. 1, 332.
21 Ibid. 333.
22 Ibid.
23 Ibid. 335.
24 Llorca (1980) 107.
25 Huerga (1978–88) Vol. 1, 467.
26 Ibid.
27 Ibid. 468.
28 Ibid.
29 Ibid. Vol. 4, 179–313, 389, 485–6; AHN, Inquisición, Legajo 2962.
30 The relevance of this to the sexual nature of the neuroses of the *alumbradas* of Extremadura was noted by Menéndez y Pelayo (1945: Vol. 5, 262).
31 Fernández (2003) 12–13.
32 Foucault (1976) 110–11.
33 Monter (1990) 279.
34 Vainfas (1989) 206.
35 Mott (1988) 14; see IAN/TT, CGSO, Livro 100, folio 43r for more detail on the confirmation of powers to try sodomy by Pope Gregory XIII to Cardinal Henry.
36 IAN/TT, CGSO, Livro 96, folio 1r.
37 Bellini (1989) 17–29.
38 Vainfas (1989) 207–9, 209 n.65. Nevertheless, the offence was still mentioned in the rules of operation for the Inquisition of Goa as late as 1774 (Rêgo (1983: 115)).
39 Vassberg (1996) 129.
40 Fernández (2003) 271–3.
41 IAN/TT, Inquisição de Évora, Livro 92, folios 34v–35r.
42 Ibid. folios 31v–34r.
43 Vainfas (1989) 205.
44 Fernández (2003) 80.
45 Mott (1992) 704.
46 Palmer (1976) 58–9.
47 IAN/TT, Inquisição de Lisboa, Livro 243, folio 62r.
48 IAN/TT, Inquisição de Lisboa, Livro 246, folios 3r–v; this is where the whole of this story is derived from.
49 See for example the case of Francisco Barradas from IAN/TT, Inquisição de Lisboa, Livro 212, folio 127v.
50 IAN/TT, Inquisição de Lisboa, Livro 236, folios 381r–v.
51 Rêgo (ed.) (1971) 191.
52 Dellon (1815) 13.

53 AHN, Inquisición, Legajo 5345, Expediente 4. This had also occurred in Spain; there are numerous examples in AHN, Inquisición, Libro 1153.
54 Cervantes (1994) 102–5; this is the source for the remainder of the information distilled here on the activities of Sister Margaret.
55 Freud (1961b) 72.
56 BL, Additional MS 23726, folio 85r.
57 The question posed by Bernardo de Iriarte to Ana Farina in 1775 (Pinta Llorente (1961) 130).
58 This derives from Cervantes (1994: 114–24).
59 This material is from Huerga (1978–88) Vol. 3, 85–94.
60 Ibid. 447–8.
61 Ibid. 352–3.
62 Ibid. 354.
63 Ibid. 358–9.
64 Ibid. 360.
65 Ibid. 139.
66 Sarrión Mora (2003) 145–53 and 208.
67 Ibid. 284, 288.
68 Ibid. 295.
69 Ibid. 297–8.
70 Huerga (1978–88) Vol. 1, 468.
71 BL, Additional MS 23726, folios 9r, 15r.
72 Ibid. folio 82v.
73 Ibid. folio 83r–v.
74 Ibid. folios 90r–v.
75 Ibid. folio 91r.
76 Benassar (1979b) 85–6.
77 Ibid. 86.
78 Ibid.
79 García Mercadal (ed.) (1999) Vol. 1, 292.
80 Ibid. Vol. 2, 288.
81 Fernández (2003) 14.
82 Fernández-Armesto (1982) 181–3.
83 Ibid. 273.
84 Ibid. 14.
85 IAN/TT, CGSO, Livro 433, folio 106v; the case of Catherina Galves from the see of Porto, from 1625.
86 Fernández Vargas (1980) 934.
87 Menéndez y Pelayo (1945) Vol. 6, 118.
88 All this information is derived from CA: *Relacion de los Reos que Salieron en el Auto Particular de Fe que el Santo Oficio de la Inquisición de Cuenca Celebró en la Iglesia del Convento de San Pablo (1721); Relacion del Auto Particular de Fe que Celebró el Santo Oficio de la Inquisición de Valladolid (1722); Relacion del Auto Particular de Fe que Celebró el Santo Oficio de la Inquisición de la Ciudad y Reyno de Granada, el dia 31 de Enero de este Presente Año de 1723.*

89 Ibid. folio 305v.
90 Ibid.; there were numerous Brazilian prisoners taken from America to Lisbon in the first half of the 18th century, with many of them accused of crimes of sorcery and divining as well as for crypto-Judaism (this last particularly in the newly wealthy Rio de Janeiro, the port for the goldfields of Minas Gerais: Souza (1987: 158–65 and 323)).
91 PD.
92 Marti Gilabert (1975) 22–3.
93 AHN, Inquisición, Legajo 3727, Expediente 159; I have modernized some of the punctuation of this passage.
94 Ibid.
95 Ibid.
96 Ibid.
97 Sánchez Ortega (1992) 48–9.
98 Ibid. 48.
99 IAN/TT, Inquisição de Lisboa, Livro 792, folios 409–17, 453.
100 Toribio Medina (1887) Vol. 1, 313.
101 Millar Carvacho (1997) 347.
102 AHN, Inquisición, Legajo 4518, Expediente 14.
103 AHN, Inquisición, Legajo 1808, Expediente 12, folio 33r.

Thirteen – Paranoia

1 AHN, Inquisición, Legajo 3730, Expediente 7, as with all the details of this case.
2 Blázquez Miguel (1990) 285. For a full examination of the circumstances surrounding the bull *In Eminenti* and its impact in the Catholic world, see Ferrer Benimeli (1976–7) Vol. 1, 178–236.
3 Ferrer Benimeli (1976–7) Vol. 1, 54–70.
4 Ferrer Benimeli (1984) 83–90.
5 Ferrer Benimeli (1976–7) Vol. 2, 137, 189.
6 Ibid. 189; Coustos (1803) 19–21, 63–72, 78.
7 Ferrer Benimeli (1984) 84.
8 Ibid. 85.
9 Ibid. 86.
10 Ferrer Benimeli (1976–7) Vol. 1, 213.
11 Ferrer Benimeli (1976–7) Vol. 3, 22–3.
12 Ibid. 409: '*per quanto si dice*'.
13 Ibid. 52 n.193 and 56.
14 Ibid. 79.
15 Ibid.
16 Ibid. 80.
17 Ibid. 98.
18 Ibid. 124.

19 Ibid. 86–7, 139–40.
20 Ibid. 320–6, 351–61.
21 Kamen (1965).
22 Ferrer Benimeli (1976–7) Vol. 3, 57.
23 These are much more numerous than there was space to cite in the relevant passages in Chapter Seven; for another example, see AHN, Inquisición, Legajo 4529, Expediente 2, or Valencia (1997: 74): '[the *moriscos*] make a conspiracy and agreement among themselves for wickedness'.
24 Saraiva (1985) 128–9.
25 Pinto Crespo (1983) 107.
26 Delumeau (1978) 22–3.
27 This, it must be recognized, is contrary to the prevailing academic view that the Inquisition is best studied on the basis of individual tribunals. This book can and should be taken as a counter-argument to this fashionable thesis.
28 Jiménez Monteserín (ed.) (1980) 760.
29 Ibid. 760–1.
30 Ibid. 761–2.
31 Ibid. 762–5.
32 Ibid. 769–70.
33 Ibid. 770–2.
34 Ibid. 772–3.
35 Henningsen (1980) 32–6, 51.
36 Ibid. 54, 57, 108–12.
37 Ibid. 136.
38 Ibid. 150, 185–6.
39 Ibid. 232–307.
40 Saugnieux (1975) 80.
41 Mestre (1984) 1247–8.
42 Tomsich (1972) 25–7.
43 Saugnieux (1975) 10.
44 Ibid.
45 Ibid. 31; Tomsich (1972) 72.
46 Ibid. 65–72.
47 Saugnieux (1975) 23.
48 Ibid. 26, 55; Tomsich (1972) 45.
49 Saugnieux (1975) 59; Tomsich (1972) 31–2; Menéndez y Pelayo (1945: Vol. 6, 40–61, 148–150) is the key work linking Jansenists to regalists, although he exaggerates the connections.
50 Ibid. 78.
51 Defourneaux (1963) 27.
52 Ibid. 28.
53 Ibid. 32–3; this was Father José Casani.
54 Ibid. 33 n.4.
55 Ibid. 34.
56 Poliakov (2003) 243 n.3.

57 Oliveira (ed.) (1887–1910) Vol. 16, 139.
58 Ibid.
59 Ibid. Vol. 16, 140.
60 Maxwell (1995) 24; Serrão (1982) 27–8.
61 Oliveira (ed.) (1887–1910) Vol. 16, 141.
62 Pageaux (1971) 83; the view of the Frenchman Etienne de Silhouette 1729–30.
63 Oliveira (1887–1910) Vol. 16, 140.
64 Serrão (1982) 31–2.
65 Ibid. 46–7; celebrations were held up and down the kingdom in June, and in July Pombal's brother Francisco Xavier de Mendonça Furtado was made secretary of state.
66 Fleches (1982–3) 300–8.
67 Ibid. 314. Pombal cannot be excused promotion of himself here, since the Jesuit kingdom in Paraguay stood in the way of the commercial company of the Grão Pará and Maranhão, which he had founded in 1755 as a state monopoly company to exploit these regions of Brazil, and in which he and members of his family had important commercial interests (Ibid. 300).
68 Ibid. 312.
69 Pereira (1982–3) 368–70.
70 Santos (1982–3) 118.
71 Ibid. 313.
72 Maxwell (1995) 91.
73 Rêgo (1984) 335; the full text of the decree is published ibid. 330–6.
74 Ibid. 311.
75 Baião (1945) 284–5; the statistics here make this emphasis clear, with the vast majority of cases in the 18th century for this crime.
76 Ibid. 285.
77 This idea obviously derives significantly from the Freudian notion of the 'return of the repressed'.
78 Moreno Mancebo (1984) 1265–6.
79 AHN, Inquisición, Legajo 1866, Expediente 1, folio 2v.
80 Ibid. folio 5v.
81 Ibid. folios 6v, 10r.
82 Ibid. folio 10v.
83 Ibid. folios 153v–154r.
84 Ibid. folio 30r.
85 Ibid. folios 30r, 38v, 45v, 47v, 54v, 78r, 83v
86 Saínz Rodríguez (1962) 97.
87 AHN, Inquisición, Legajo 1866, Expediente 1, folios 151r, 157v.
88 AHN, Inquisición, Legajo 1866, Expediente 9. Note that this file has no folio numbers.
89 Ibid.
90 AHN, Inquisición, Legajo 1866, Expediente 2, folio 568v.
91 Moreno Mancebo (1984) 1275.

92 AHN, Inquisición, Legajo 1866, Expediente 1, folio 153v.
93 Moreno Mancebo (1984) 1274: *Olavide es luterano / es francmason, es ateísta / es gentil, es calvinista / es judío, es arriano.*
94 AHN, Inquisición, Legajo 1866, Expediente 5.
95 Mestre (1984) 1250.
96 AHN, Inquisición, Legajo 4465, Expediente 5.
97 AHN, Inquisición, Legajo 4465, Expediente 17.
98 Ibid. folio 2r.
99 Mestre (1984) 1251.
100 Defourneaux (1963) 46.
101 Marti Gilabert (1975) 44–5.
102 Defourneaux (1963) 43 n.1.
103 Mestre (1984) 1252.
104 Bethencourt (1994) 174.
105 Saugnieux (1975) 40–1.
106 Pinta Llorente (1961) 123.
107 Ibid. 130–1.
108 Ibid. 125.
109 Ibid. 126.
110 Ibid. 131–2.
111 Ibid. 137.
112 Ferrer Benimeli (1976–7) Vol. 3, 81.
113 Ibid. 330–1.
114 Rêgo (1971) 125.

Fourteen – The Failure of Fear and the Fear of Failure

1 Defourneaux (1963) 100.
2 AHN, Inquisición, Legajo 4493, Expediente 8.
3 AHN, Inquisición, Legajo 4518, Expediente 3.
4 AHN, Inquisición, Legajo 4469, Expediente 33.
5 AHN, Inquisición, Legajo 4492, Expediente 12.
6 Paz y Melia (1947) 141.
7 Ibid. 143.
8 AHN, Inquisición, Legajo 4506, Expediente 7.
9 García Camarero and García Camarero (eds.) (1970) 48.
10 Ibid. 49.
11 Ibid. 51.
12 Ibid. 52.
13 Ibid. 114.
14 Ibid.
15 Cirac Estopañán (1942) 68–9.
16 Ibid. 80.
17 AHN, Inquisición, Legajo 3730, Expediente 15.

18 Cirac Estopañán (1942) 250; Menéndez y Pelayo (1945) Vol. 3, 352.
19 Trevor-Roper (1984) 115.
20 Boyajian (1993) 172–4; Ruiz (1987) 39.
21 Blázquez Miguel (1990) 34.
22 Saínz Rodríguez (1962) 96.
23 García Cárcel and Moreno Martínez (2000) 38.
24 Ibid. 64–5.
25 Souza (1987) 101.
26 Lithgow (1640) 484–5.
27 IAN/TT, CGSO, Livro 433: the case of Manuel Fernandes in the Auto of 24 July 1569.
28 Ibid. folio 22v (2 cases); folios 83r–84r, a total of seven Old Christians from Coimbra hiding *conversos* or warning them to flee from 1619.
29 This was not limited to the case of Pimienta outlined below. Other cases can be found ibid. folio 72r; also IAN/TT, CGSO, Livro 435, folio 29r (the case of Diogo de Asumpção from Lisbon in 1603, who was burnt alive). Many of the people adopting crypto-Judaism in west Africa and Latin America in these years were also Old Christians – see Green (2007) Part III, Chapter 3.
30 I derive the details for the case of Pimienta from Gottheil (1971).
31 Jiménez Lozano (1987).
32 Bernáldez (1962) 96–7. That this remained associated with the Jews is confirmed by subsequent inquisitorial cases; see for example IAN/TT, Inquisição d'Évora, Livro 89, folio 184r, a case of someone accused of making a 'meal of meat with onion fried in oil . . . in the manner in which the *conversos* keep the Jewish ceremonies'.
33 Amílcar Paulo (n.d.), 43–4; Wachtel (2001a) 331ff.
34 Egido (1986); Marti Gilabert (1975) 22–3.
35 On these various attempts at reform see Jiménez Monteserín (1984) 1430–54.
36 Marti Gilabert (1975) 14.
37 Ibid. 81.
38 Ibid. 59, 86.
39 Ibid. 63.
40 Ibid. 19.
41 Ibid. 14.
42 Ibid. 35.
43 Blázquez Miguel (1990) 133.
44 Menéndez y Pelayo (1945) Vol. 5, 443.
45 Mirsky (2006) 37.
46 One of the noble and brilliant exceptions to this rule is Piccini (1992). Yet the depth of the problem is revealed through the fact that Piccini is herself a psychoanalyst.
47 Marti Gilabert (1975) 150.
48 DP, 227.
49 Marti Gilabert (1975) 169.

50 González Obregón (ed.) (n.d.) 167, 169.
51 Ibid. 170.
52 Ibid. 171.
53 Ibid. 208.
54 Ibid.
55 Jiménez Monteserín (1984) 1476–7.
56 Rêgo (ed.) (1971) 7.
57 Rêgo (ed.) (1983) 18.
58 Mendonça and Moreira (1980) 128.
59 Marti Gilabert (1975) 297–308; Alonso Tejada (1969) 23.
60 Alonso Tejada (1969) 24–5.
61 Ibid. 28.
62 Blázquez Miguel (1990) 135.

Bibliography

Abbreviations

ACE *An Account of the Cruelties Exercis'd by the Inquisition in Portugal* (1708)
AG *As Gavetas da Torre do Tombo*, Rêgo, A. (1960–75)
AGI Archivo General de las Indias, Seville
AHN Archivo Histórico Nacional, Madrid
ASV Archivio Segreto Vaticano, Vatican State
BA Biblioteca da Ajuda, Lisbon
BAGN *Boletín del Archivo General de la Nación de México*
BL British Library Manuscripts Collection, London
CA *Collection of Autos, 1723–1724*. British Library shelfmark 4071.i.3.(30)
CDIHE *Colección de Documentos Históricos para la Historia de España, Colección Fernández Navarrete*
CGSO *Conselho Geral do Santo Officio*, archival collection in IAN/TT
CRP *Crónica de Rui de Pina*, Almeida (1977)
DH *Fray Bartolomé Carranza: Documentos Históricos*, Tellechea Idigoras (1962–6)
DP *Discusión del Proyecto de Decreto Sobre el Tribunal de la Inquisición*
ENE Epistolario de la Nueva España, Pasoty Troncoso (1934)
HGCV *Historia Geral de Cabo Verde*, Albuquerque and Santos (1988–90)
IAN/TT Instituto dos Arquivos Nacionais da Torre do Tombo, Lisbon
IT *Copilación de las Instrucciones del Officio de la Sancta Inquisición, Hechas por el Muy Reverendo Señor Fray Thomas de Torquemada* (1576)
MMA *Monumenta Misionária Africana, Segunda Serie*, Brásio (1960–2004)
PD *Concordias Hechas y Firmadas Entre la Iurisdiccion Real y el Santo Oficio de la Inquisición*. British Library shelfmark 4625.g.i
PV *Primeira Visitação do Santo Officio Ás Partes do Brasil: Denunciações da Bahia, 1591–1593* (1925)
TA *Traslado Autentico de Todos os Privilegios Concedidos Pelos Reis Destes Reinos, e Senhorios de Portugal aos Officiaes, e Familiares do Santo Officio* (1768)

MANUSCRIPT SOURCES

I have not listed all the manuscripts which I have consulted for this book. For those so inclined, the notes reveal archival sources where appropriate. I have used collections in the following archives in the preparation of this book:

Archivio Segretto Vaticano, Vatican State
Archivo General de las Indias, Seville
Archivo Histórico Nacional, Madrid
Biblioteca da Ajuda, Lisbon
British Library Manuscripts Collection, London
Instituto dos Arquivos Nacionais da Torre do Tombo, Lisbon

For similar reasons of space, I have not included all the books consulted, but only those cited in the notes or most relevant to the subject.

PRIMARY SOURCES (PUBLISHED MATERIAL)

Alberti, L. de and Wallis Chapman, A.B. (eds) (1912): *English Merchants and the Spanish Inquisition in the Canaries: Extracts from the Archives in Possession of the Most Hon. The Marquess of Bute*. London: Offices of the Royal Historical Society.

Albuquerque, Luis de and Santos, Maria Emília Madeira (eds) (1988–90): *História Geral de Cabo Verde: Corpo Documental*. Lisbon: Instituto de Investigação Científica Tropical; 2 vols.

Almeida, M. Lopes de (ed.) (1977): *Crónicas de Rui de Pina*. Porto: Lello & Irmão – Editores.

An Account of the Cruelties Exercis'd by the Inquisition in Portugal – Written by One of the Secretaries to the Inquisition (1708). London: R. Burrough and J. Baker.

Anonymous (1551/2?): 'Navegação de Lisbon á Ilha de S. Thome, escrita por um Piloto Portugues' in *Colecção de Noticias* . . . (1812), Vol. II, no. II.

Anonymous (ed.) (1964): *Documentos de la Época de los Reyes Católicos*. Vaduz: Kraus Reprint of CDIHE Vol. 8.

Azpilcueta Navarro, Martim de (1560): *Manual de Confessores e penitentes, que clara e brevemente contem a universal decisam de quasi todas as duvidas q em as confissões soem ocorrer dos pecados, absoluições, restituyções, censuras, e irregularidades*. Coimbra: Joan de Barreyra.

Barrios, Manuel (1991): *El Tribunal de la Inquisición en Andalucía: Selección de Textos y Documentos*. Seville: J. Rodríguez Castillejo S.A.

Beinart, Haim (ed.) (1974–85): *Records of the Trials of the Spanish Inquisition in Ciudad Real*. Jerusalem: Israel National Academy of Sciences and Humanities, 4 vols.

Bernáldez, Andres (1962): *Memorias del Reinado de los Reyes Católicos*. Madrid: Real Academia de la Historia.

Biarnés i Biarnés, Carmen (ed.) (1981): *Els Moriscos a Catalunya: Apunts d'Historia d'Asco: Documents Inèdits*. Asco: Gràfiques Moncunill.

Boletín del Archivo General de la Nación (1935–7). Mexico City: Archivo General de la Nación; Vols 6–8.

Brásio, António (ed.) (1960–2004): *Monumenta Misionaria Africana: África Ocidental:*

Segunda Série – Vol. 1 (1958), Vol. 2 (1963), Vol. 3 (1964), Vol. 4 (1968), Vol. 5 (1979), Vol. 6 (1989), Vol. 7 (2004). Lisbon: Agência Geral do Ultramar, 7 vols.

Camões, Luís de (1973): *Os Lusiadas*. Oxford: Clarendon Press.

Carletti, Francesco (1965): *My Voyage Around the World*. London: Methuen & Co.

Cohen, Martin A. (ed. and trans.) (1971b, first published 1935): 'The Autobiography of Luis de Carvajal, the Younger' in Cohen, Martin A. (ed.) (1971b), Vol. I., pp. 201–42.

Colección de Documentos Inéditos para la Historia de España. Madrid (1847): Imprenta de la Viuda de Calero.

Collection of Autos, 1723–1724. British Library shelfmark 4071.i.3.(30).

Concordias Hechas y Firmadas Entre la Iurisdiccion Real y el Santo Oficio de la Inquisición. British Library shelfmark 4625.g.i.

Conway, G.R.G. (ed.) (1927): *An Englishman and the Mexican Inquisition 1556–1560 – Being an Account of the Voyage of Robert Tomson to New Spain, His Trial for Heresy in the City of Mexico and Other Contemporary Historical Documents*. Mexico City: privately printed.

Copilación de las Instrucciones del Officio de la Sancta Inquisición, Hechas por el Muy Reverendo Señor Fray Thomas de Torquemada (1576). Madrid: Alonso Gomez.

Coustos, John (1803): *Procedures Curieuses de l'Inquisition de Portugal Contre les Francs-Maçons*. Vallée de Josephat: L.T.V.I.L.R.D.M.

Dellon, Charles (1698): *A Voyage to the East Indies*. London: D. Browne, A. Roper and T. Leigh.

Dellon's Account of the Inquisition at Goa (1815). London: Baldwin, Craddock and Joy.

Discusión del Proyecto de Decreto Sobre el Tribunal de la Inquisición (1813). Cádiz.

Eymeric, Nicolas (1972): *Manual de los Inquisidores*. Buenos Aires: Rodolfo Afonso Editor; Gioia, Amanda Furns de (trans.).

Fernández Álvarez, Manuel (1971–83): *Corpus Documental de Carlos V*. Salamanca: Ediciones Universidad de Salamanca, 5 vols.

Fernández del Castillo, Francisco (ed.) (1982): *Libros y Libreros en el Siglo XVI*. Mexico City: Fondo de Cultura Económica.

Fleckno, Richard (n.d. – *c.* 1660): *A Relation of Ten Years Travels in Europe, Asia, Affrique, and America*. London: privately printed.

Fonseca, Damián (1612): *Iusta Expulsión de los Moriscos de España*. Rome: Iacomo Mascardo.

Ford, J.D.M. (ed. and trans.) (1931): *Letters of John III, King of Portugal*. Cambridge, Mass.: Harvard University Press.

Freire, Anselmo Bramcamp et al. (eds) (1903–18): *Archivo Histórico Portuguez*. Lisbon: Of. Tip., 11 vols.

Gandavo, Pero de Magalhães (1858): *Historia da Provincia Santa Cruz, a que Vulgarmente Chamamos Brasil*. Lisbon: Na Typographia da Academia das Sciencias.

García Fuentes, José Maria (1981): *La Inquisición en Granada en el Siglo XVI: Fuentes Para su Estudio*. Granada: Talleres Gráficos Arte de Maracena.

García Mercadal, J. (ed.) (1999): *Viajes de Extranjeros por España y Portugal*. Salamanca: Junta de Castilla y León, 5 vols.

Góis, Damião de (1949, first published 1566): *Crónica do Felicíssimo Rei D. Manuel*. Coimbra: Por Ordem da Universidade, 2 vols.

González Obregón, Luis (ed.) (1935): *Procesos de Luis de Carvajal (El Mozo)*. Mexico City: Talleres Gráficos de la Nación.

González Obregón, Luis (ed.) (n.d.): *La Santa Inquisición en los Albores de la Independencia: Los Procesos Militar e Inquisitorial del Padre Hidalgo y de Otros Caudillos Insurgentes*. Mexico City: Ediciones Fuente Cultural.

Gracia Boix, Rafael (ed.) (1982): *Colección de Documentos para la Historia de la Inquisición de Córdoba*. Cordoba: Publicaciones del Monte de Piedad y Caja de Ahorros de Córdoba.

Hakluyt, Richard (ed.) (1600): *The Third and Last Volume of the Voyages, Navigations, Traffiques and Discoveries of the English Nation*. London: George Bishop, Ralph Newberie and Robert Barker.

Hawkins, John (1569): *A True Declaration of the Troublesome Voyage of M. John Hawkins to the Parties of Guynea and the West Indies, in the Yeares of Our Lord 1567, and 1568*. London: Thomas Purfoote.

Jiménez Monteserín, Miguel (ed.) (1980): *Introducción a la Inquisición Española*. Madrid: Editora Nacional.

Jiménez Rueda, Julio (ed.) (1945): *Corsarios Franceses e Ingleses en la Inquisición de la Nueva España, Siglo XVI*. Mexico City: Archivo General de la Nación, Imprenta Universitaria.

Kagan, Richard L. and Dyer, Abigail (eds and trans.) (2004): *Inquisitorial Inquiries: Brief Lives of Secret Jews and Other Heretics*. Baltimore and London: Johns Hopkins Press.

Léry, Jean de (1975): *Histoire d'un Voyage Fait en la Terre du Brésil*. Geneva: Librairie Droz.

Liebman, Seymour B. (ed. and trans.) (1974): *Jews and the Inquisition of Mexico: The Great Auto de Fe of 1649*. Lawrence, Ka.: Coronado Press.

Lithgow, William (1640): *The Total Discourse, Of the rare Adventures, and painefull Peregrinations of long nineteen yeares Travailes from* Scotland, *to the most famous Kingdomes in Europe, Asia and Affrica*. London: I. Okes.

Llorca, Bernardino (ed.) (1949): *Bulario Pontificio de la Inquisición Española – En su Período Constitucional (1478–1525)*. Rome: Pontificia Università Gregoriana.

López, Don Fray Joan (1613): *Tercera Parte de la Historia General de Sancto Domingo, y de su Orden de Predicadores*. Valladolid: Francisco Fernández de Cordova.

Mariana, Juan de (1751): *Historia General de España, Vol. 8*. Antwerp: Marcos-Miguel Bousquet y Compañía.

Mauny, R., Monod, Th. and Teixeira da Mota, A. (eds) (1951): *Description de la Côte Occidentale d'Afrique (Sénégal au Cap de Monte, Archipels) par Valentim Fernandes (1506–1510).* Bissau: Centro de Estudos da Guiné Portuguesa.

Mello, José Antônio Gonsalves de (ed.) (1970): *Confissões de Pernambuco, 1594–1595.* Recife: Universidade Federal de Pernambuco.

Mello, José Antônio Gonsalves de (ed.) (1982): *Diálogos das Grandezas do Brasil.* Recife: Imprenta Universitária.

Montaigne, Michel de (1998): *Essais.* Paris: Pocket.

Monteiro, Pedro (1750): *Historia da Santa Inquisição do Reino de Portugal e Suas Conquistas.* Lisbon: Na Regia Oficina Sylviana e da Academia Real, 2 vols.

Monterroso y Alvarado, Gabriel de (1571): *Pratica Civil y Criminal & Instruccion de Escrivanos.* Alcala de Henares: Casa de Andres Angulo.

Oliveira, Eduardo Freire de (ed.) (1887–1910): *Elementos para a Historia do Municipio de Lisbon.* Lisbon: Typographia Universal, 17 vols.

Ortega-Costa, Milagros (ed.) (1978): *Proceso de la Inquisición Contra Maria de Cazalla.* Madrid: Fundación Universitaria Española.

Osorio, Jerónimo (1944, first published 1571): *Da Vida e Feitos de el-Rei D. Manuel.* Porto: Livraria Civilização Editôra, 2 vols.

Pageaux, David-Henri (1971): *Images du Portugal Dans les Lettres Françaises (1700–1755).* Paris: Fundação Calouste Gulbenkian.

Paso y Troncoso, Francisco (ed.) (1934): *Epistolario de la Nueva España.* Mexico City: Antigua Librerí Robredo, de José Porrúa e Hijos, 24 vols.

Pereira, Isaías da Rosa (ed.) (1987): *Documentos para a História da Inquisição em Portugal (Século XVI).*Lisbon.

Pérez de Guzmán, Fernán (1965): *Generaciones y Semblanzas.* London: Tauris Books Limited, R.B. Tate (ed.).

Pinta Llorente, Miguel de la and Palacio y Palacio, Jose Maria de (eds) (1964): *Procesos Inquisitoriales Contra la Familia Judía de Juan Luis Vives.* Madrid-Barcelona: Instituto Arias Montano.

Pitta, Sebastião da Rocha (1880, first published 1724): *Historia da America Portugueza Desde o Anno 1500 Até o de 1724.* Lisbon: Editor Francisco Arthur da Silva.

Primeira Visitação do Santo Officio Ás Partes do Brasil: Denunciações da Bahia, 1591–1593 (1925). São Paulo: Homenagem de Paulo Prado.

Pulgar, Fernando del (1943): *Crónica de los Reyes Católicos por su Secretario Fernando del Pulgar.* Madrid: Espasa-Calpe S.A., 2 vols.

Pyrard de Laval, François (1619): *Voyage de François Pyrard de Laval.* Paris: Samuel Thibost et la Veuve Remy Dallin; 2 vols.

Rat, Maurice (ed.) (1941): *Montaigne: Essais.* Paris: Librairie Gamier Frères, 3 vols.

Regimento dos Familiares do Santo Officio (1739). Lisbon: Officina de Manoel Fernandes da Costa.

Rêgo, A. Da Silva (ed.) (1960–75): *As Gavetas da Torre do Tombo.* Lisbon: Centro de Estudos Históricos Ultramarinos da Junta de Investigações Científicas do Ultramar, 11 vols.

Rêgo, Raul (ed.) (1971): *O Ultimo Regimento da Inquisição Portuguesa.* Lisbon: Edições Excelsior.

Rêgo, Raul (ed.) (1983): *O Último Regimento e o Regimento da Economia da Inquisição de Goa.* Lisbon: Biblioteca Nacional.

Rojas, Fernando de (1985): *Celestina: Tragicomedia de Calisto y Melibea.* Urbana: University of Illinois Press.

Ruiz de Pablos, Francisco (ed. and trans.) (1997): *Artes de la Santa Inquisición Española por Reinaldo González Montes.*

Salazar de Miranda (1788): *Vida y Sucesos Prosperos y Adversos de Don Bartolomé de Carranza y Miranda.* Madrid: Joseph Doblado.

Sanches, Francisco (1988): *'That Nothing is Known' (Quod Nihil Scitur).* Cambridge: Cambridge University Press, Thompson, Douglas F.S. (trans.)

Splendiani, Anna María (1997): *Cincuenta Años de Inquisición en el Tribunal de Cartagena de las Indias, 1610–60.* Santafé de Bogotá: Centro Editorial Javeriano CEJA, 4 vols.

Suárez Fernández, Luis (ed.) (1964): *Documentos Acerca de la Expulsión de los Judíos.* Valladolid: Ediciones Aldecoa, S.A.

Tellechea Idigoras, José Ignacio (1962–6): *Fray Bartolomé de Carranza: Documentos Históricos.* Madrid: Archivo Documental Español.

Toro, Alfonso (ed.) (1932): *Los Judíos de la Nueva España: Selección de Documentos del Siglo XVI, Correspondientes al Ramo de la Inquisición.* Mexico City: Talleres Gráficos de la Nación.

Traslado Autentico de Todos os Privilegios Concedidos pelos Reis destes Reinos, e Senhorios de Portugal aos Officiaes, e Familiares do Santo officio da Inquisição, Impressos por Comissão, e Mandado dos Senhores do Supremo Conselho da Santa, e Geral Inquisição (1768). Lisbon: Na Officina de Miguel Manescal da Costa, Impressor do Santo Officio.

Trasmiera, Garcia de (1664): *Epitome de la Sancta Vida y Relacion de la Gloriosa Muerte del Venerable Pedro de Arbues, Inquisidor Apostolico de Aragon A Quien la Obstinacion Hebrea Dió Muerte Temporal, y la Liberalidad Divina, Vida Eterna.* Madrid: Diego Diaz de la Carrera.

Usque, Samuel (1989): *Consolação às Tribulações de Israel.* Lisbon: Fundação Calouste Gulbenkian, 2 vols.

Valencia, Pedro de (1997): *Tratado Acerca de los Moriscos de España.* Málaga: Editorial Algazara.

Valera, Mosén Diego de (1927): *Crónica de los Reyes Católicos.* Madrid: José Molina.

Wadsworth, James (1630): *The English Spanish Pilgrime.* London: T. Cotes.

Wolf, Lucien (ed. and trans.) (1926): *Jews in the Canary Islands, Being a Calendar of Jewish Cases Extracted From the Records of the Canariote Inquisition of the Marquess of Bute.* London: Jewish Historical Society of England.

Zurita, Jerónimo de (1610): *Anales de la Corona de Aragón.* Zaragoza: Colegio de San Vicente Ferrer.

REFERENCE

Farinha, Maria do Carmo Jasmins Dias (1990): *Os Arquivos da Inquisição*. Lisbon: Arquivo Nacional da Torre do Tombo.

Guerra, Luiz de Bivar (1972): *Inventário dos Processos da Inquisição de Coimbra (1541–1820)*. Paris: Fundação Calouste Gulbenkian; 2 vols.

Liebman, Seymour B. (1964): *A Guide to Jewish References in the Mexican Colonial Era 1521–1821*. Philadelphia: University of Pennsylvania Press.

Llamas Martínez, Enrique (1975): *Documentación Inquisitorial: Manuscritos Españoles del Siglo XVI Existentes en el Museo Británico*. Madrid: Fundación Universitaria Española.

Martínez Bara, José Antonio (1970): *Catálogo de Informaciones Genealógicas de la Inquisición de Córdoba Conservados en el Archivo Histórico Nacional*. Madrid: Dirección General de Archivos y Bibliotecas, Diputación Provincial de Jaén, 2 vols.

Paz y Melia, A. (ed.) (1947): *Papeles de Inquisición: Catálogo y Extractos*. Madrid: Patronato del Archivo Histórico Nacional.

Roncancio Parra, Andrés (ed.) (2000): *Índice de Documentos de la Inquisición de Cartagena de Indias: Programa de Recuperación, Sistematización y Divulgación de Archivos*. Santafé de Bogotá: Instituto Colombiano de Cultura Hispánica.

Singerman, Robert (1975): *The Jews in Spain and Portugal: A Bibliography*. New York: Garland Publishing, Inc.

Tovar, Conde do (1932): *Catálogo dos Manuscritos Portugueses Existentes no Museu Britânico*. Lisbon: Academia das Ciências.

GENERAL

Abellán, José Luis (1995): 'Función Cultural de la Presencia Judía en España Antes y Después de la Expulsión' in Alcalá, Angel (ed.) (1995), pp. 395–407.

Ackerman, Nathan W. and Jahoda, Marie (1950): *Anti-Semitism and Emotional Disorder: A Psychoanalytic Interpretation*. New York: Harper and Brothers.

Ackroyd, Peter (1998): *The Life of Thomas More*. London: Chatto & Windus.

Adler, Elkan Nathan (1971, first published 1904): 'The Inquisition in Peru' in Cohen, Martin A. (ed.) (1971a) Vol. II., pp. 6–38.

Adorno, Theodor W. et al. (1950): *The Authoritarian Personality*. New York: Harper and Row.

Aguirre Bellver, Joaquín (1994): *Los Secretos de la Celestina*. Madrid: Jafuibel.

Albuquerque, Luís de and Santos, María Emilia Madeira (eds) (1991): *História Geral de Cabo Verde, Vol. I*. Coimbra: Imprensa de Coimbra.

Alcalá, Angel (ed.) (1987): *The Spanish Inquisition and the Inquisitorial Mind*. Boulder, Col.: Columbia University Press.

Alcalá, Angel (ed.) (1995): *Judíos. Sefarditos. Conversos – La Expulsión de 1492 y sus Consecuencias*. Valladolid: Ámbito Ediciones.

Alcalá Galve, A. (1984): 'Los Hechos y las Actividades Inquisitoriales en España: Control de Espirituales' in Pérez Villanueva, Joaquín and Escandell Bonet, Bartolomé (eds) (1984) pp. 780–841.

Almeida, Fortunato de (1967): *A História da Igreja em Portugal*. Porto: Portucalense Editora, 4 vols.

Alonso Tejada, Luis (1969): *Ocaso de la Inquisición en los Últimos Años del Reinado de Fernando VII: Juntas de Fe, Juntas Apostólicas, Conspiraciones Realistas*. Algorta: Zero S.A.

Alpert, Michael (2001): *Cryptojudaism and the Spanish Inquisition*. Basingstoke: Palgrave.

Alvarez Alonso, Fermina (1999): *La Inquisición en Cartagena de Indias Durante el Siglo XVII*. Madrid: Fundación Universitaria Española.

Amador de los Ríos, José (1960, first published 1875): *Historia Social Política y Religiosa de los Judíos de España y Portugal*. Madrid: Aguilar S.A. de Ediciones.

Anderson, Benedict (1991 revised edition, first published 1983): *Imagined Communities: Reflections on the Origin and Spread of Nationalism*. London: Verso.

Arbell, Mordechai (2002): *The Jewish Nation of the Caribbean: The Spanish-Portuguese Jewish Settlement in the Caribbean and the Guianas*. Jerusalem: Gegen Publishing House.

Arendt, Hannah (1986, first published 1951): *The Origins of Totalitarianism*. London: André Deutsch.

Arzona, Tarsicio de (1980): 'La Inquisición Española Procesada por la Congregación General de 1508' in Pérez Villanueva, Joaquín (ed.) (1980), pp. 89–163.

Avilés Fernández, M. (1984): 'Los Acontecimientos: El Santo Oficio en la Primera Etapa Carolina', in Pérez Villanueva, Joaquín and Escandell Bonet, Bartolomé (eds) (1984) pp. 443–72.

Azevedo, Elvira Cunha (1974): *O Sefardismo na Cultura Portuguesa*. Porto: Paisagem.

Azevedo, João Lucio d' (1922): *Historia dos Christãos Novos Portugueses*. Lisbon: Livraria Clássica Editora.

Azevedo, João Lucio d' (1929): *Épocas de Portugal Económico: Esboços da História*. Lisbon: Livraria Clássica Editora.

Aznar Vallejo, Eduardo (1994): 'The Conquests of the Canary Islands' in Schwartz, Stuart B. (ed.) (1994), pp. 134–56.

Baer, Yitzhak (1966): *A History of the Jews in Christian Spain*. Philadelphia: Jewish Publication Society of America, 2 vols, Schoffman, Louis (trans.).

Baião, António (1921): *A Inquisição em Portugal e no Brazil: Subsídios para a sua História*. Lisbon: Of. Tip.

Baião, António (1942): *El Rei D. João IV e a Inquisição*. Lisbon: Academia Portuguesa da História.

Baião, António (1945): *A Inquisição de Goa: Tentativa de Historia da Sua Origem, Estabelecimento, Evolução e Extinção.* Lisbon: Academia das Ciências.

Baião, António (1972): *Episódios Dramáticos da Inquisição Portuguesa.* Lisbon: Seara Nova.

Baião, António et al. (eds) (1937): *História da Expansão Portuguesa no Mundo.* Lisbon: Editorial Ática, 3 vols.

Baleno, Ilídio Cabral (1991); 'Pressões Externas. Reassões ao Corso e à Piratarí', in HGCV, Vol. II, pp. 125–88.

Barnett, R.D. (ed.) (1971): *The Sephardi Heritage: Essays on the History and Cultural Contribution of the Jews of Spain and Portugal.* London: Valentine, Mitchell & Co., 2 vols.

Barrios Aguilera, Manuel (2002): *Granada Morisca: La Convivencia Negada.* Granada: Editorial Comares.

Bataillon, Marcel (1937): *Érasme et l'Espagne: Recherches sur l'Histoire Spirituelle du XVIe Siècle.* Paris: Librairie E. Droz.

Bataillon, Marcel (1952): *Études sur le Portugal au Temps de l'Humanisme.* Coimbra: Por Ordem da Universidade.

Beinart, Haim (1971a): 'The Converso Community in 15th Century Spain', in Barnett, R.D. (ed.) (1971) Vol. I., pp. 425–56.

Beinart, Haim: (1971b): 'The Converso Community in 16th and 17th Century Spain', in Barnett, R.D., (ed.) (1971), Vol. I., pp. 457–478.

Beinart, Haim (1980): *Trujillo: A Jewish Community in Extremadura on the Eve of the Expulsion from Spain.* Jerusalem: Magnes Press.

Beinart, Haim (1981): *Conversos on Trial: The Inquisition in Ciudad Real.* Jerusalem: Magnes Press, Guiladi, Yael (trans.).

Beinart, Haim (ed.) (1992a): *Moreshet Sepharad: The Sephardi Legacy.* Jerusalem: Magnes Press, 2 vols.

Beinart, Haim (1992b): 'The Conversos and their Fate', in Kedourie, Elie (ed.) (1992) pp. 92–122.

Beinart, Haim (1995): 'Vuelta de Judíos a España Después de la Expulsión', in Alcalá, Angel (ed.) (1995) pp. 181–94.

Bellini, Ligia (1989): *A Coisa Obscura: Mulher, Sodomia e Inquisição no Brasil Colonial.* São Paulo: Editora Brasiliense.

Benassar, Bartolomé (1979a): *L'Inquisition Espagnole: XVe-XIXe Siècle.* Paris: Hachette.

Benassar, Bartolomé (1979b): *The Spanish Character: Attitudes and Mentality From the Sixteenth to the Nineteenth Century.* Berkeley: University of California Press.

Benassar, Bartolomé (1987): 'Patterns of the Inquisitorial Mind as the Basis for a Pedagogy of Fear' in Alcalá, Angel (ed.) (1987) pp. 177–84.

Benítez Sánchez-Blanco, Rafael (1983): 'Un Plan para la Aculturación de los Moriscos Valencianos: "Les Ordinacions" de Ramírez de Haro (1540)' in Cardaillac, Louis (ed.) (1983), pp. 127–57.

Benito Ruano, Eloy (1961): *Toledo en el Siglo XV: Vida Política*. Madrid: Consejo Superior de Investigaciones Científicas, Escuela de Estudios Medievales.

Benito Ruano, Eloy (2001): *Los Orígenes del Problema Converso*. Madrid: Real Academía de la Historia.

Bernardini, Paolo and Fiering, Norman (eds) (2001): *The Jews and the Expansion of Europe to the West, 1450–1800*. New York: Berghahn Books.

Bernis, Carmen (1978): *Trajes y Modas en la España de los Reyes Católicos*. Madrid: Instituto Diego Velázquez del Consejo Superior de Investigaciones Científicas, 2 vols.

Bethencourt, Francisco (1994): *História das Inquisições: Portugal, Espanha e Italia*. Lisbon: Circulo de Leitores.

Bethencourt, Francisco and Chaudhuri, Kirti (eds) (1998a): *História da Expansão Portuguesa: Vol. 1, A Formação do Império (1415–1570)*. Navarra: Temas e Debates e Autores.

Bethencourt, Francisco and Chaudhuri, Kirti (eds) (1998b): *Historia da Expansão Portuguesa, Vol. 2: Do Índico ao Atlântico (1570–1697)*. Lisbon: Círculo de Leitores.

Bethencourt, Francisco and Havik, Philip (2004): 'A África e a Inquisição Portuguesa: Novas Perspectivas' in *Revista Lusófona de Ciência das Religiões*, Ano III, 2004, no.5/6, pp. 21–7 – also published at http://cienciareligioes.ulusofona.pt.

Blázquez Miguel, Juan (1985): *La Inquisición en Albacete*. Albacete: Instituto de Estudios Albacetenses.

Blázquez Miguel, Juan (1986a): *El Tribunal de la Inquisición en Murcia*. Murcia: Edición de la Academia Alfonso X el Sabio.

Blázquez Miguel, Juan (1986b): *La Inquisición en Castilla-La Mancha*. Madrid: Librería Anticuaria Jerez y Servicios de Publicaciones Universidad de Córdoba.

Blázquez Miguel, Juan (1988): *Inquisición y Criptojudaismo*. Madrid: Ediciones Kaydeda.

Blázquez Miguel, Juan (1989): *Toledot: Historia del Toledo Judío*. Toledo: Editorial Arcano.

Blázquez Miguel, Juan (1990): *La Inquisición en Cataluña: El Tribunal del Santo Oficio de Barcelona (1487–1820)*. Toledo: Editorial Arcano.

Böhm, Günter (1948): 'Los Judíos en Chile Durante la Colonia' in *Boletín de la Academia Chilena de la Historia*, no. 38, pp. 21–100.

Böhm, Günter (1963): *Nuevos Antecedentes para una Historia de los Judíos en Chile Colonial*. Santiago de Chile: Editorial Universitaria.

Böhm, Gunter (1984). *Historia de los Judios En Chile: Volumen I: Periodo Colonial: Judios y Judiosconversos en Chile Colonial Durante Los Siglos XVI y XVII*. Santiago de Chile: Editorial Andres Bello, Editorial Universitaria.

Böhm, Gunter (2001): 'Crypto-Jews and New Christians in Colonial Peru and Chile' in Bernardini, Paolo and Fiering, Norman (eds) (2001) pp. 203–12.

Borja Gómez, Jaime Humberto et al. (eds) (1996): *Inquisición, Muerte y Sexualidad en el Nuevo Reino de Granada*. Santa Fé de Bogotá: Editorial Ariel.

Bostos, José Timoteo da Silva (1983): *História da Censura Intelectual em Portugal*. Lisbon: Moraes Editores, 2nd edition.

Boucharb, Ahmed (1983): 'Spécificité du problème Morisque au Portugal: Une Colonie Étrangère refusant l'Assimilation et Souffrant d'un Sentiment de Déracinement et de Nostalgie' in Cardaillac, Louis (ed.) (1983) pp. 219–33.

Boxer, C.R. (1948): *Fidalgos in the Far East: Fact and Fancy in the History of Macao*. The Hague: Martinus Nijhoff.

Boxer, C.R. (1969): *The Portuguese Seaborne Empire 1415–1825*. London: Hutchinson.

Boyajian, James C. (1983): *Portuguese Bankers at the Court of Spain, 1626–1650*. New Brunswick, New Jersey: Rutgers University Press.

Boyajian, James C. (1993): *Portuguese Trade in Asia Under the Habsburgs, 1580–1640*. Baltimore: Johns Hopkins University Press.

Bradley, Edward Sculley (1931): *Henry Charles Lea: A Biography*. Philadelphia: University of Pennsylvania Press.

Braudel, Fernand (1966, first published 1949): *La Méditérranée et le Monde Méditérranéen à l'Époque de Philippe II*. Paris: Librairie Armand Colin, 2 vols.

Braudel, Fernand (1967): *Civilisation Matérielle et Capitalisme (XVe–XVIIIe Siècle)*. Paris: Librairie Armand Colin.

Canabrava, Alicia (1944): *O Comércio Portugues no Rio da Prata (1580–1640)*. São Paulo: Faculdade de Filosofia, Ciências e Letras.

Cardaillac, Louis (1978): *Morisques et Chrétiens: Un Affrontement Polémique (1492–1640)*. Paris: Klincksieck.

Cardaillac, Louis (ed.) (1983): *Les Morisques et Leur Temps*. Paris: Éditions du Centre National de la Recherche Scientifique.

Cardaillac, Louis (ed.) (1990): *Les Morisques et l'Inquisition*. Paris: Published.

Cardaillac, Louis and Dedieu, Jean-Pierre (1990): 'Introduction à l'Histoire des Morisques' in Cardaillac, Louis (ed.) (1990) pp. 11–28.

Carneiro, Maria Luiza Tucci (1983): *Preconceito Racial no Brasil Colonial: Os Cristãos Novos*. São Paulo: Editora Brasiliense, S.A.

Caro Baroja, Julio (1968): *El Señor Inquisidor y Otras Vidas por Oficio*. Madrid: Alianza Editorial.

Caro Baroja, Julio (1970): *Inquisición, Brujería y Criptojudaismo*. Barcelona: Editorial Ariel.

Caro Baroja, Julio (1976): *Los Moriscos del Reino de Granada*. Madrid: Ediciones Istmo, 2nd edition.

Caro Baroja, Julio. (1978): *Los Judíos en la España Moderna y Contemporánea*. Madrid: Taurus Ediciones, 3 vols., 2nd edition.

Carrasco, Rafael (1983): 'Le Refus d'Assimilation des Morisques: Aspects Politiques et Culturels d'Après les Sources Inquisitoriales' in Cardaillac, Louis (ed.) (1983) pp. 171–216.

Carvalho, Joaquim Barradas de (1981): *Portugal e as Origens do Pensamento Moderno*. Lisbon: Livros Horizonte.

Casey, James (1999): *Early Modern Spain: A Social History*. London: Routledge.

Castañeda Delgado, Paulino and Hernández Aparicio, Pilar (1989): *La Inquisición de Lima (1570–1635)*. Madrid: Editorial DEIMOS.

Castañeda Delgado, Paulino and Hernández Aparicio, Pilar (1995): *La Inquisición de Lima (1635–1696)*. Madrid: Editorial DEIMOS.

Castro, Américo (1954): *La Realidad Histórica de España*. Mexico City: Editorial Porrua.

Castro, Américo (1972, first published 1963): *De la Edad Conflictiva: Crisis de la Cultura Española en el Siglo XVII*. Madrid: Taurus Ediciones.

Ceballos Gómez, Diana Luz (1994): *Hechicería, Brujería e Inquisición en el Nuevo Reino de Granada*. Medellín: Editorial Universidad Nacional.

Cervantes, Fernando (1994): *The Devil in the New World: The Impact of Diabolism in New Spain*. New Haven and London: Yale University Press.

Chinchilla Aguilar, Ernesto (1952): *La Inquisición en Guatemala*. Guatemala City: Editorial del Ministerio de Educación Pública.

Cirac Estopañán, Sebastián (1942): *Los Procesos de Hechicerias en la Inquisición de Castilla la Nueva (Tribunales de Toledo y Cuenca)*. Madrid: Consejo Superior de Investigaciones Científicas, Instituto Jerónimo Zurita.

Coates, Timothy J. (2001): *Convicts and Orphans: Forced and State-Sponsored Colonizers in the Portuguese Empire, 1550–1755*. Stanford, Calif.: Stanford University Press.

Coelho, António Borges (1987): *Inquisição de Évora*. Lisbon: Editorial Caminho.

Cohen, Mario (1995): 'Lo que Hispanoamérica Perdío: El Impacto de la Expulsión en su Atraso Cultural y Económico' in Alcalá, Angel (ed.) (1995), pp. 434–54.

Cohen, Mario (2000): *América Colonial Judía*. Buenos Aires: Centro de Investigación y Difusión de la Cultura Sefardí.

Cohen, Martin A. (ed.) (1971a): *The Jewish Experience in Latin America*. Waltham, Mass.: American Jewish Historical Association, 2 vols.

Cohen, Martin A. (1971b): 'The Letters and Last Will and Testament of Luis de Carvajal, the Younger', in Cohen, Martin A. (ed.) (1971a) pp. 243–312.

Cohen, Martin A. (2001, first published 1973): *Martyr: Luis de Carvajal, a Secret Jew in Sixteenth-Century Mexico*. Albuquerque: University of New Mexico Press.

Cohen, Martin A. and Peck, Abraham J. (eds) (1993): *Sephardim in the Americas: Studies in Culture and History*. Tuscaloosa: University of Alabama Press.

Cohn, Norman (1975): *Europe's Inner Demons: An Enquiry Inspired by the Great Witch-Hunt*. London: Sussex University Press.

Collantes de Terán, Antonio (1977): *Sevilla en la Baja Edad Media*. Seville: Sección de Publicaciones del Excmo. Ayuntamiento.

Comas, Juan (1951): *Racial Myths*. Paris: UNESCO.

Contreras, Jaime (1982): *El Santo Oficio de la Inquisición en Galicia 1560–1700: Poder, Sociedad y Cultura*. Madrid: Akal Editor.

Contreras, Jaime (1984): 'El Sentido de la Coyuntura: La Fase Conversa y Morisca' in Pérez Villanueva, Joaquín and Escandell Bonet, Bartolomé (eds) (1984), pp. 427–33.

Contreras, Jaime (1987): 'The Impact of Protestantism in Spain 1520–1600' in Haliczer, Stephen P. (ed.) (1987) pp. 47–66.

Contreras, Jaime and Henningsen, Gustav (1986): 'Forty-four Thousand Cases of the Spanish Inquisition (1540–1700): Analysis of a Historical Data Bank' in Henningsen, Gustav and Tedeschi, John (eds) (1986) pp. 100–29.

Correia e Silva, António Leáo (1996): *Histórias de um Sahel Insular*. Praia, Spleen-Ediçoes.

Correia-Afonso, John (ed.) (1981): *Indo-Portuguese History: Sources and Problems*. Bombay: Oxford University Press.

Crews, Frederick (1993): 'The Unknown Freud' in *New York Review of Books*, Vol. 40, no. 19. pp. 55–66.

Croitoru Rotbaum, Itic (1967): *De Sefarad al Neosefardismo: Contribución a la Historia de Colombia*. Bogotá: Editorial Kelly.

David, Maurice (1933): *Who was 'Columbus'? His Real Name and Fatherland – A Sensational Discovery Among the Archives of Spain*. New York: Research Publishing Company.

Davis, David Brion (1994): 'The Slave Trade and the Jews', in *New York Review of Books*, Vol. 41, no 21, 22 December 1994, pp. 14–16.

Dedieu, Jean-Pierre (1983): 'Les Morisques de Daimiel et l'Inquisition – 1502–1526' in Cardaillac, Louis (ed.) (1983) pp. 495–522.

Dedieu, Jean-Pierre (1989): *L'Administration de la Foi: L'Inquisition de Tolède (XVIe–XVIIIe Siècles)*. Madrid: Casa de Velázquez.

Dedieu, Jean-Pierre (1997): 'L'Inquisition Face Aux Morisques: Aspects Juridiques' in Cardaillac, Louis (ed.) (1990) pp. 110–27.

Dedieu, Jean-Pierre and García-Arenal, Mercedes (1997): 'Les Tribunaux de Nouvelle Castille' in Cardaillac, Louis (ed.) (1990) pp. 276–95.

Dedieu, Jean-Pierre and Vincent, Bernard (1990): 'Face à l'Inquisition: Jugements et Attitudes des Morisques à l'Égard du Tribunal' in Cardaillac, Louis (ed.) (1990) pp. 81–93.

Defourneaux, Marcelin (1963): *L'Inquisition Espagnole et les Livres Français au XVIIIe Siècle*. Paris: Presses Universitaires de France.

Delumeau, Jean (1978): *La Peur en Occident (XIVe-XVIIIe Siècles): Une Cité Assiégée*. Paris: Fayard.

Dias, Manuel Nunes (1963–4): *O Capitalismo Monárquico Português: Contribuição para o Estudo das Orignes do Capitalismo Moderno*. Coimbra: Faculdade de Létras da Universidade de Coimbra, Instituto de Estudos Históricos Dr. António de Vasconcelos, 2 vols.

Dias, J.S. da Silva (1975): *O Erasmismo e a Inquisição em Portugal: O Processo de Fr. Valentim da Luz*. Coimbra: Universidade de Coimbra.

Diffie, Bailey W. and Winius, George D. (1977): *Foundations of the Portuguese Empire 1415–1580*. Minneapolis: University of Minnesota Press.

Disney, Anthony (1981): 'The Portuguese Empire in India, *c.* 1550–1650' in Correia-Afonso, John (ed.) (1981) pp. 148–62.

Domínguez Ortiz, Antonio (1971): *Los Judeoconversos en España y América.* Madrid: Ediciones Istmo.

Domínguez Ortiz, Antonio (1993, first published 1991): *Los Judeoconversos en la España Moderna.* Madrid: Editorial Mapfre.

Domínguez Ortiz, Antonio and Vincent, Bernard (1978): *Historia de los Moriscos: Vida y Tragedia de una Minoria.* Madrid: Editorial Revista de Occidente.

Douglas, Mary (1984; first published 1966): *Purity and Danger: An Analysis of the Concepts of Pollution and Taboo.* London: Routledge.

Drescher, Seymour (2001): 'Jews and New Christians in the Atlantic Slave Trade' in Bernardini, Paolo and Fiering, Norman (eds) (2001) pp. 439–70.

Dufourcq, Ch.-E. and Gautier Dalché, J. (1976): *Histoire Économique et Sociale de l'Espagne Chrétienne au Moyen Âge.* Paris: Armand Colin.

Edwards, John (1999): *The Spanish Inquisition.* Stroud: Tempus Publishing.

Egido, T. (1984a): 'La España del Siglo XVIII' in Pérez Villanueva, Joaquín and Escandell Bonet, Bartolomé (eds) (1984) pp. 1204–10.

Egido, T. (1984b): 'Los Hechos y las Actividades Inquisitoriales' in Pérez Villanueva, Joaquín and Escandell Bonet, Bartolomé (eds) (1984) pp. 1227–47.

Epalza, Míkel de (1992): *Los Moriscos Antes y Después de la Expulsión.* Madrid: Editorial Mapfre.

Epalza, Mikel de (1997): 'Le Lexique Religieux des Morisques et la Litterature Aljamiado-Morisque' in Cardaillac, Louis (ed.) (1990) pp. 51–64.

Escandell Bonet, Bartolomé (1980): 'Una Lectura Psico-Social de los Papeles del Santo-Oficio: Inquisición y Sociedad Peruana en el Siglo XVI' in Pérez Villanueva (ed.) (1980), pp. 437–67.

Escandell Bonet, Bartolomé (1984a): 'El "Fenomeno Inquisitorial": Naturaleza Sociológica e Infraestructura Histórica' in Pérez Villanueva, Joaquín and Escandell Bonet, Bartolomé (eds) (1984) pp. 220–7.

Escandell Bonet, Bartolomé (1984b): 'El Tribunal Peruano en la Época de Felipe II' in Pérez Villanueva, Joaquín and Escandell Bonet, Bartolomé (eds) (1984), pp. 919–37.

Escandell Bonet, Bartolomé (1984c): 'La Coyuntura Ideológica: Procesos y Carácteres de la Etapa' in Pérez Villanueva, Joaquín and Escandell Bonet, Bartolomé (eds) (1984) pp. 434–43.

Escandell Bonet, Bartolomé (1984d): 'Las Adecuaciones Estructurales: Establecimiento de la Inquisición en Indias' in Pérez Villanueva, Joaquín and Escandell Bonet, Bartolomé (eds) (1984) pp. 713–29.

Espejo, Cristóbal and Paz, Julián (1908): *Las Antiguas Ferias de Medina del Campo.* Valladolid: La Nueva Pincia.

Eysenck, Hans (1985): *Decline and Fall of the Freudian Empire.* Harmondsworth: Penguin.

Faur, José (1992): *In the Shadow of Modernity: Jews and* Conversos *at the Dawn of Modernity*. Albany: State University of New York Press.

Fernández, André (2003): *Au Nom du Sexe: Inquisition et Répression Sexuelle en Aragon (1560–1700)*. Paris: Éditions L'Harmattan.

Fernández-Armesto, Felipe (1982): *The Canary Islands After the Conquest: The Making of a Colonial Society in the Early Sixteenth Century*. Oxford: Clarendon Press.

Fernández-Armesto, Felipe (1995): 'Medieval Atlantic Exploration: The Evidence of Maps' in Winius, George D. (ed.) (1995) pp. 41–70.

Fernández García, María de los Angeles (1995): 'Criterios Inquisitoriales Para Detectar al Marrano: Los Criptojudíos en Andalucía en los Siglos XVI y XVII' in Alcalá, Angel (ed.) (1995) pp. 478–502.

Fernández Nieto, F. J. et al. (eds) (1998): *Luis Vives y el Humanismo Europeo*. Valencia: Universitat de València.

Fernández Santamaría, José A. (1990): *Juan Luis Vives: Escepticismo y Prudencia en el Renacimiento*. Salamanca: Ediciones Universidad de Salamanca.

Fernández Vargas, Valentina (1980): 'Dos Noticias Sobre la Inquisición Española: Una Primera Aproximación Sobre Ciertos Aspectos de la Incidencia del Santo Oficio en la Vida Cotidiana de la España del Siglo XVII' in Pérez Villanueva, Joaquín (ed.) (1980) pp. 931–5.

Ferrer Benimeli, José Antonio (1976–7): *Masonería, Iglesia e Ilustración: Un Conflicto Ideológico-Político-Religioso*. Madrid: Fundación Universitaria Española, Seminario Cisneros.

Ferrer Benimeli, José A. (1984): 'Pombal y la Masonería', in Santos, Maria Helena Carvalho dos (ed.) (1984), Vol. 1, pp. 75–95.

Fleches, Claude-Henri (1982–3): 'Pombal et la Compagnie de Jesus: La Campagne de Pamphlets' in Torgal, Luís Reis and Vargues, Isabel (eds) (1982–3), Vol. 1, pp. 299–327.

Fletcher, Richard (1992): *Moorish Spain*. London: Weidenfeld & Nicolson.

Fonseca, Luis Adão da (1995): 'The Discovery of Atlantic Space' in Winius, George D. (ed.) (1995) pp. 5–18.

Foucault, Michel (1976): *Histoire de la Sexualité*. Paris: Gallimard.

Fredrickson, George M. (2002): *Racism: A Short History*. Princeton: Princeton University Press.

Freud, Sigmund (1961a): 'The Loss of Reality in Neurosis and Psychosis' in *The Standard Edition of the Complete Psychological Works of Sigmund Freud*, ed. Strachey, James (ed.) (London: Hogarth Press) Vol. 19, pp. 183–7.

Freud, Sigmund (1961b): 'A Seventeenth-Century Demonological Neurosis' in *The Standard Edition of the Complete Psychological Works of Sigmund Freud*, Strachey, James (ed.) (London: Hogarth Press) Vol. 19, pp. 72–105.

Fromm, Erich (1951): *Psychoanalysis and Religion*. London: Victor Gollancz.

García, Angelina (1987): *Els Vives: Una Familia de Jueus Valencians*. València: Edifeu Climent, Editor.

García-Arenal, Mercedes (1978): *Inquisición y Moriscos: Los Procesos del Tribunal de Cuenca*. Madrid: Siglo XXI de España Editores S.A.

García-Arenal, Mercedes (1996): *Los Moriscos*. Granada: Universidad de Granada.

García Camarero, Ernesto and Enrique (eds) (1970): *La Polémica de la Ciencia Española*. Madrid: Alianza Editorial.

García Cárcel, Ricardo (1976): *Orígenes de la Inquisición Española: El Tribunal de Valencia, 1478–1530*. Barcelona: Ediciones Península.

García Cárcel, Ricardo (1997): 'L'Inquisition de Valence' in Cardaillac, Louis (ed.) (1990) pp. 153–70.

García Cárcel, Ricardo and Moreno Martínez, Doris (2000): *Inquisición: Historia Crítica*. Madrid: Ediciones Temas de Hoy.

Garrett, Don (ed.) (1996): *The Cambridge Companion to Spinoza*. Cambridge: Cambridge University Press.

Gil, Juan (2000–1): *Los Conversos y la Inquisición Sevillana*. Sevilla: Universidad de Sevilla – Fundación El Monte, 5 vols.

Gilman, Stephen (1972): *The Spain of Fernando de Rojas: The Intellectual and Social Landscape of La Celestina*. Princeton: Princeton University Press.

Gitlitz, David M. (1996): *Secrecy and Deceit: The Religion of the Crypto-Jews*. Philadelphia and Jerusalem: Jewish Publication Society.

Godinho, Vitorino Magalhães (1969): *L'Économie de l'Empire Portugais aux XVe et XVIe Siècles*. Paris: S.E.V.P.E.N.

Godinho, Vitorino Magalhães (1981): *Os Descobrimentos e a Economia Mundial*. Lisbon: Editorial Presença, 4 vols.

Gómez-Menor, José-Carlos (1995): 'Linaje Judío de los Escritores Religiosos y Místicos Españoles del Siglo XVI' in Alcalá, Angel (ed.) (1995) pp. 587–600.

Gonsalves de Mello, José Antônio (1996): *Gente da Nação: Cristãos-novos e Judeus em Pernambuco, 1542–1654*. Recife: Fundação Joaquim Nabuco, Editora Massangana.

González Gónzalez, Enrique (1998): 'La Crítica de los Humanistas a las Universidades. El Caso de Vives' in F. J. Fernández Nieto et al. (eds) (1998), pp. 13–40.

Gottheil, Richard (1971, first published 1901): 'Fray Joseph Diaz Pimienta, Alias Abraham Diaz Pimienta, And the Auto-da-Fé Held at Seville, July 25, 1720', in Cohen, Martin A. (ed.) (1971a) Vol. II, pp. 56–65.

Gouhier, Henri (1958): *Les Premières Pensées de Descartes: Contribution à l'Histoire de l'Anti-Renaissance*. Paris: Librairie Philosophique J. Vrin.

Gracia Guillén, Diego (1987): 'Judaism, Medicine, and the Inquisitorial Mind in Sixteenth-Century Spain' in Alcalá, Angel (ed.) (1987) pp. 375–400

Graizbord, David L. (2004): *Souls in Dispute: Converso Identities in Iberia and the Jewish Diaspora, 1580–1700*. Philadelphia: University of Pennsylvania Press.

Green, Tobias (2005): 'Further Considerations on the Sephardim of the Petite Cote', in *History in Africa* 32 (2005), pp. 165–83.

Green, Tobias (2006): 'Fear and Atlantic History: Some Observations Derived From the Cape Verde Islands and the African Atlantic' in *Journal of Atlantic Studies* 3, Vol. 1, pp. 25–43.

Green, Tobias (2007): *Masters of Difference: Creolization and the Jewish Presence in Cabo Verde, 1497–1672*. Birmingham: University of Birmingham, (unpublished PhD thesis).

Green, Toby (2004): *Thomas More's Magician: A Novel Account of Utopia in Mexico*. London: Weidenfeld & Nicolson.

Greenleaf, Richard E. (1969): *The Mexican Inquisition of the Sixteenth Century*. Albuquerque: University of New Mexico Press.

Grendler, Paul F. (1977): *The Roman Inquisition and the Venetian Press, 1540–1605*. Princeton: Princeton University Press.

Griffiths, Nicholas (1997): 'Popular Religious Scepticism in Post-Tridentine Cuenca' in Twomey Leslie (ed.) (1997), pp. 95–126.

Guibovich Pérez, Pedro (1998): *En Defensa de Dios: Estudios y Documentos Sobre la Inquisición en el Perú*. Lima: Ediciones del Congreso del Perú.

Guibovich Pérez, Pedro (2000): *La Inquisición y la Censura de Libros en el Perú Virreinal (1570–1813)*. Lima: Ediciones del Congreso del Perú.

Gutwirth, Eleazar (1992): 'Towards Expulsion: 1391–1492' in Kedourie, Elie (ed.) (1992) pp. 51–75.

Haliczer, Stephen (ed. and trans.) (1987): *Inquisition and Society in Early Modern Europe*. London: Croom Helm.

Hall, Trevor P. (1992): *The Role of Cape Verde Islanders in Organizing and Operating Maritime Trade Between West Africa and Iberian Territories, 1441–1616*. Baltimore: Johns Hopkins University, 2 vols (unpublished PhD thesis).

Hamilton, Alastair (1992): *Heresy and Mysticism in Sixteenth-Century Spain: The* Alumbrados. Cambridge: James Clarke & Co.

Havik, Philip (2004a): 'La Sorcellerie, L'Acculturation et le Genre: La Persécution Religieuse de l'Inquisition Portugaise Contre les Femmes Africaines Converties en Haut Guinée (XVIIe Siècle)' in *Revista Lusófona de Ciência das Religiões*, Ano III, 2004, no. 5/6, pp. 99–116 – also published at http://cienciareligioes.ulusofona.pt

Havik, Philip J. (2004b): *Silences and Soundbytes: The Gendered Dynamics of Trade and Brokerage in the pre-Colonial Guinea Bissau Region*. Muenster/New York: Lit Verlag/Transaction Publishers.

Henningsen, Gustav (1980): *The Witches' Advocate: Basque Witchcraft and the Spanish Inquisition (1609–1614)*. Reno: University of Nevada Press.

Henningsen, Gustav and Tedeschi, John (eds) (1986): *The Inquisition in Early Modern Europe: Studies and Sources on Methods*. Dekalb, Ill.: Northern Illinois University Press.

Herculano, A (1854): *Da Origem e Estabelecimento da Inquisição em Portugal: Tentativas Históricas*. Lisbon: Imprensa Nacional, 3 vols.

Hirschberg, H.Z. (J.W.) (1974): *A History of the Jews in North Africa*. Leiden: E.J. Brill, Eichelberg, M. (trans.).

Huerga, Álvaro (1978–88): *Historia de Los Alumbrados (1570–1630)*. Madrid: Fundación Universitaria Española, 4 vols.

Huerga, Álvaro (1984): 'El Tribunal de México en la Época de Felipe II' in Pérez Villanueva, Joaquín and Escandell Bonet, Bartolomé (eds) (1984) pp. 937–69.

Isaac, Benjamin (2004): *The Invention of Racism in Classical Antiquity*. Princeton: Princeton University Press.

Israel, Jonathan I. (1982): *The Dutch Republic and the Hispanic World, 1606–1661*. Oxford: Oxford University Press.

Israel, Jonathan I. (1990): *Empires and Entrepots: The Dutch, The Spanish Monarchy and the Jews, 1585–1713*. London and Ronceverte: Hambledon Press.

Israel, Jonathan I. (1992a): 'The Sephardi Contribution to Economic Life and Colonization in Europe and the New World (16th–18th centuries)', in Beinart, Haim (1992a) Vol. II, pp. 365–98.

Israel, Jonathan (1992b): 'The Sephardim in the Netherlands' in Kedourie, Elie (ed.) (1992), pp. 189–212.

Israel, Jonathan I. (1998a, 3rd edition): *European Jewry in the Age of Mercantilism, 1550–1750*. London and Portland, Oreg.: Littman Library of Jewish Civilisation.

Israel, Jonathan I. (1998b): *The Dutch Republic: Its Rise, Its Greatness, Its Fall*. Oxford: Oxford University Press.

Israel, Jonathan I. (2002): *Diasporas Within a Diaspora: Jews, Crypto-Jews and the World Maritime Empires (1540–1740)*. Leiden: Brill.

Jama, Sophie (2001): *L'Histoire Juive de Montaigne*. Paris: Flamarrion.

Jiménez Lozano, José (1987): 'The Persistence of Judaic and Islamic Cultures in Spanish Society, or the Failure of the Inquisition' in Alcalá, Angel (ed.) (1987) pp. 401–18.

Jiménez Monteserín, M. (1984): 'La Abolición del Tribunal (1808–1834)' in Pérez Villanueva, Joaquín and Escandell Bonet, Bartolomé (eds) (1984) pp. 1424–86.

Jiménez Rueda, Julio (1946): *Herejras y Supersticiones en la Nueva España (los Heterodoxos en México)*. Mexico City: Imprenta Universitaria.

Kamen, Henry (1965): *The Spanish Inquisition*. London: Weidenfeld & Nicolson.

Kamen, Henry (1987): 'Notes on Witchcraft, Sexuality and the Inquisition' in Alcalá, Angel (ed.) (1987) pp. 237–48.

Kamen, Henry (1992): 'The Expulsion: Purpose and Consequence' in Kedourie, Elie (ed.) (1992), pp. 74–91.

Kamen, Henry (1997): *The Spanish Inquisition: An Historical Revision*. London: Weidenfeld & Nicolson.

Kaplan, Yosef (ed.) (1985): *Jews and Conversos: Studies in Society and the Inquisition*. Jerusalem: Magnes Press.

Kaplan, Yosef (1996): *Judíos Nuevos en Amsterdam: Estudio Sobre la Historia Social y Intelectual del Judaísmo Sefardí en el Siglo XVII*. Barcelona: Editorial Gedisa S.A.

Kedourie, Elie (ed.) (1992): *Spain and the Jews: The Sephardi Experience 1492 and After*. London: Thames & Hudson.

Kinder, A. Gordon (1997): 'Spain's Little-Known "Noble Army of Martyrs" and the Black Legend', in Twomey, Lesley K. (ed.) (1997) pp. 61–83.

Klever, W.N.A. (1996): 'Spinoza's Life and Works' in Garrett, Don (ed.) (1996) pp. 13–60.

Kohut, George Alexander (1971, first published 1896): 'Jewish Martyrs of the Inquisition in South America' in Cohen, Martin A. (ed.) (1971a) Vol. I, pp. 1–87.

Kriegel, Maurice (1995): 'El Edicto de Expulsión: Motivos, Fines, Contexto', in Alcalá, Angel (ed.) (1995) pp. 134–49.

La Mantia, Vito (1977): *Origine e Vicende dell'Inquisizione in Sicilia*. Palermo: Sellerio Editore, 2nd edition.

Ladero Quesada, Miguel Angel (1976): *La Ciudad Medieval (1248–1492)*. Seville: Secretaria de Publicaciones de la Universidad de Sevilla.

Ladero Quesada, Miguel Ángel (1992): 'Los Judeoconversos en Castilla del Siglo XV' in *Historia* 16 (1992), pp. 42–44.

Ladero Quesada, Miguel Angel (1995): 'El Número de Judíos en la España de 1492: Los que se Fueron', in Alcalá, Angel (ed.) (1995), pp. 170–80.

Ladero Quesada, Miguel Angel (1999): *La España de los Reyes Católicos*. Madrid: Alianza Editorial.

Lea, H.C. (1906–7): *A History of the Inquisition of Spain*. New York: Macmillan Company, 3 vols.

Lea, H.C. (1908): *The Inquisition in the Spanish Dependencies: Sicily, Naples, Sardinia, Milan, the Canaries, Mexico, Peru, New Granada*. New York: Macmillan Company.

Lea, H.C. (1963): *The Inquisition of the Middle Ages: Its Organization and Operation*. London: Eyre and Spottiswoode.

Lea, H.C. (2001): *Los Moriscos Españoles: Su Conversión y Expulsión*. Alicante: Publicaciones de la Universidade de Alicante, Miralles, Jaime Lorenzo (trans.).

León Tello, Pilar (1979): *Judíos de Toledo*. Madrid: Consejo Superior de Investigaciones Científicas, Instituto 'B Arias Montano', 2 vols.

Lewin, Boleslao (1960): *Los Judíos Bajo la Inquisición en Hispanoamérica*. Buenos Aires: Editorial Dedalo.

Lewin, Boleslao (1967): *La Inquisición en Hispano américa: Judíos, Protestantes y Patriotas*. Buenos Aires: Editorial Paidos.

Liebman, Seymour B. (1970): *The Jews in New Spain: Faith, Flame and Inquisition*. Coral Gables: University of Miami Press.

Liebman, Seymour B. (1971): 'The Secret Jewry in the Spanish New World Colonies: 1500–1820' in Barnett, R.D. (ed.) (1971), Vol. II, pp. 474–96.

Liebman, Seymour B. (1992): 'The Religion and Mores of the Colonial New World Marranos' in Novinsky, Anita and Carneiro, Maria Luiza Tucci (eds) (1992) pp. 49–71.

Lipiner, Elias (1969): *Os Judaizantes nas Capitanias da Cima (Estudos Sôbre os Cristãos Novos do Brasil nos Séculos XVI e XVII).* São Paulo: Editôra Brasiliense.

Lipiner, Elias (1977): *Santa Inquisição: Terror e Linguagem.* Rio de Janeiro: Editora Documentário.

Lipiner, Elias (1985): 'O Cristão-Novo: Mito ou Realidade' in Kaplan, Yosef (ed.) (1985) pp. 124–38.

Llamas Martínez, Enrique (1972): *Santa Teresa de Jesús y la Inquisición Española.* Madrid: Consejo Superior de Investigaciones Científicas.

Llorca, Bernardino (1980): *La Inquisición Española y los Alumbrados (1509–1667).* Salamanca: Universidad Pontificia.

Llorente, J.-A. (1818): *Historie Critique de l'Inquisition: depuis l' époque de son établissement par Fernando V, jusqu' au règne de Fernando VII: tirée des pièces originales des archives du Conseil de la Suprême et de celles des tribunaux subalternes du Saint-office.* Paris: Treuttel et Wurtz, Pellier, Alexis (trans.) 4 vols.

Llorente, J.-A. (1841): *Anales de la Inquisición: Desde que fue Instituido Aquel Tribunal Hasta su Total Extinción en el año 1834.* Madrid: Imp. Calle Angosta de S. Bernardo num. 22.

Lobo, António de Sousa Silva Costa (1979, first published 1903): *História da Sociedade en Portugal no Século XV e Outros Estudos Históricos.* Lisbon: Cooperativa Editora.

Loeb, I (1887): 'Le Nombre des Juifs de Castille et d'Espagne' in *Revue des Études Juives*, Vol. 14, pp. 161–83.

Lopes, Edmundo Correia (1944): *Escravatura: Subsídios para a sua Historia.* Lisbon: Agência Geral do Ultramar.

López Martínez, Nicolás (1954): *Los Judaizantes Castellanos y la Inquisición en Tiempo de Isabel la Católica.* Burgos: Publicaciones del Seminario Metropolitano de Burgos.

Malvezin, Théophile (1875): *Michel de Montaigne: Son Origine, Sa Famille.* Bordeaux: Charles Lefebvre, Librairie-Éditeur.

Mann, Charles C. (2005): *Ancient Americans: Rewriting the History of the New World.* London: Granta.

Marañon, Gregorio (2004): *Expulsión y Diaspora de los Moriscos Españoles.* Madrid: Santillana Ediciones Generales.

Marques, A.H. de Oliveira (1972): *History of Portugal.* New York: Columbia University Press, 2 vols.

Marquez, Antonio (1972): *Los Alumbrados: Orígenes y Filosofía 1525–1559.* Madrid: Taurus Ediciones.

Marquez, Antonio (1980): *Literatura e Inquisición en España (1478–1834).* Madrid: Taurus Ediciones.

Marti Gilabert, Francisco (1975): *La Abolición de la Inquisición en España.* Pamplona: Ediciones Universidad de Navarra S.A.

Martín, Melquiades Andres (1975): *Los Recogidos: Nueva Visión de la Mística Española.* Madrid: Fundación Universitaria Española.

Martínez de Bujanda, Jesús (1980): 'Literatura e Inquisición en España en el Siglo XVI' in Pérez Villanueva, Joaquín (ed.) (1980) pp. 579–92.

Martínez Millán, José (1984): *La Hacienda de la Inquisición (1478–1700)*. Madrid: Consejo Superior de Investigaciones Científicas – Instituto Enrique Flores.

Martínez Millán and Dedieu, Jean-Pierre (1990): 'Les Morisques et les Finances Inquisitoriales' in Cardaillac, Louis (ed.) (1990) pp. 128–48.

Masson, Jeffrey (1990): *Against Therapy*. London: Fontana.

Mauro, Frédéric (1991): *O Império Luso-Brasileiro 1620–1750*. Lisbon: Editorial Estampa.

Maxwell, Kenneth (1995): *Pombal: Paradox of the Enlightenment*. Cambridge: Cambridge University Press.

Mea, Elvira Cunha de Azevedo (1997): *A Inquisição de Coimbra no Século XVI: A Instituição, Os Homens e a Sociedade*. Porto: Fundação Eng. António de Almeida.

Mello, José Antônio Gonsalves de (1996, first published 1992): *Gente da Nação: Cristãos-Novos e Judeus em Pernambuco, 1542–1654*. Recife: Fundação Joaquim Nabuco, Editora Massangana.

Mendes, António de Almeida (2004): 'Le Rôle de l'Inquisition en Guinée: Vicissitudes des Présences Juives Sur la Petite Côte (XVe–XVIIe Siècles)', in *Revista Lusófona de Ciência das Religiões*, Ano III, 2004, no.5/6, pp. 137–55, also published at http://cienciareligioes.ulusofona.pt

Mendonça, José Lourenço D. de and Moreira, António Joaquim (1980, first published 1842): *História dos Principais Actos e Procedimentos da Inquisição em Portugal*. Lisbon: Imprensa Nacional, Casa da Moeda.

Menéndez y Pelayo, Marcelino (1945): *Historia de los Heterodoxos Españoles*. Buenos Aires: Emecé Editores S.A., 8 vols.

Mesa Bernal, Daniel (1996): *De los Judíos en la Historia de Colombia*. Santa Fe de Bogotá: Planeta Colombiana Editorial.

Meseguer Fernández, Juan (1980): 'Fernando de Talavera, Cisneros y la Inquisición en Granada' in Pérez Villanueva, Joaquín (ed.) (1980) pp. 371–400.

Meseguer Fernández, Juan (1984): 'El Periodo Fundacional (1478–1517): Los Hechos' in Pérez Villanueva, Joaquín and Escandell Bonet, Bartolomé (eds) (1984) pp. 281–370.

Mestre, A. (1984): 'Inquisición y Corrientes Ilustradas', in Pérez Villanueva, Joaquín and Escandell Bonet, Bartolomé (eds) (1984) pp. 1247–65.

Millar Carvacho, René (1997): *Inquisición y Sociedad en el Virreinato Peruano: Estudios Sobre el Tribunal de la Inquisición en Lima*. Santiago de Chile: Ediciones Universidad Católica de Chile.

Millares Torres, Agustín (1981, first published 1874): *Historia de la Inquisición en las Islas Canárias*. Santa Cruz de Tenerife: Editorial Benchoma.

Mirsky, Jonathan (2006): 'China: The Shame of the Villages' in *New York Review of Books*, Vol. 53 no. 8, pp. 37–9.

Monín, José (1939): *Los Judíos en la América Española, 1492–1810*. Buenos Aires: Biblioteca Yavne.

Monteiro, Yara Nogueira (1992): 'Os Portugueses e a Ação Inquisitorial no Peru: Aspectos de Uma Perseguição Política' in Novinsky, Anita and Carneiro, Maria Luiza Tucci (eds) (1992) pp. 337–54.

Monter, William (1990): *Frontiers of Heresy: The Spanish Inquisition from the Basque Lands to Sicily*. Cambridge: Cambridge University Press.

Moore, R.I. (1987): *The Formation of a Persecuting Society: Power and Deviance in Western Europe, 950–1250*. Oxford and Cambridge, Mass.: Blackwell.

Moreno, Humberto Baquero (1985): 'Movimentos Sociais Anti-Judaicos em Portugal no Século XV' in Kaplan, Yosef (ed.) (1985) pp. 62–73.

Moreno Mancebo, M. (1984): 'Más Sobre el Proceso Inquisitorial de Pablo de Olavide' in Pérez Villanueva, Joaquín and Escandell Bonet, Bartolomé (eds) (1984) pp. 1265–76.

Mota, Avelino Teixeira de (1978): *Some Aspects of Portuguese Colonization and Sea Trade in West Africa in the 15th and 16th Centuries*. Bloomington: Indiana University.

Mott, Luiz (1988): *O Sexo Proibido: Virgens, Gays e Escravos nas Garras da Inquisição*. Campinas: Papyrus Editora.

Mott, Luiz (1992): 'Justitia et Misericordia: A Inquisição Portuguesa e a Repressão ao Nefando Peccado de Sodomía' in Novinsky, Anita and Carneiro, Maria Luiza Tucci (eds) (1992) pp. 703–38.

Netanyahu, B. (1966): *The Marranos of Spain: from the late XIVth to the early XVIth century, according to contemporary Hebrew sources*. New York: American Academy of Jewish Research.

Netanyahu, B. (1995a): *The Origins of the Inquisition in Fifteenth Century Spain*. New York: Random House.

Netanyahu, B. (1995b): 'Una Visión Española de la História Judía en España: Sánchez Albornoz', in Alcalá, Angel (ed.) (1995) pp. 89–121.

Netanyahu, B. (1997): *Towards the Inquisition: Essays on Jewish and Converso History in Late Medieval Spain*. Ithaca: Cornell University Press.

Newitt, Malyn (1995): *A History of Mozambique*. London: Hurst & Company.

Newitt, Malyn (2005): *A History of Portuguese Overseas Expansion, 1400–1668*. Abingdon: Routledge.

Nieto, José C. (1970): *Juan de Valdes and the Origins of the Spanish and Italian Reformation*. Geneva: Librairie Droz.

Nirenberg, David (1998, first published 1996): *Communities of Violence: Persecution of Minorities in the Middle Ages*. Princeton: Princeton University Press.

Novalín, José Luis G. (1968–71): *El Inquisidor General Fernando de Valdés (1483–1568)*. Oviedo: Universidad de Oviedo, 2 vols.

Novinsky, Anita (1971): 'Sephardim in Brazil: The New Christians', in Barnett, R. D. (ed.) (1971), Vol. 2, pp. 431–44.

Novinsky, Anita (1972): *Cristãos Novos na Bahia*. São Paulo: Editôra Perspectiva.

Novinsky, Anita (1995): 'Consideraciones Sobre los Criptojudíos Hispano-Portugueses: El Caso de Brasil' in Alcalá, Angel (ed.) (1995) pp. 513–22.

Novinsky, Anita and Carneiro, Maria Luiza Tucci (eds) (1992): *Inquisição: Ensaios Sobre Mentalidade, Heresias e Arte*. São Paulo: Editora Expressão e Cultura.

Osorio Osorio, Alberto (1980): *Judaismo e Inquisición en Panamá Colonial*. Panamá: Litho-Impresora Panamá S.A.

Paiva, José Pedro (1997): *Bruxaria e Superstição num País sem 'Caça às Bruxas', 1600–1774*. Lisbon: Editorial Notícias.

Palmer, Colin A. (1976): *Slaves of the White God: Blacks in Mexico, 1570–1650*. Cambridge, Mass.: Harvard University Press.

Patai, Raphael and Jennifer (1989, revised edition): *The Myth of the Jewish Race*. Detroit: Wayne State University Press.

Paulo, Amílcar, (n.d.): *Os Criptojudeus*. Porto: Livraria Athena.

Pedraza Jiménez, Felipe B. et al. (eds) (2001): *La Celestina: V Centenario (1499–1999)*. Cuenca: Ediciones de la Universidad Castilla La Mancha.

Perceval, José María (1997): *Todos Son Uno: Arquetipos, Xenofobia y Racismo. La Imagen del Morisco en la Monarquía Española Durante los Siglos XVI y XVII*. Almería: Instituto de Estudios Almerienses.

Pereira, Isaías da Rosa (1982–3): 'O Auto-da-Fé de 1761' in Torgal, Luís Reis and Vargues, Isabel (eds) (1982–3), Vol. 1, pp. 367–376.

Pereira, Isaías Rosa (1993): *A Inquisição em Portugal: Séculos XVI–XVII – Período Filipino*. Lisbon: Vega Gabinete de Edições.

Pérez Castro, Federico (1971): 'España y los Judíos Españoles' in Barnett, R.D. (ed.) (1971), Vol. I, pp. 275–313.

Pérez Canto, P. (1984): 'Tribunal de Lima' in Pérez Villanueva, Joaquín and Escandell Bonet, Bartolomé (eds) (1984) pp. 1133–41.

Pérez Villanueva, Joaquín (ed.) (1980): *La Inquisición Española: Nueva Visión, Nuevos Horizontes*. Madrid: Siglo XXI de España Editores, S.A.

Pérez Villanueva, Joaquín (1984): 'Felipe IV y su Política' in Pérez Villanueva, Joaquín and Escandell Bonet, Bartolomé (eds) (1984) pp. 1006–79.

Pérez Villanueva, Joaquín and Escandell Bonet, Bartolomé (eds) (1984): *Historia de la Inquisición en España y América*. Madrid: Biblioteca de Autores Cristianos.

Perry, Mary Elizabeth (1987): 'Beatas and the Inquisition in Early Modern Seville' in Haliczer, Stephen P. (1987) pp. 147–68.

Piccini, Amina Maggi (1992): 'Visão Psicoanalítica do Imaginário dos Inquisidores e das Bruxas' in Novinsky, Anita and Carneiro, Maria Luiza Tucci (eds) (1992) pp. 72–93.

Pieroni, Geraldo (2003): *Banidos: A Inquisição e a Lista dos Cristãos-Novos Condenados a Viver no Brasil*. Rio de Janeiro: Bertrand Brasil.

Pinta Llorente, Miguel de la (1953–58): *La Inquisición Española y los Problemas de la Cultura y de la Intolerancia*. Madrid: Ediciones Cultura Hispánica, 2 vols.

Pinta Llorente, Miguel de la (1961): *Aspectos Históricos del Sentimiento Religioso en*

España: Ortodoxía y Heterodoxía. Madrid: Consejo Superior de Investigaciones Científicas, Escuela de Historia Moderna.

Pinto Crespo, Virgilio (1983): *Inquisición y Control Ideológico en la España del Siglo XVI*. Madrid: Taurus Ediciones.

Pinto Crespo, Virgilio (1987): 'Thought Control in Spain' in Haliczer, Stephen P. (ed.) (1987) pp. 171–88.

Poliakov, Léon (2003, first published 1973): *The History of Anti-Semitism, Volume II: From Mohammed to the Marranos*. Philadelphia: University of Pennsylvania Press, Gerardi, Natalie (trans.).

Popkin, Richard H. (1960): *The History of Scepticism from Erasmus to Descartes*. Assen: Van Gorcum & Comp. N.V., Dr H.J. Prakke and H.M.G. Prakke.

Rawlings, Helen (2006): *The Spanish Inquisition*. Oxford: Blackwell.

Reglà, Joan (1974): *Estudios Sobre los Moriscos*. Barcelona: Ariel Quicencal, 3rd edition.

Rêgo, Raul (1984): 'O Marquês de Pombal, os Cristãos Novos e a Inquisição' in Santos, Maria Helena Carvalho dos (ed.) (1984) Vol. 1, pp. 307–35.

Remedios, J. Mendes dos (1895–1928): *Os Judeus em Portugal*. Coimbra: F. França Amado-Editor, 2 vols.

Remedios, J. Mendes dos (1911): *Os Judeus Portugueses em Amsterdam*. Coimbra: Atlantida Editora.

Reparaz, Gonçalo de (1976): *Os Portugueses no Vice-Reinado do Peru (Séculos XVI e XVII)*. Lisbon: Instituto de Alta Cultura.

Révah, I.S. (1957): 'Une Famille de "nouveaux-chrétiens": les Bocarro-Francês' in *Revue des Études Juives*, no. 116, (1957), pp. 73–86.

Révah, I.S. (1959): 'Les Marranes' in *Revue des Études Juives*, no. 118, pp. 29–77.

Révah, I.S. (1960): *La Censure Inquisitoriale Portugaise au XVIe Siècle*. Lisbon: Instituto de Alta Cultura.

Révah, I.S. (1971): 'Les Marranes Portugais et l'Inquisition au XVIe Siècle' in Barnett, R.D. (ed.) (1971) Vol. I., pp. 479–526.

Ribenboim, José Alexandre (1995): *Senhores de Engenho: Judeus em Pernambuco Colonial 1542–1654*. Recife: 20–20 Comunicação e Editora.

Riley, Carlos (1998): 'Ilhas Atlânticas e Costa Africana' in Bethencourt, Francisco and Chaudhuri, Kirti (eds) (1998a) pp. 137–62.

Rivkin, Ellis (1995): 'Los Cristianos Nuevos Portugueses y la Formación del Mundo Moderno' in Alcalá, Angel (ed.) (1995) pp. 409–19.

Roth, Cecil (1959, first published 1932): *A History of the Marranos*. New York: Meridian Books, Inc.

Roth, Norman (1994): *Jews, Visigoths and Muslims in Medieval Spain: Cooperation and Conflict*. Leiden: E.J. Brill.

Roth, Norman (2002, 2nd edition): *Conversos, Inquisition, and the Expulsion of the Jews From Spain*. Madison: University of Wisconsin Press.

Rowland, Robert (2001): 'New Christian, Marrano, Jew' in Bernardini, Paolo and Fiering, Norman (eds) (2001) pp. 129–48.

Ruiz, Teófilo F. (1987): 'The Holy Office in Medieval France and in Late

Medieval Castile: Origins and Contrasts' in Alcalá, Angel (ed.) (1987) pp. 33–52.

Rumeu de Armas, Antonio (1940): *Historia da la Censura Literaria Gubernativa en España*. Madrid: M. Aguilar Editor.

Rumeu de Armas, Antonio (1956): *España en el Africa Atlántica*. Madrid: Instituto de Estudios Africanos, Consejo Superior de Investigaciones Científicas.

Russell-Wood, A.J.R. (1978): 'Iberian Expansion and the Issue of Black Slavery: Changing Portuguese Attitudes, 1440–1770' in *American Historical Review*, Vol. 83, no. 1, pp. 16–42.

Russell-Wood, A.J.R. (1998): *The Portuguese Empire, 1415–1808: A World on the Move*. Baltimore: Johns Hopkins University Press.

Sabatini, Rafael (1928): *Torquemada and the Spanish Inquisition*. London: Stanley Paul & Co. Ltd.

Saínz Rodríguez, Pedro (1962): *Evolución de las Ideas Sobre la Decadencia Española*. Madrid: Ediciones Rialp, S.A.

Salvador, José Gonçalves (1969): *Cristãos-Novos, Jesuítas e Inquisição: Aspectos de sua Actuação nas Capitanias do Sul, 1530–1680*. São Paulo: Editôra da Universidade de São Paulo.

Salvador, José Gonçalves (1976): *Os Cristãos-Novos: Povoamento e Conquista do Solo Brasileiro (1530–1680)*. São Paulo: Livraria Pioneira Editora.

Salvador, José Gonçalves (1978): *Os Cristãos-Novos e o Comércio no Atlântico Meridional (com enfoque nas Capitanias do Sul 1530–1680)*. São Paulo: Livraria Pioneira Editora.

Salvador Miguel, Nicasio (2001): 'La Identidad de Fernando de Rojas' in Pedraza Jiménez, Felipe B. et al (eds) (2001) pp. 23–47.

Samuel, Edgar R. (1971): 'The Trade of the "New Christians" of Portugal in the 17th Century' in Barnett, R.D. (ed.) (1971) Vol. II, pp. 100–14.

Samuel, Edgar R. (2004): *At the Ends of the Earth: Essays on the History of the Jews in England and Portugal*. London: Jewish Historical Society of England.

Sánchez B., José Enrique (1996): 'La Herejía: Una Forma de Resistencia del Negro Contra la Estructura Social Colonial (1610–1636)' in Borja Gómez, Jaime Humberto et al. (eds) (1996) pp. 42–67.

Sánchez Ortega, María Helena (1980): 'Un Sondeo en la Historia de la Sexualidad Sobre Fuentes Inquisitoriales' in Pérez Villanueva, Joaquín (ed.) (1980) pp. 917–30.

Sánchez Ortega, María Helena (1992): *La Mujer y la Sexualidad en el Antiguo Régimen: La Perspectiva Inquisitorial*. Madrid: Ediciones Akal.

Sanmartín Bastida, Rebeca and Vidal Doval, Rosa (eds) (2005): *Las Metamorfosis de la Alegoría: Discurso y Sociedad en la Península Ibérica desde la Edad Media hasta la Edad Contemporánea*. Vervuert: Iberoamericana.

Santos, Maria Helena Carvalho dos (ed.) (1984): *Pombal Revisitado*. Lisbon: Editorial Estampa, 2 vols.

Santos, Maria Emília Madeira (ed.) (1995): *Historia Geral de Cabo Verde (1560–1650), Vol. II*. Lisbon: Instituto de Investigação Científica Tropical.

Saraiva, António (1985, first published 1969): *Inquisição e Cristãos-Novos*. Lisbon: Editorial Estampa.

Sarrión Mora, Adelina (2003): *Beatas y Endemoniadas: Mujeres Heterodoxas Ante la Inquisición, Siglos XVI a XIX*. Madrid: Alianza Editorial.

Saugnieux, Joël (1975): *Le Jansénisme Espagnole du XVIIIe Siècle: Ses Composantes et ses Sources*. Oviedo: Catedra Feijoo.

Saunders, A.C. de C.M. (1982): *A Social History of Black Slaves and Freedmen in Portugal, 1441–1555*. Cambridge: Cambridge University Press.

Scammell, G.V. (1981): 'Indigenous Assistance in the Establishment of Portuguese Power in the Indian Ocean' in Correia-Afonso, John (1981) (ed.) pp. 163–73.

Schorsch, Jonathan (2004): *Jews and Blacks in the Early Modern World*. Cambridge: Cambridge University Press.

Schwartz, Stuart B. (1985): *Sugar Plantations in the Formation of Brazilian Society: Bahia, 1550–1835*. Cambridge: Cambridge University Press.

Schwartz, Stuart B. (ed.) (1994): *Implicit Understandings: Observing, Reporting, and Reflecting on the Encounters Between Europeans and Other Peoples in the Early Modern Era*. Cambridge: Cambridge University Press.

Selke, Angela (1980): 'El Iluminismo de los Conversos y la Inquisición: Cristianismo Interior de los Alumbrados: Resentimiento y Sublimación' in Pérez Villanueva, Joaquín (ed.) (1980) pp. 617–36.

Selke, Angela (1986): *The Conversos of Majorca: Life and Death in a Crypto-Jewish Community in XVII Century Spain*. Jerusalem: Magnes Press.

Serrão, Joaquim Veríssimo (1982): *Historia de Portugal, Vol. 6: O Despotismo Iluminado (1750–1807)*. Lisbon: Editorial Verbo.

Shastry, B.S. (1981): *Studies in Indo-Portuguese History*. Bangalore: Ibh Prakashana.

Shaw, L.M.E. (1989): *Trade, Inquisition and the English Nation in Portugal, 1650–1690*. Manchester: Carcanet.

Sicroff, Albert A. (1985): *Los Estatutos de Limpieza de Sangre: Controversias entre los Siglos XV y XVII*. Madrid: Taurus Ediciones, Armiño, Mauro (trans.).

Sierra Corella, Antonio (1947): *La Censura de Libros y Papeles en España y Los Índices y Catálogos Españoles de los Prohibidos y Expurgados*. Madrid: Cuerpo Facultativo de Archiveros, Bibliotecários y Arqueólogos.

Silva, Filipa Ribeiro da (2002): *A Inquisição na Guiné, nas Ilhas de Cabo Verde e São Tomé e Príncipe (1536–1821): contributo para o estudo da política do Santo Ofício nos Territórios Africanos*. Lisbon: Universidade Nova de Lisbon, 2 vols, unpublished MA dissertation.

Silva, Filipa Ribeiro da (2004): 'A Inquisição na Guiné, nas Ilhas de Cabo Verde e São Tomé e Príncipe', in *Revista Lusofona de Ciência das Religiões*, Ano III, 2004, no. 5/6, pp. 157–73 – also published at http://cienciareligioes.ulusofona.pt

Silva, José Gentil da (1982–3): 'A Situação Femenina em Portugal na Segunda Metade do Século XVIII' in Torgal, Luís Reis and Vargues, Isabel (eds) (1982–3), Vol. 1, pp. 143–68.

Souza, George B. (1986): *The Survival of Empire: Portuguese Trade and Society in*

China and the South China Sea, 1630–1754. Cambridge: Cambridge University Press.

Souza, Laura de Mello e (1987): *O Diabo e a Terra da Santa Cruz: Feitiçaria e Religiosidade Popular no Brasil Colonial*. São Paulo: Editora Schwarz Ltda.

Stannard, David E. (1980): *Shrinking History: On Freud and the Failure of Psychohistory*. New York and Oxford: Oxford University Press.

Suárez Fernández, Luis (1980): *Judíos Españoles en la Edad Media*. Madrid: Ediciones Rialp.

Subrahmanyan, Sanjay (1993): *The Portuguese Empire in Asia, 1500–1700*. London and New York: Longman.

Sweet, James H. (2003): *Recreating Africa: Culture, Kinship, and Religion in the African-Portuguese World, 1441–1770*. Chapel Hill: University of North Carolina Press.

Tavares, Célia Cristina da Silva (2004): *Jesuítas e Inquisidores em Goa: A Cristiandade Insular*. Lisbon: Roma Editora.

Tavares, Maria José Pimenta Ferro (1982): *Os Judeus em Portugal no Século XV*. Lisbon: Universidade Nova de Lisbon, 2 vols.

Tavares, Maria José Pimenta Ferro (1987): *Judaísmo e Inquisição – Estudos*. Lisbon: Editorial Presença.

Tavim, José Alberto Rodrigues da Silva (1997): *Os Judeus na Expansão Portuguesa em Marrocos Durante o Século XVI: Origens e Actividades duma Comunidade*. Braga: Edições APPACDM Distrital de Braga.

Tellechea Idigoras, José Ignacio (1968): *El Arzobispo Carranza y su Tiempo*. Madrid: Ediciones Guadarrama, 2 vols.

Tellechea Idigoras, J. Ignacio (1977): *Tiempos Recios: Inquisición y Heterodoxos*. Salamanca: Ediciones Sígueme.

Thomas, Hugh (1993): *The Conquest of Mexico*. London: Hutchinson.

Thomas, Hugh (1997): *The Slave Trade*. London: Picador.

Tinhorão, José Ramos (1998): *Os Negros em Portugal: Uma Presença Silenciosa*. Lisbon: Editorial Caminho.

Todorov, Tzvetan (1982): *La Conquête de l'Amérique: La Question de l'Autre*. Paris: Éditions du Seuil.

Tomás y Valiente, Francisco (1980): 'Relaciones de la Inquisición con el Aparato Institucional del Estado' in Pérez Villanueva, Joaquín (ed.) (1980) pp. 41–60.

Tomás y Valiente, Francisco (1994): *La Tortura en España*. Barcelona: Editorial Ariel, 2nd edition.

Tomsich, María Giovanna (1972): *El Jansenismo en España: Estudio Sobre Ideas Religiosas en la Segunda Mitad del Siglo XVIII*. Madrid: Siglo Veintiuno de España Editores.

Torgal, Luís Reis and Vargues, Isabel (eds) (1982–3): *O Marquês de Pombal e o Seu Tempo*. Coimbra: Universidade de Coimbra, 2 vols.

Toribio Medina, José (1887): *Historia del Santo Oficio de la Inquisición de Lima*. Santiago de Chile: Imprenta Gutenberg, 2 vols.

Toribio Medina, José (1889): *El Tribunal del Santo Oficio de la Inquisición en las Provincias del Plata*. Santiago de Chile: Imprenta Elzeviriana.

Toribio Medina, José (1890): *Historia del Tribunal del Santo Oficio de la Inquisición en Chile*. Santiago de Chile: Imprenta Ercilla.

Toribio Medina, José (1899): *Historia del Tribunal del Santo Oficio de la Inquisición en Cartagena de las Indias*. Santiago de Chile: Imprenta Elzeviriana.

Toribio Medina, José (1905): *Historia del Tribunal del Santo Oficio de la Inquisición en México*. Santiago de Chile: Imprenta Elzeviriana.

Toro, Alfonso (1944): *La Familia Carvajal: Estudio Histórico Sobre los Judíos y la Inquisición de la Nueva España en el Siglo XVI, Basado en Documentos Originales y en Su Mayor Parte Inéditos, Que Se Conservan en el Archivo General de la Nación de la Ciudad de México*. Mexico City: Editorial Patria, S.A., 2 vols.

Trevor-Roper, Hugh (1984): *Religion, The Reformation and Social Change*. London: Secker & Warburg, 2nd edition.

Twomey, Lesley K. (ed.) (1997): *Faith and Fanaticism: Religious Fervour in Early Modern Spain*. Aldershot: Ashgate.

Vainfas, Ronaldo (1989): *Trópico dos Pecados: Moral, Sexualidade e Inquisição no Brasil*. Rio de Janeiro: Editora Campus.

Valdeón Buruque, Julio (1995): 'Motivaciones Socioeconómicas de las Fricciones Entre Viejocristianos, Judíos y Conversos' in Alcalá, Angel (ed.) (1995) pp. 69–88.

Valdeón Buruque, Julio (2000): *El Chivo Expiatorio: Judíos, Revueltos y la Revolución Trastámara*. Valladolid: Ámbito Ediciones.

Vassberg, David E. (1996): *The Village and the Outside World in Golden Age Castile*. Cambridge: Cambridge University Press.

Ventura, Maria da Graça Mateus (1999): *Negreiros Portugueses na Rota das Indias de Castela (1541–1555)*. Lisbon: Edições Colibri.

Vidal, Jeanne (1986): *Quand on Brûlait les Morisques 1544–1621*. Nîmes: Imprimerie Barnier.

Vidal Doval, Rosa (2005): 'El Muro en el Peste y *La Fortaleza de la Fe*: Alegorías de la Exclusión de Minorías en la Castilla del Siglo XV', in Sanmartín Bastida, Rebeca and Vidal Doval, Rosa (eds) (2005) pp. 143–68.

Vincent, Bernard (1997): 'Le Tribunal de Grenade' in Cardaillac, Louis (ed.) (1990) pp. 199–220.

Vogt, James L. (1973): 'The Lisbon Slave House and African Trade, 1486–1521', in *Proceedings of the American Philosophical Society*, Vol. 117, no. 1, 1973, pp. 1–16.

Wachtel, Nathan (2001a): *La Foi du Souvenir: Labyrinthes Marranes*. Paris: Éditions du Seuil.

Wachtel, Nathan (2001b): 'Marrano Religiosity in Hispanic America in the Seventeenth Century' in Bernardini, Paolo and Fiering, Norman (eds) (2001) pp. 149–71.

Winius, George D. (ed.) (1995): *Portugal the Pathfinder: Journeys from the Medieval*

Toward the Modern World 1300 – ca. 1600. Madison: Hispanic Seminary of Medieval Studies.

Wittmayer Baron, Salo (1969): *A Social and Religious History of the Jews, Vol. 13*. New York: Columbia University Press.

Wiznitzer, Arnold (1954): *The Records of the Earliest Jewish Community in the New World*. New York: American Jewish Historical Society.

Wiznitzer, Arnold (1960): *Jews in Colonial Brazil*. New York: Columbia University Press.

Wiznitzer, Arnold (1971a): 'Crypto-Jews in Mexico During the Sixteenth Century' in Cohen, Martin A. (ed.) (1971a) Vol. I, pp. 88–133, first published 1962.

Wiznitzer, Arnold (1971b): 'Crypto-Jews in Mexico During the Seventeenth Century' in Cohen, Martin A. (ed.) (1971a), Vol. I, pp. 133–77, first published 1962.

Wolff, Egon and Freida (1986): *Judaizantes e Judeus no Brasil, 1500–1808: Diccionário Biográfico*. Rio de Janeiro: Cemitério Comunal Israelita.

Wolff, Egon and Freida (1989): *Judeus em Amsterdã: Seu Relacionamento com o Brasil 1600–1620*. Rio de Janeiro: ERCA Editora e Gráfica Ltda.

Yerushalmi, Yosef Haim (1981, first published 1971): *From Spanish Court to Italian Ghetto: Isaac Cardoso – A Study in Seventeeth-Century Marranism and Jewish Apologetics*. Seattle: University of Washington Press.

Yovel, Yirmiyahu (1989): *Spinoza and Other Heretics: The Marrano of Reason*. Princeton: Princeton University Press.

Index